ALBUM III

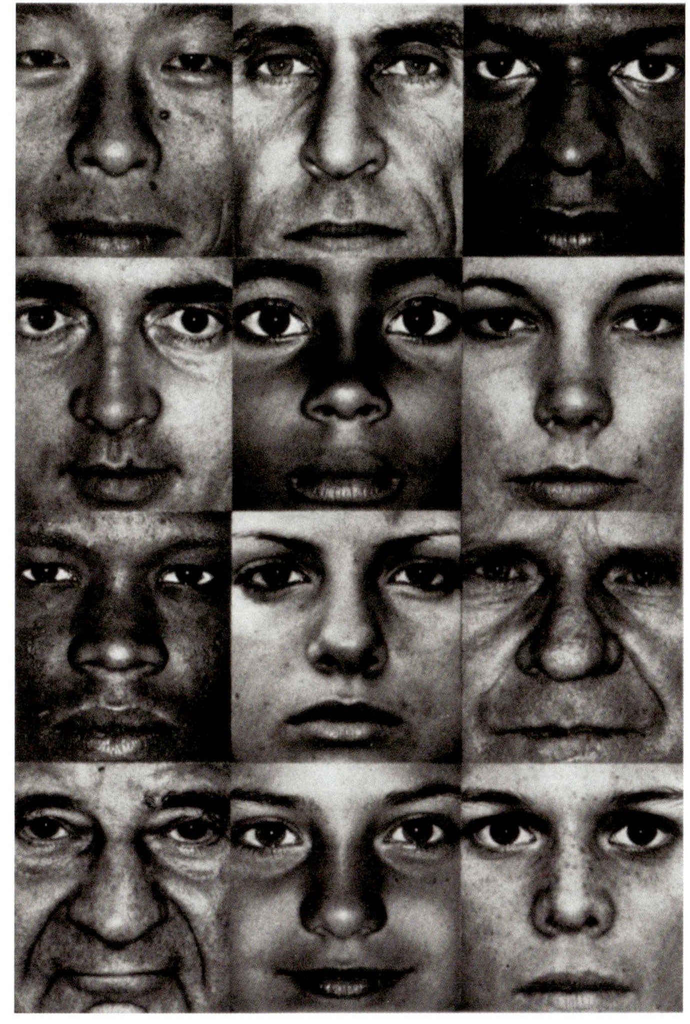

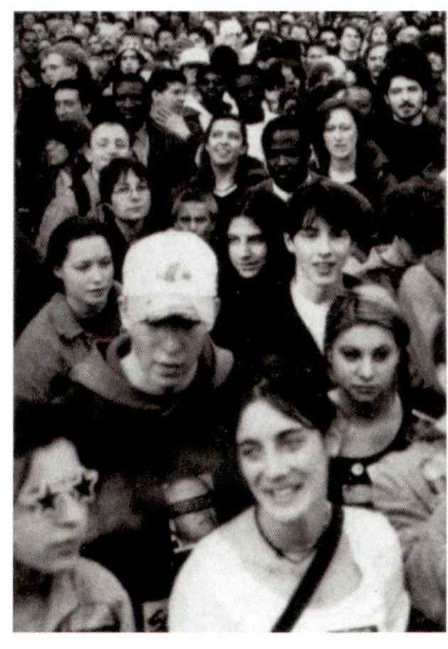

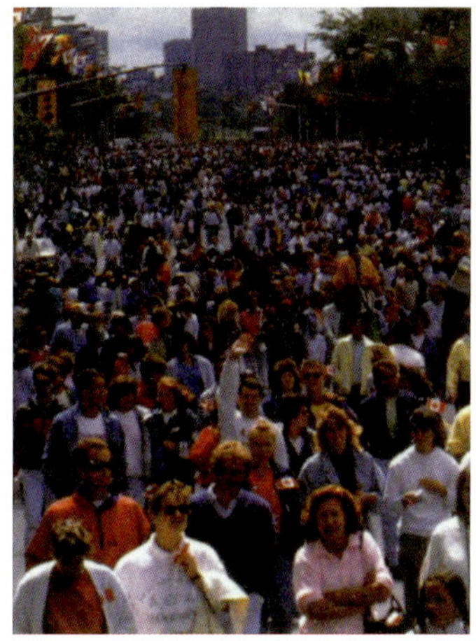

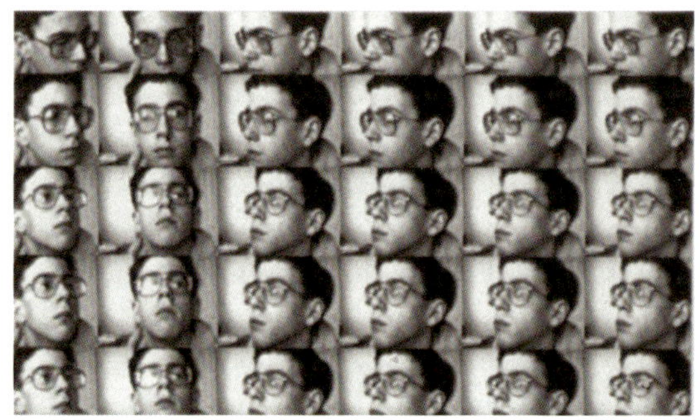

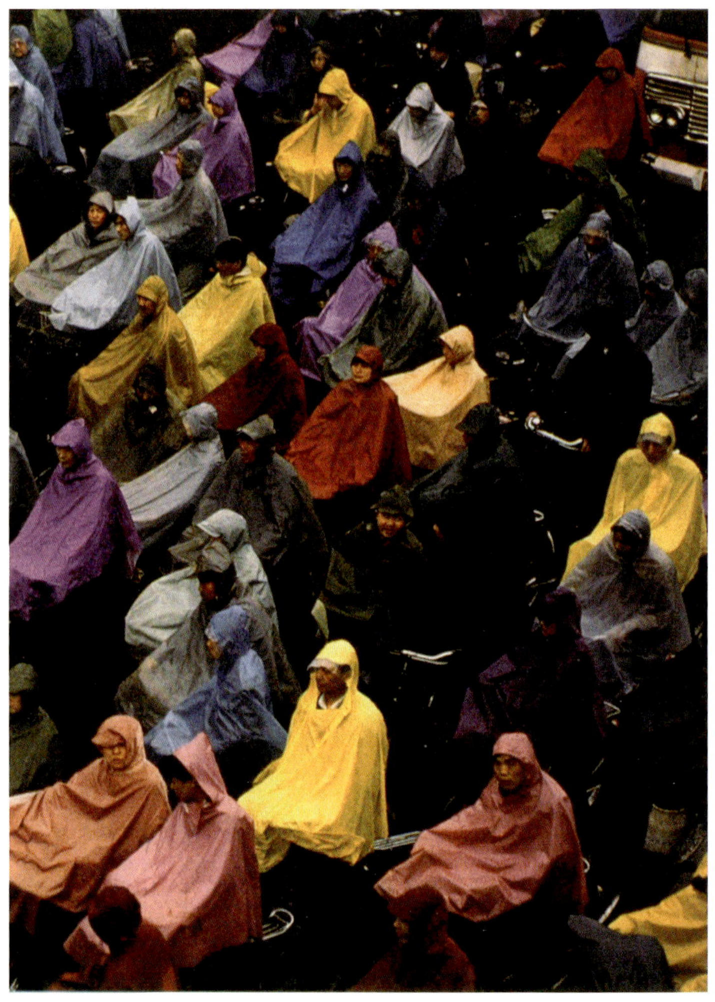

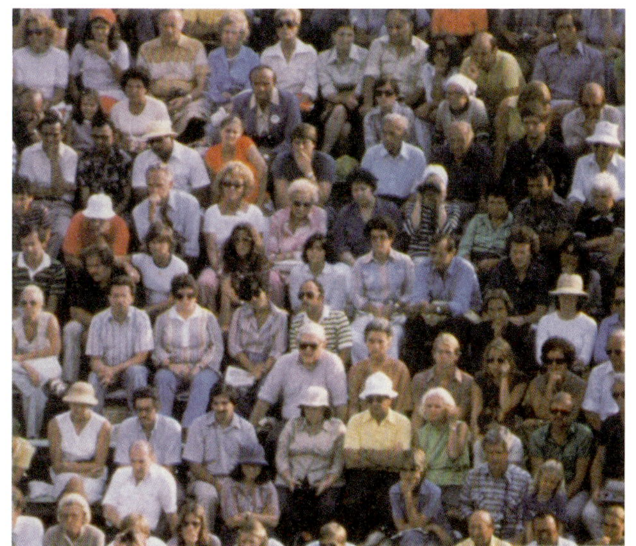
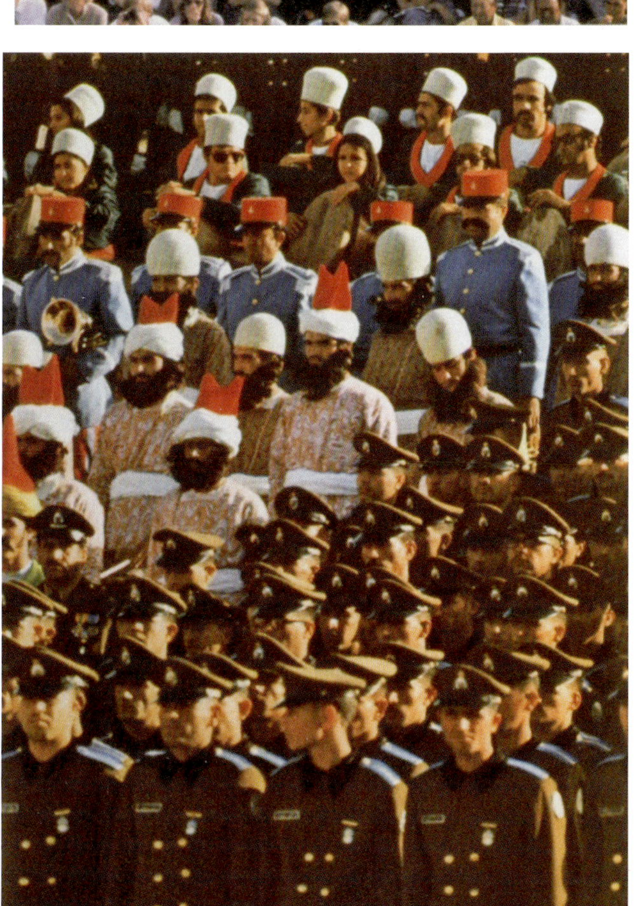
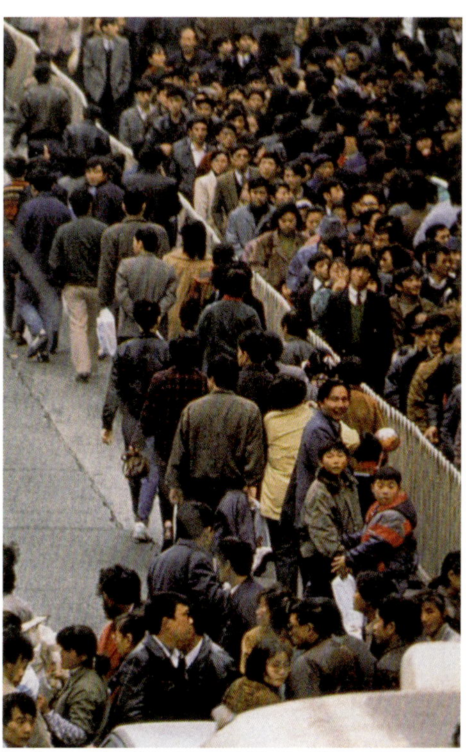
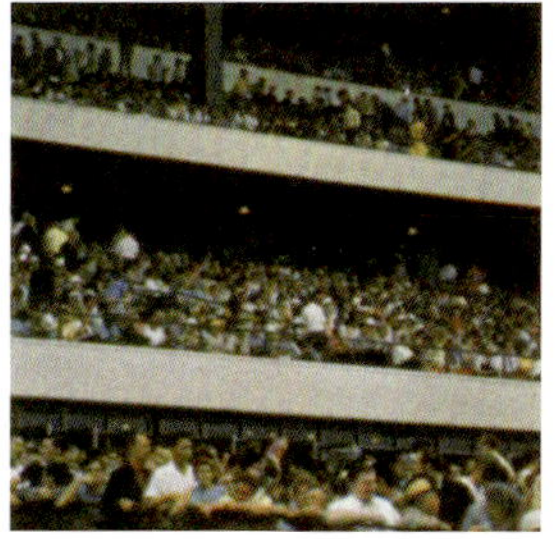

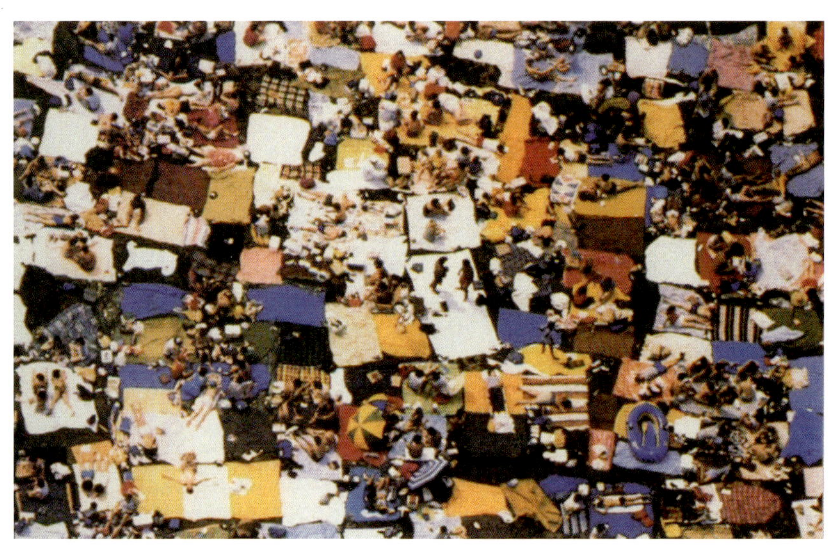

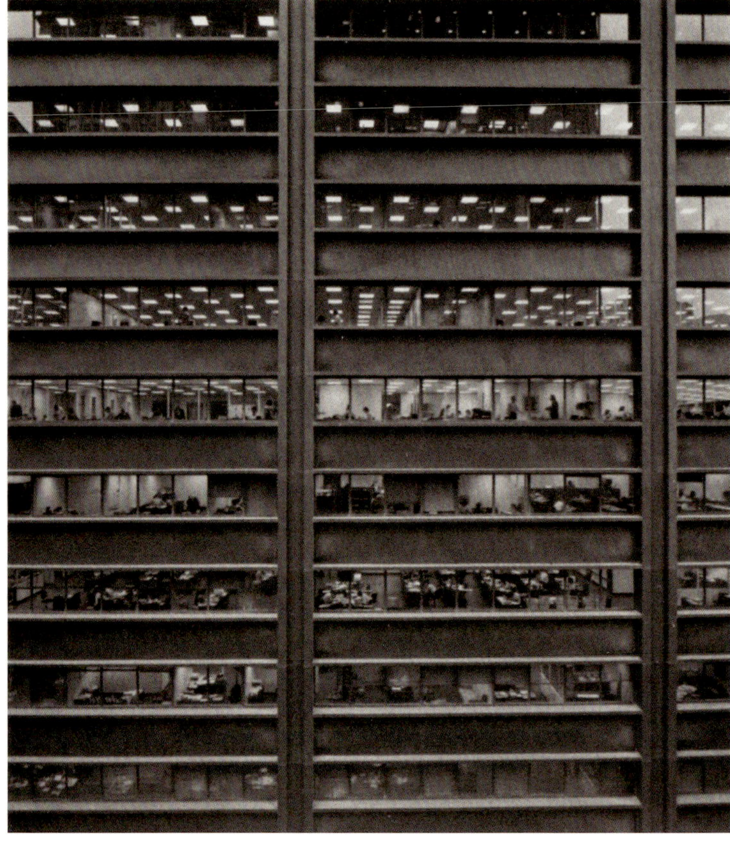

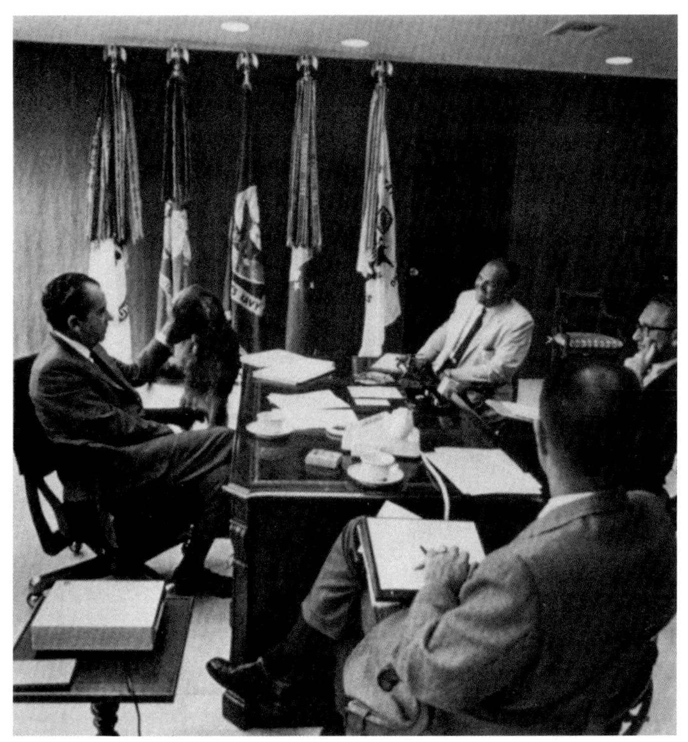

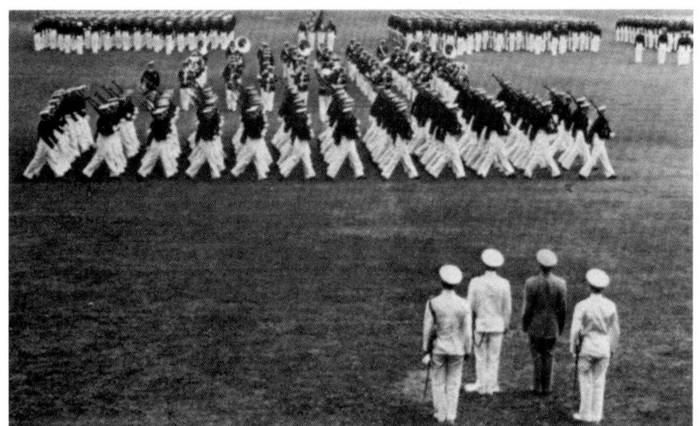

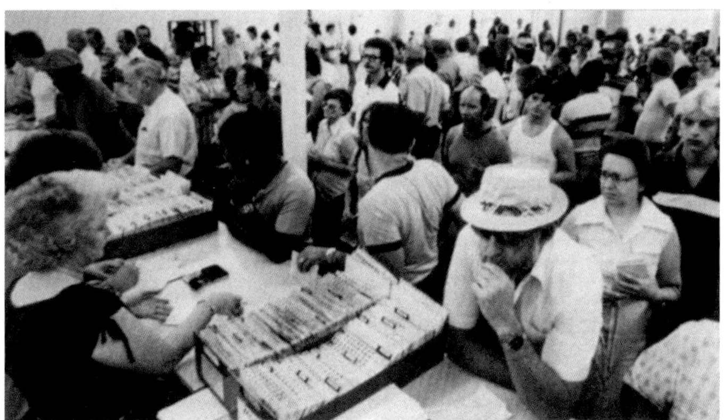

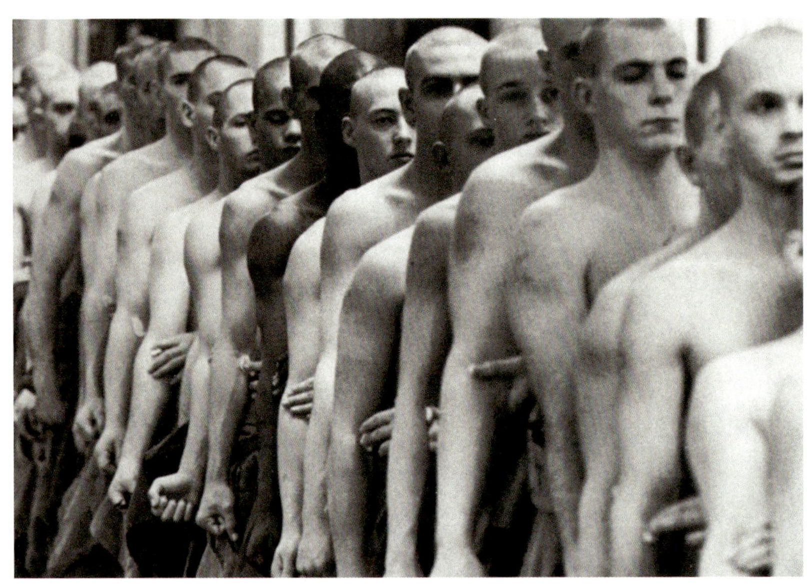

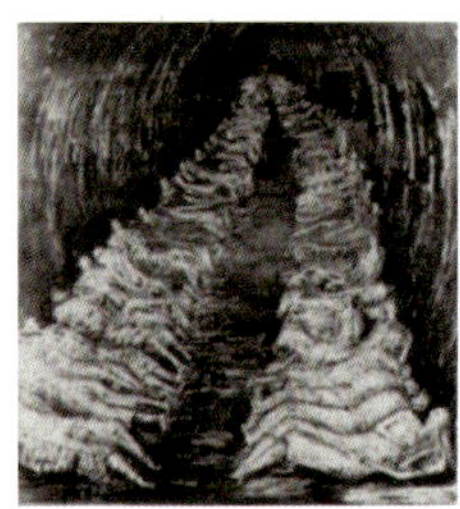

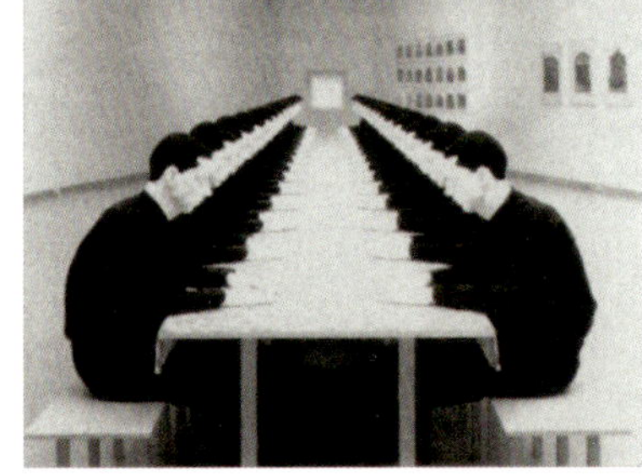

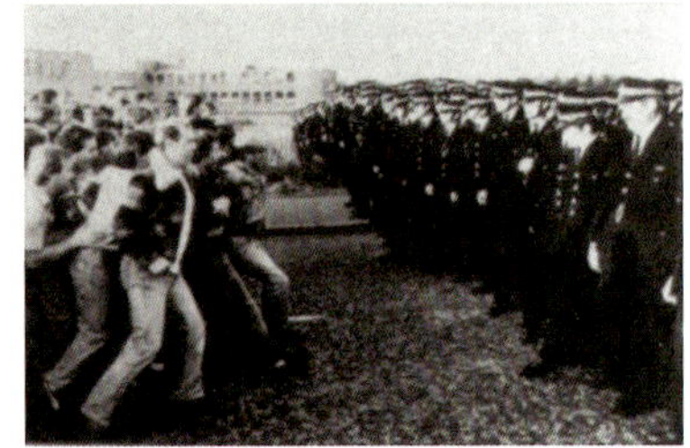

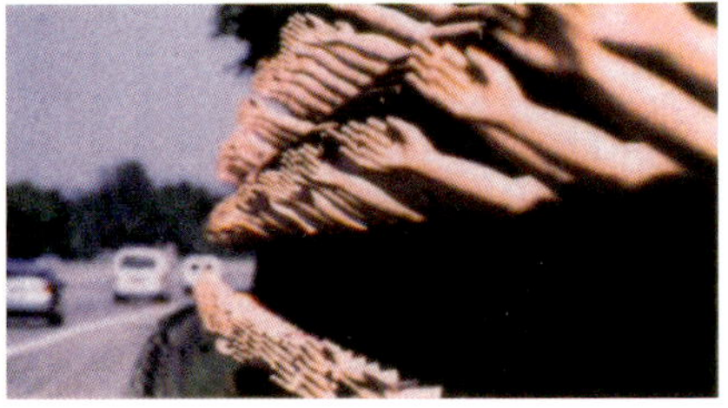

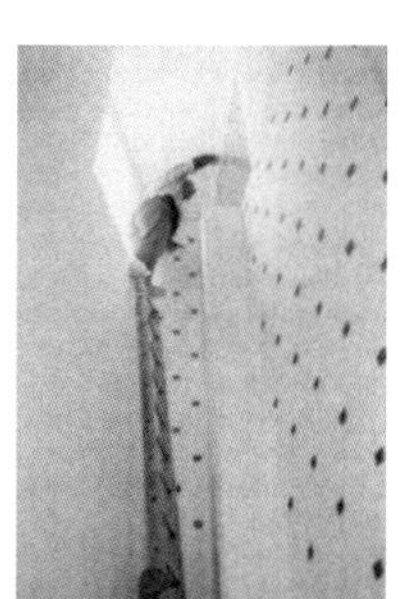
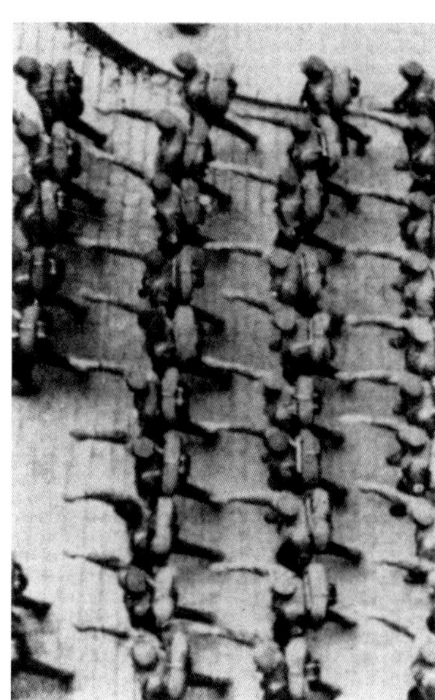
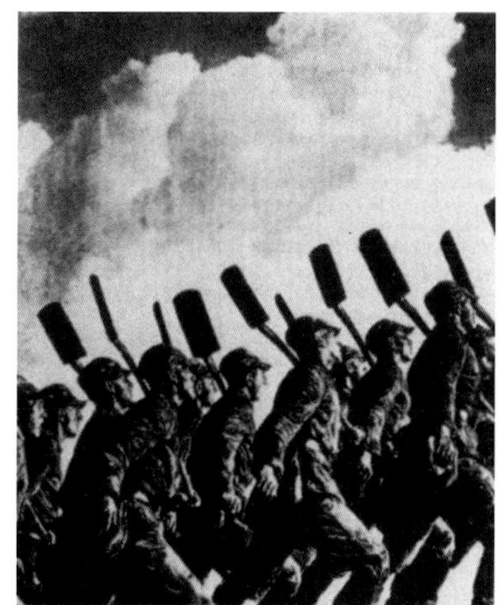
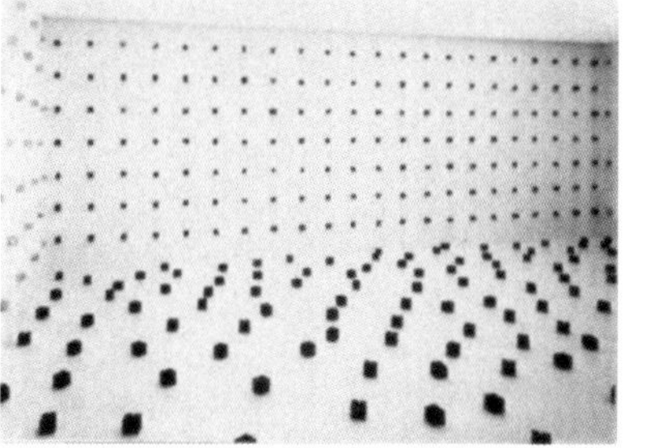

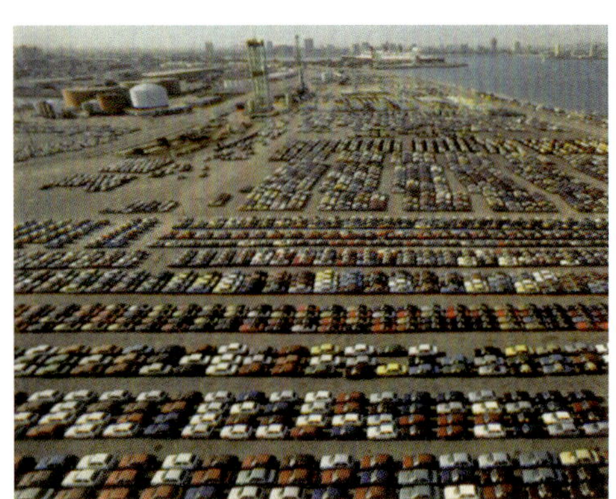

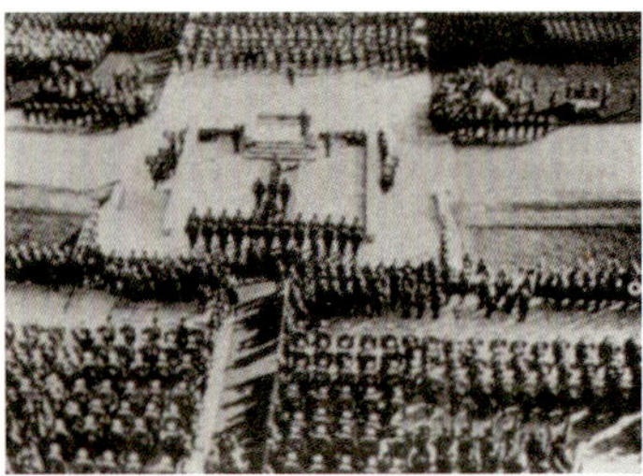

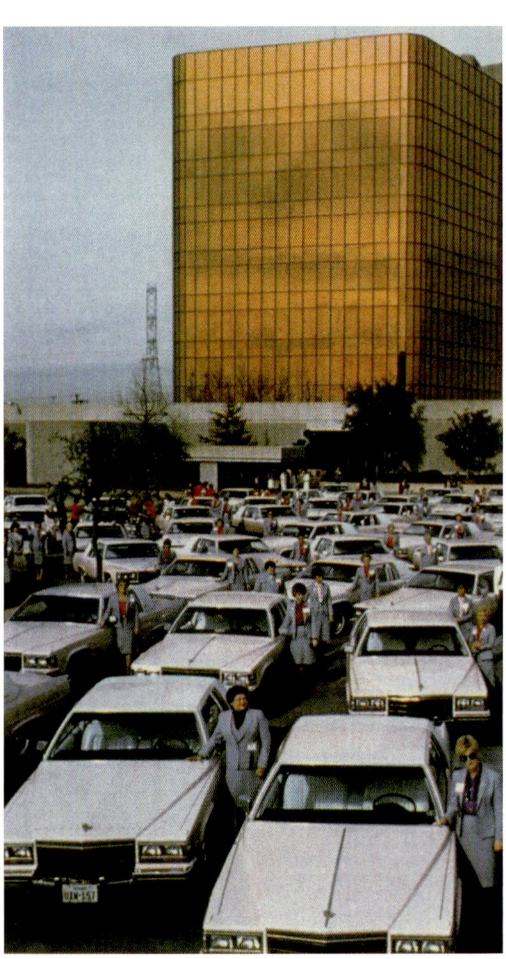

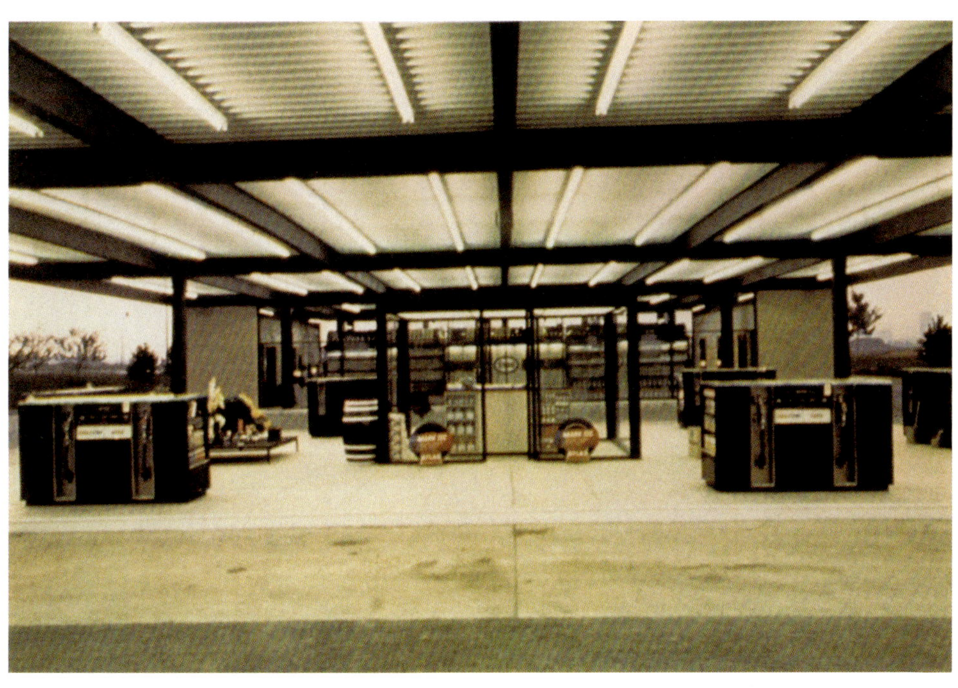

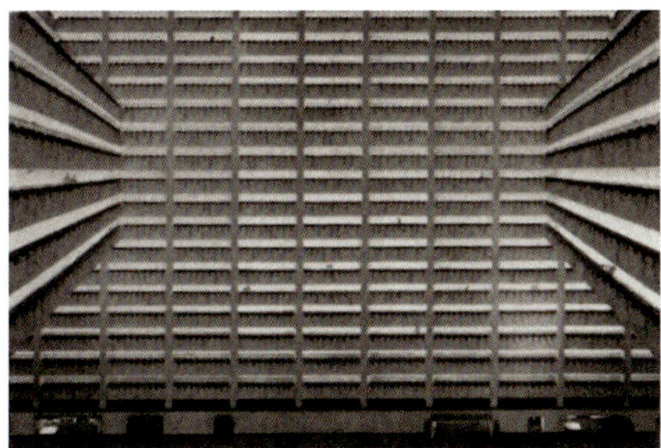

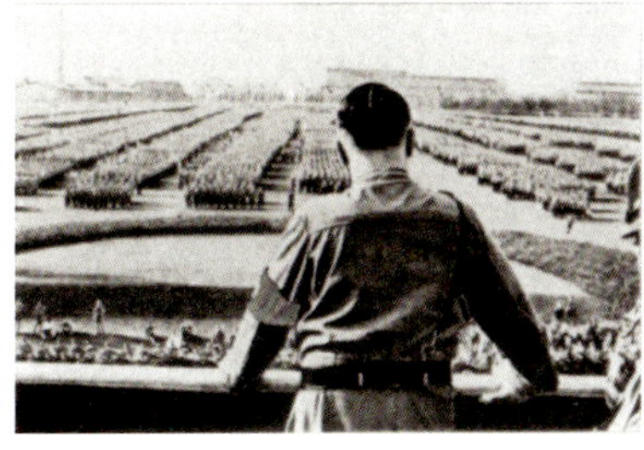

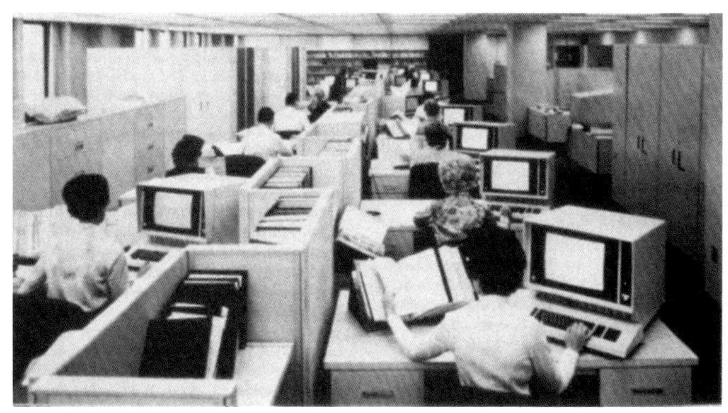

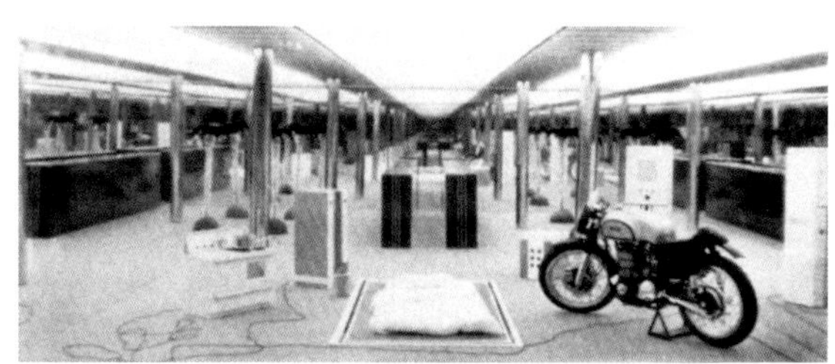

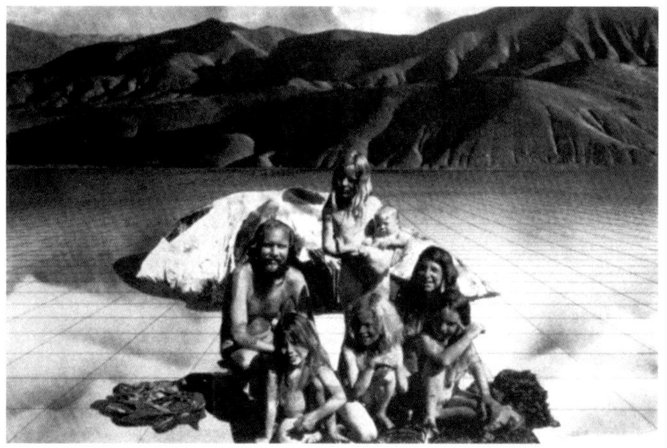

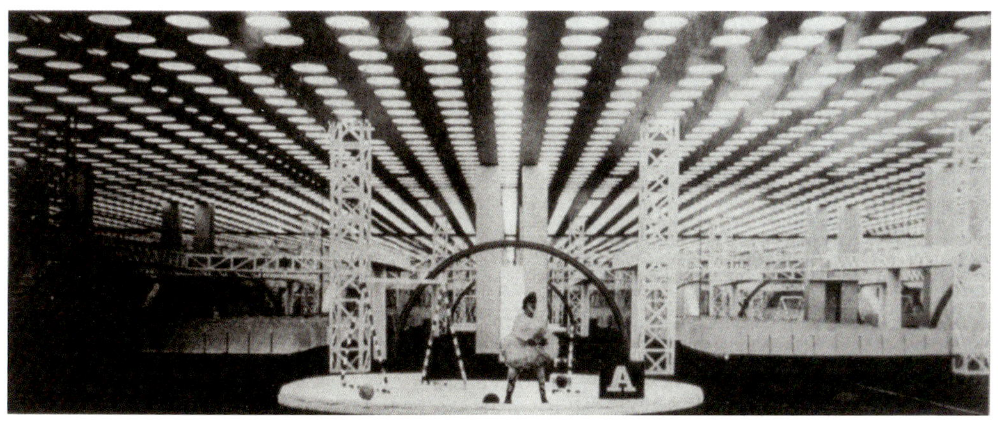

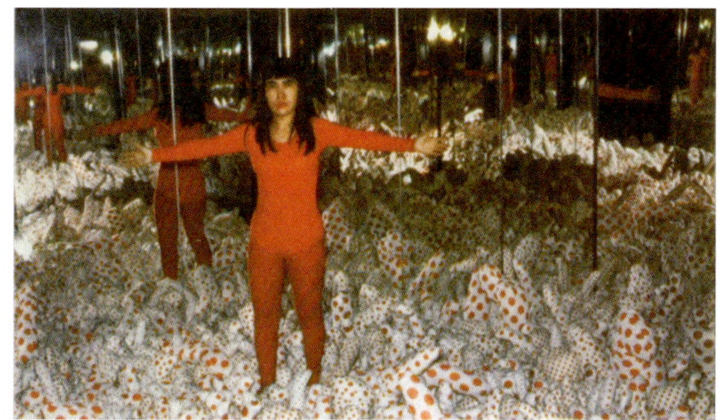

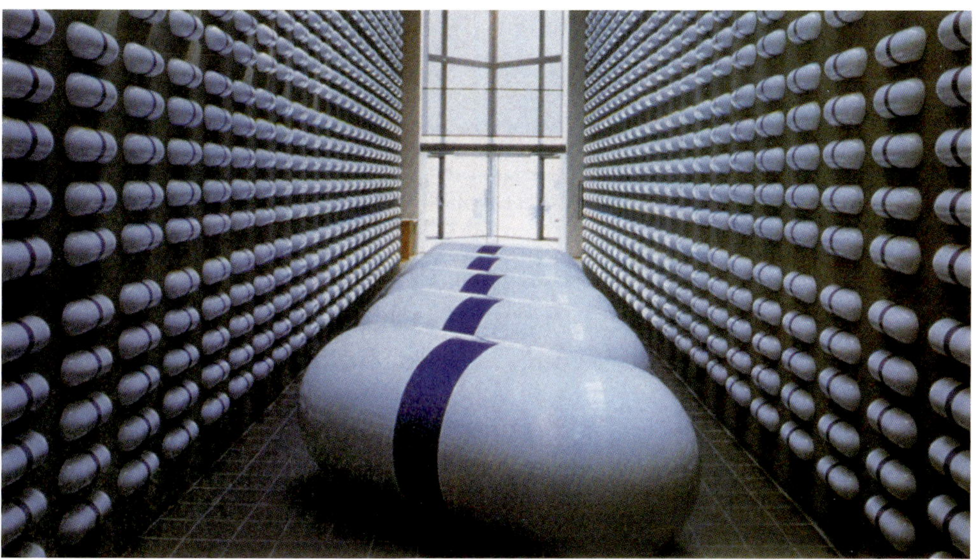

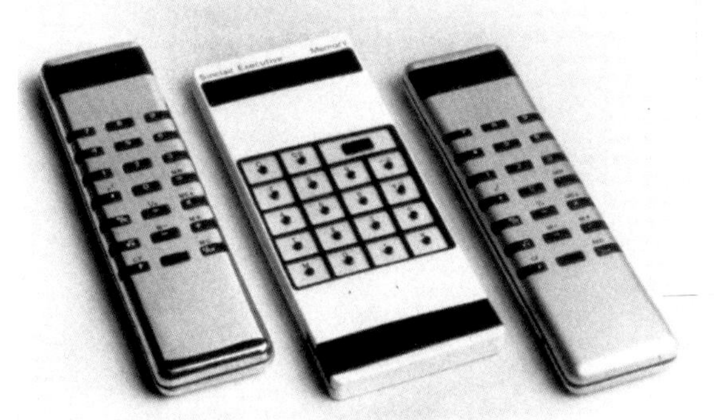

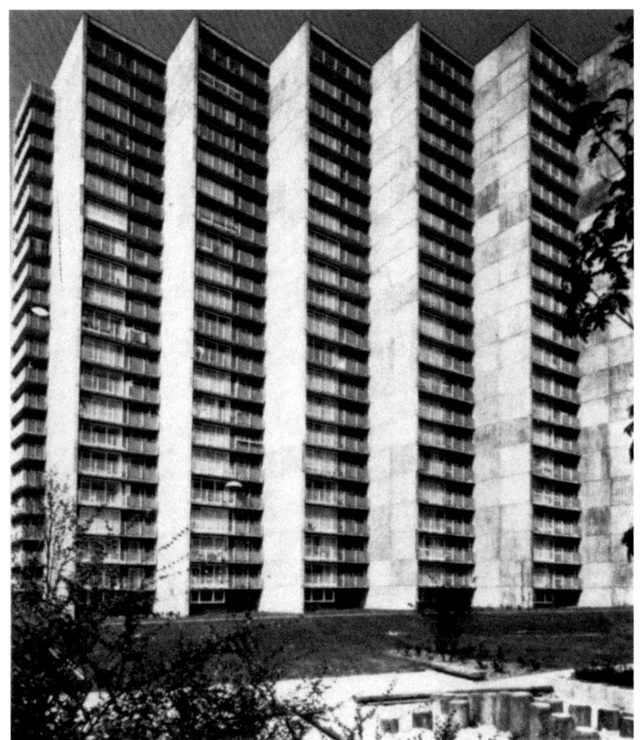

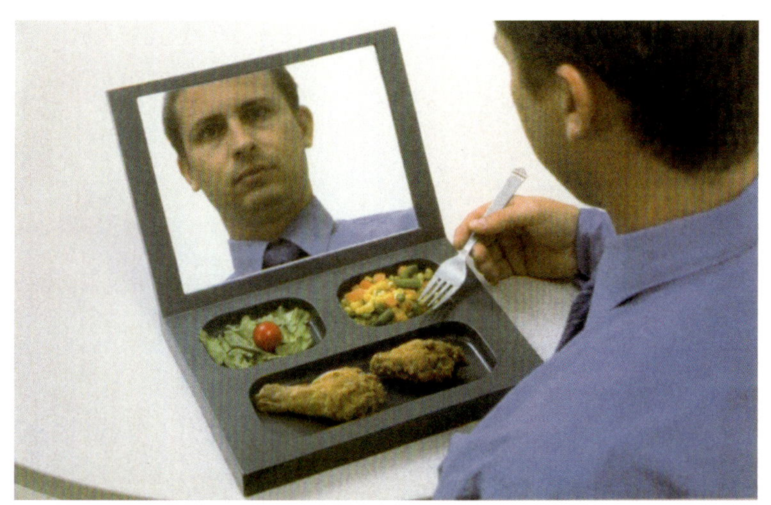

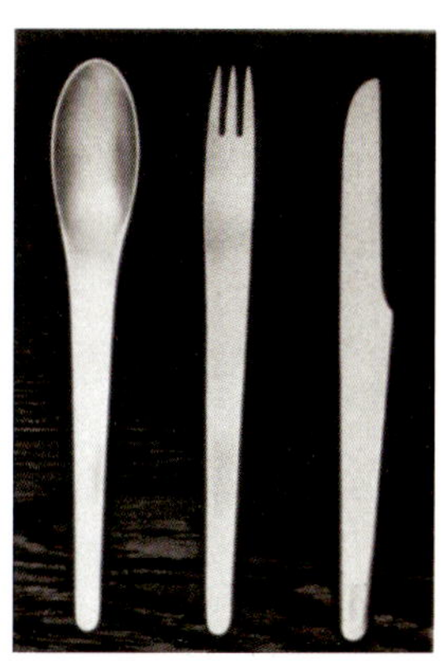

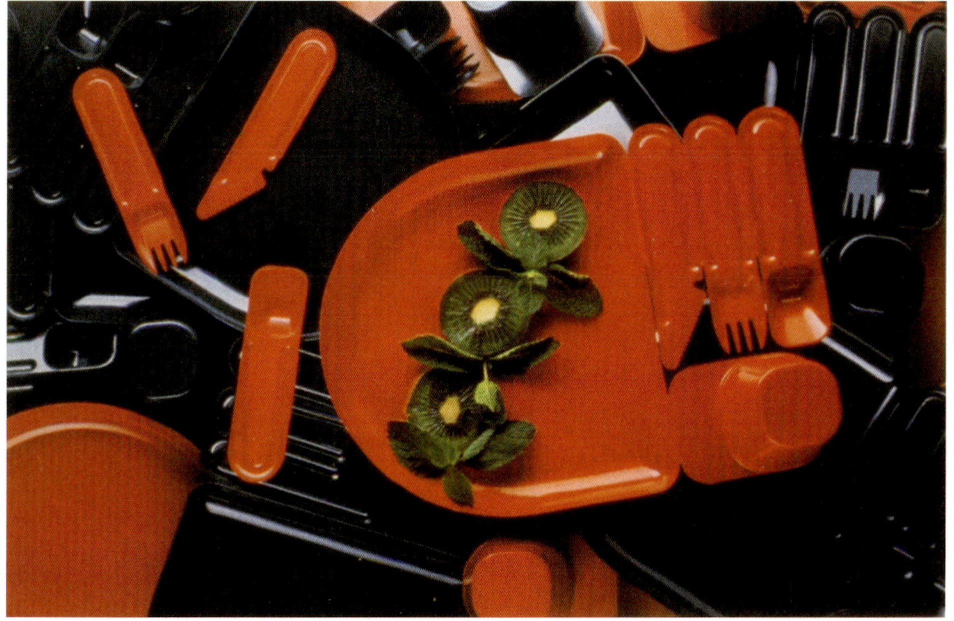

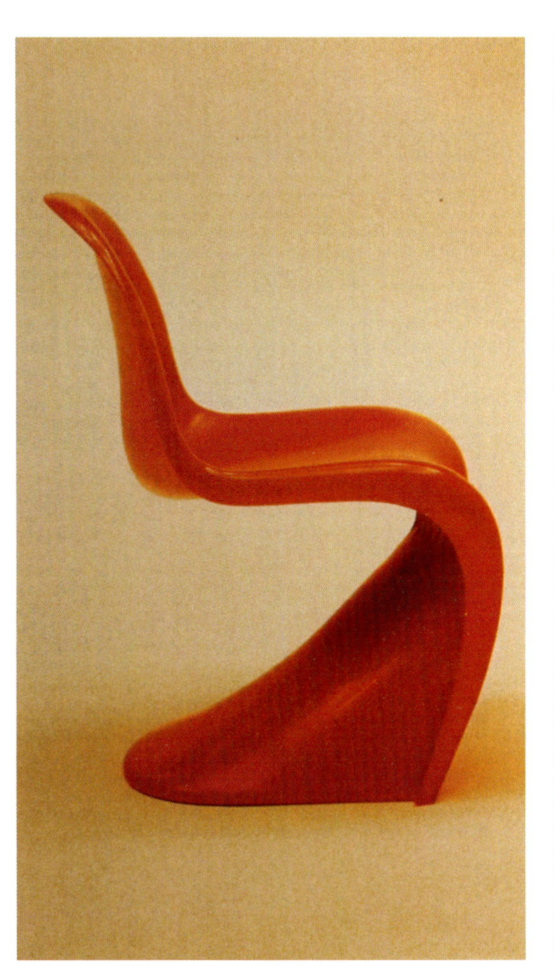

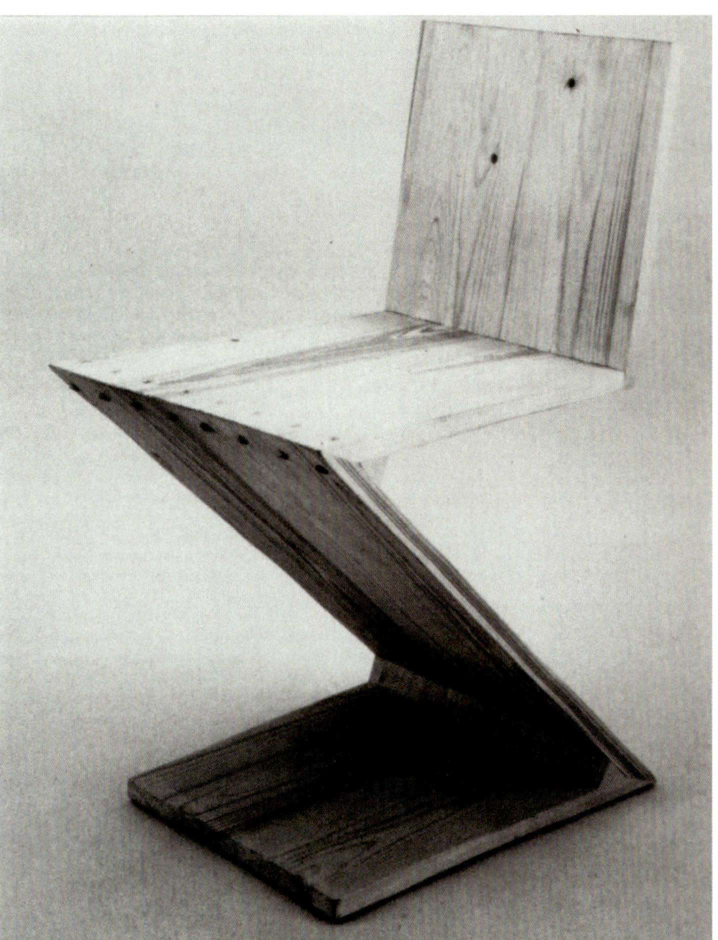

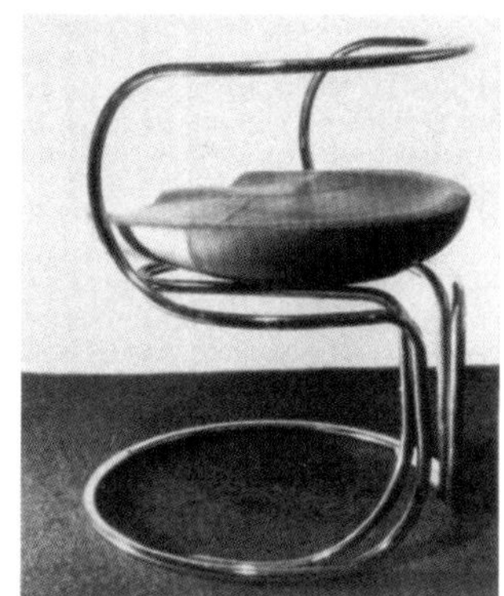

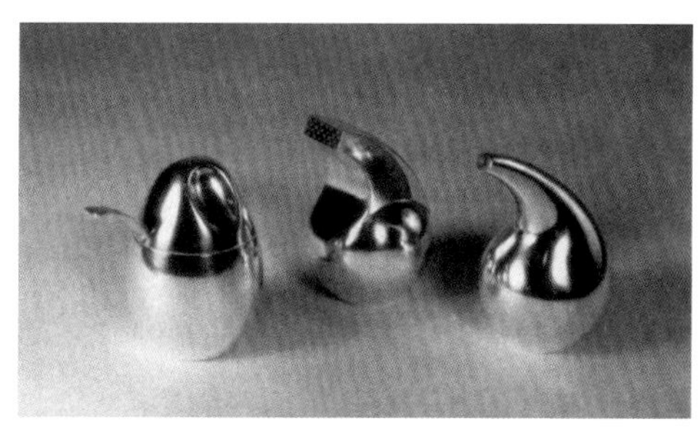

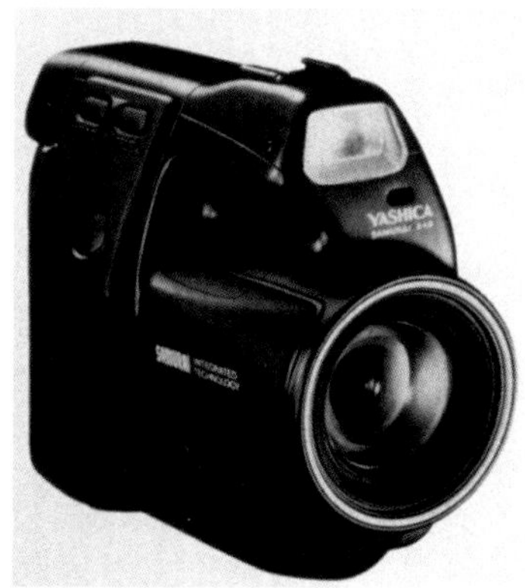

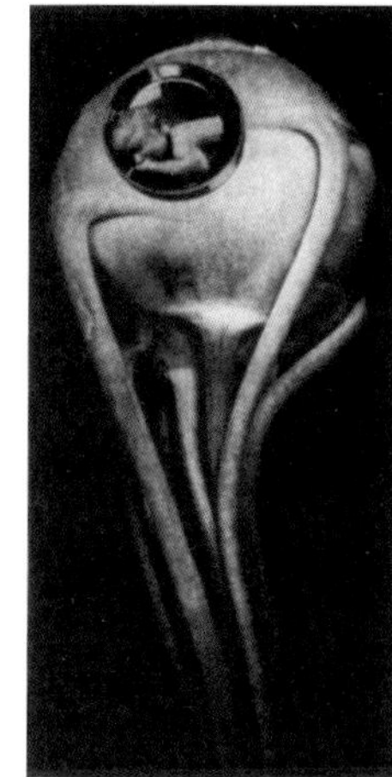

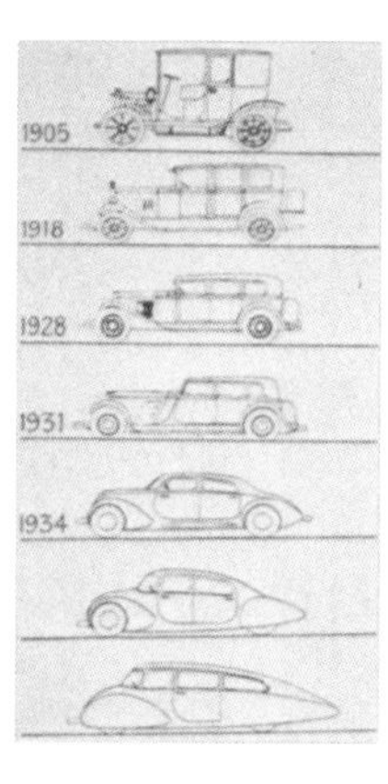
1905
1918
1928
1931
1934

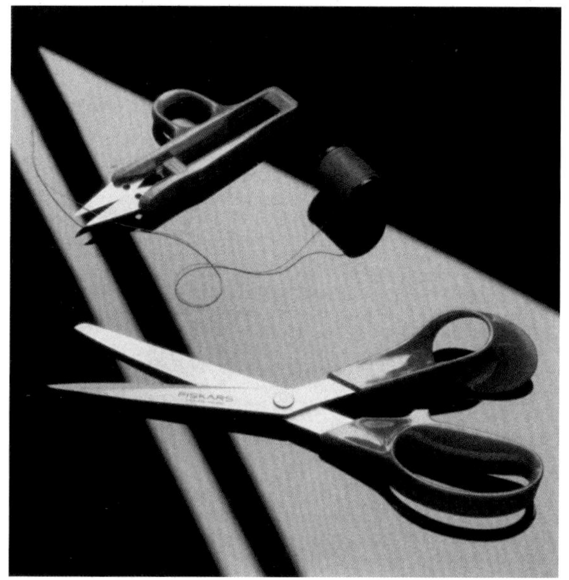
FISKARS

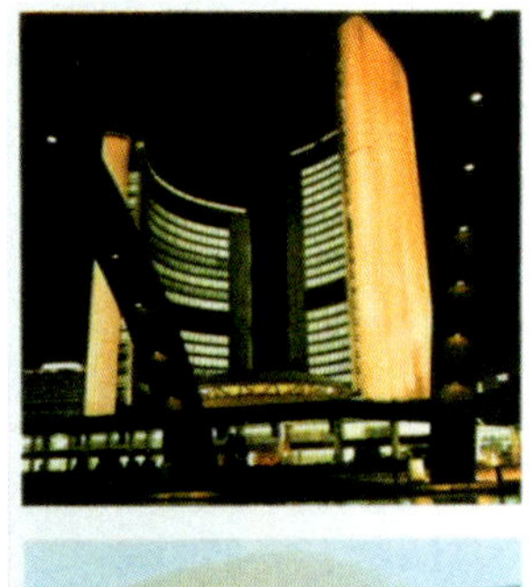
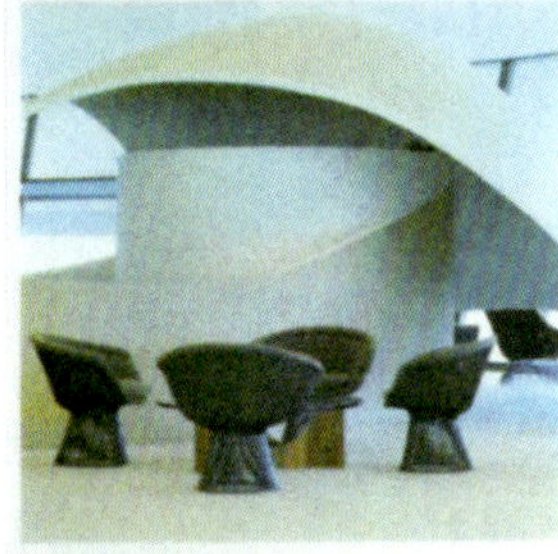
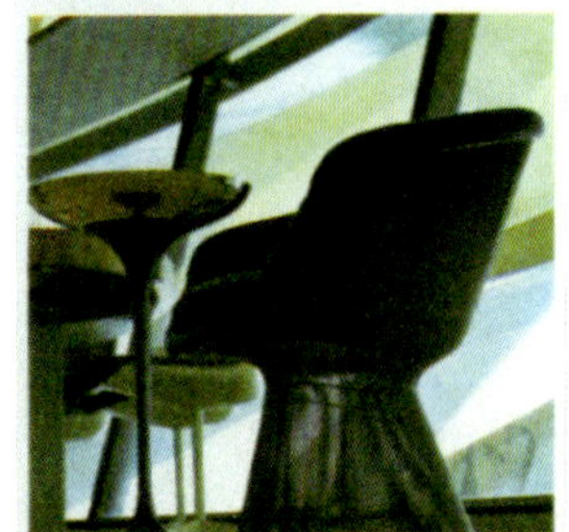
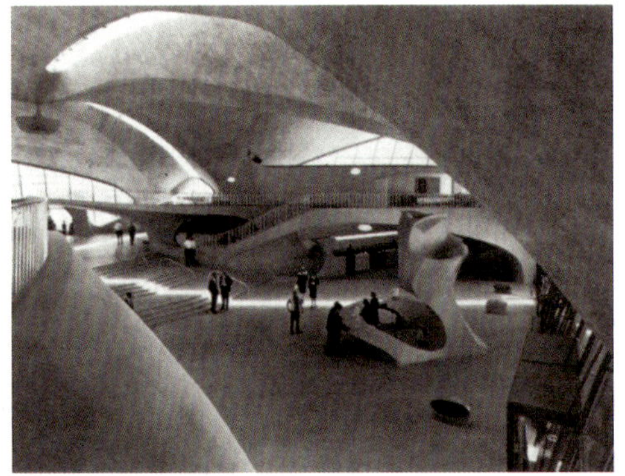
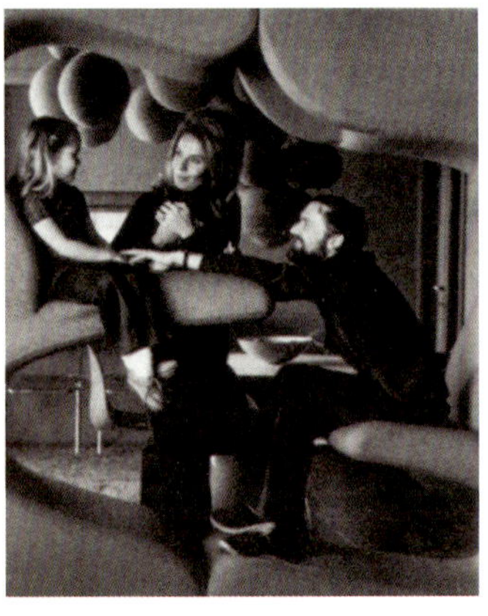
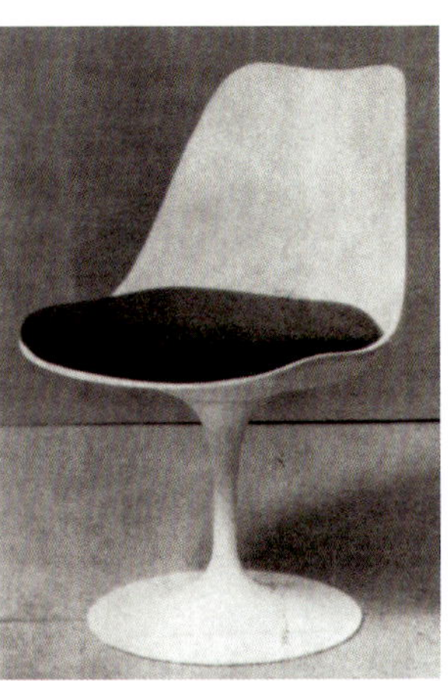
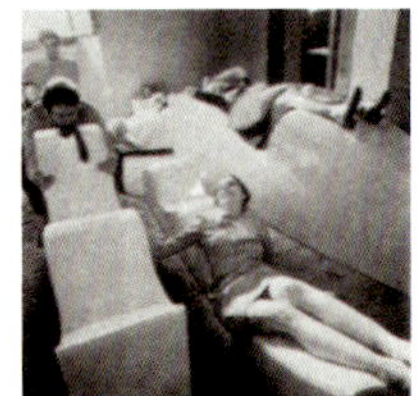
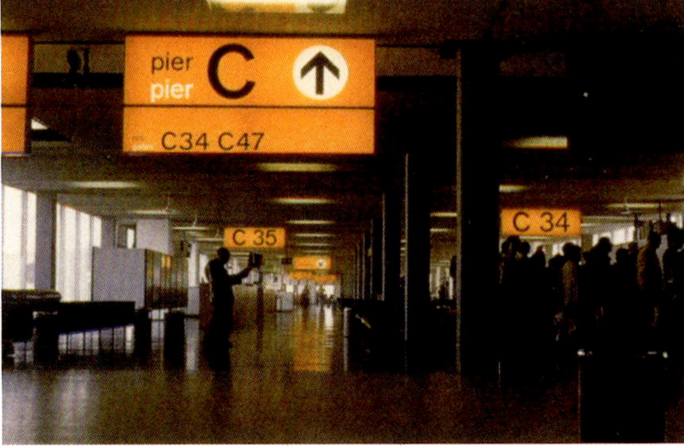
pier C
pier C
C34 C47
C 35
C 34

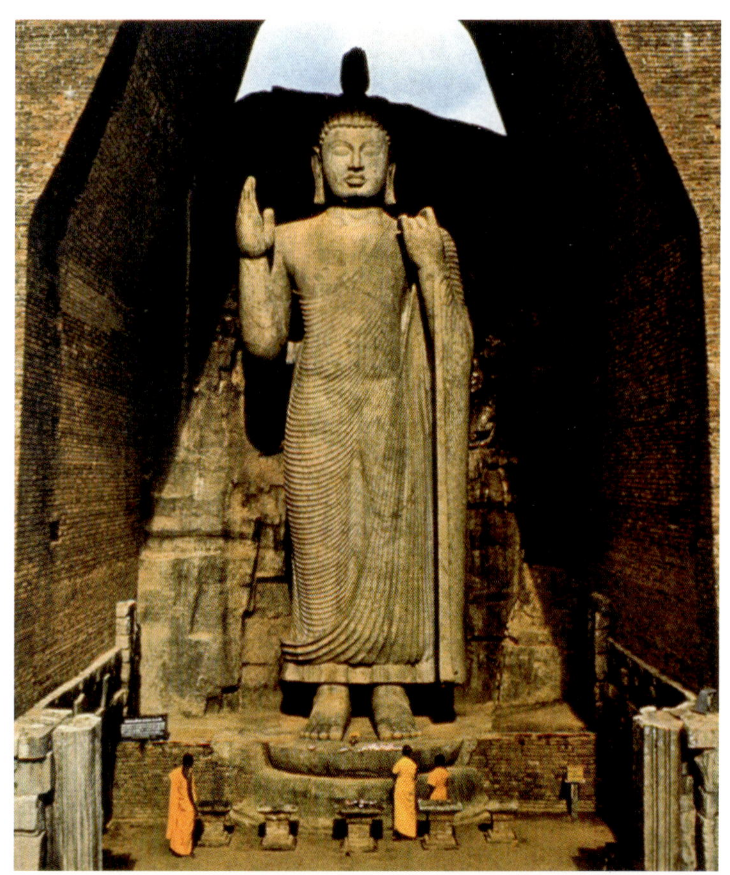

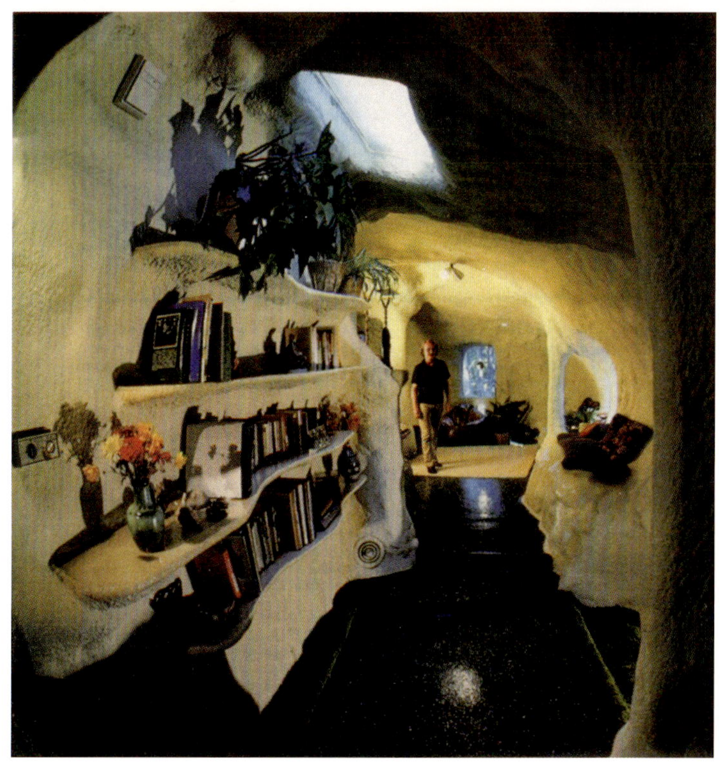

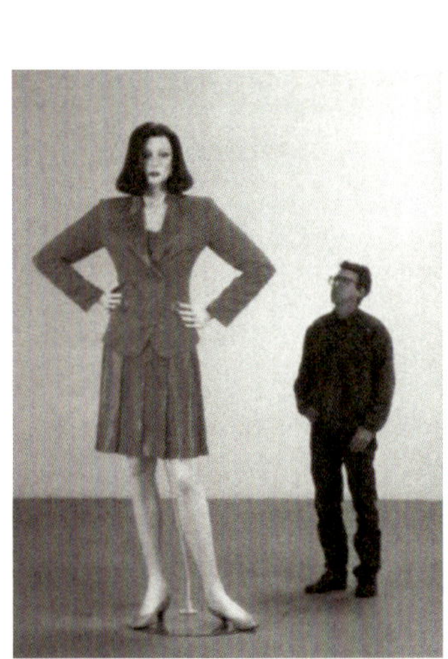

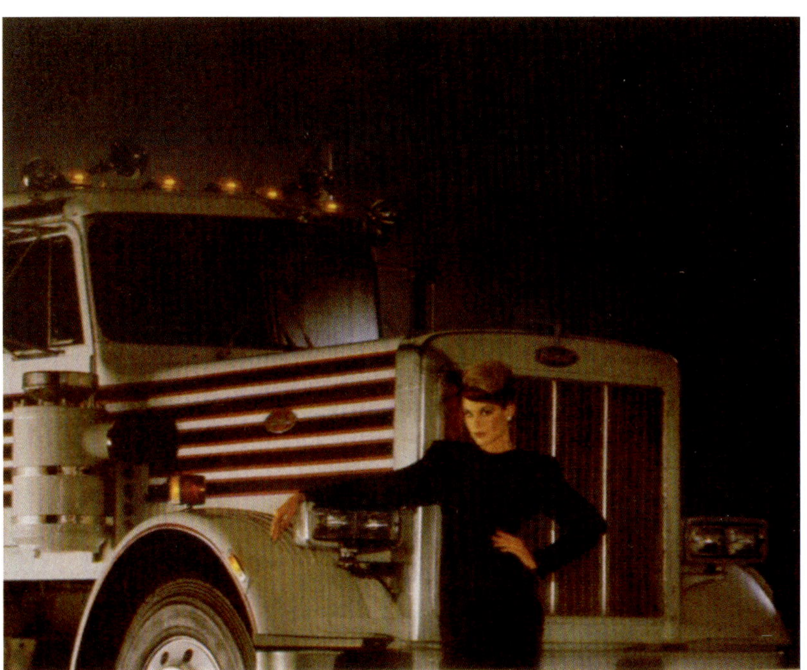

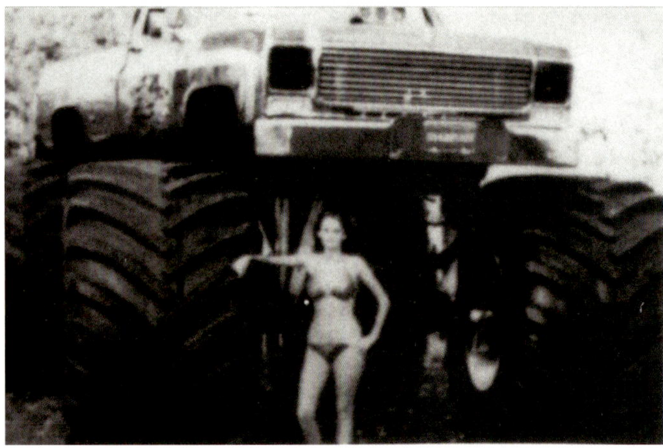

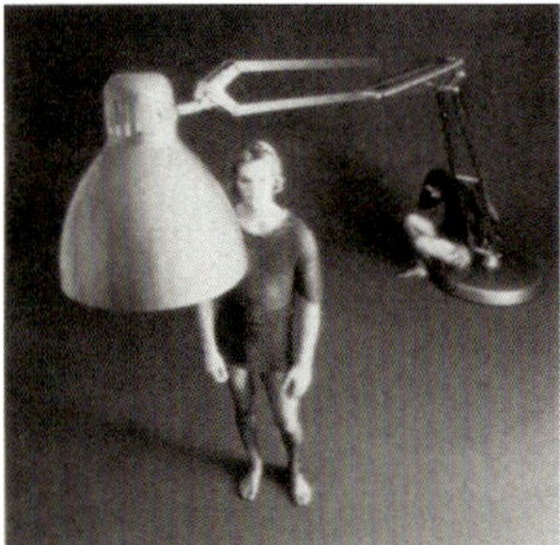

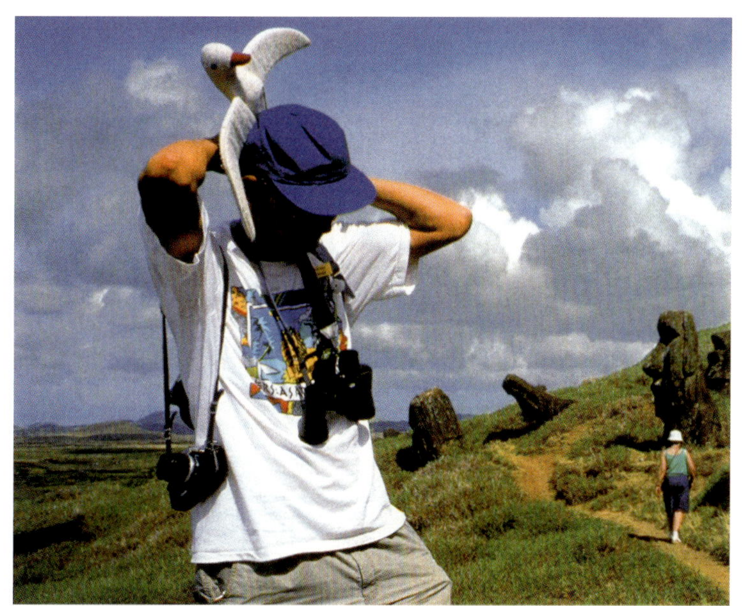

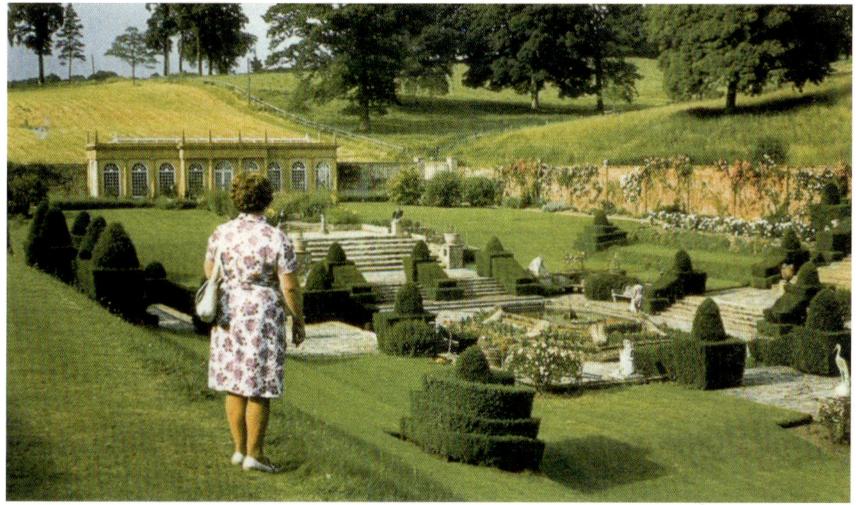

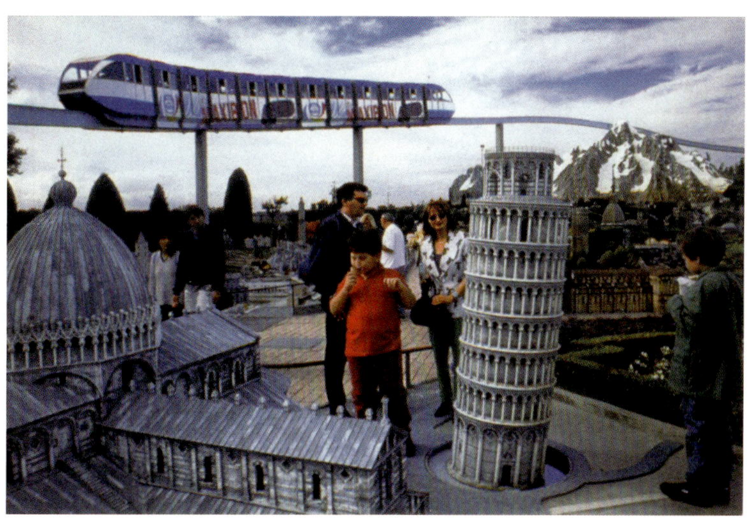

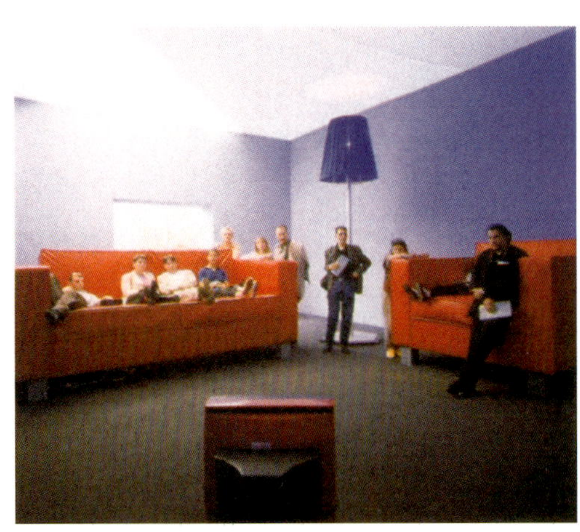

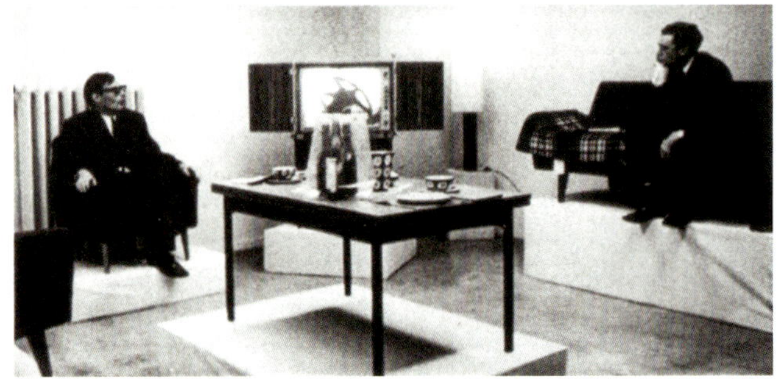

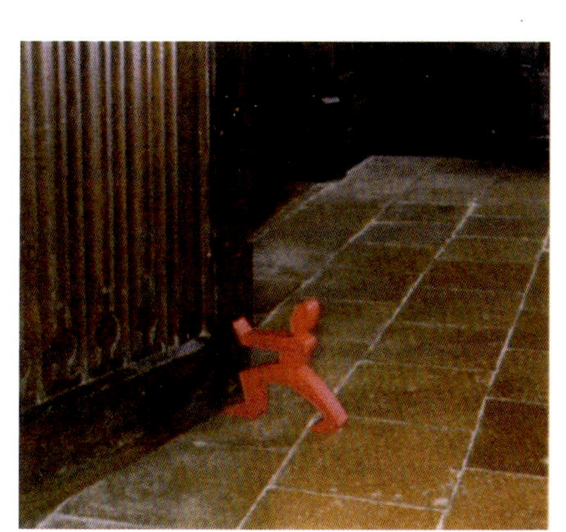
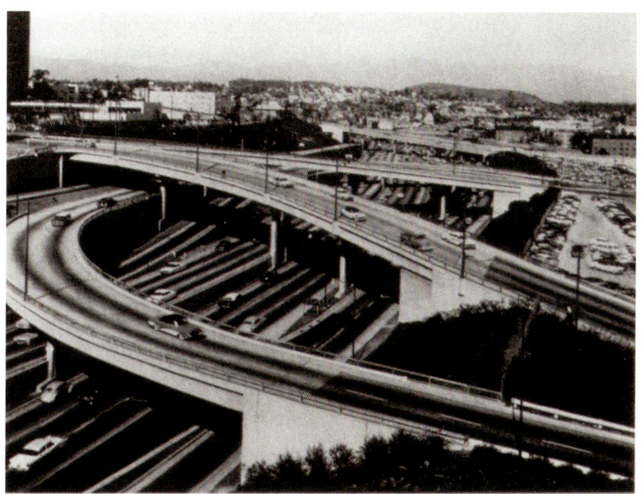
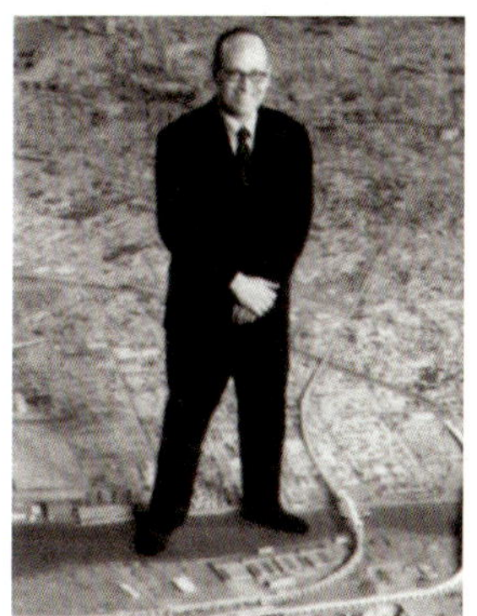
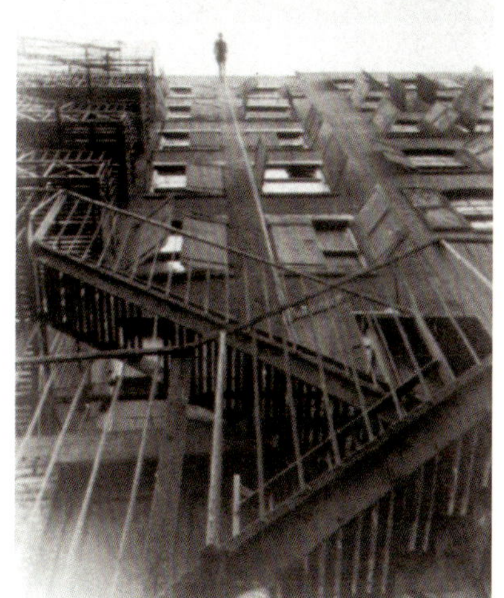
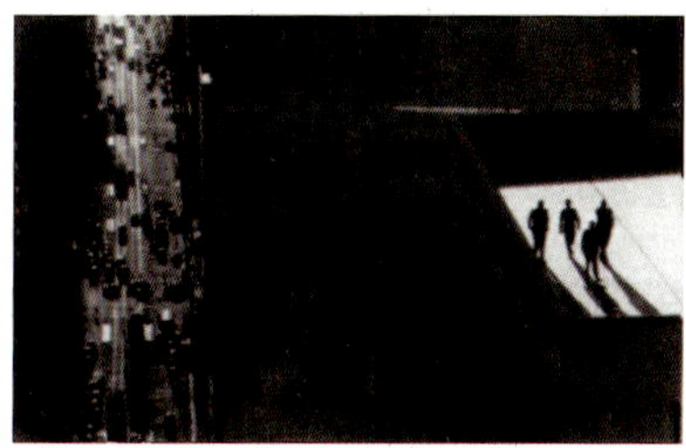

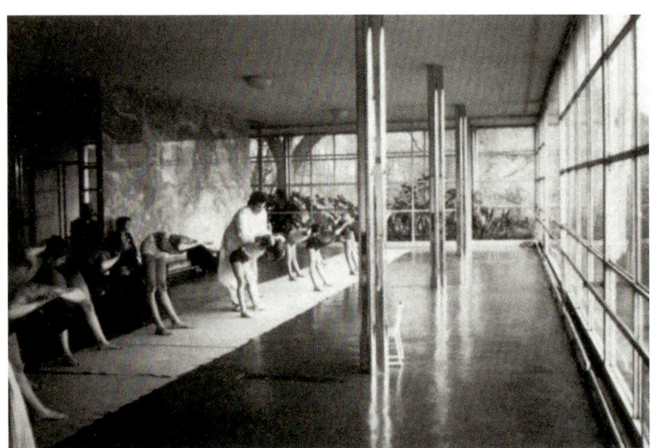

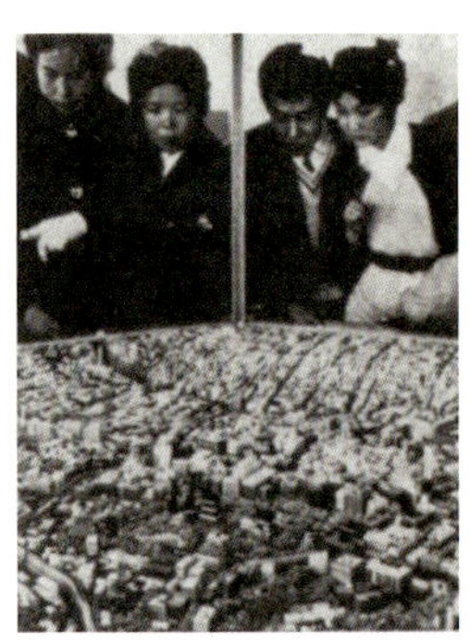

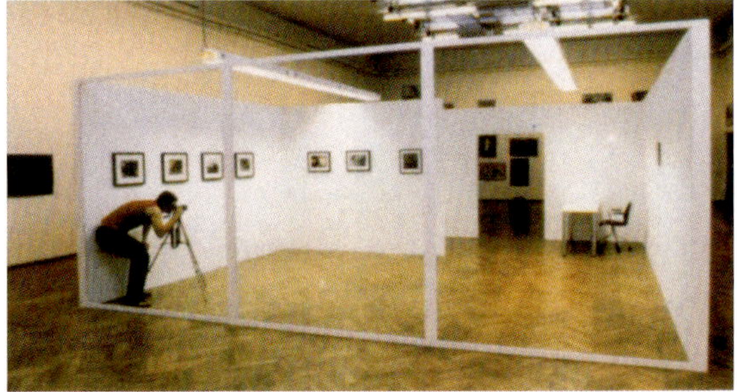

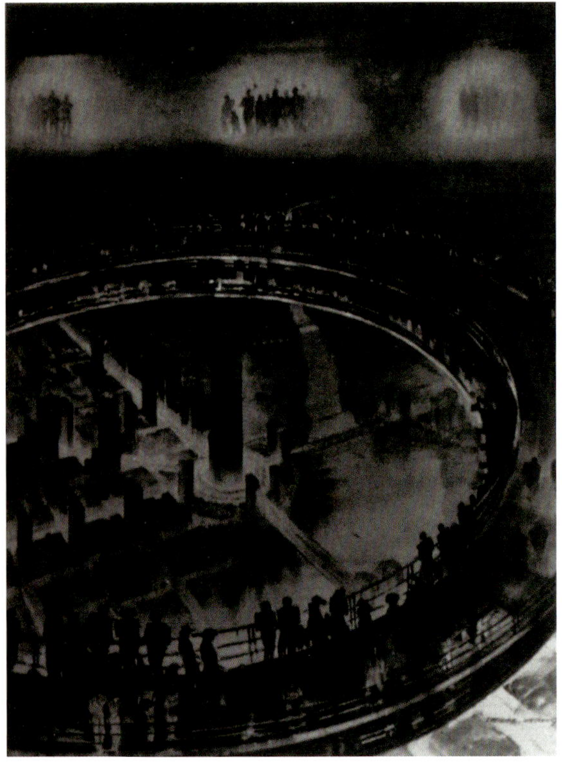

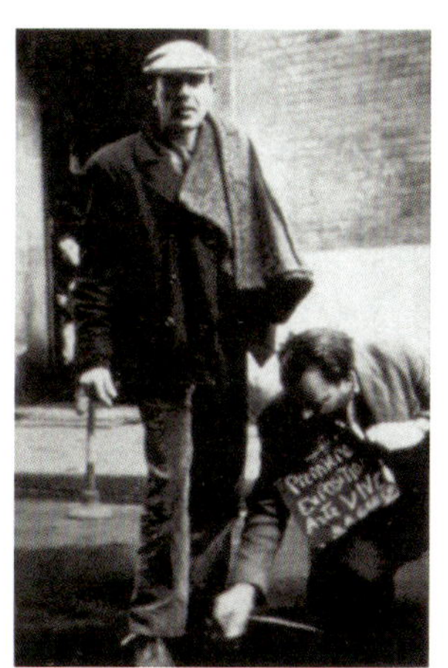
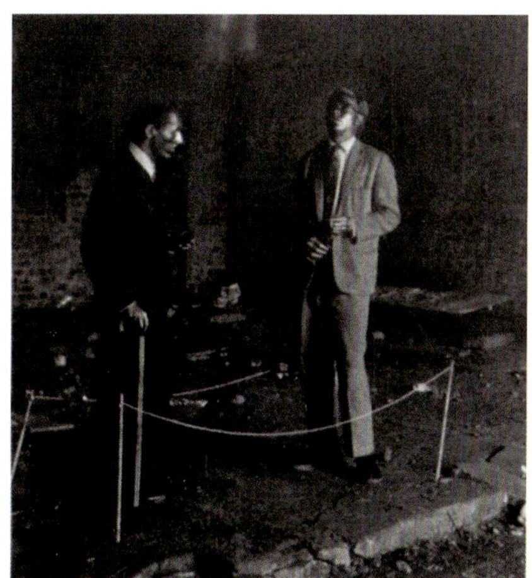
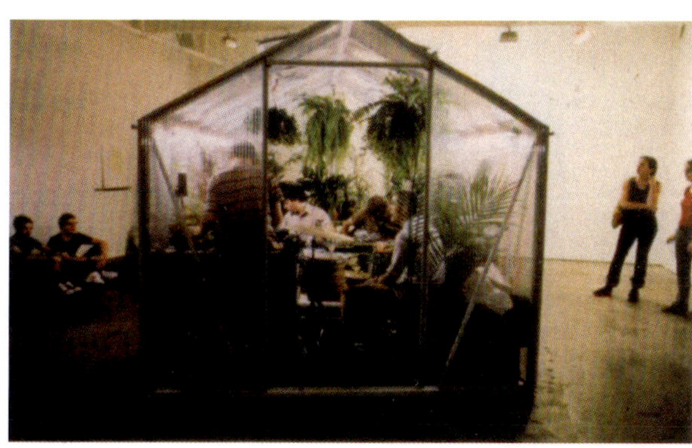
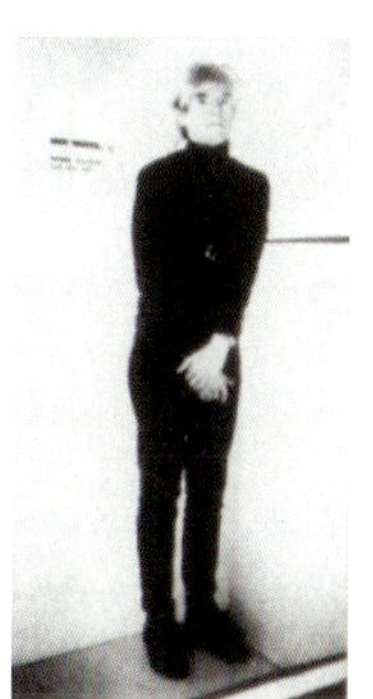
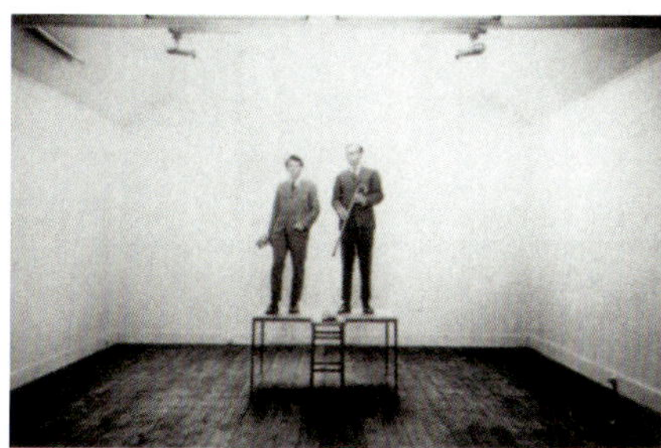
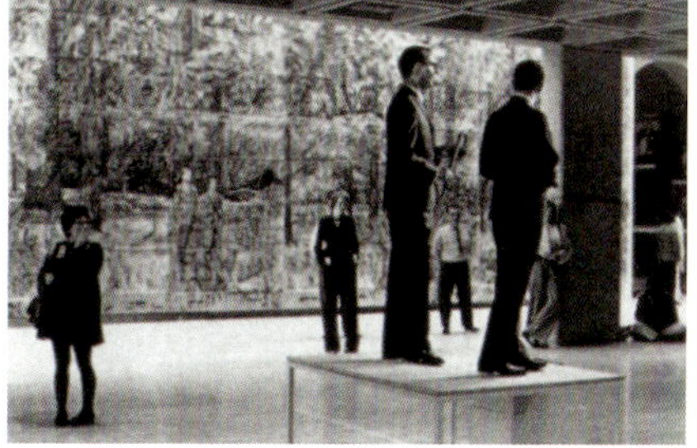

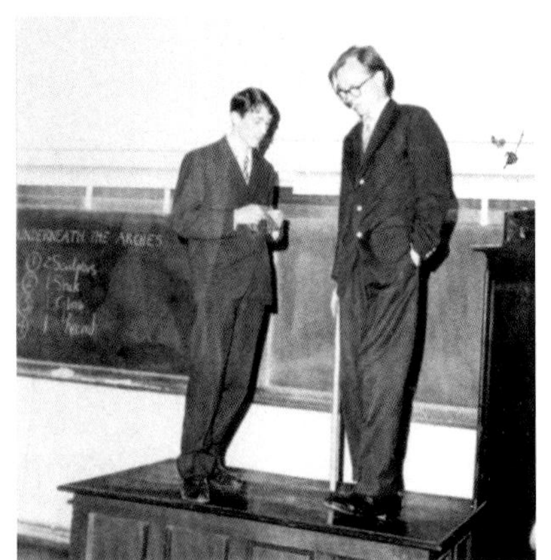

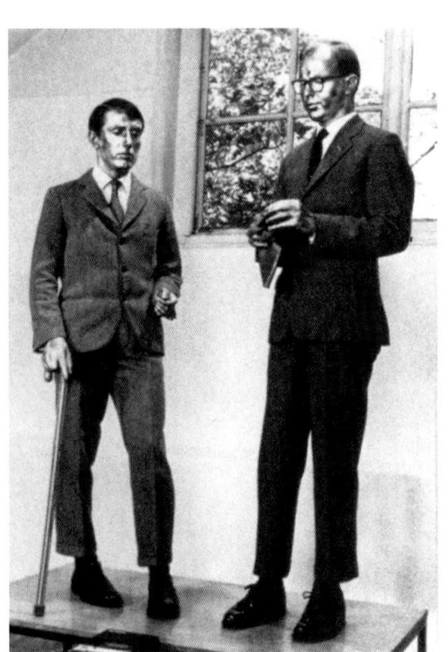

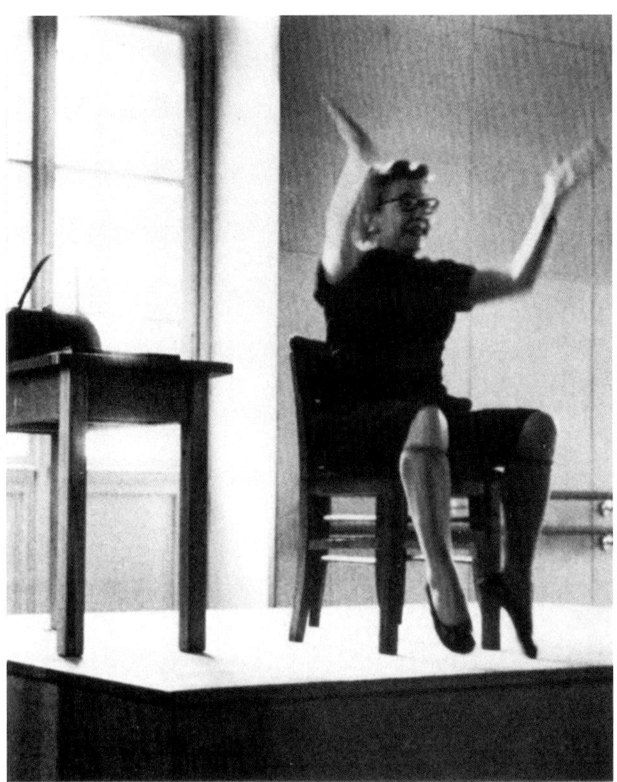

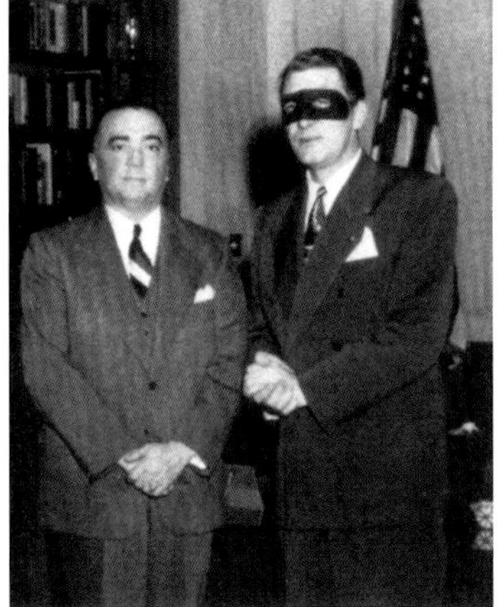

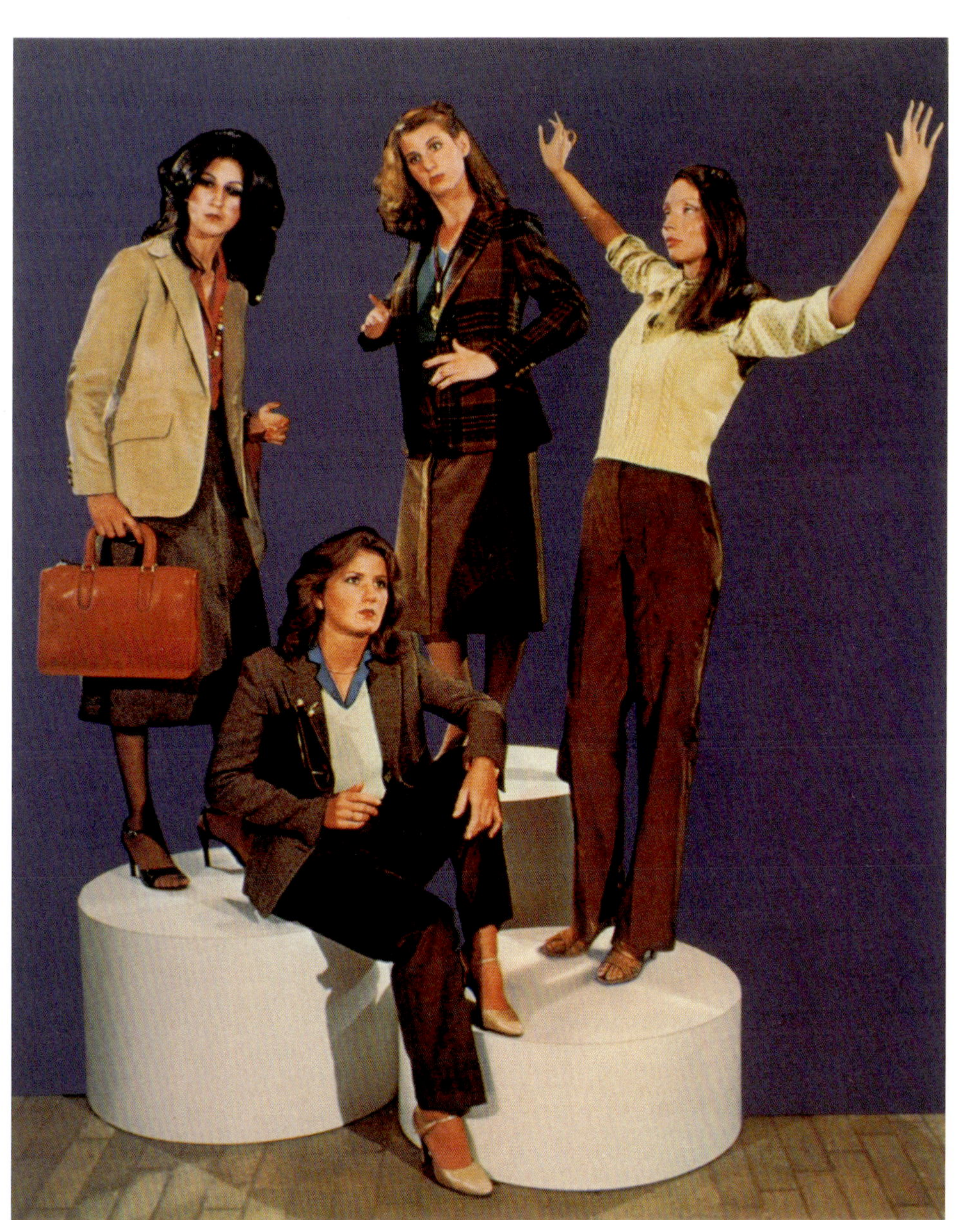

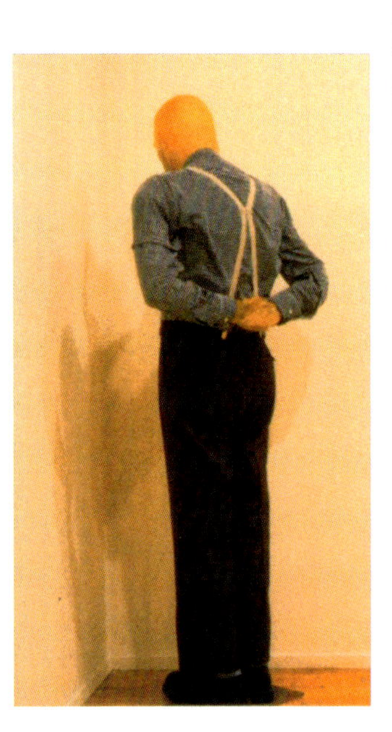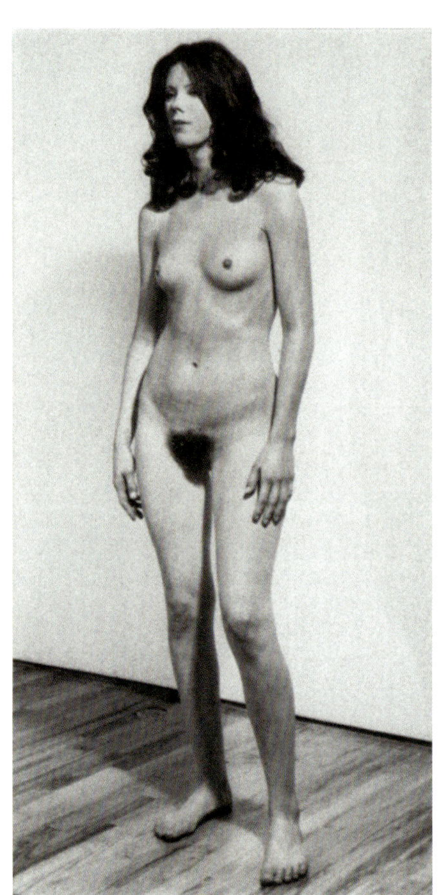

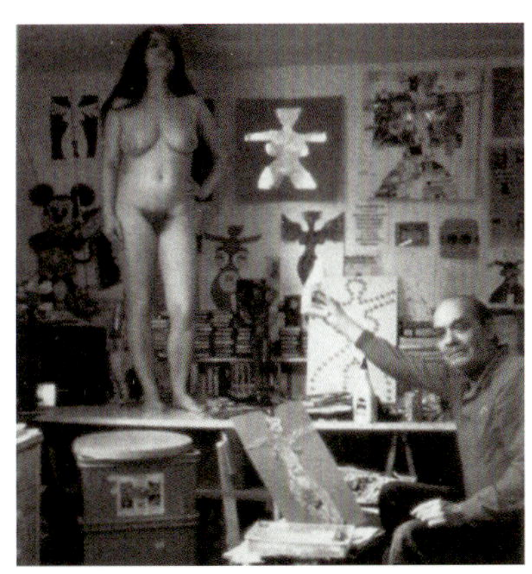

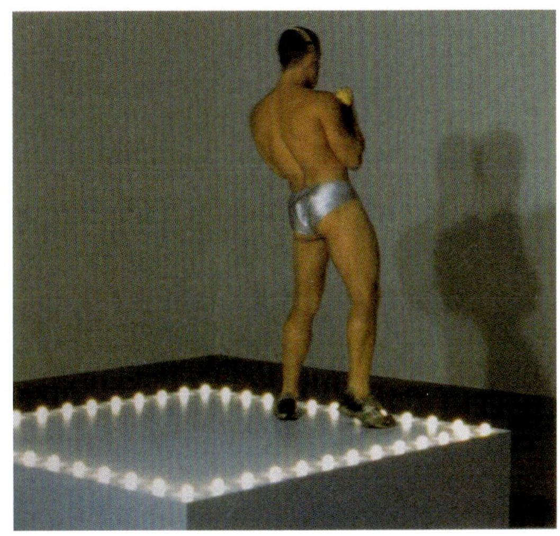

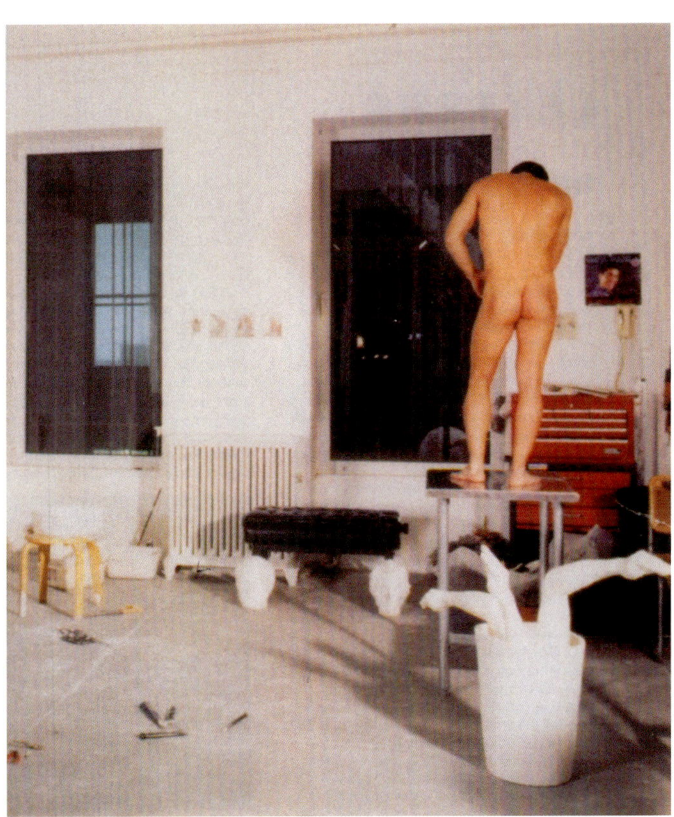

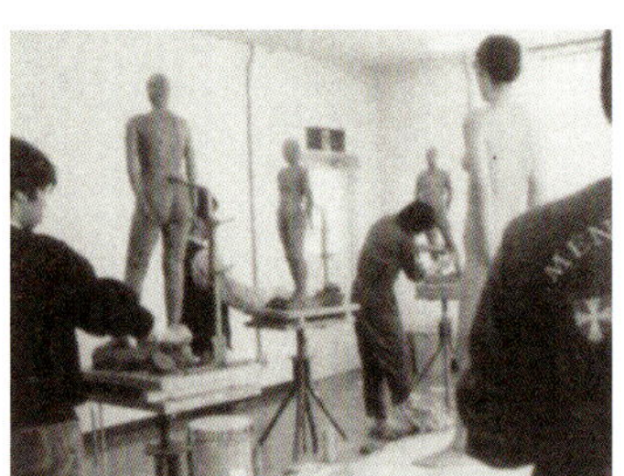
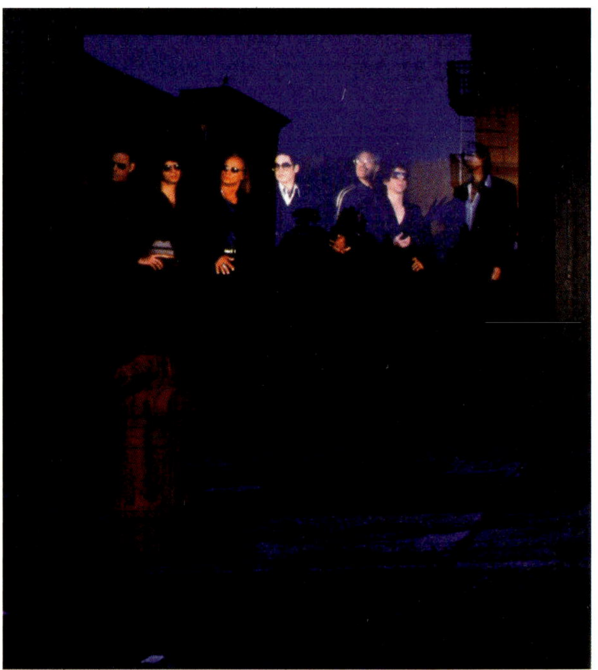
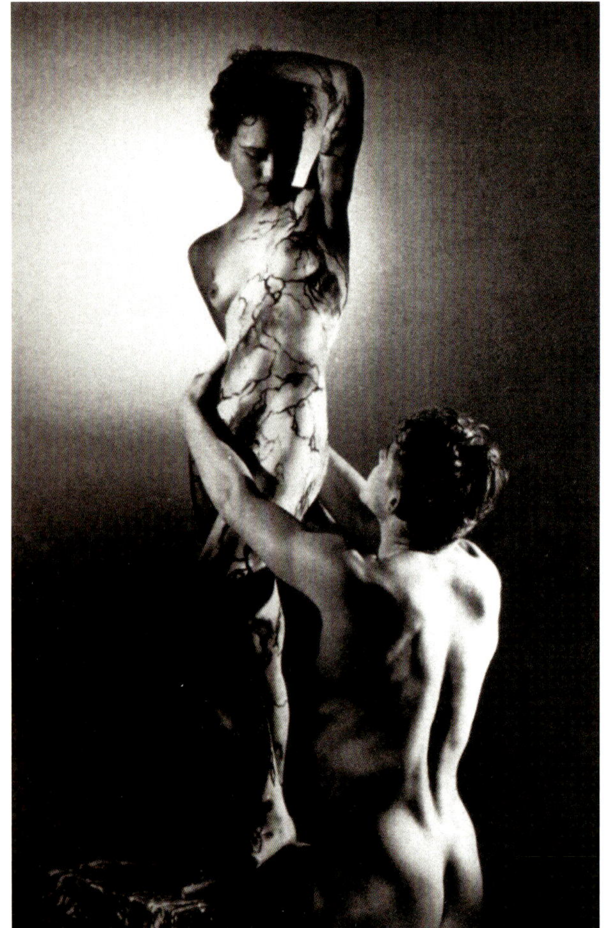
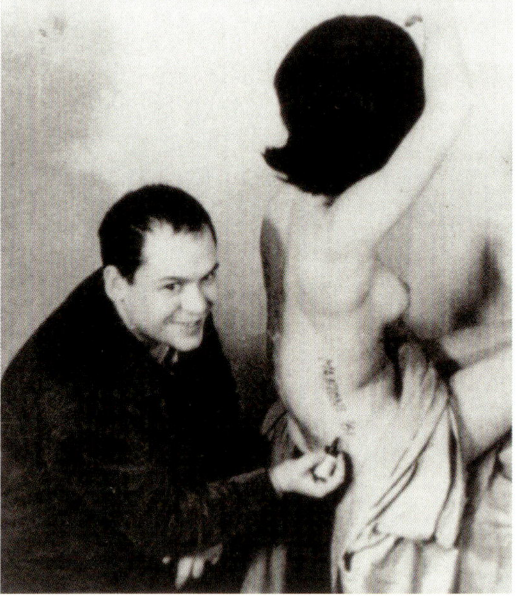

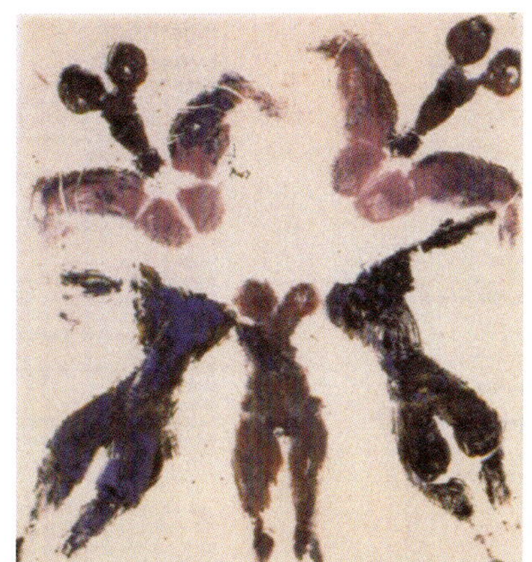

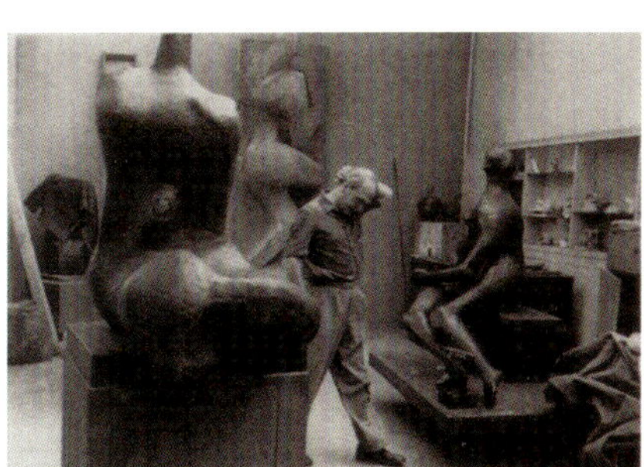

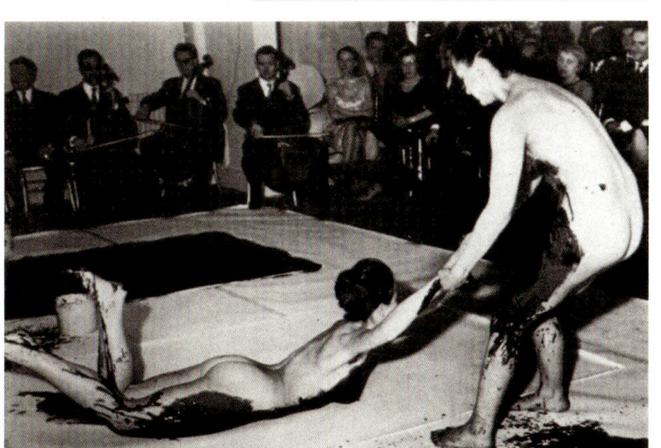

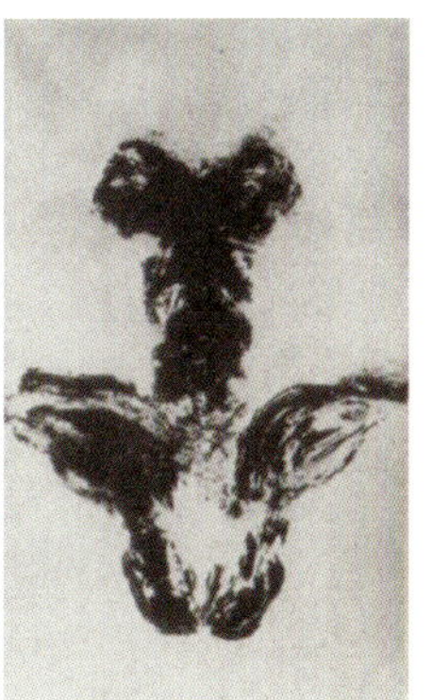

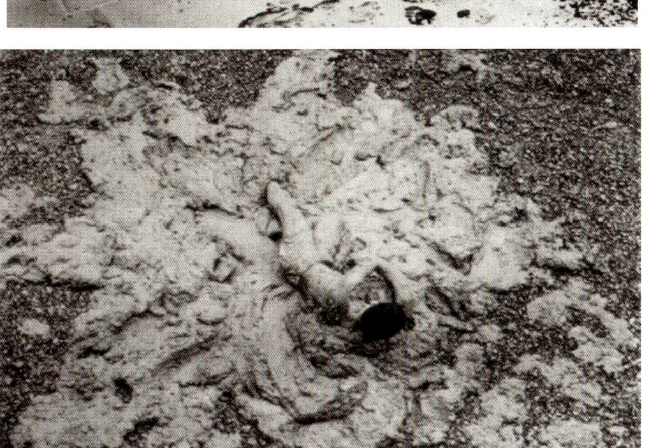

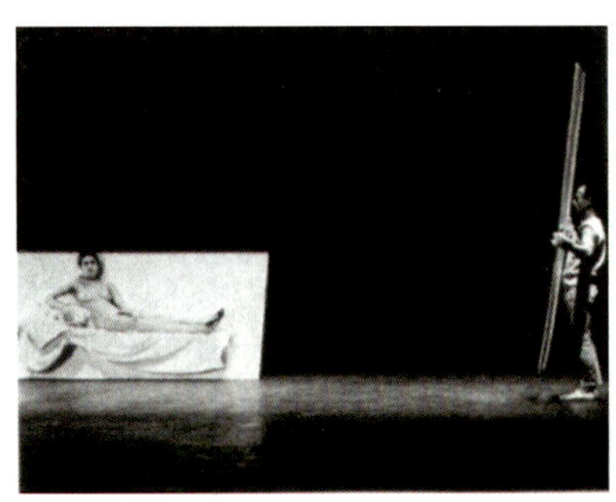

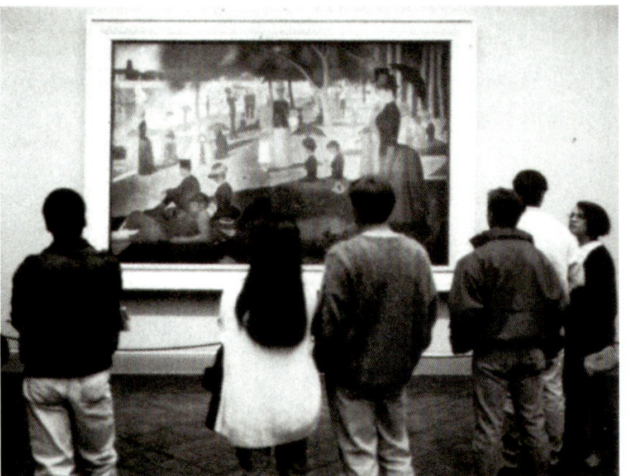

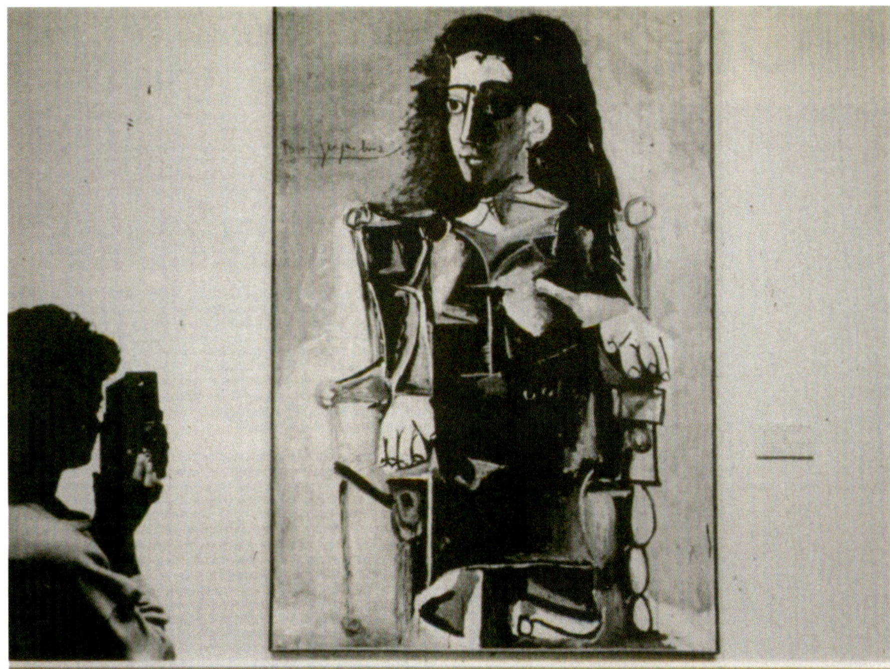

Me looking at Jacqueline's pussy through my box camera. Photo: Cheryl Simon.

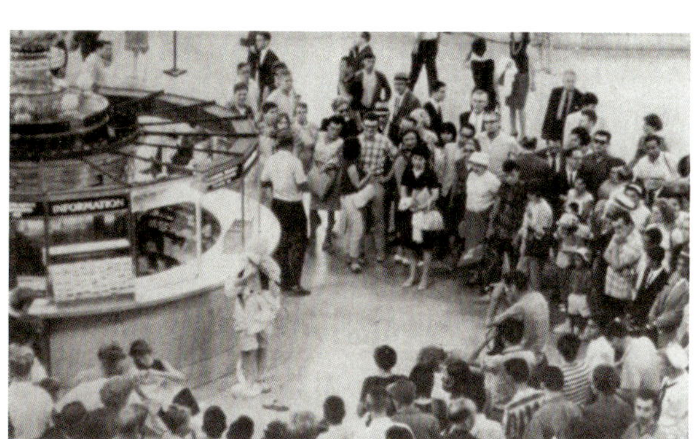
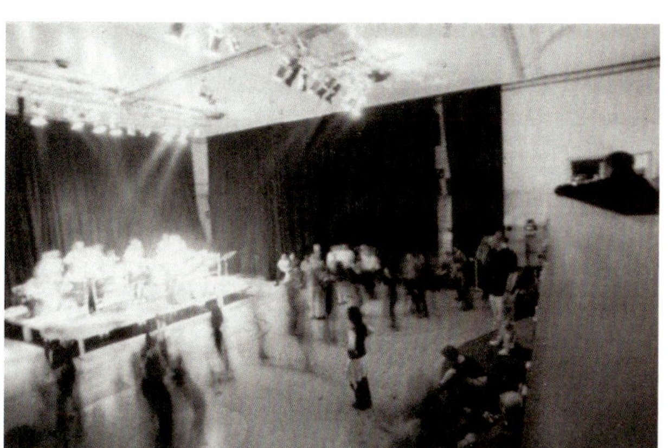
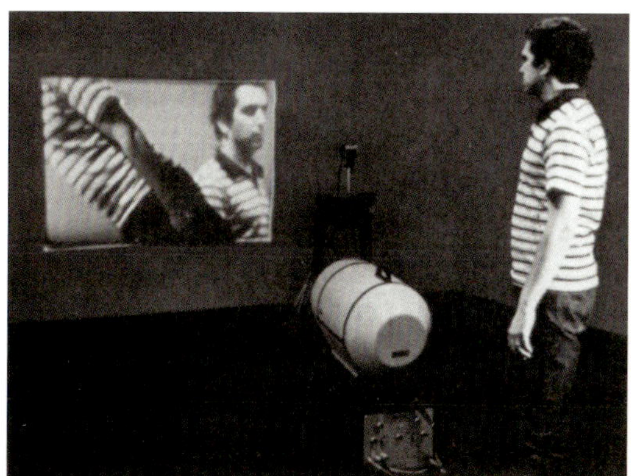
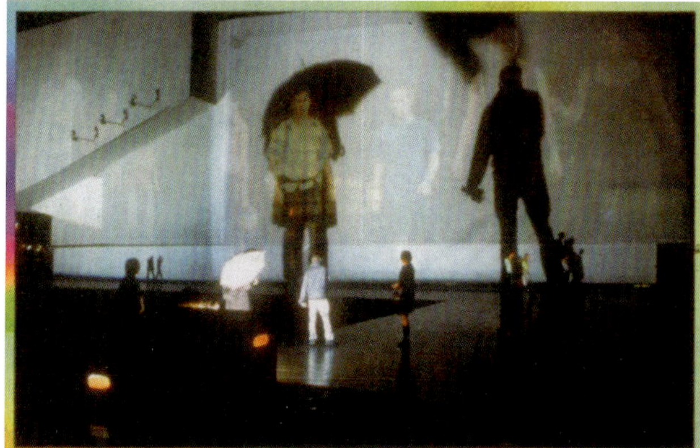
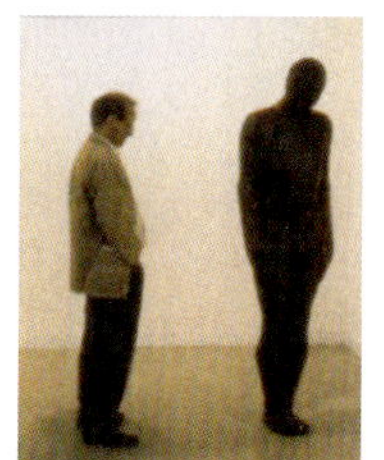
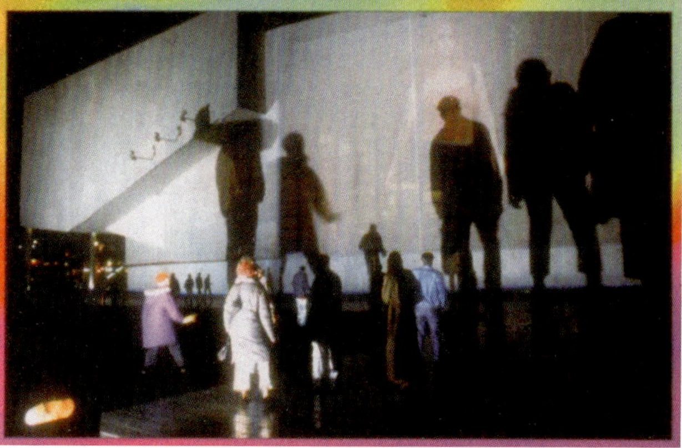

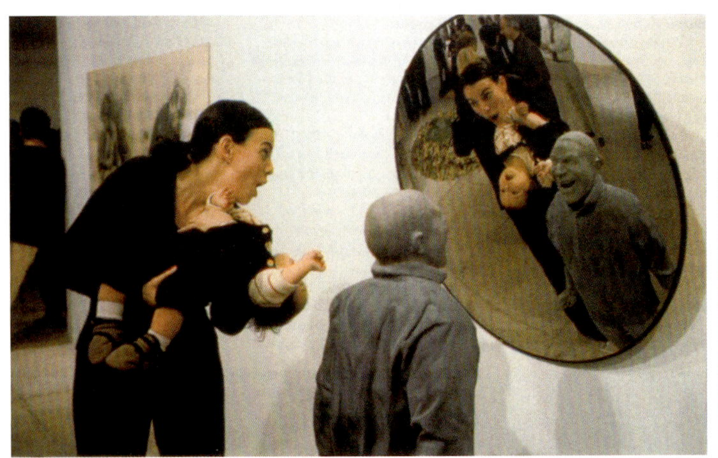
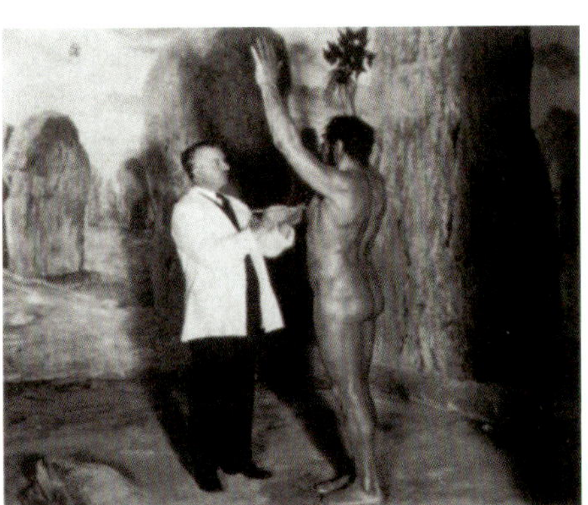
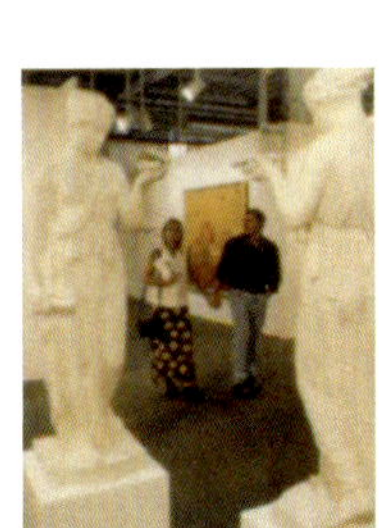
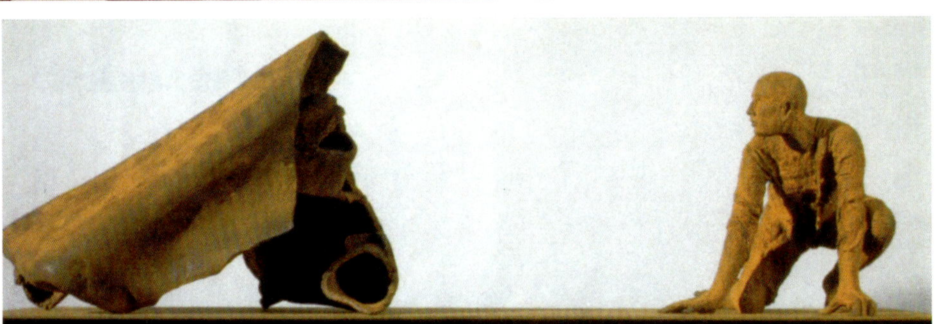
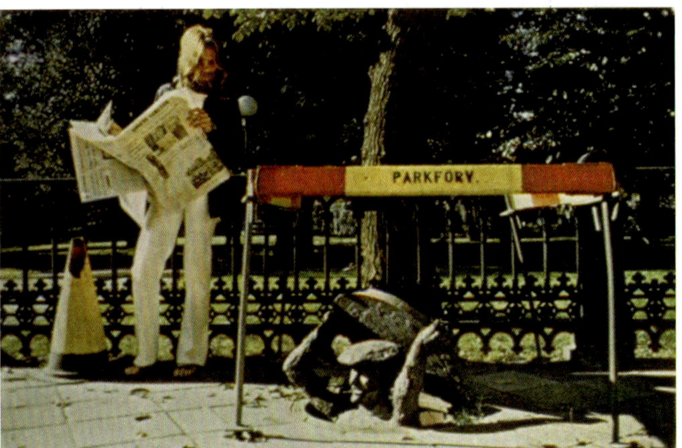
PARKFÖRV.
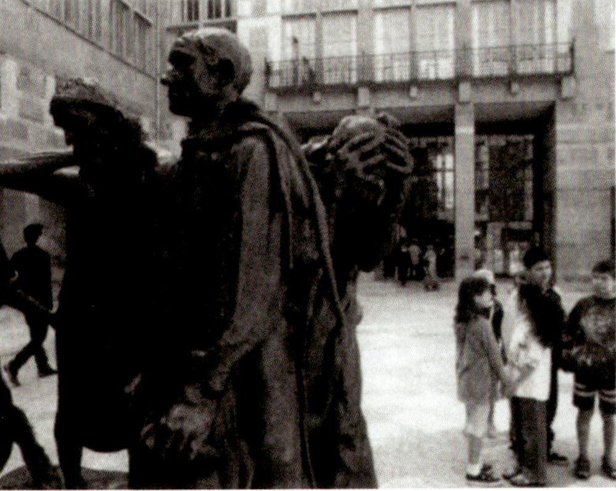

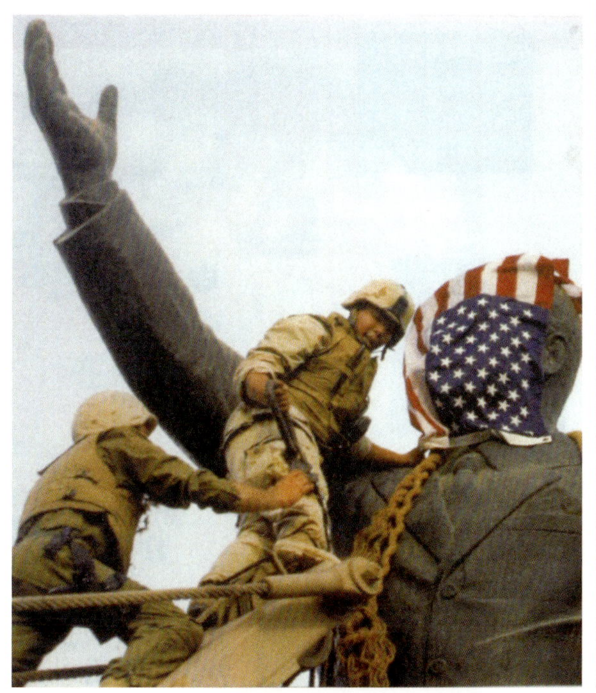

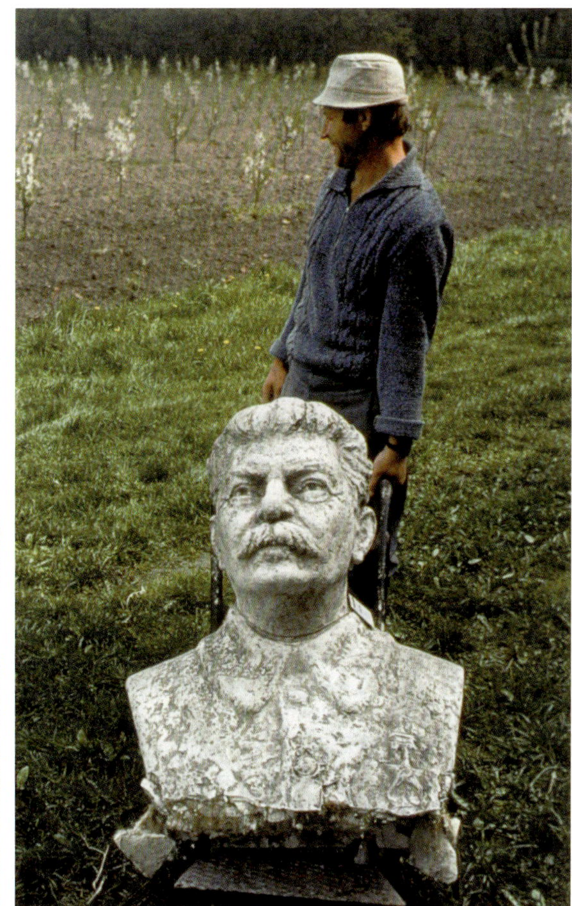

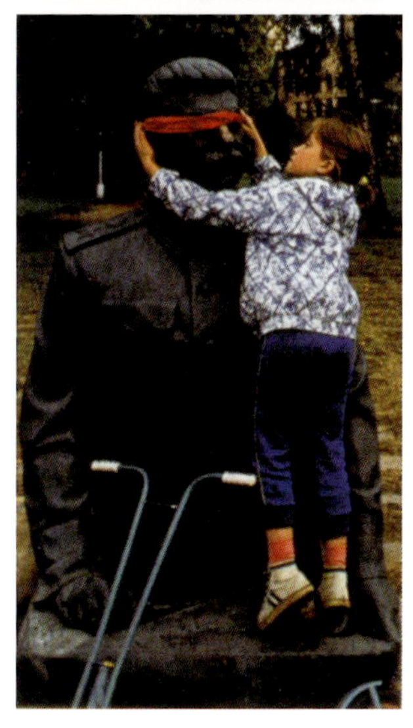

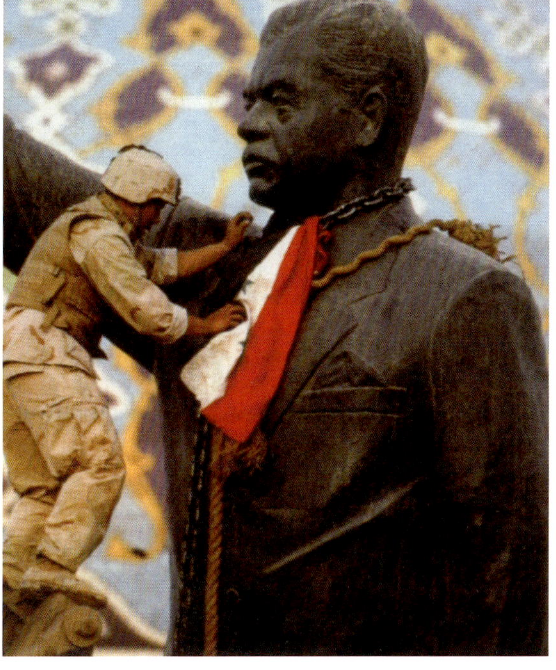

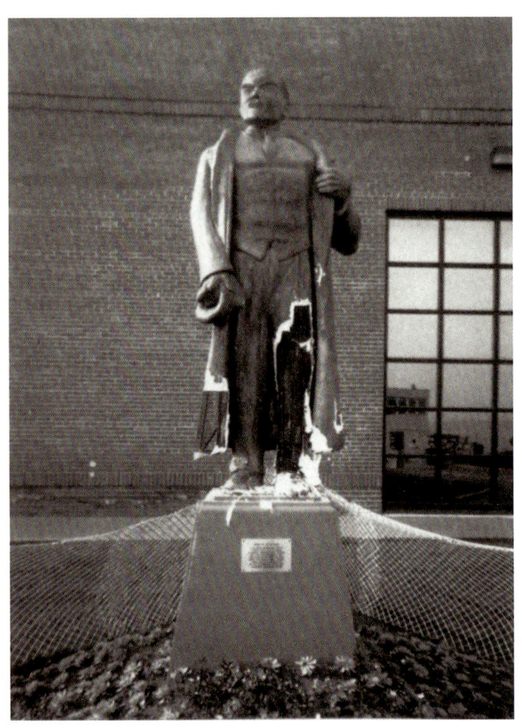
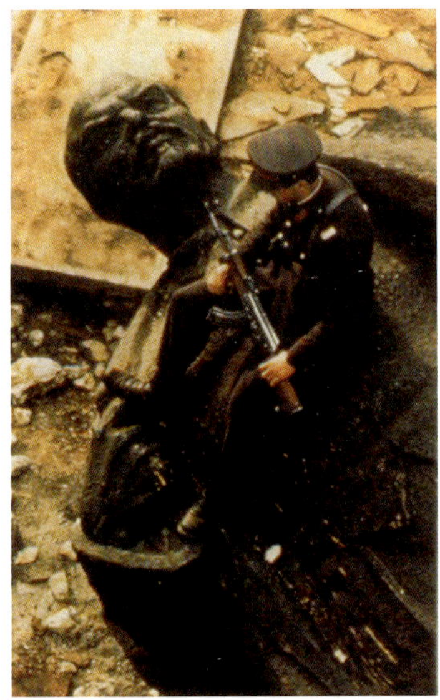
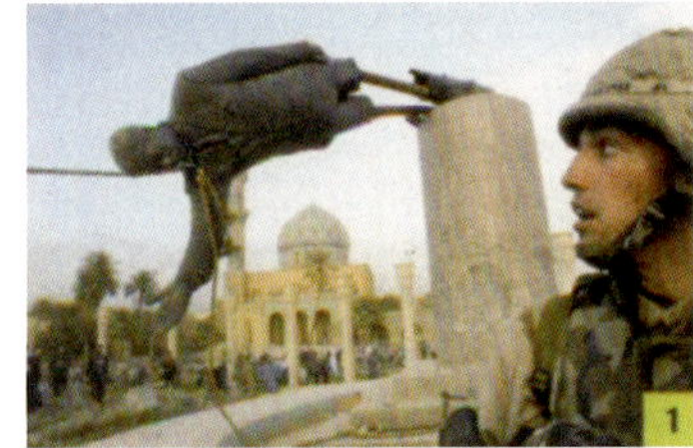
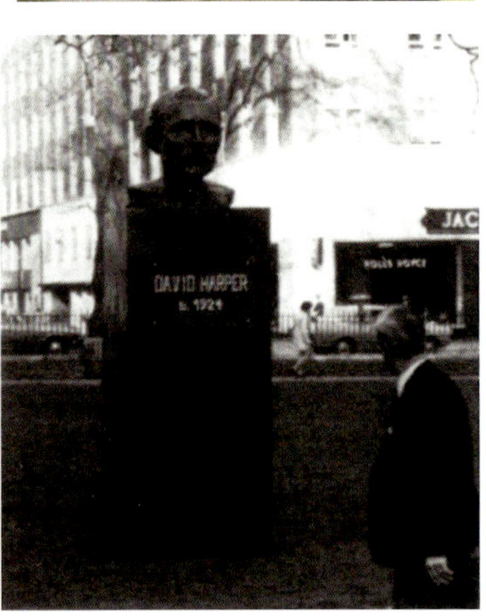

DAVID HARPER
b. 1929

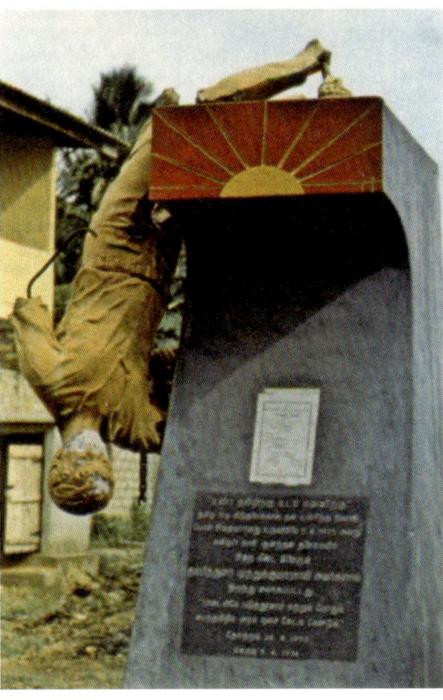

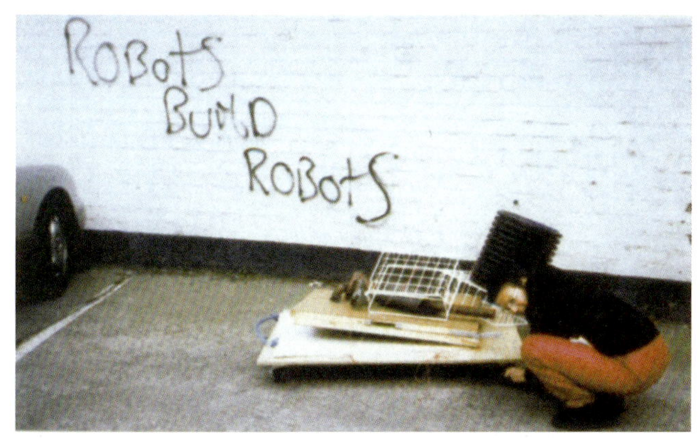

ROBOTS
BUILD
ROBOTS

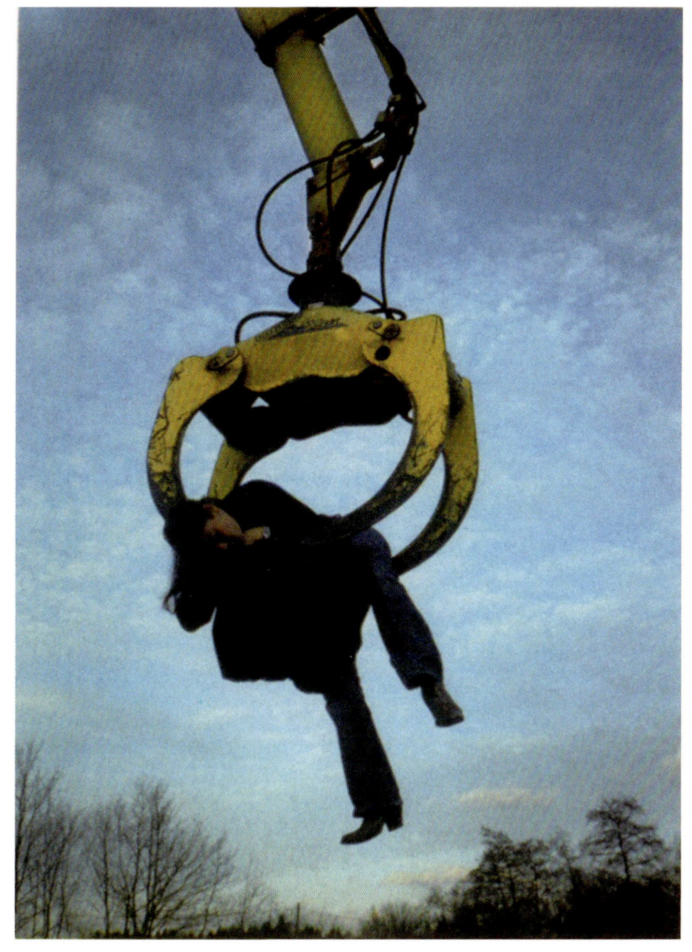

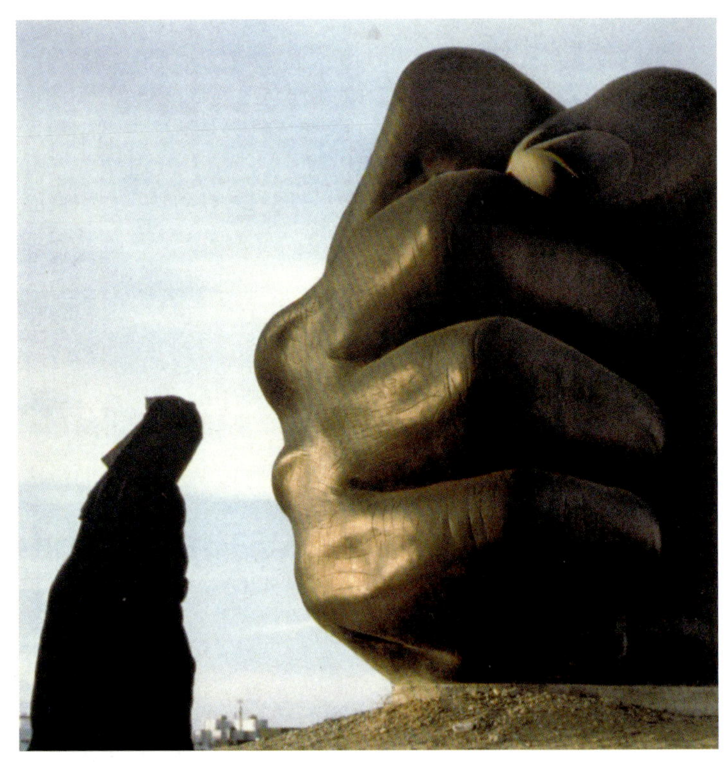

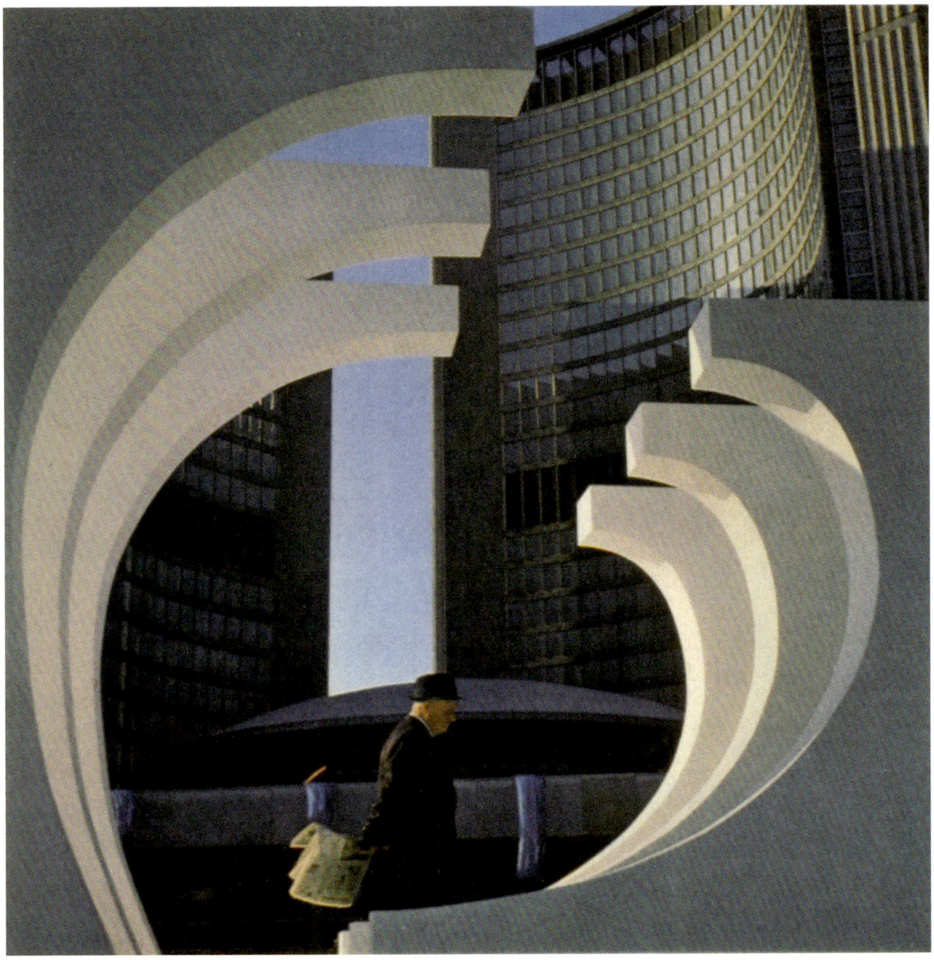

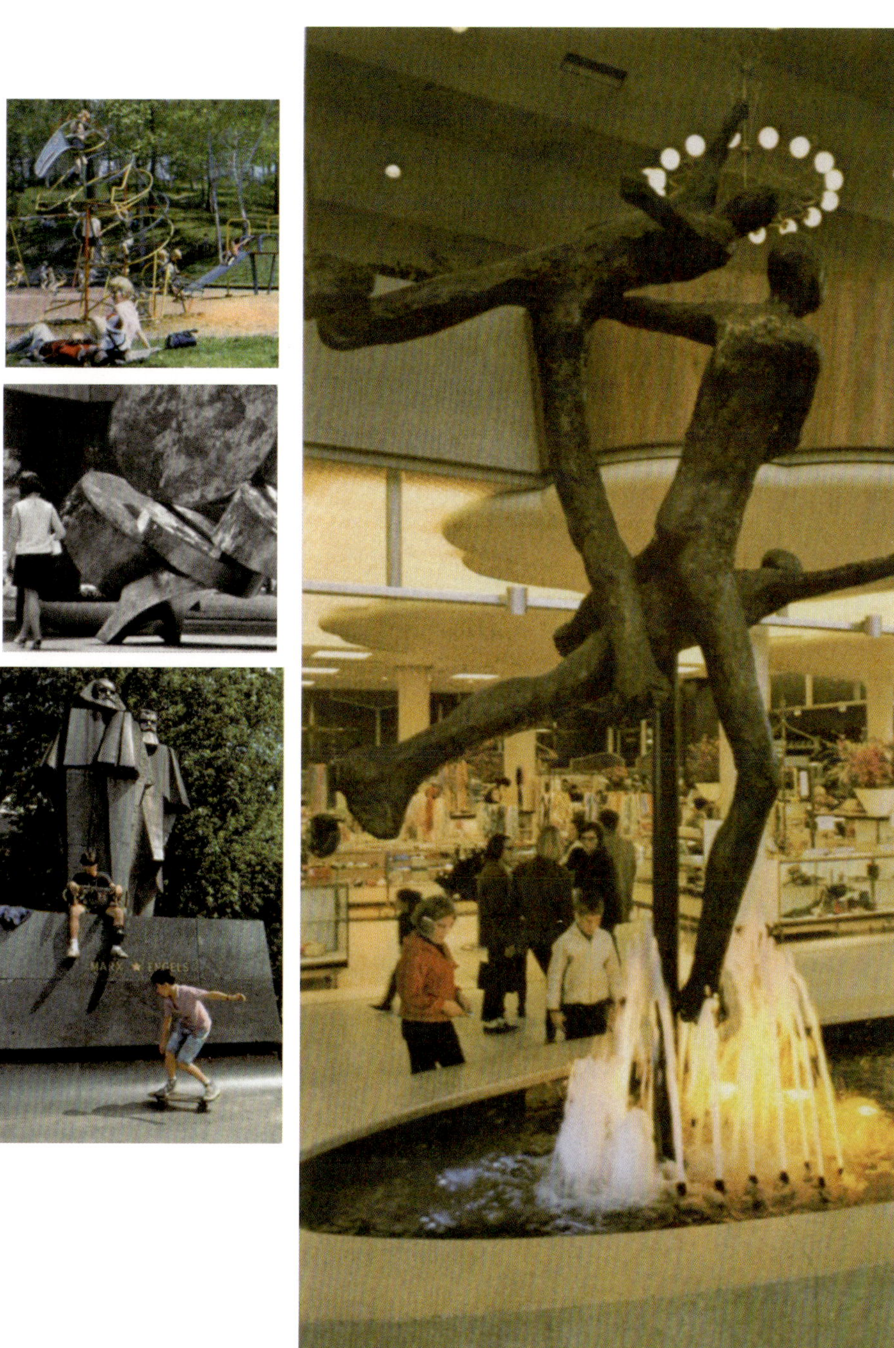

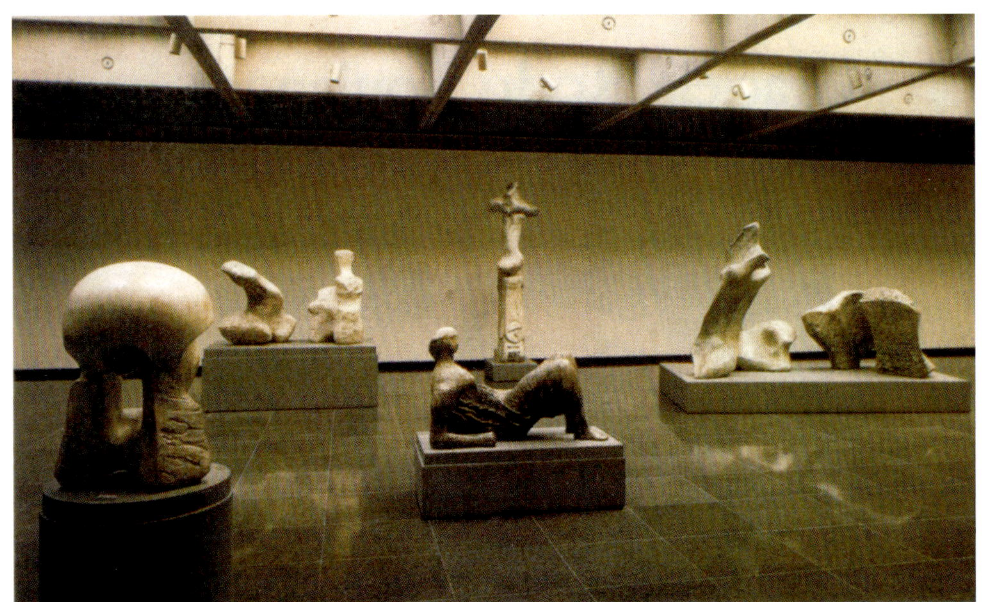

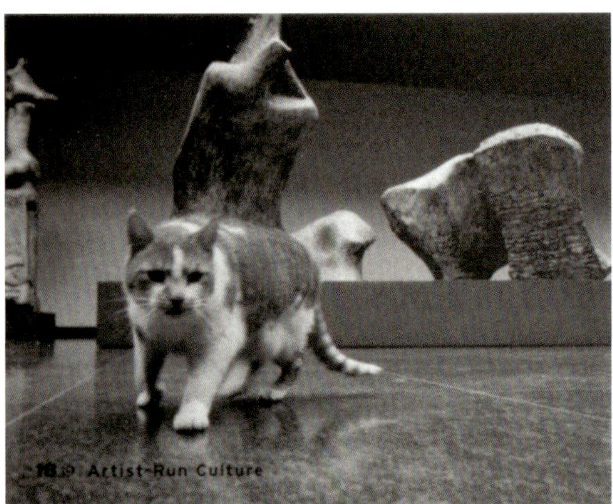
18.9 Artist-Run Culture

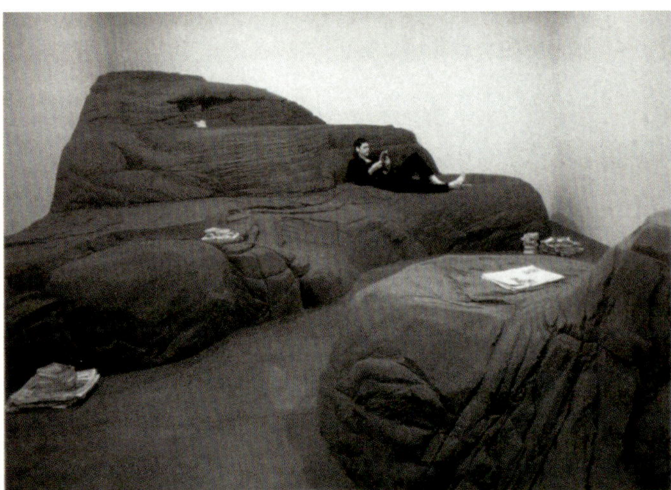

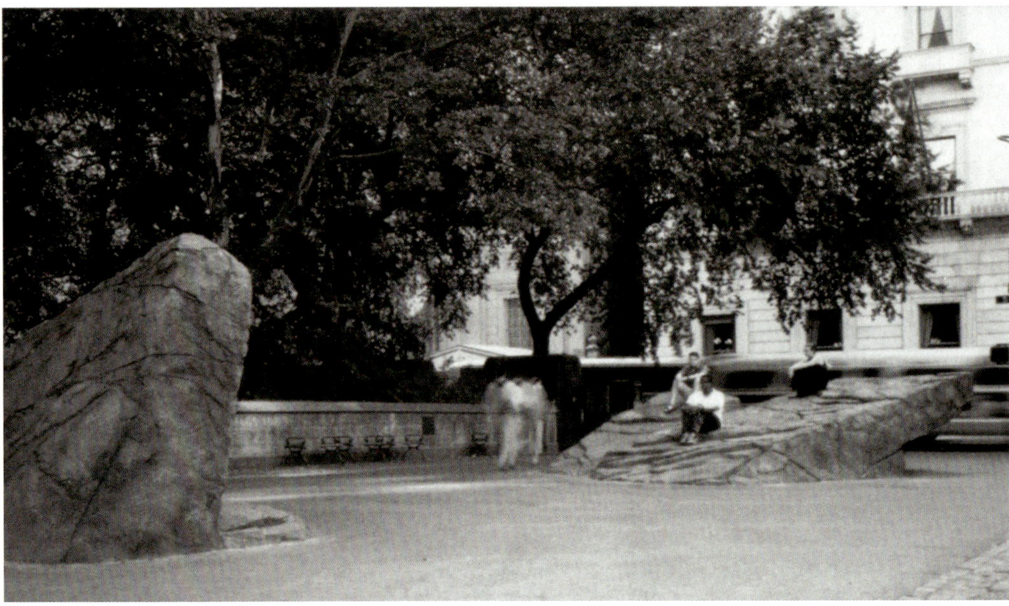

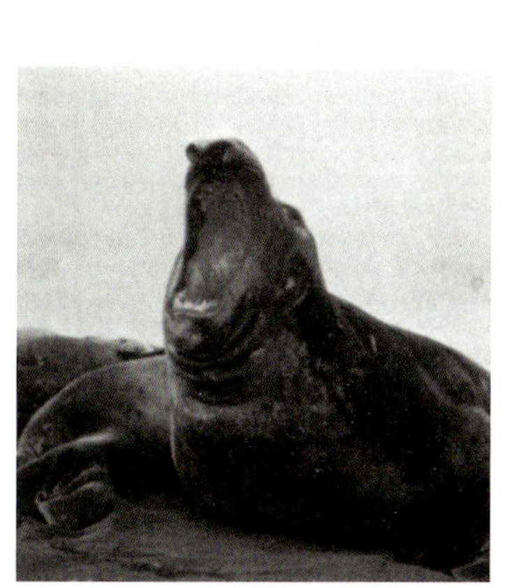

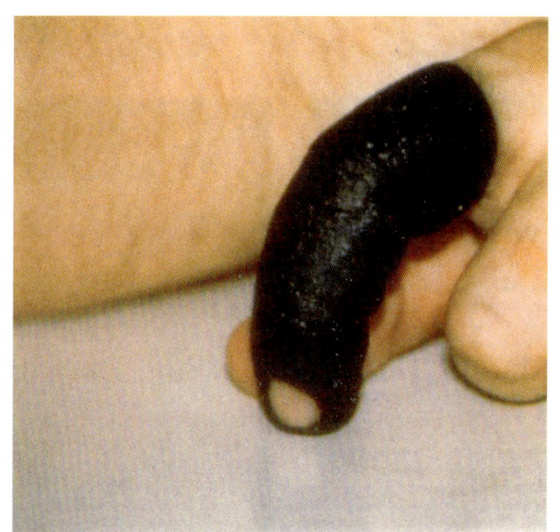

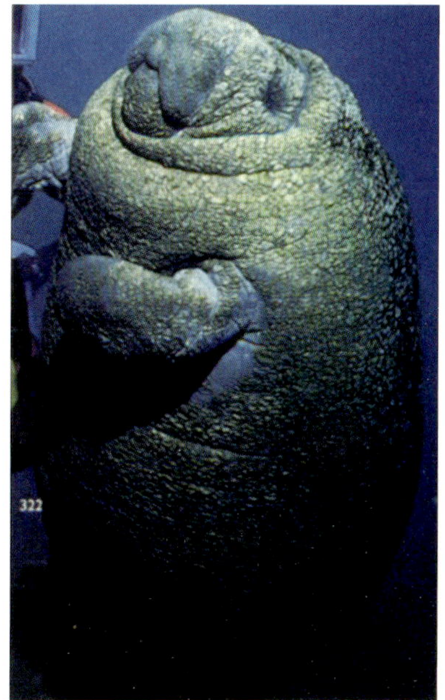

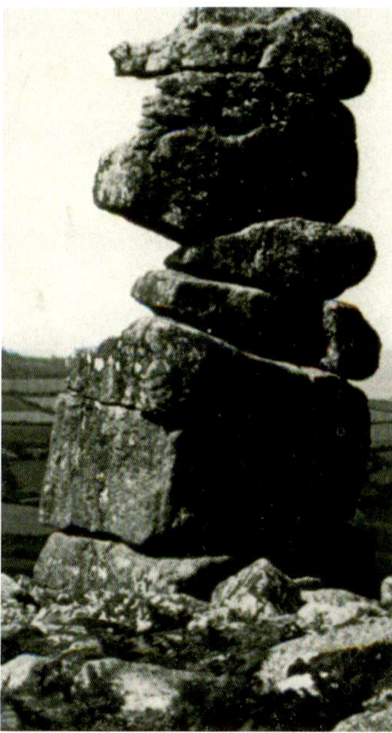

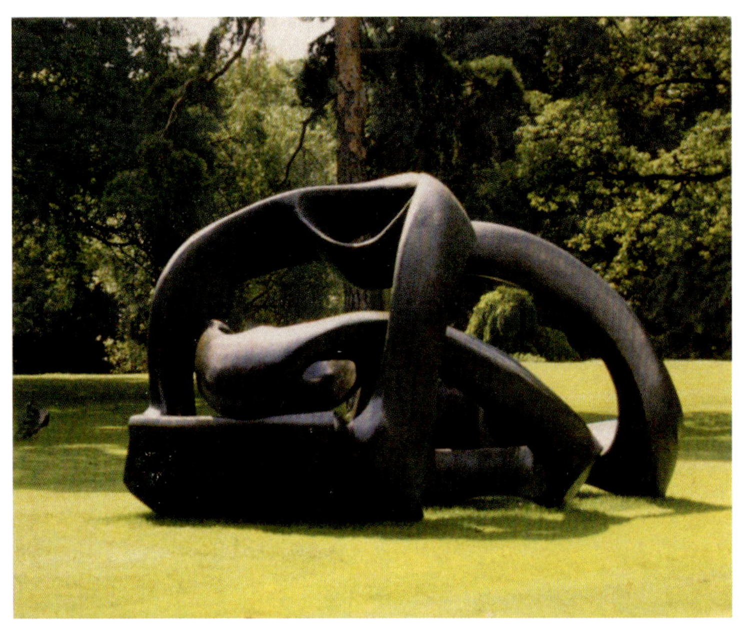

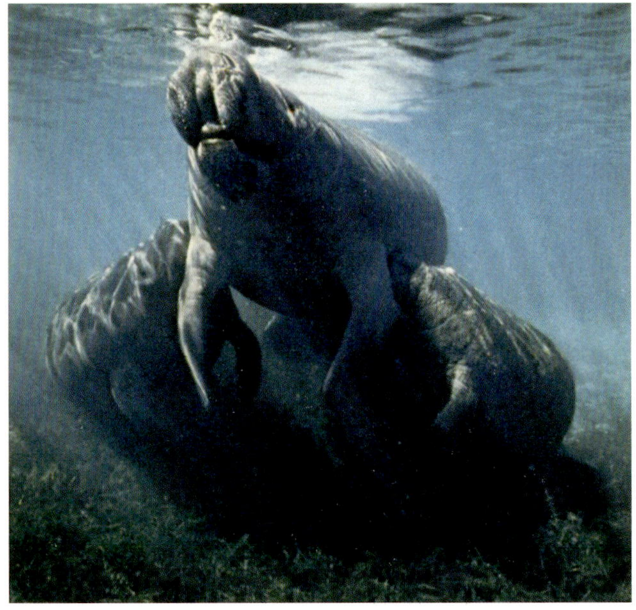

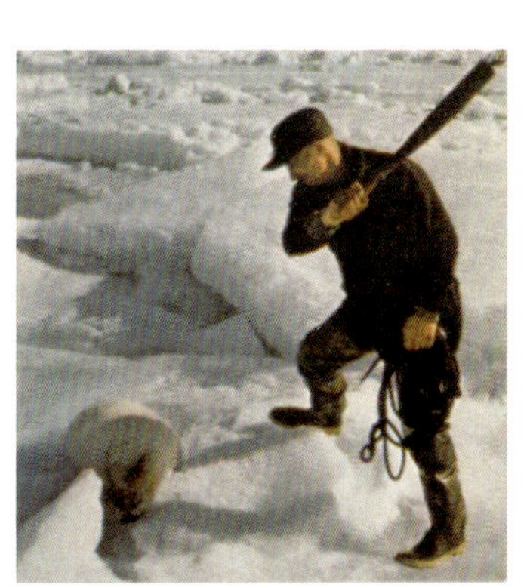
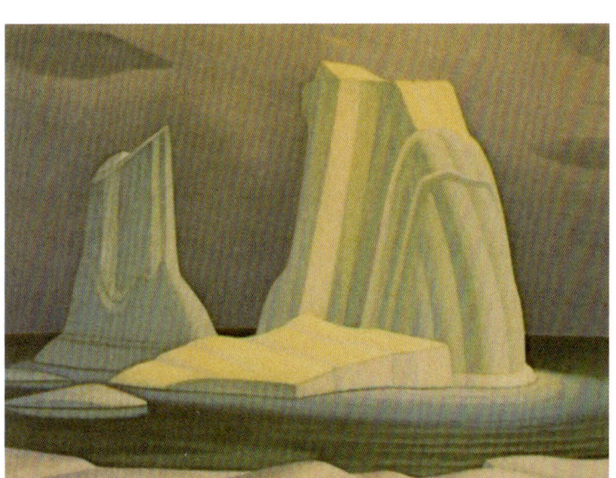
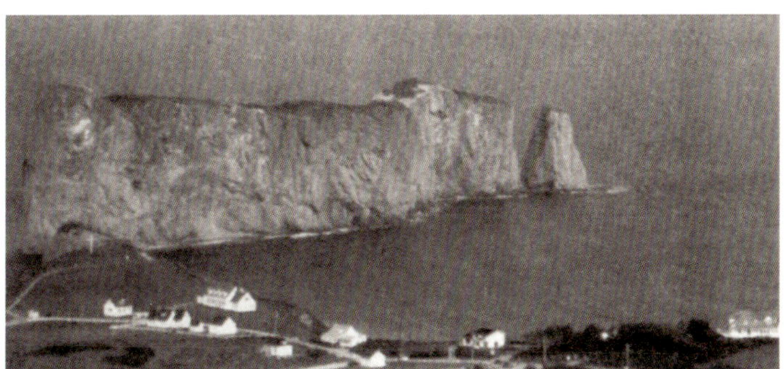
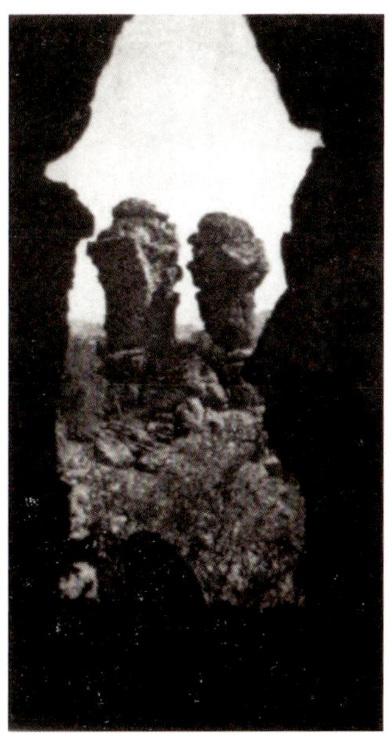
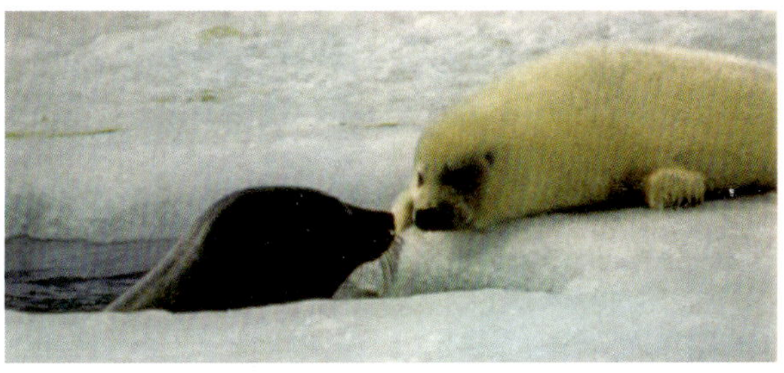

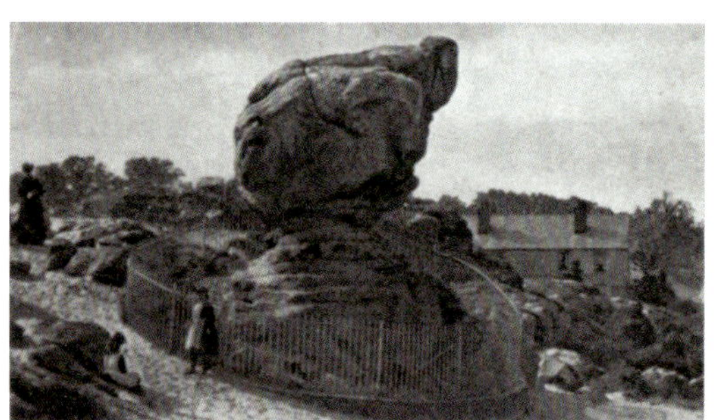

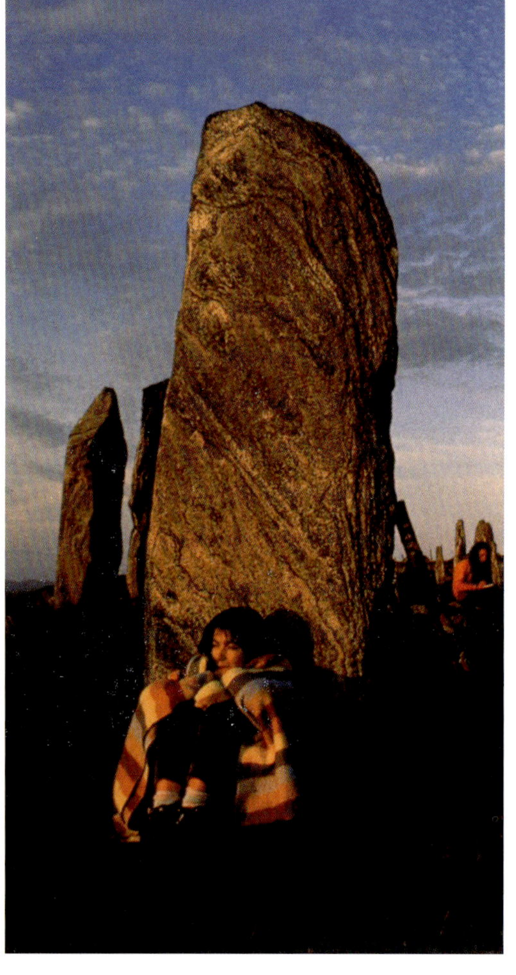

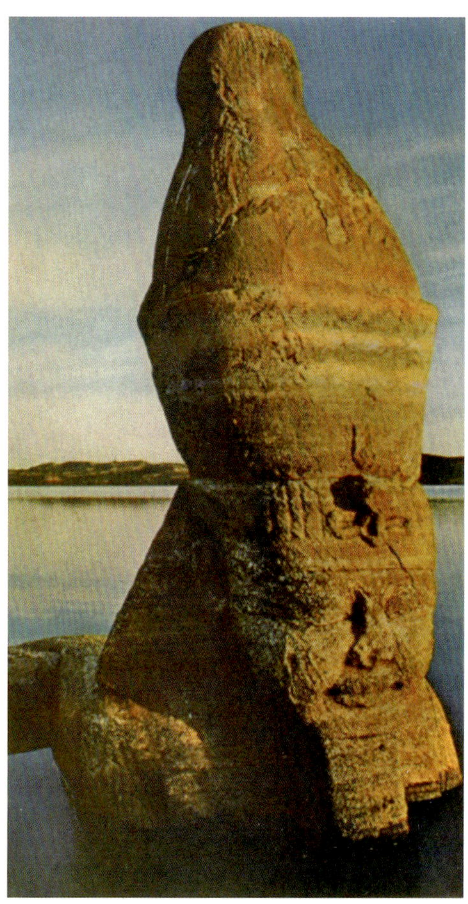

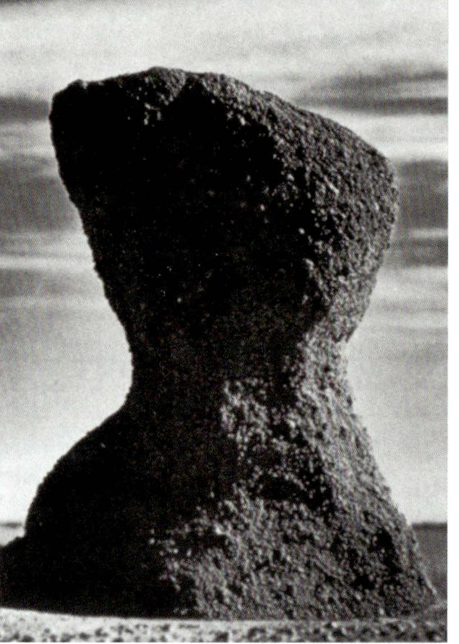

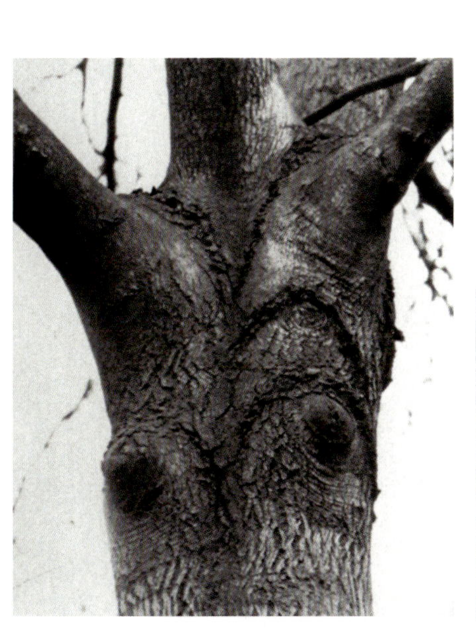
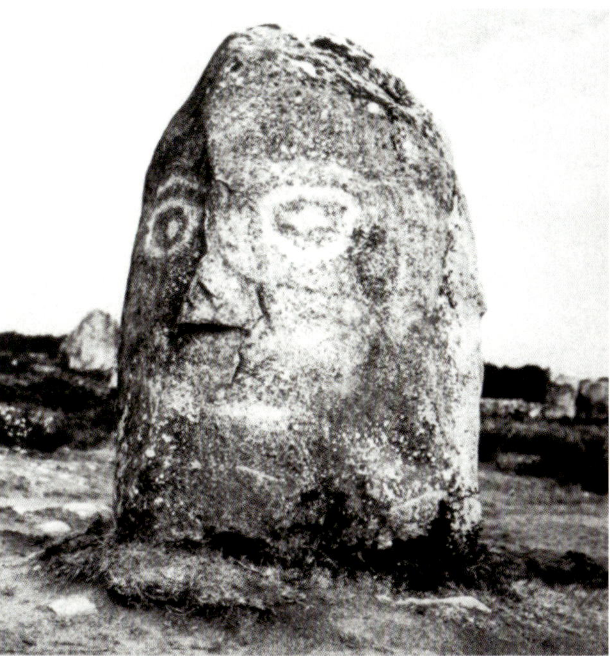
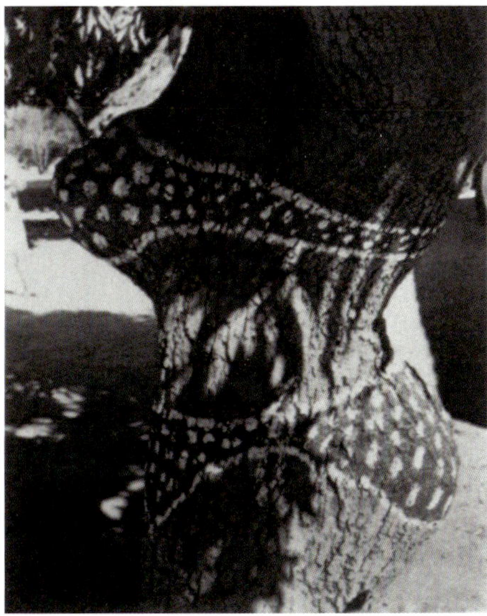
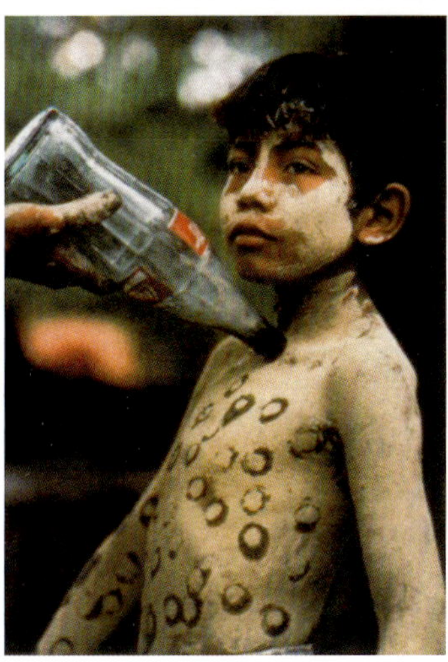

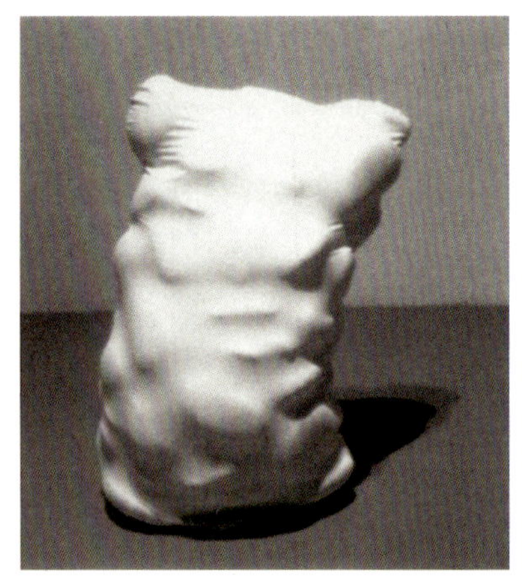
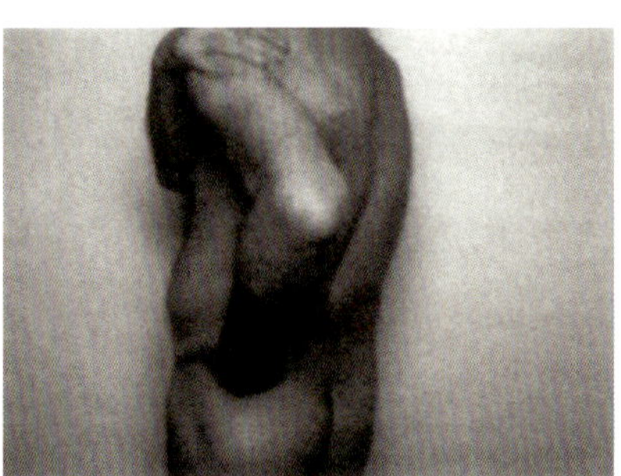
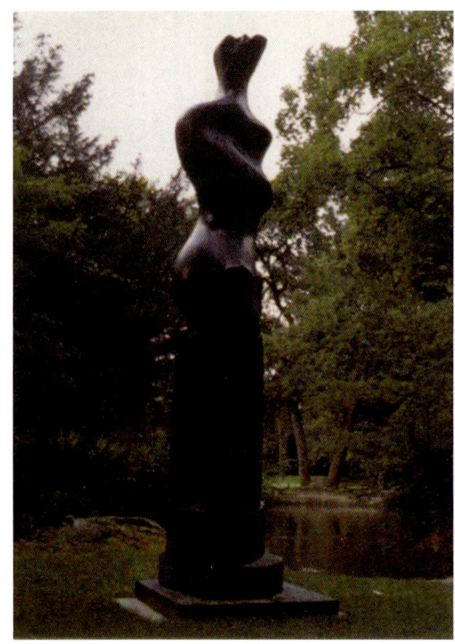
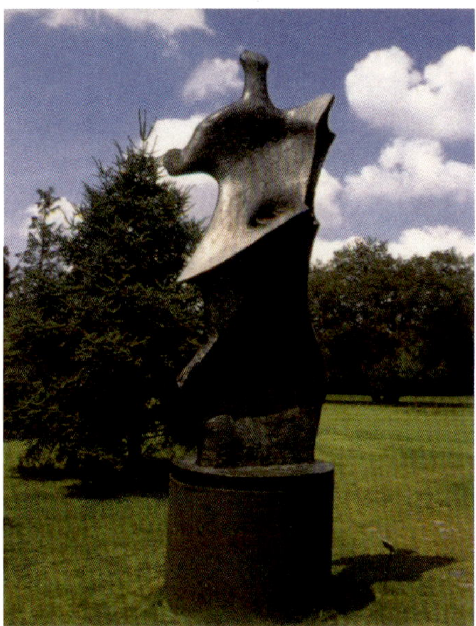

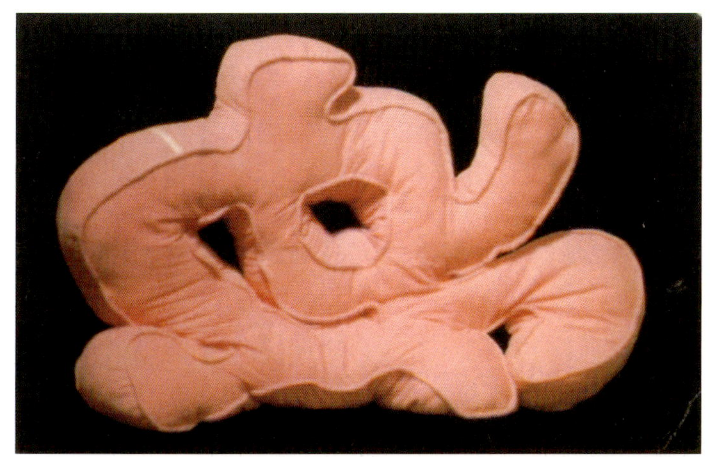
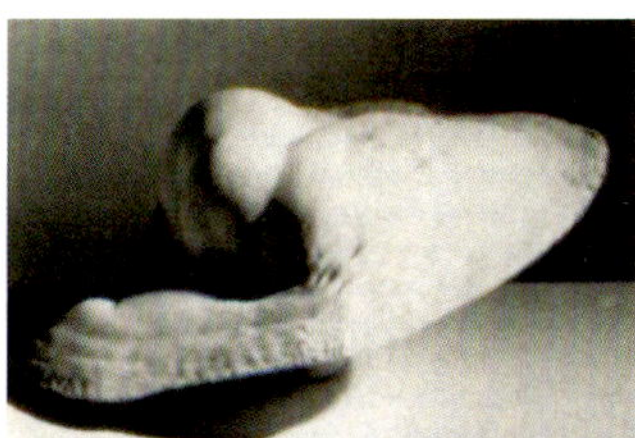

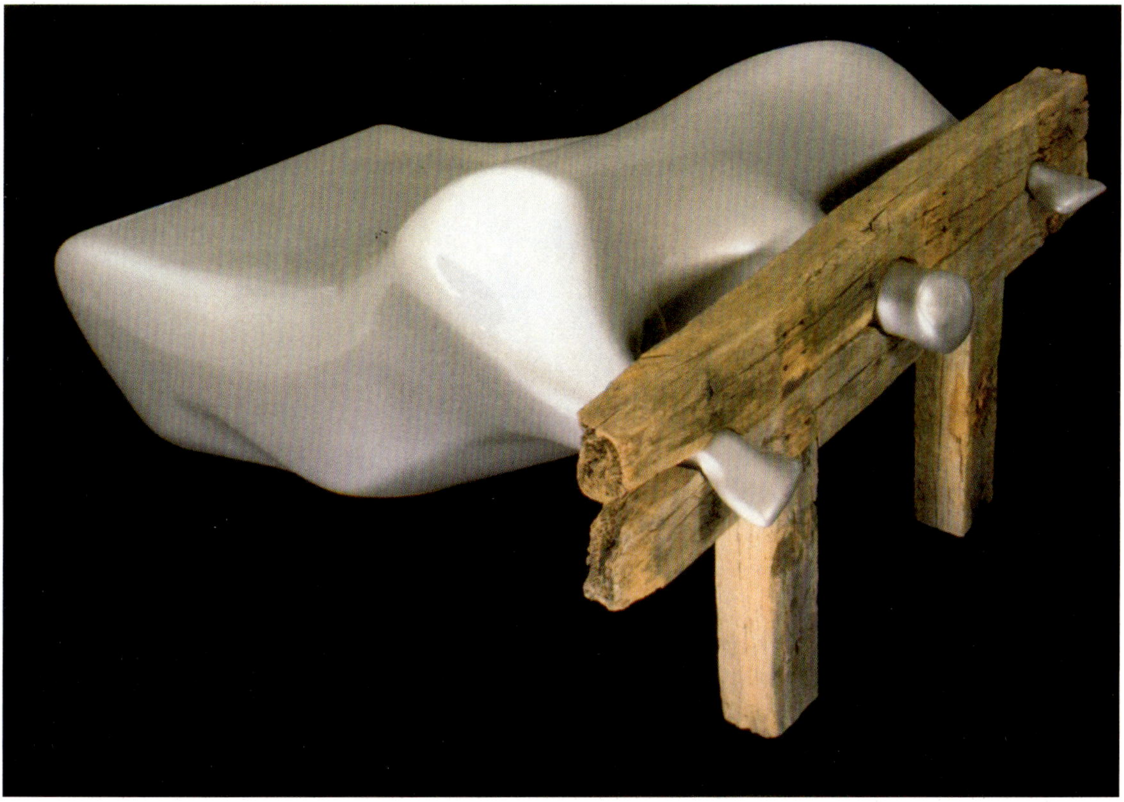

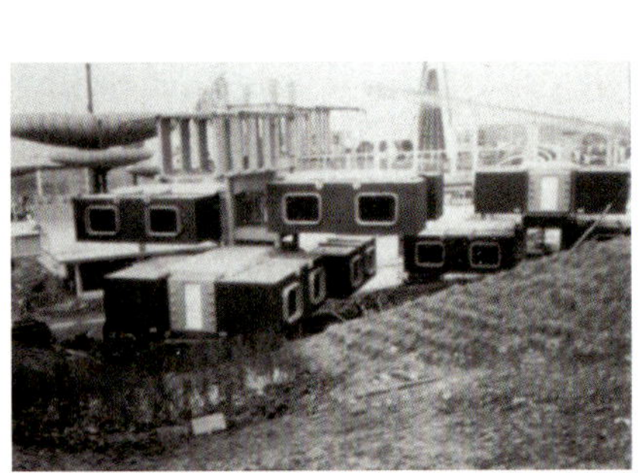
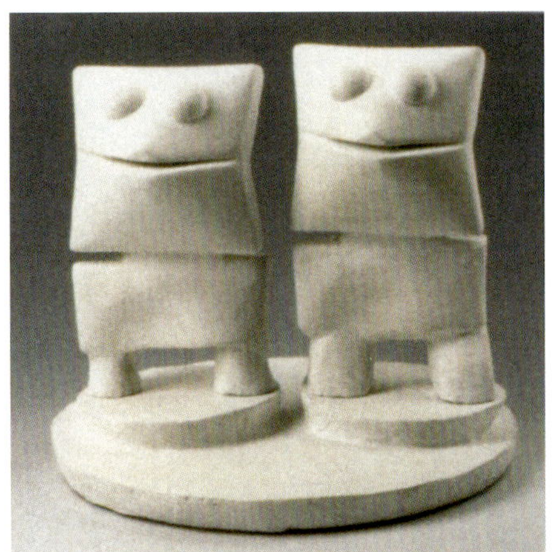
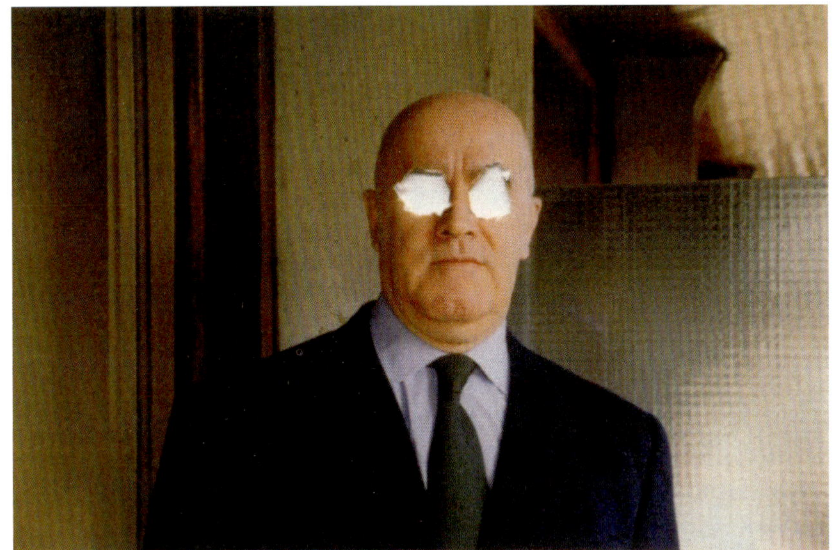
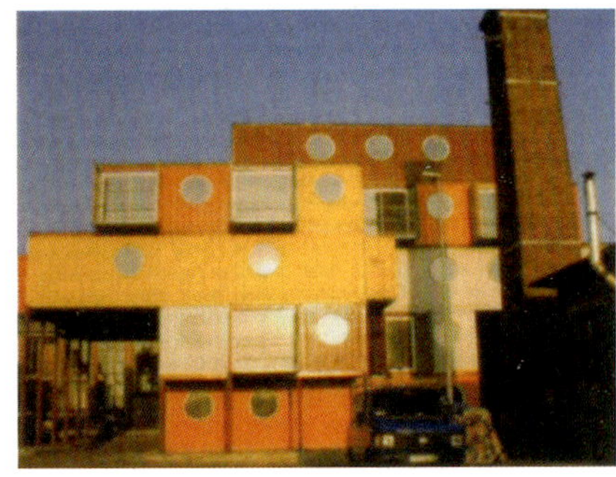
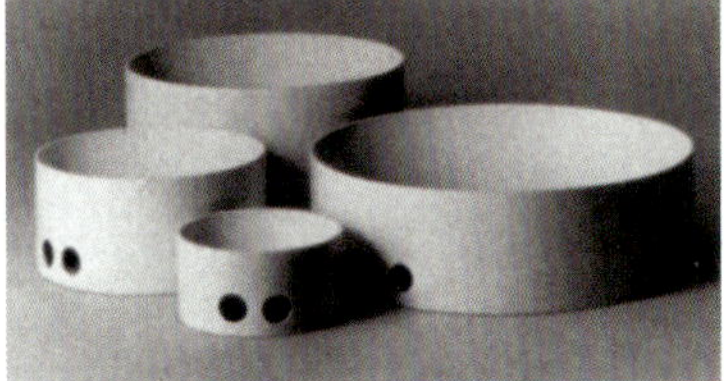

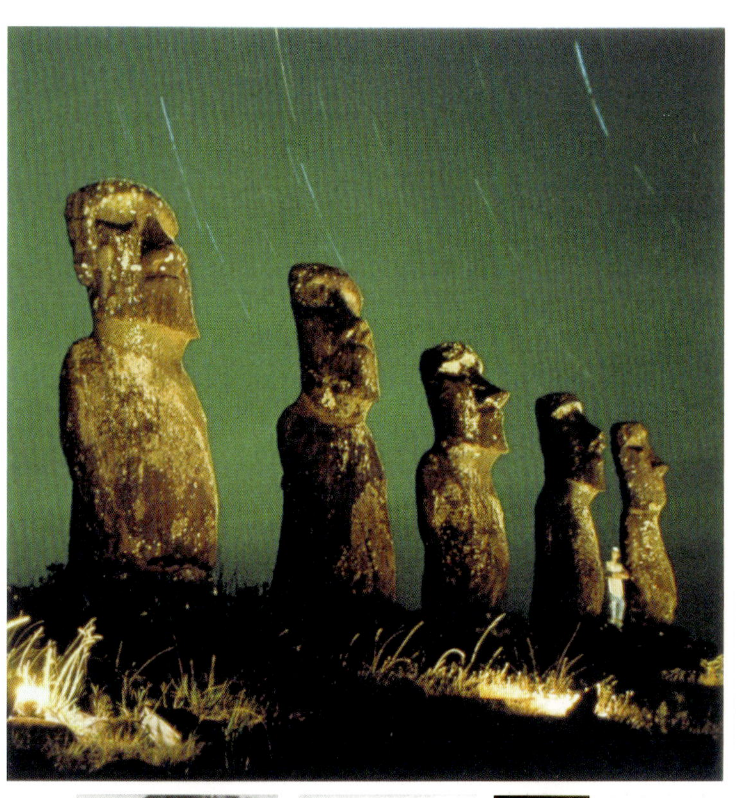
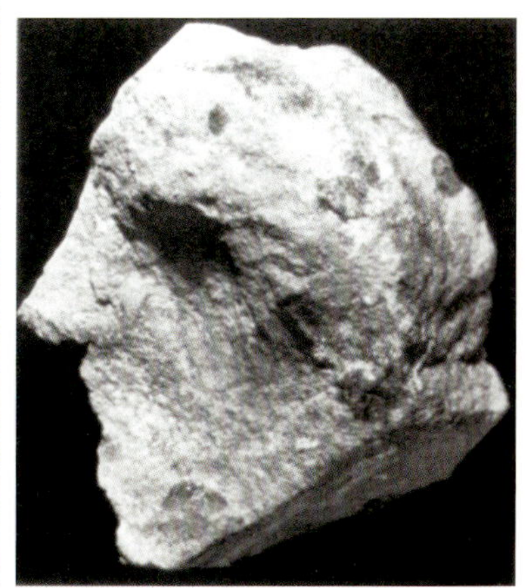
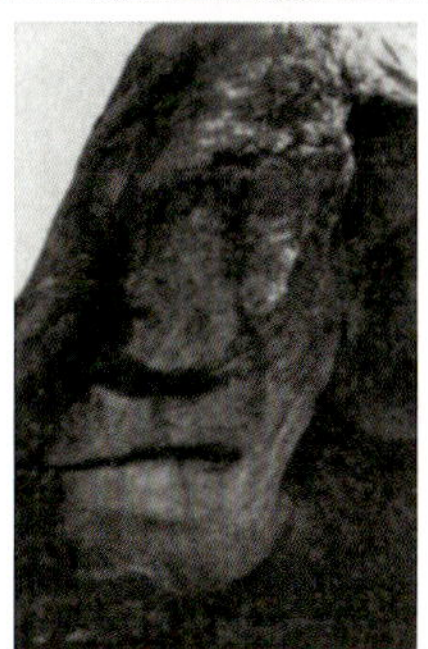
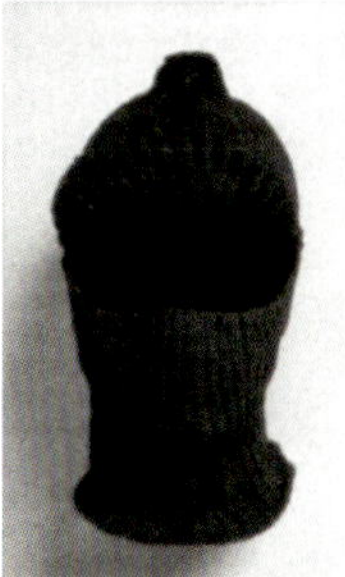
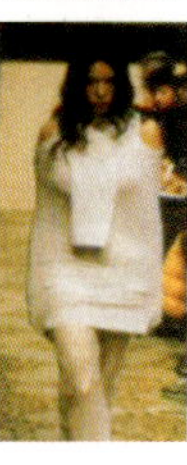
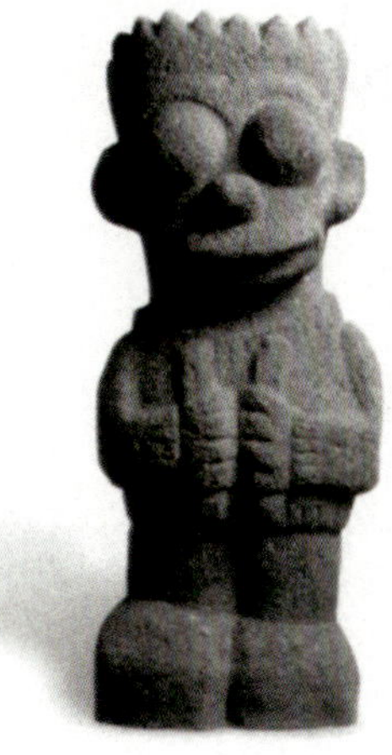

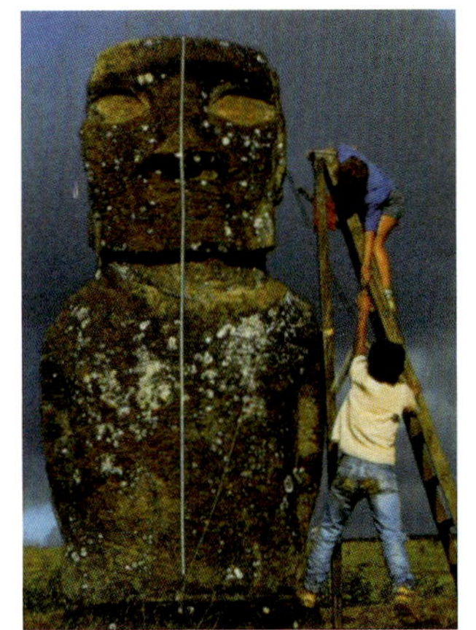
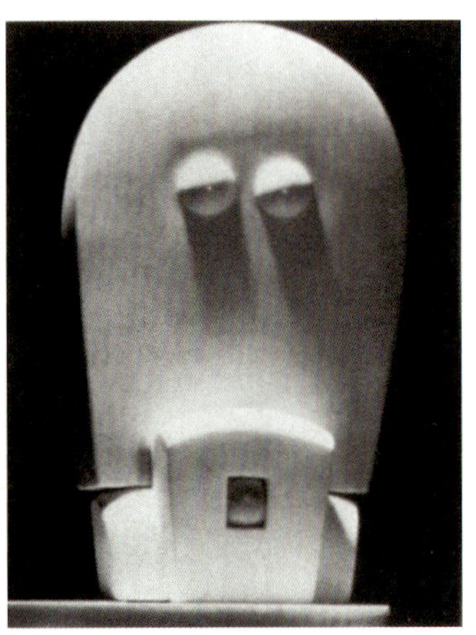
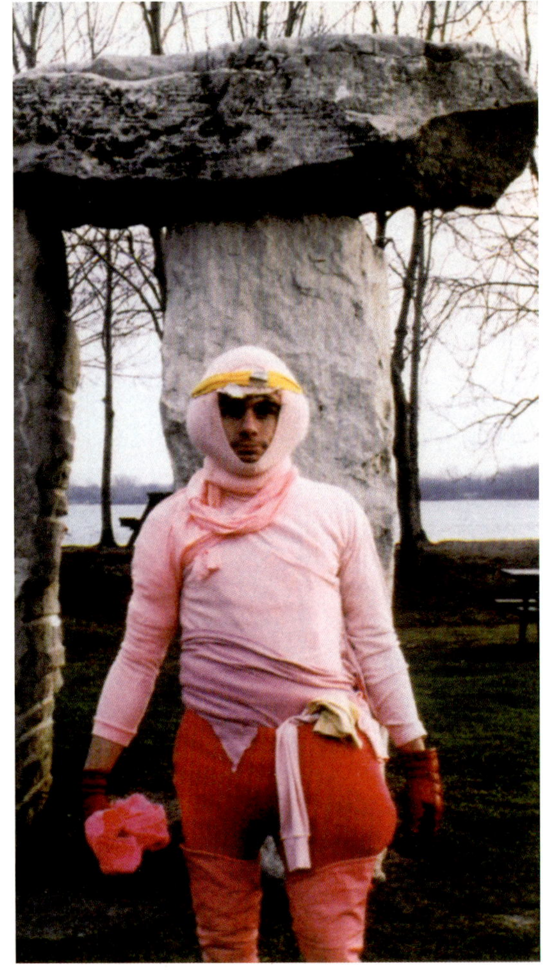

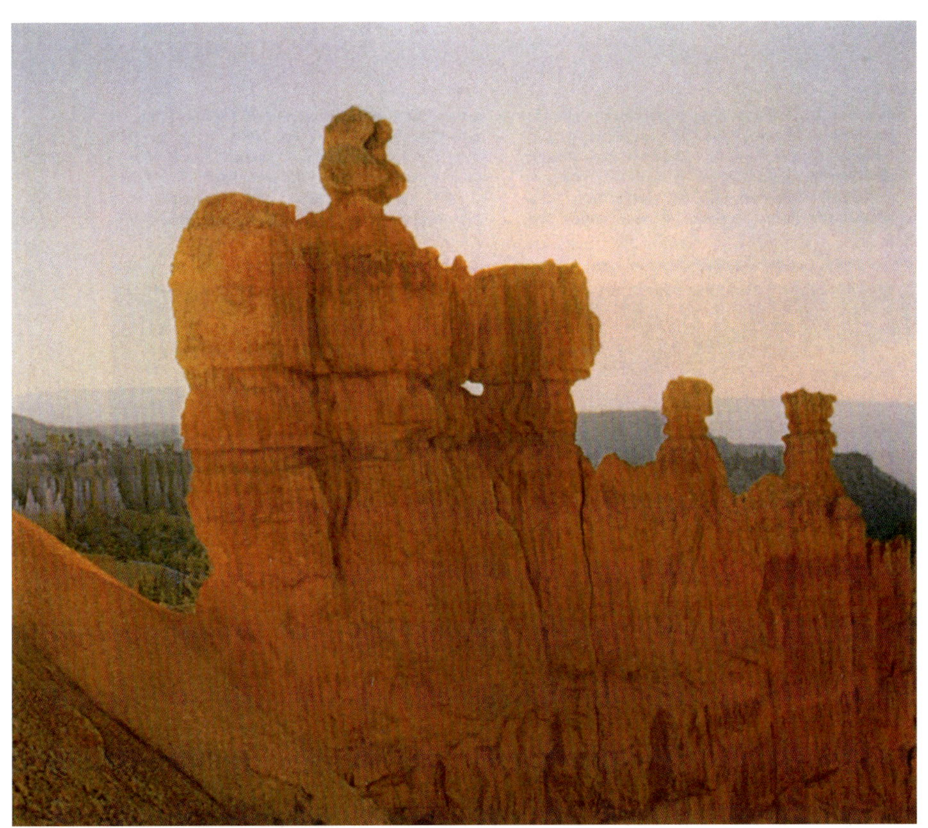

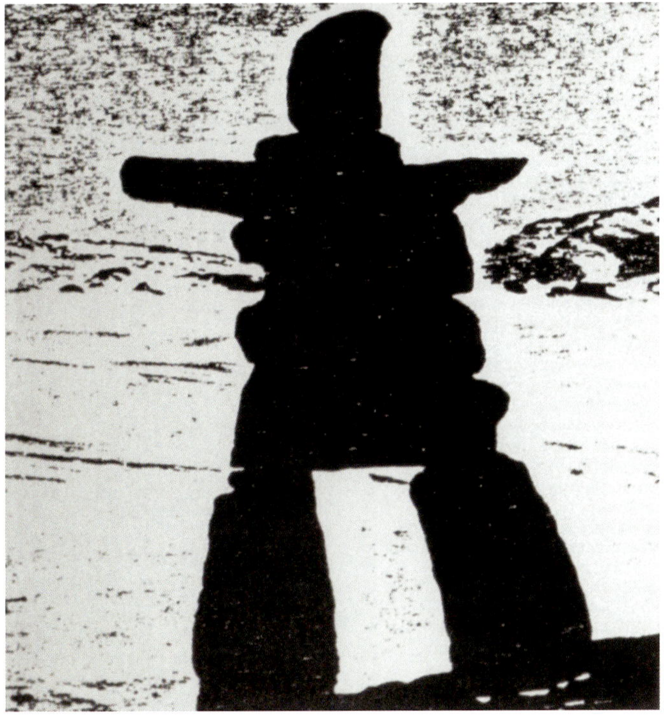

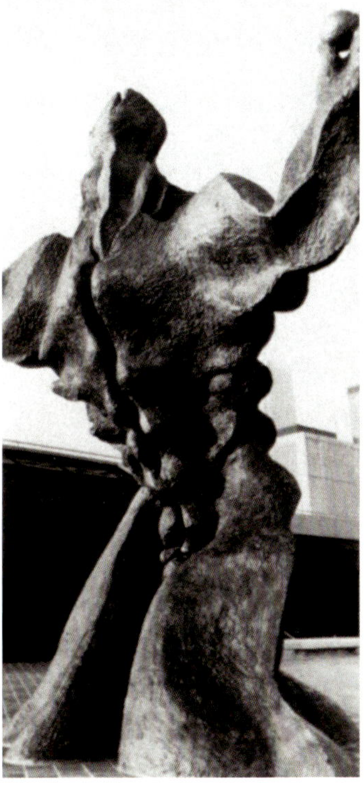

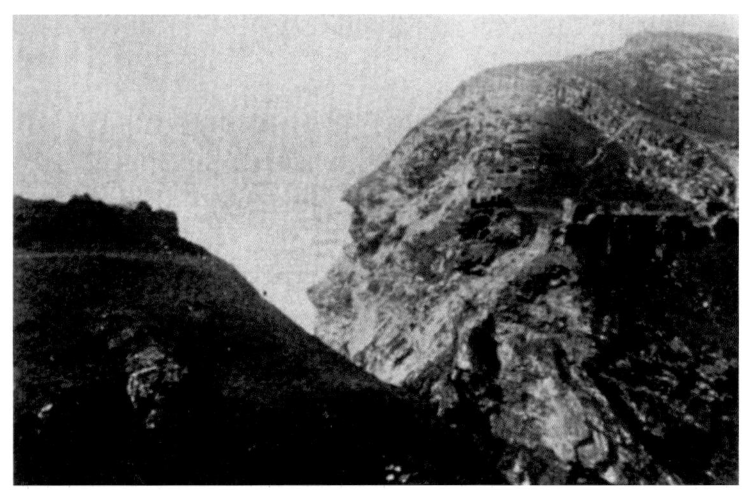

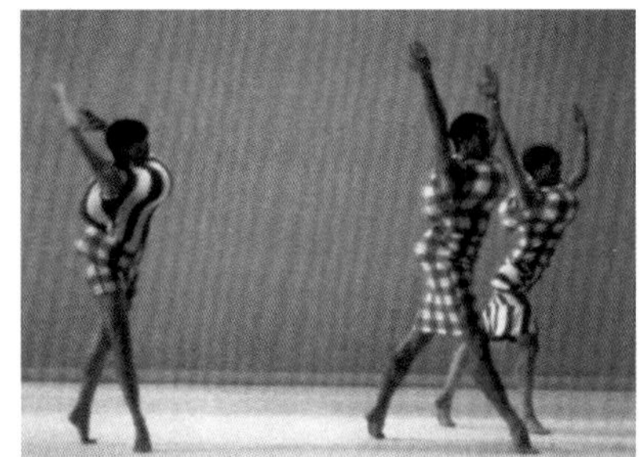

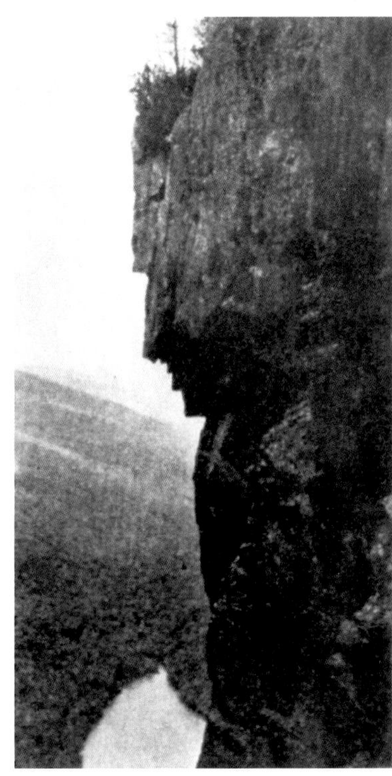

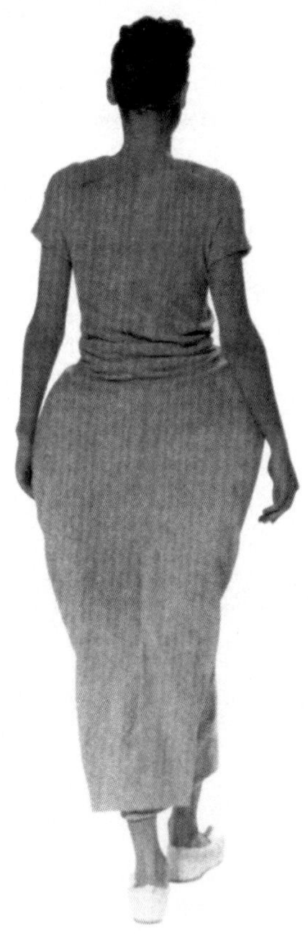

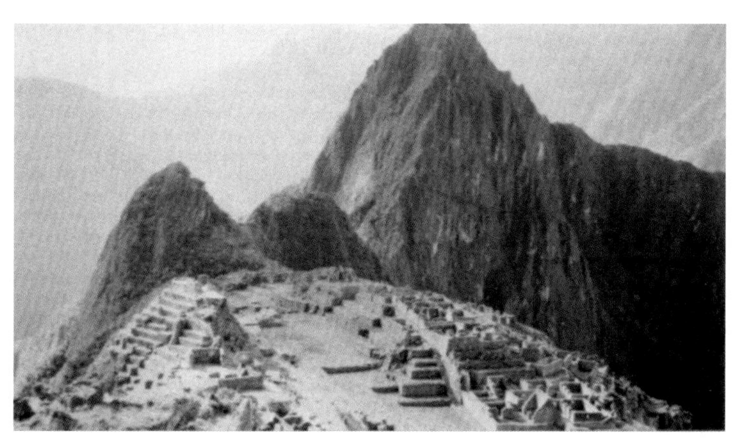

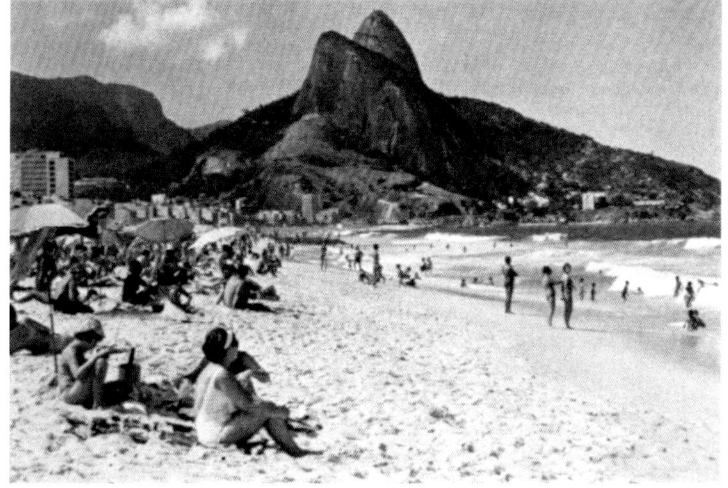

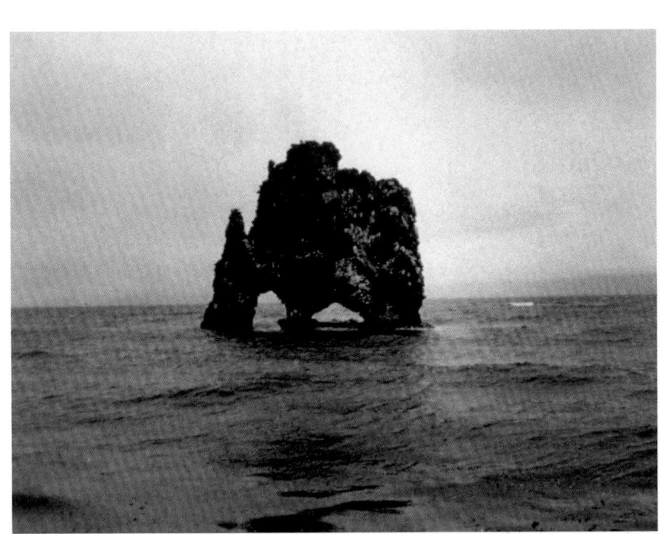 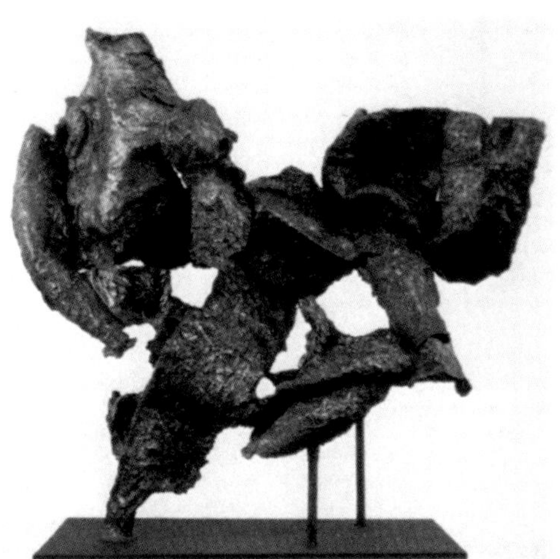

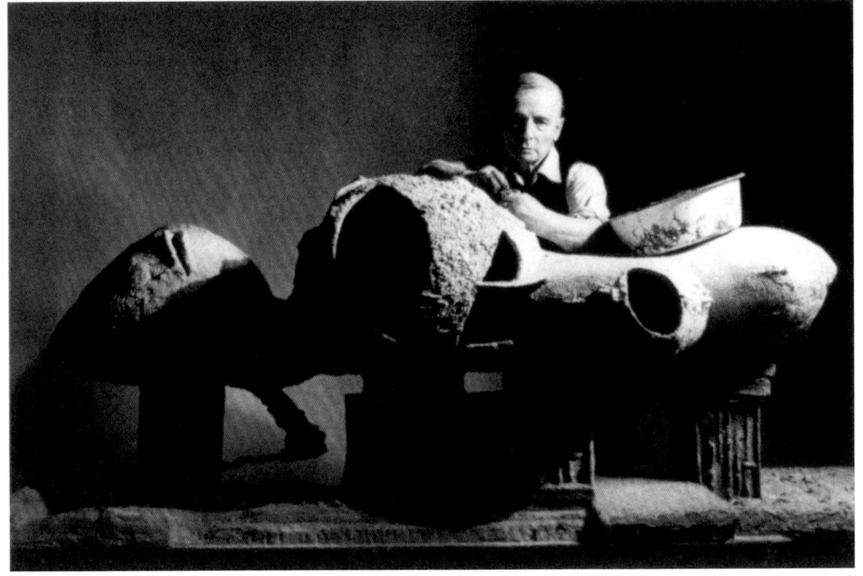

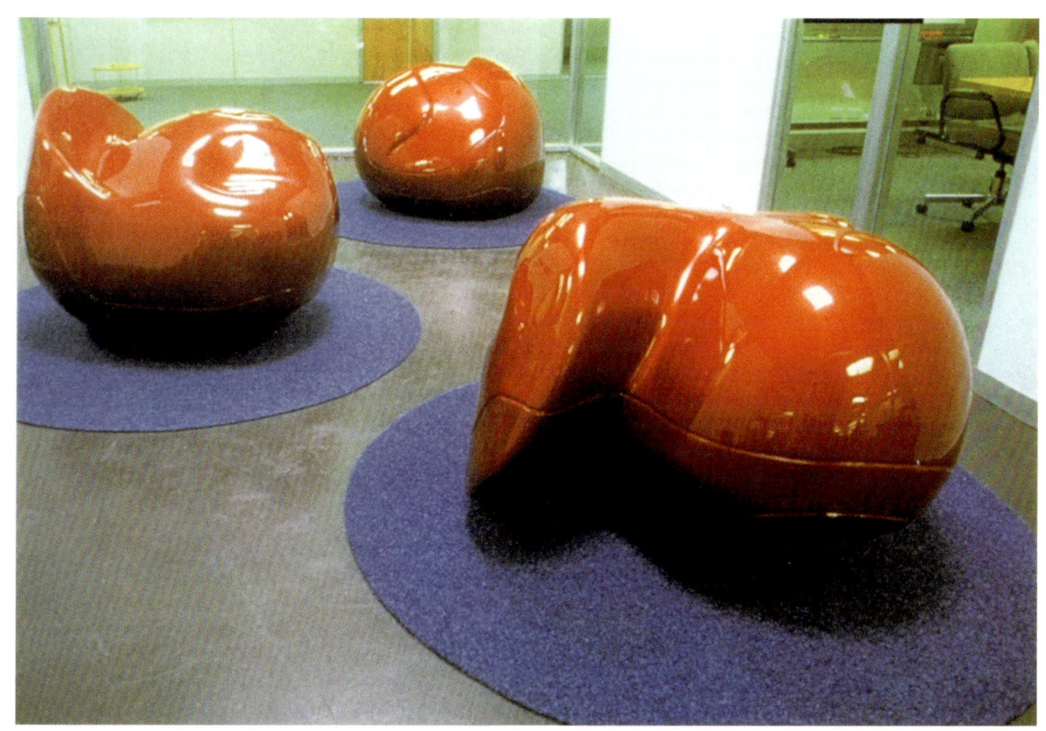

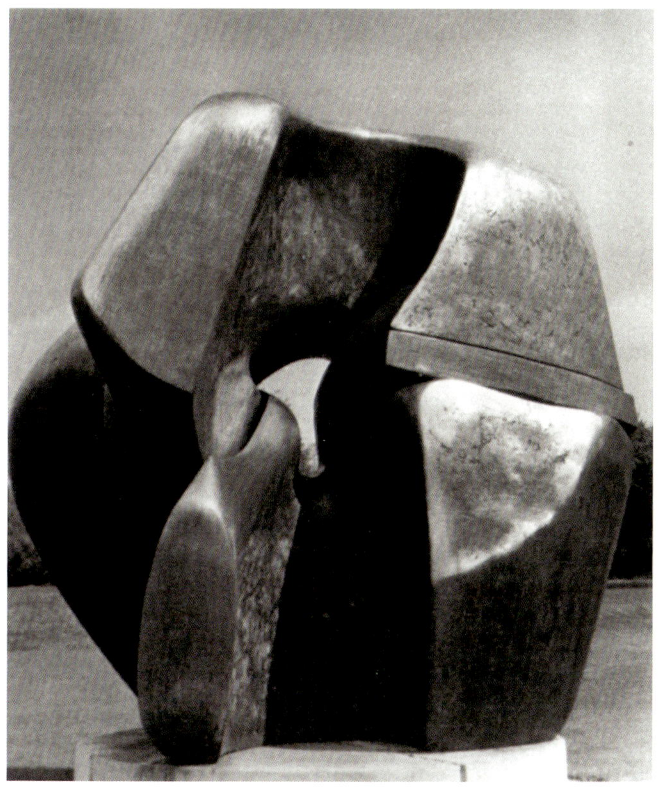

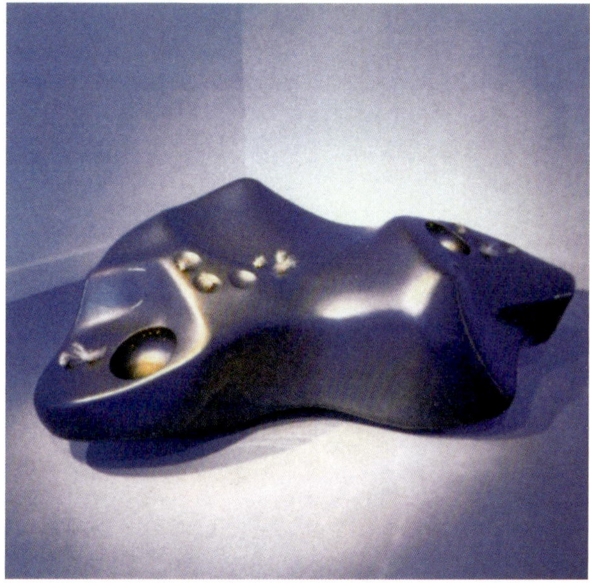

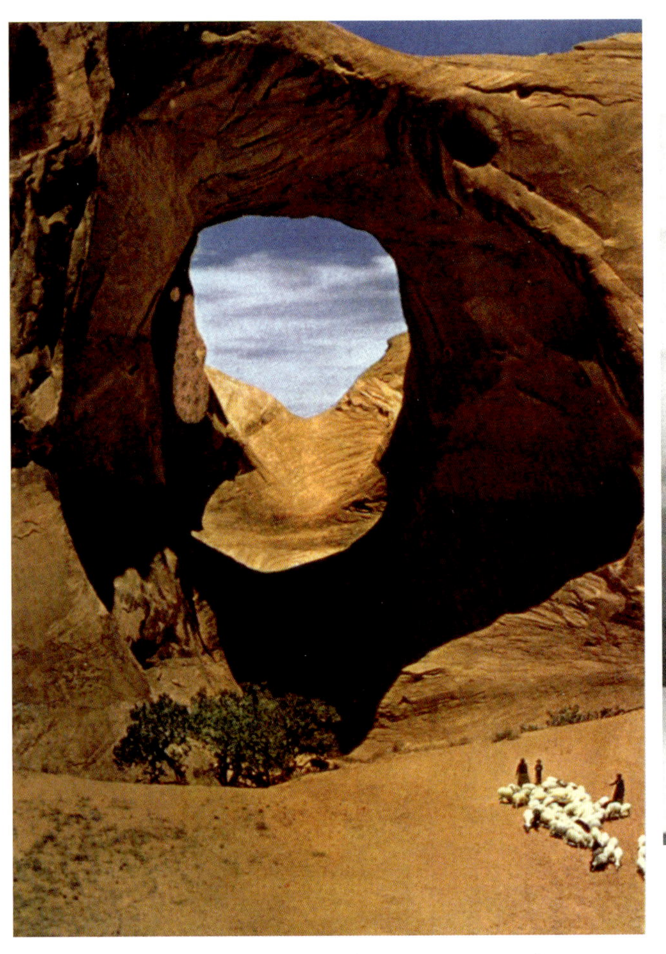

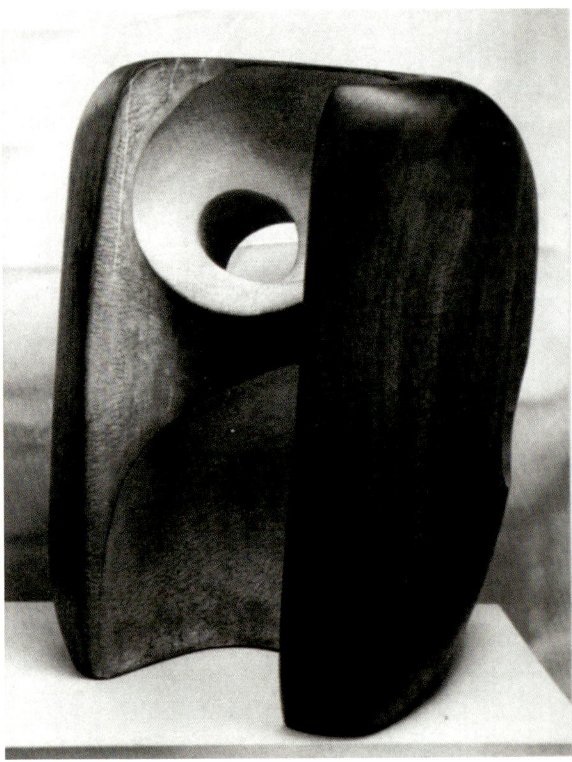

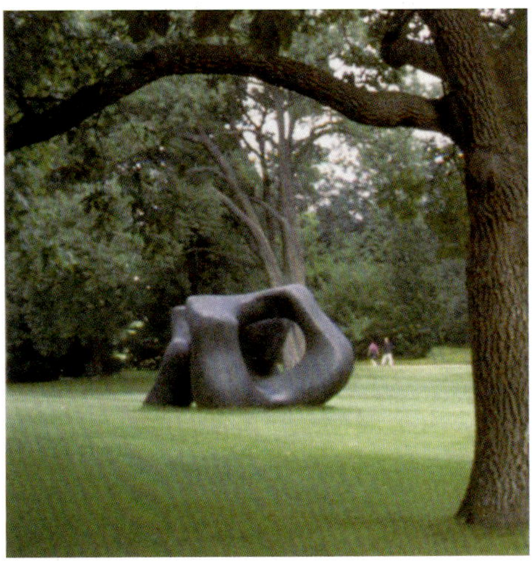

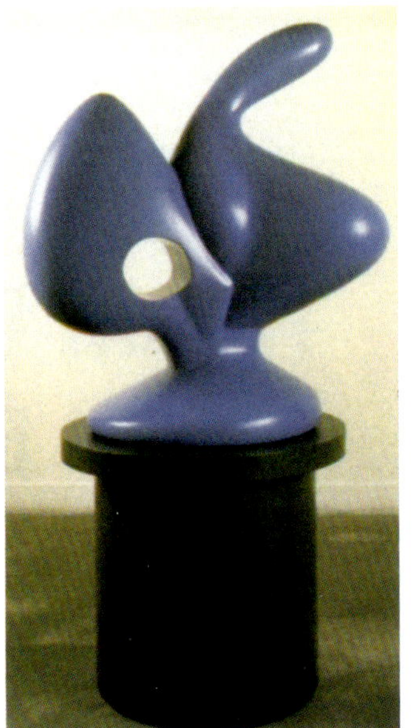

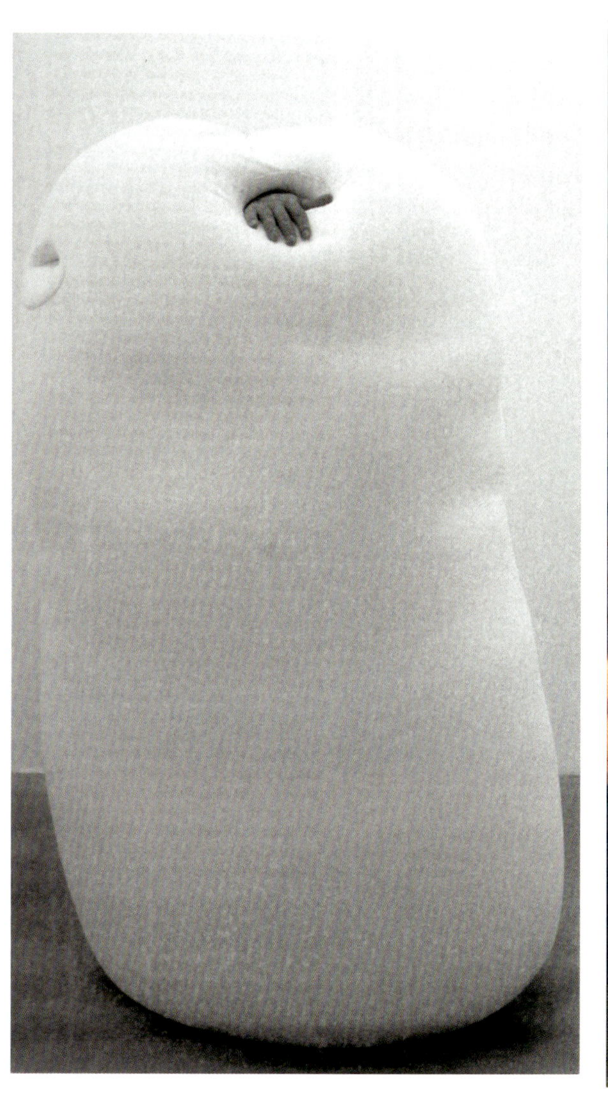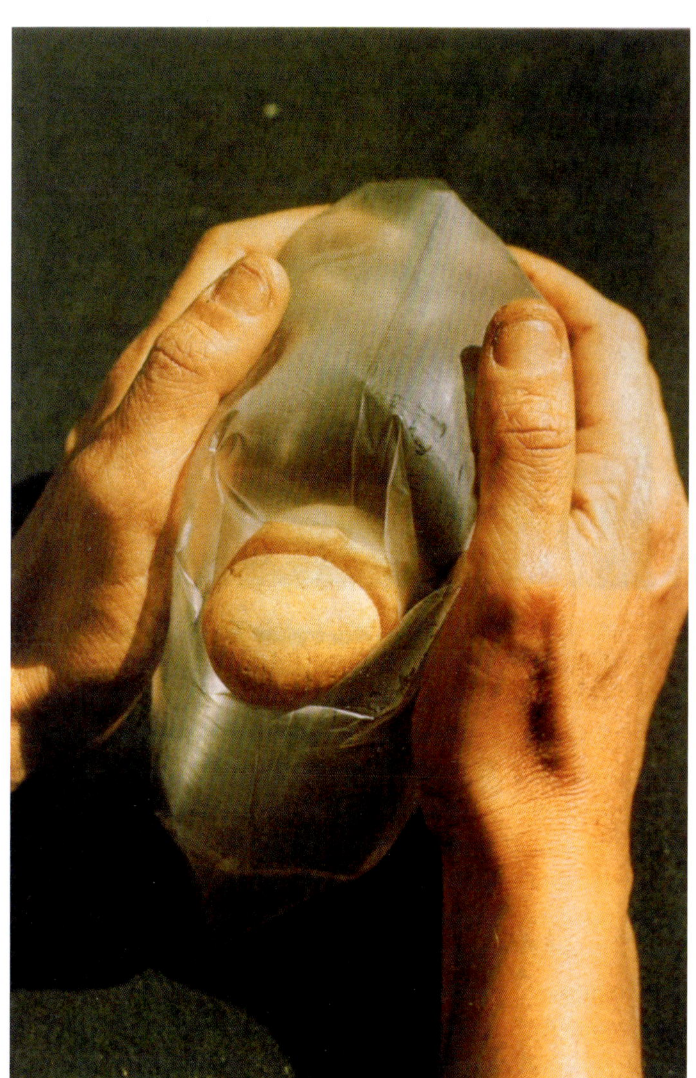

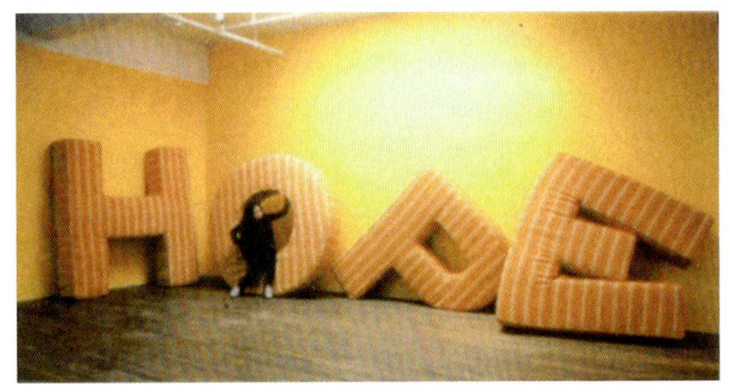

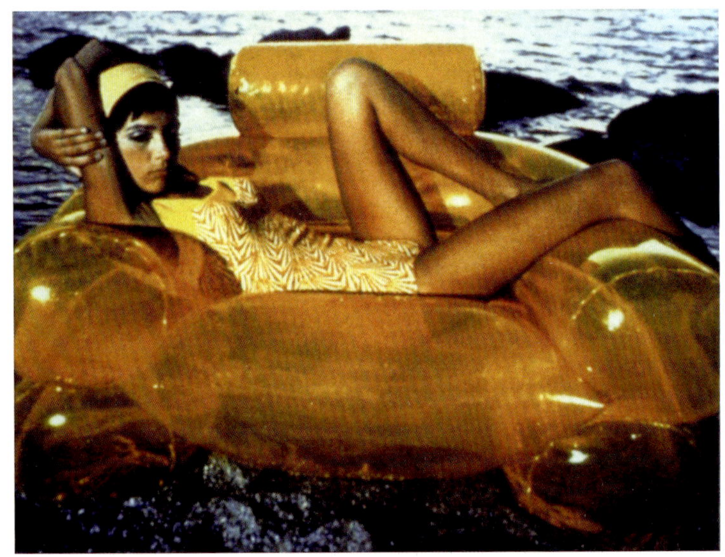

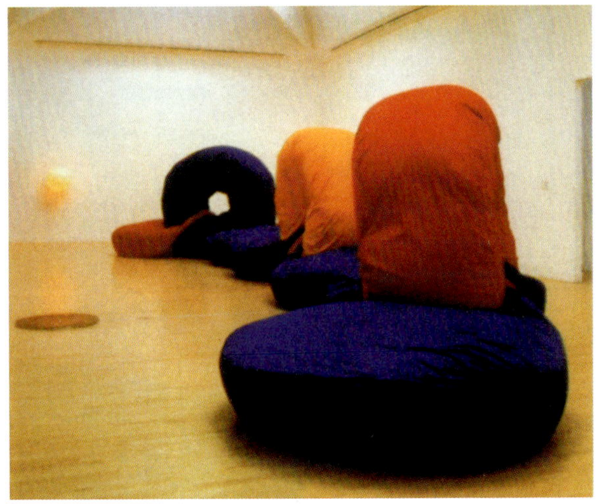

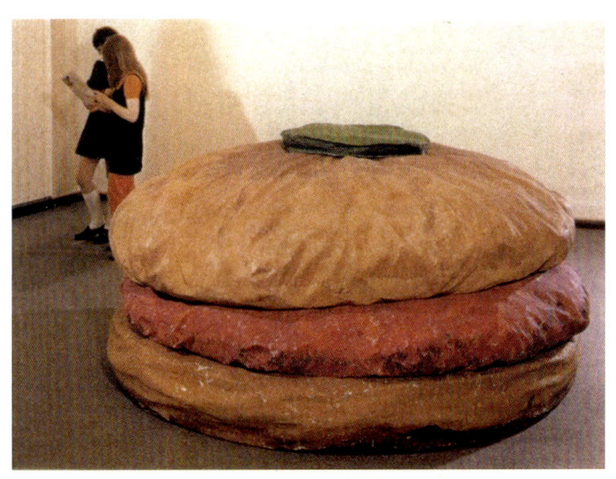

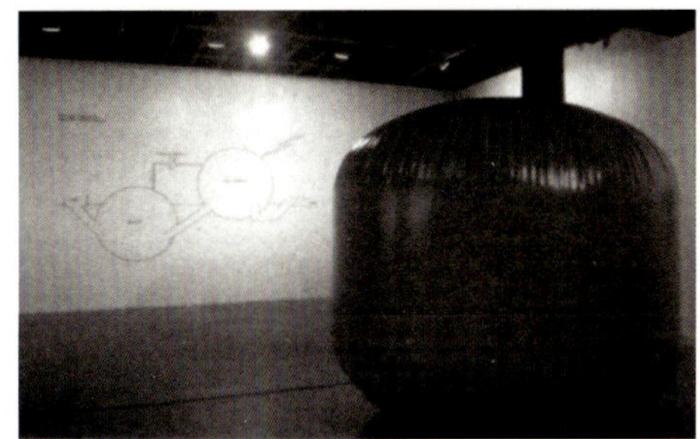

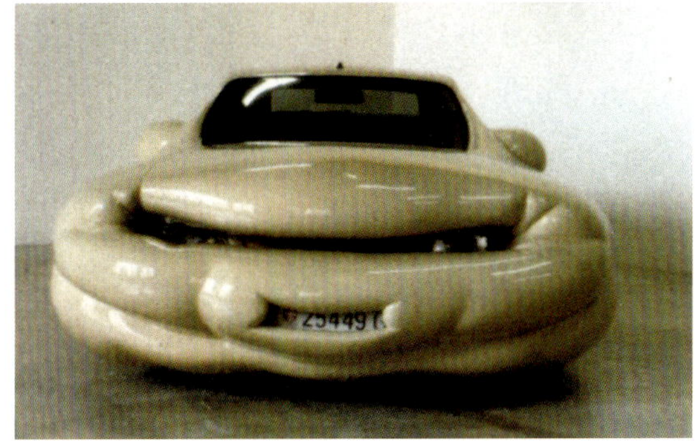

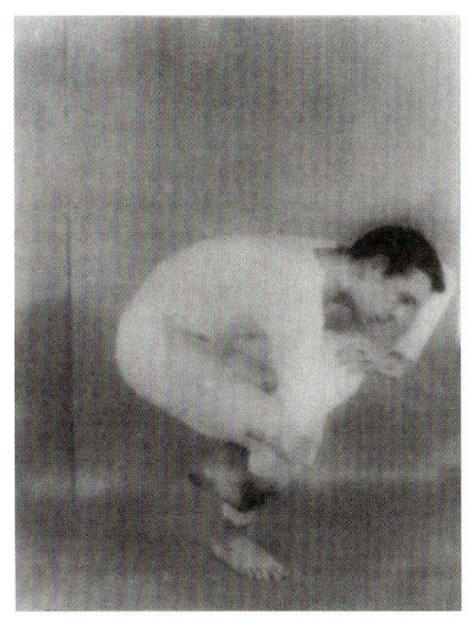
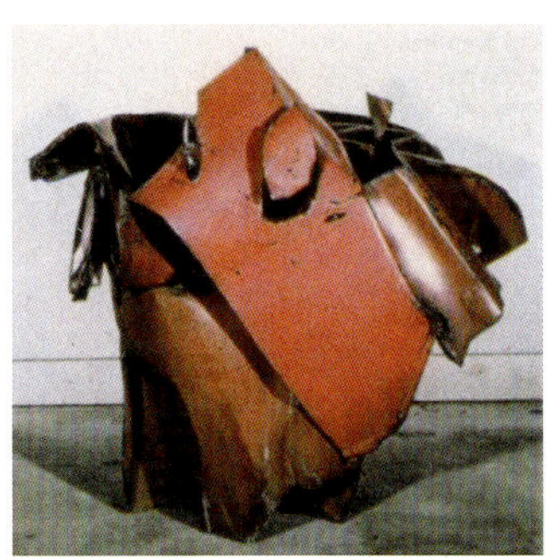
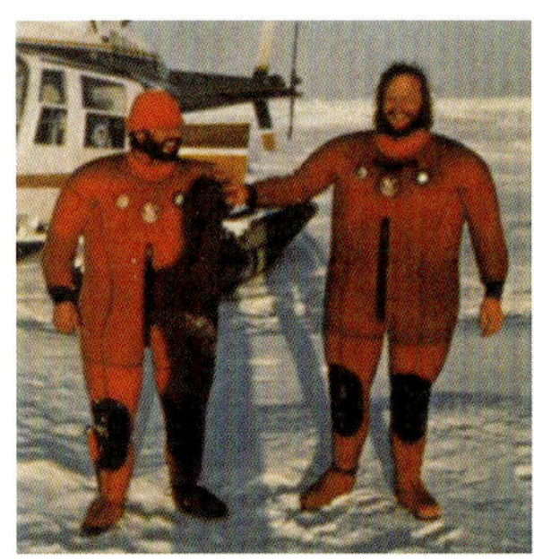
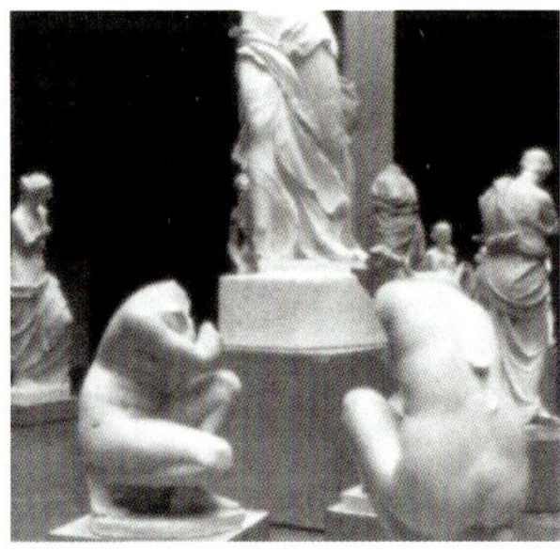
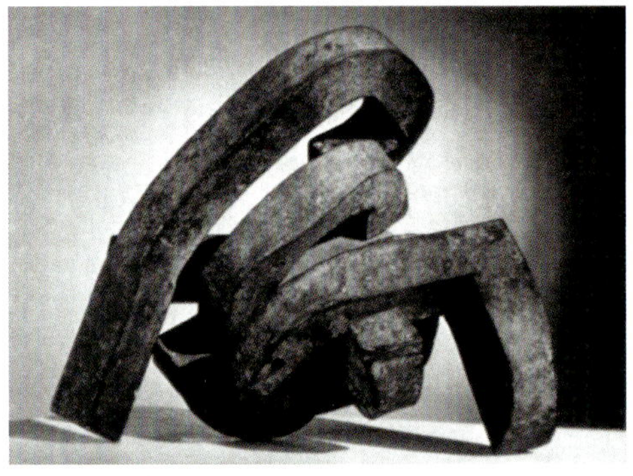
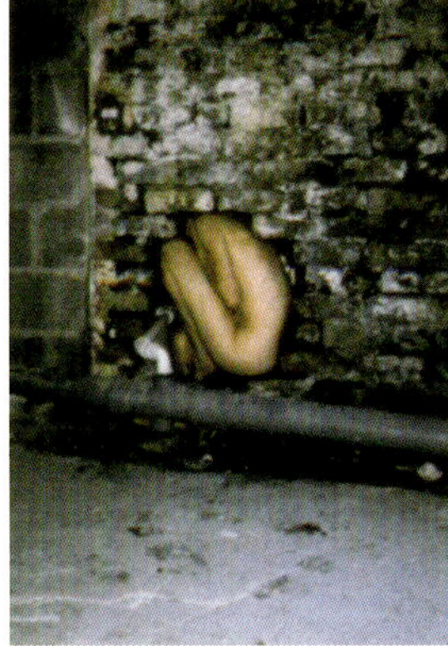

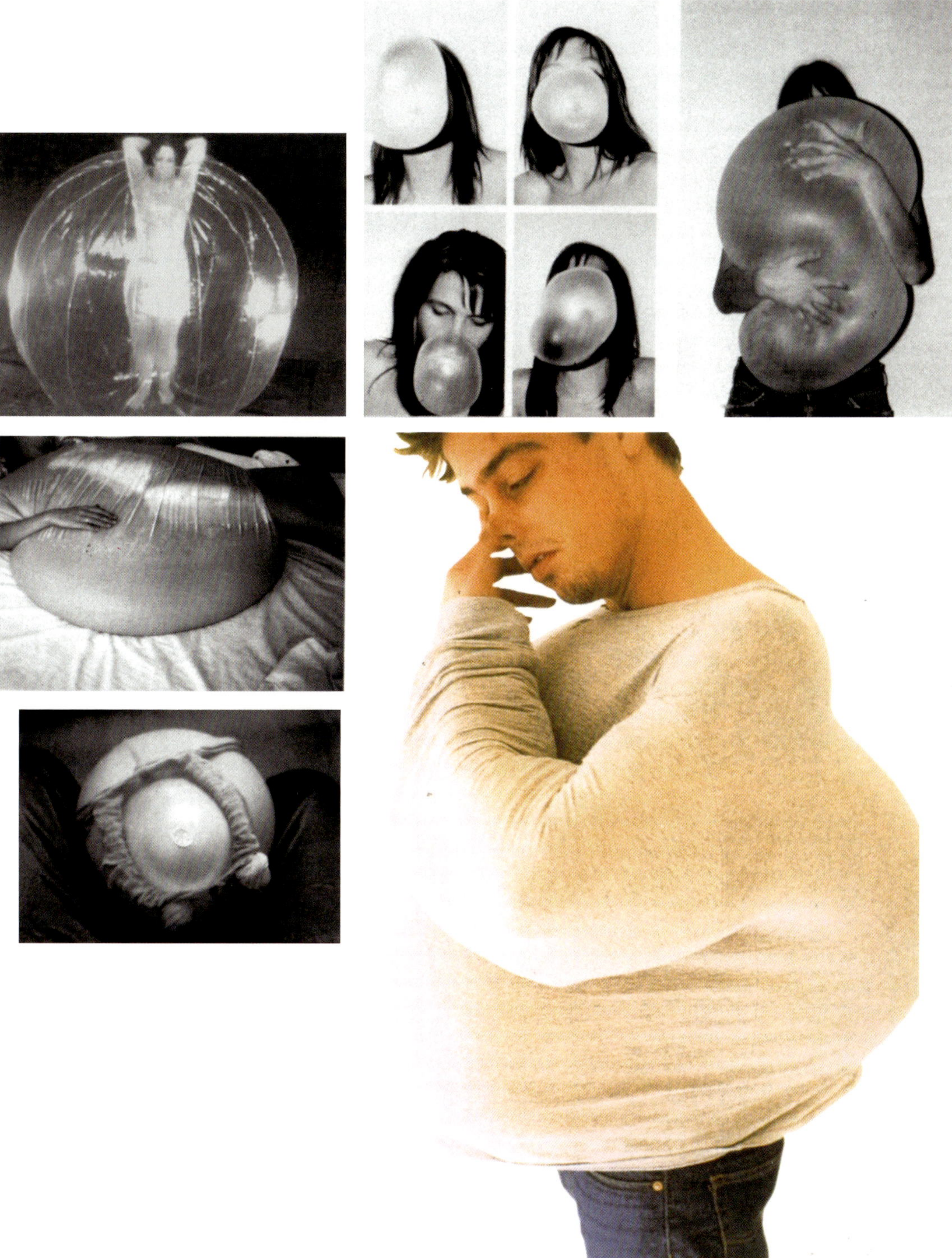

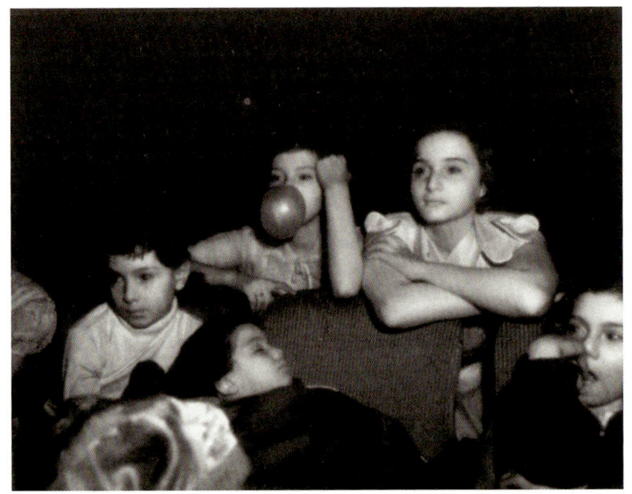

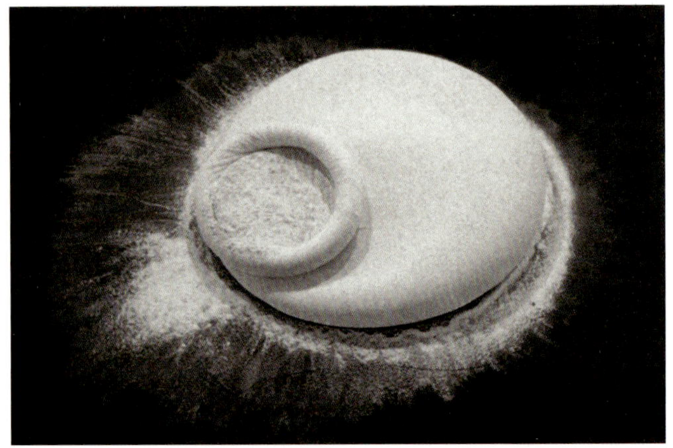

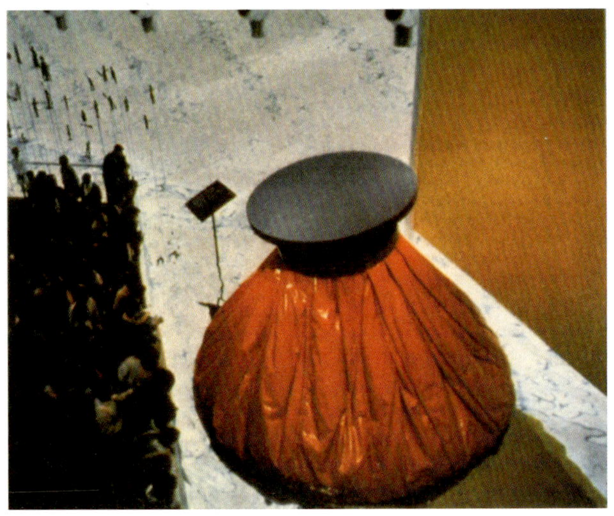

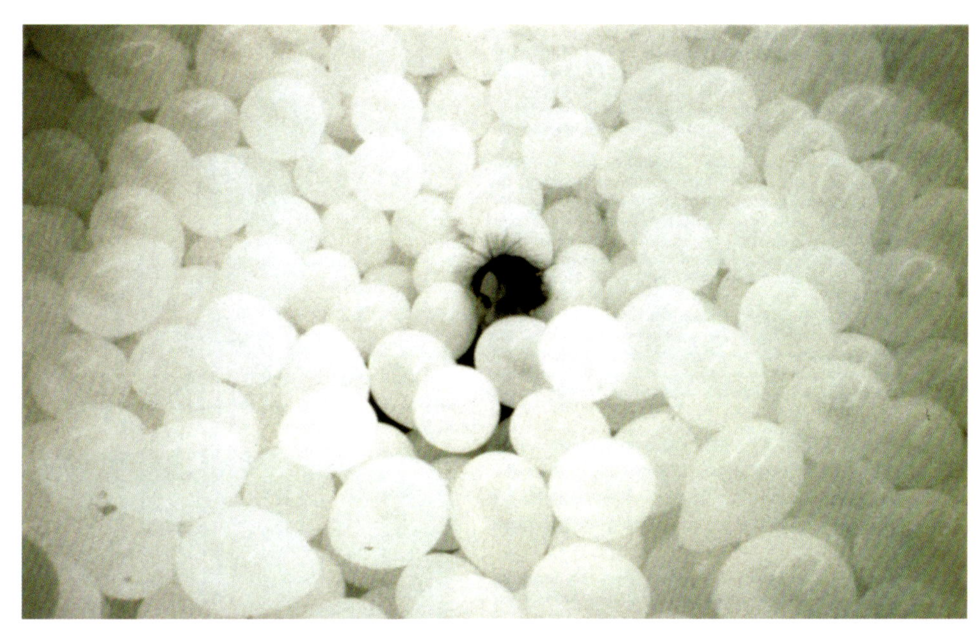

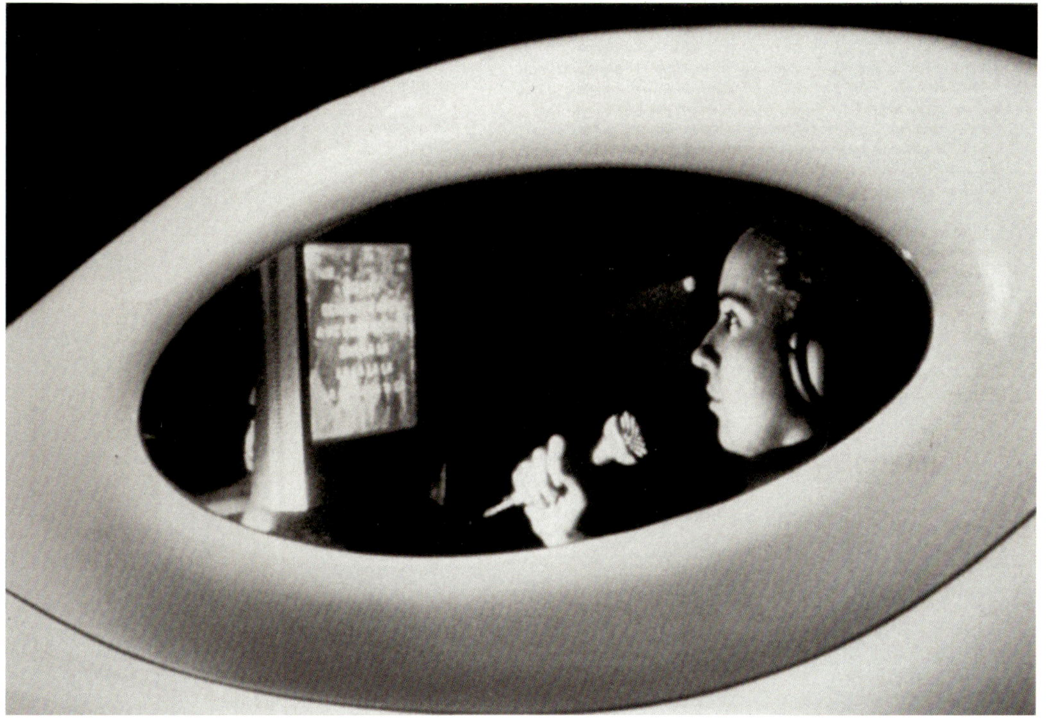

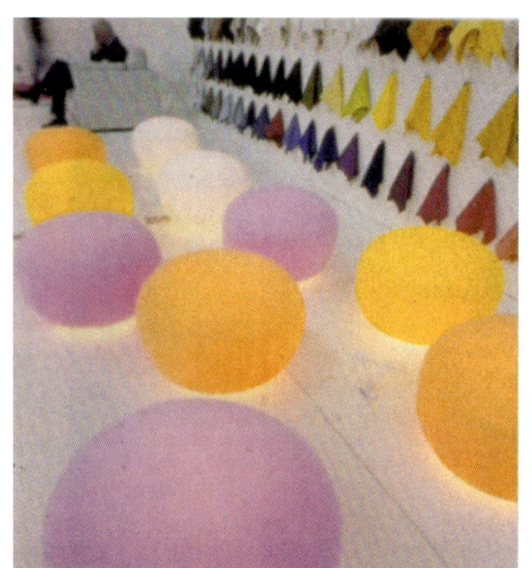
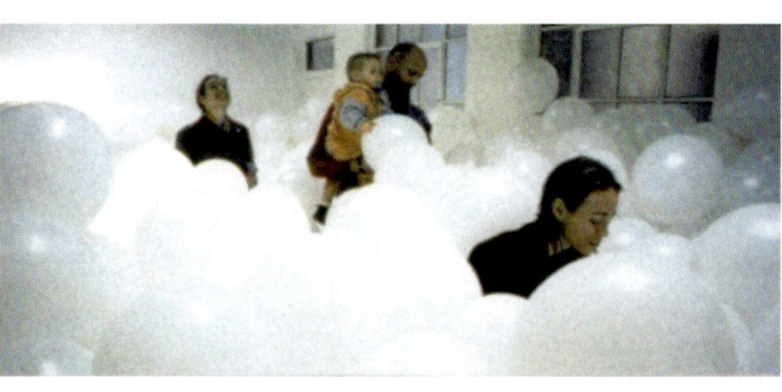
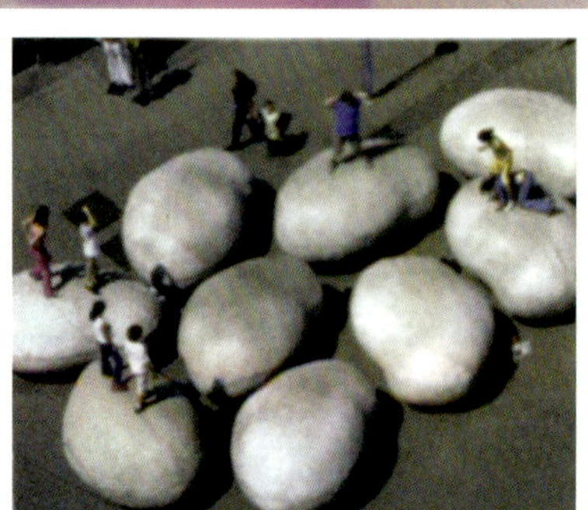
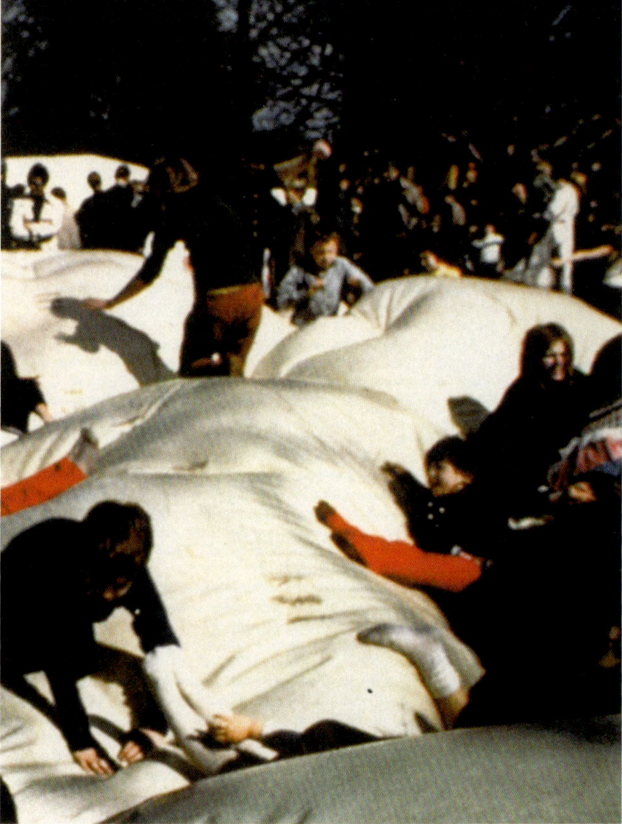
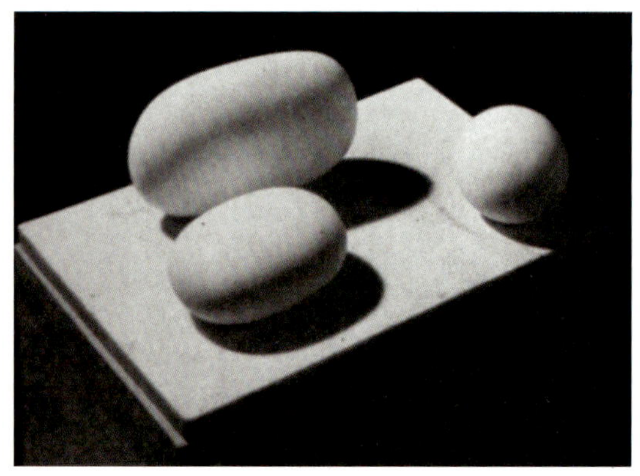

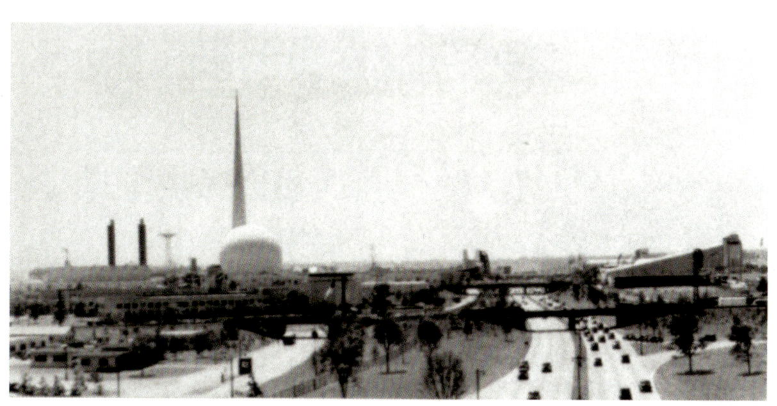

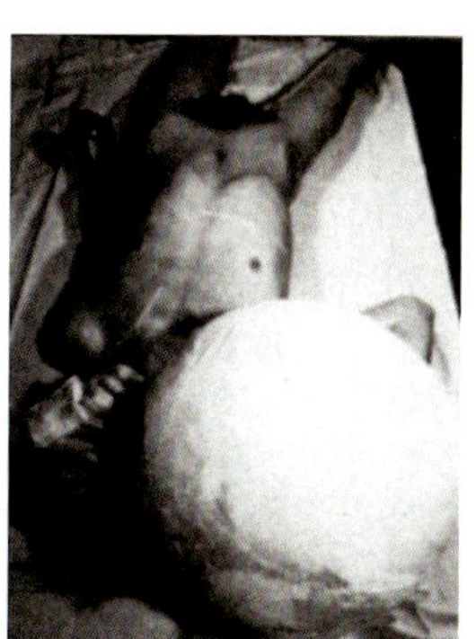

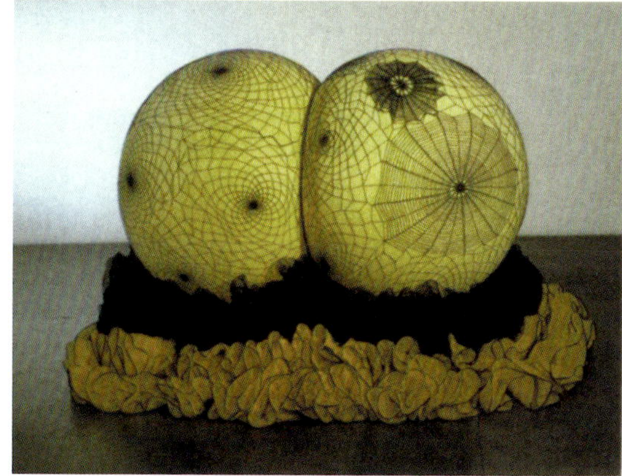

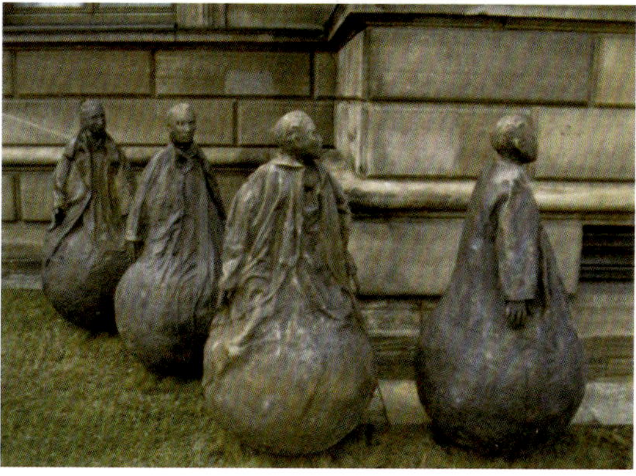

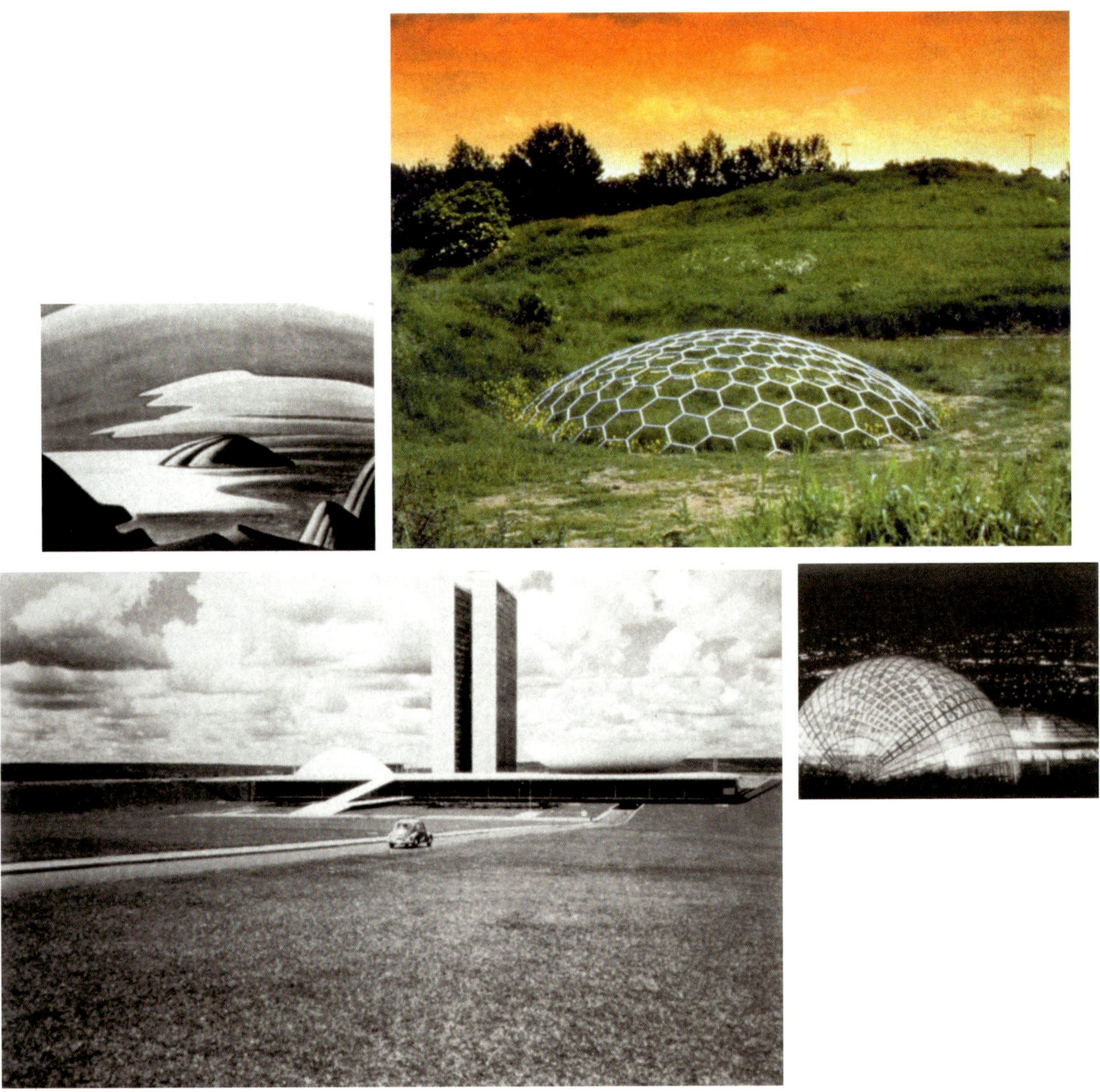

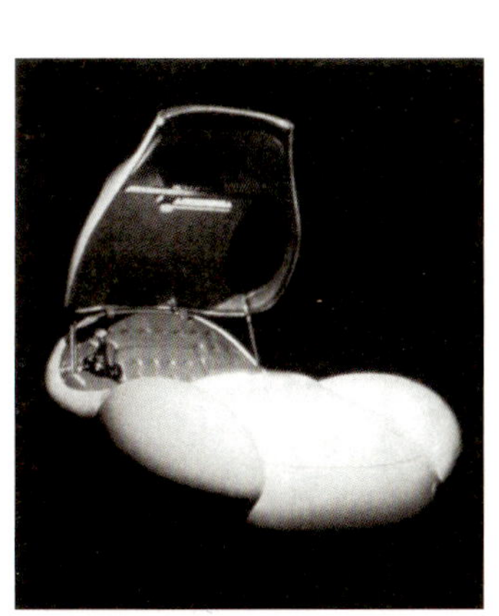
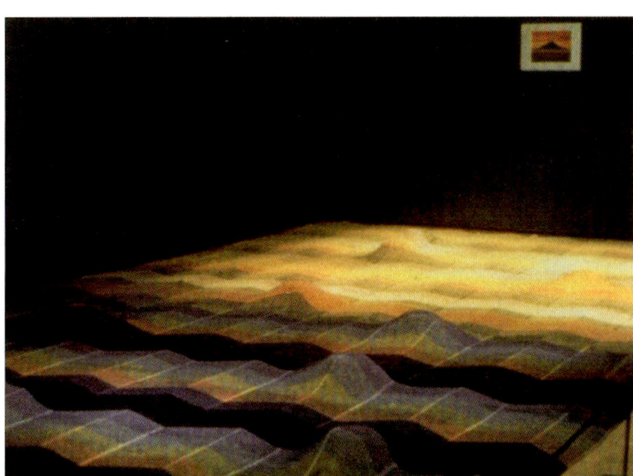
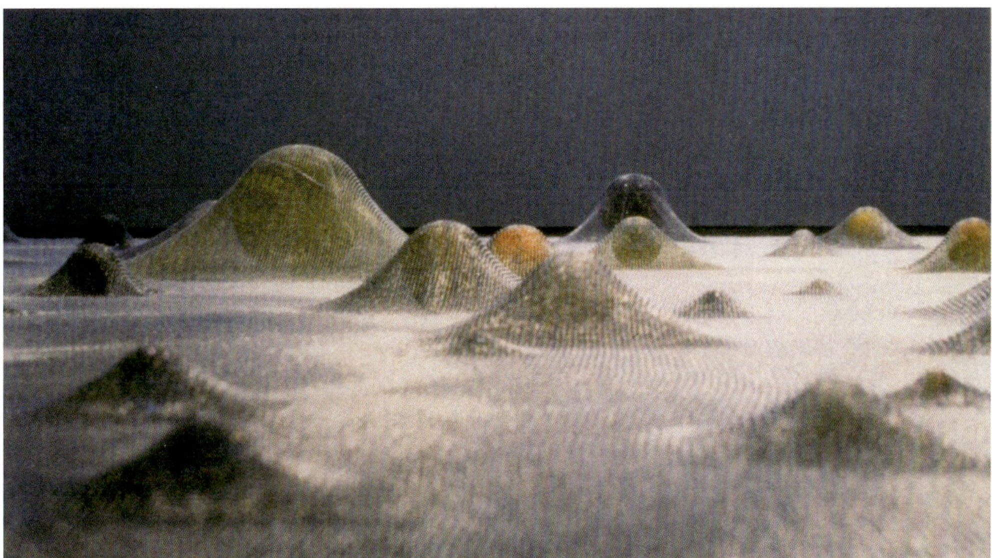

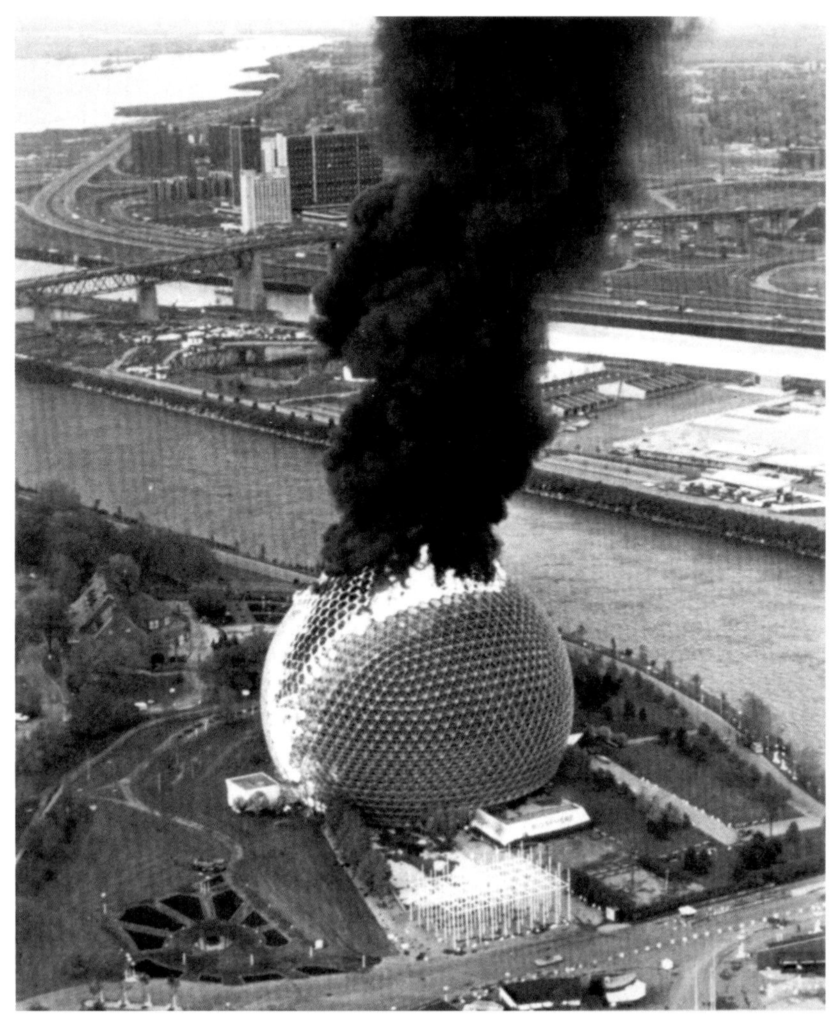

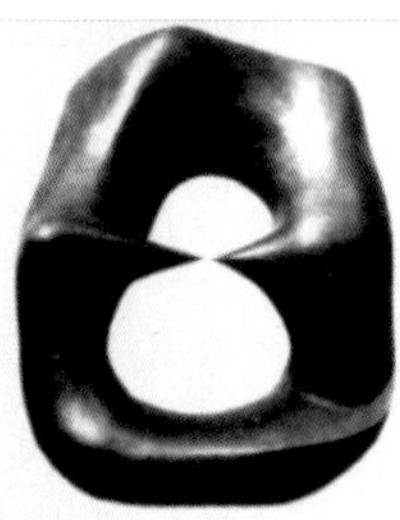

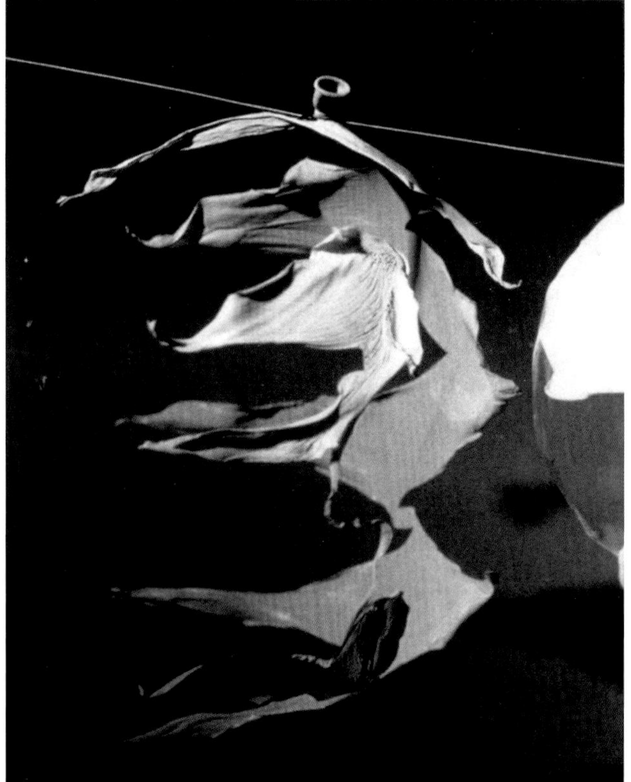

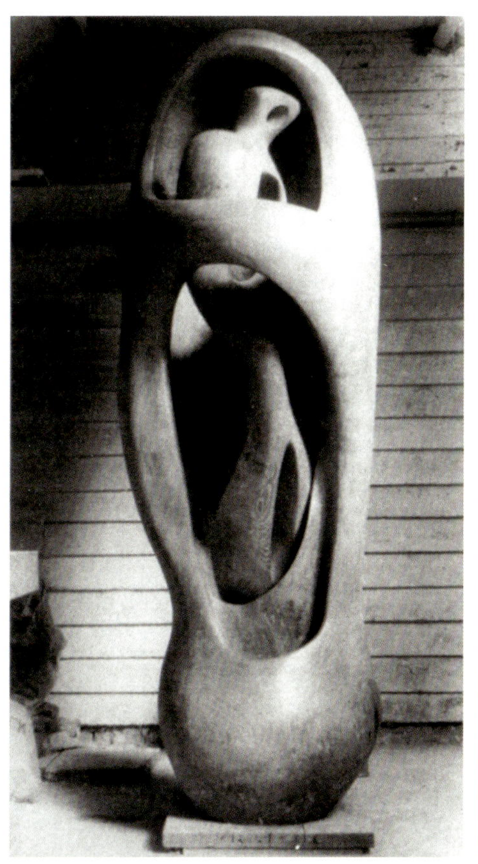
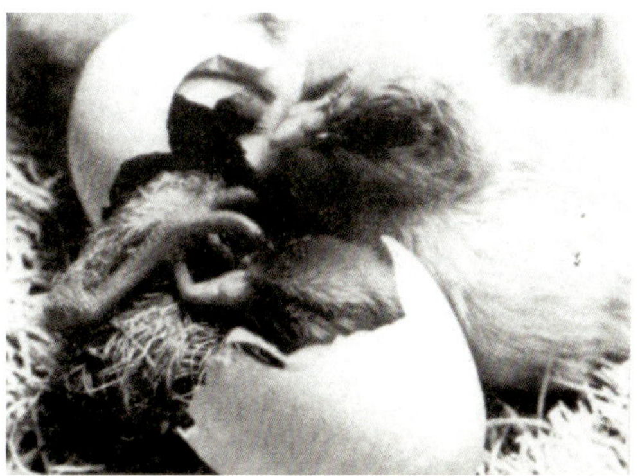
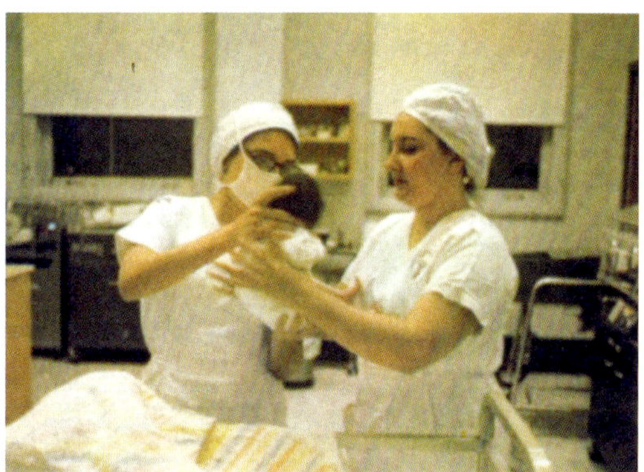
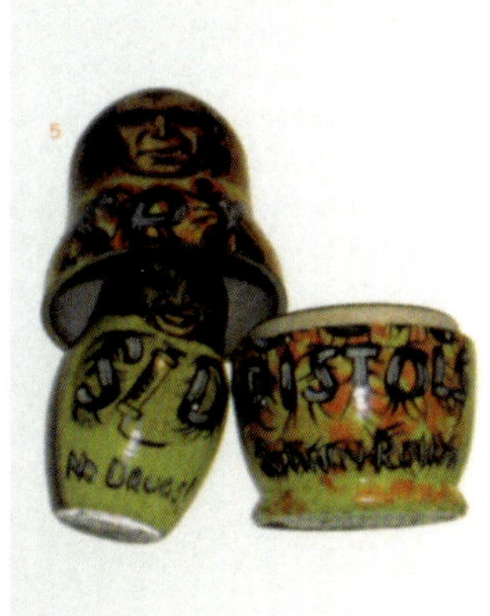
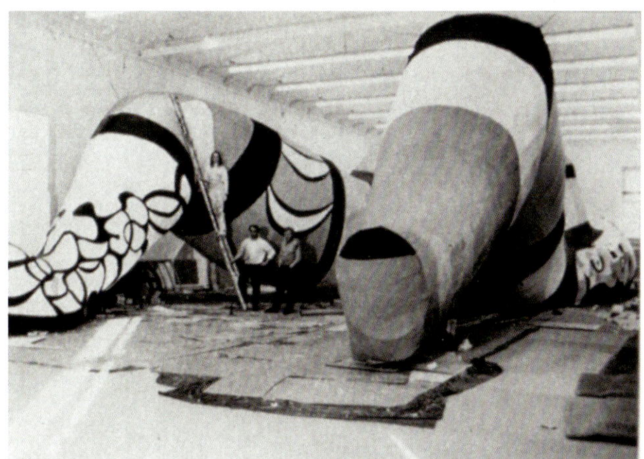
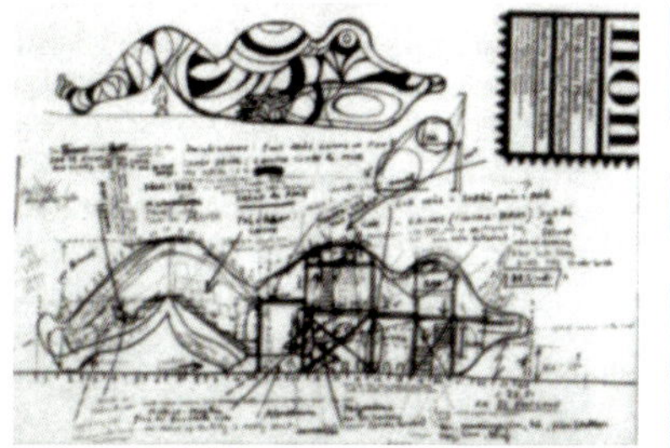
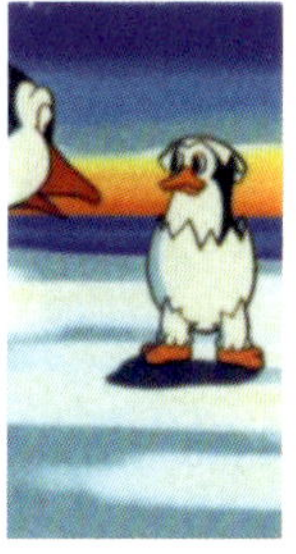

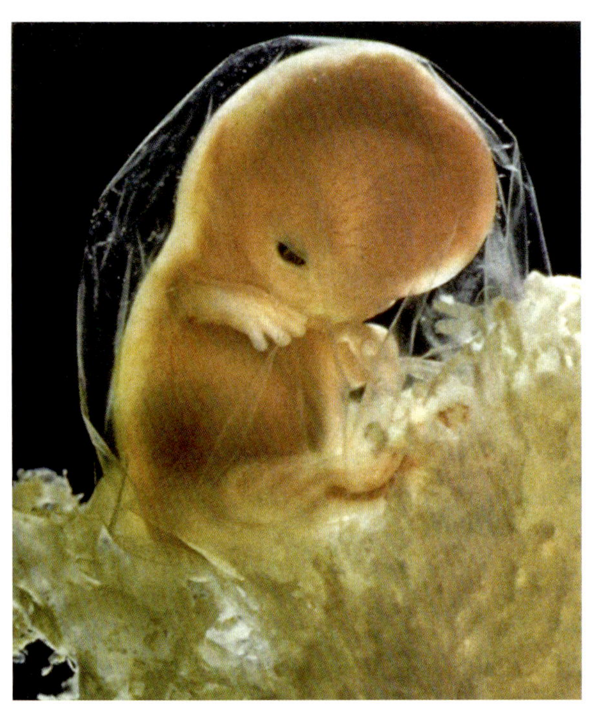
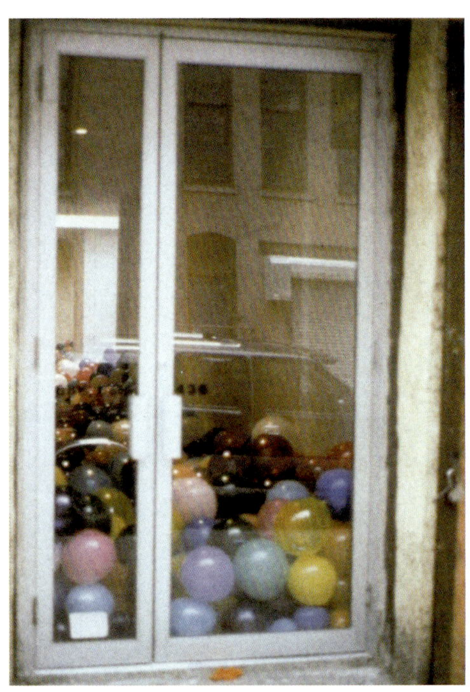
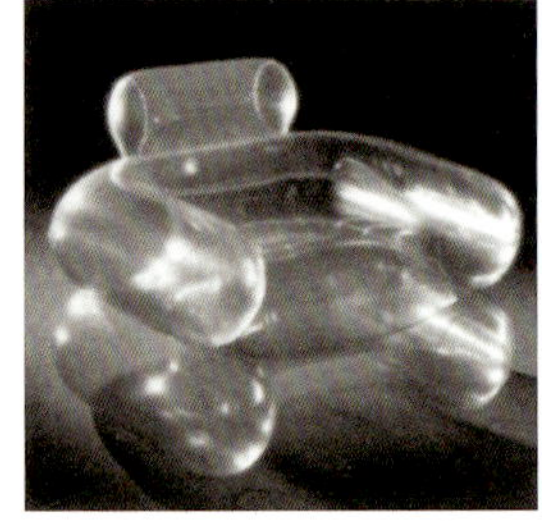
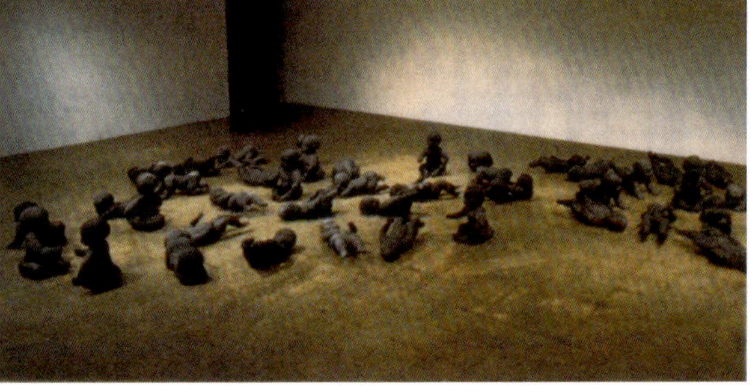

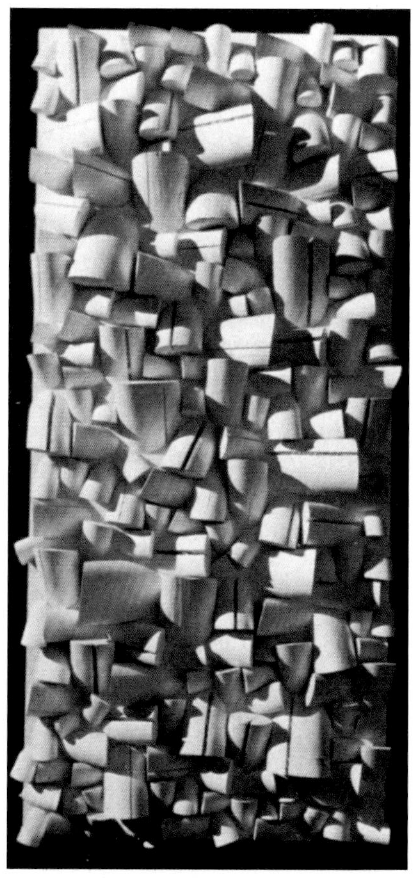
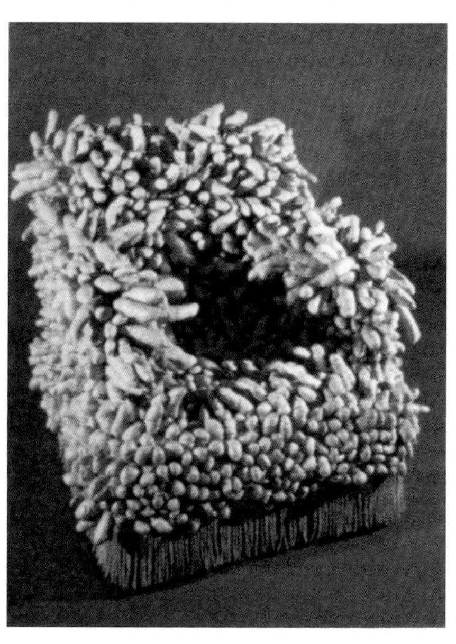
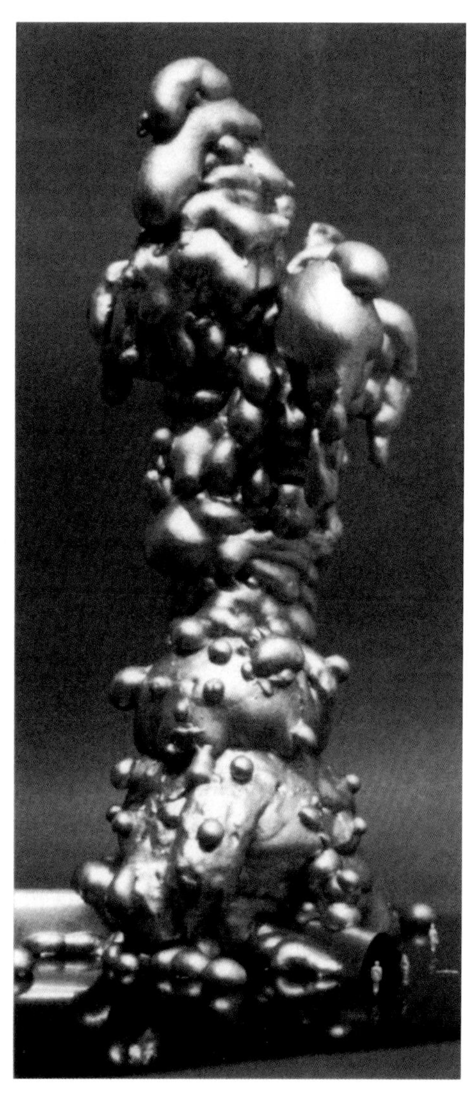

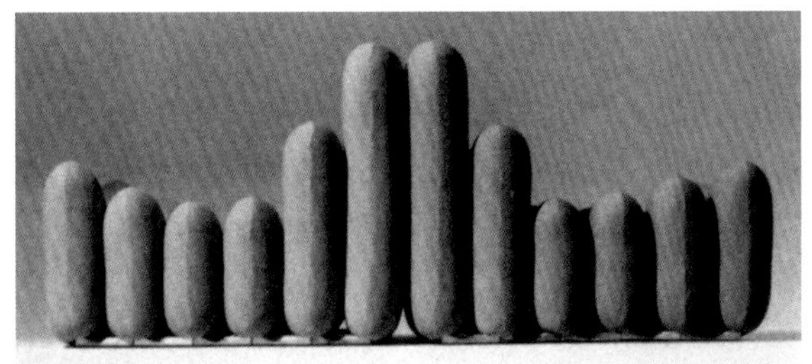

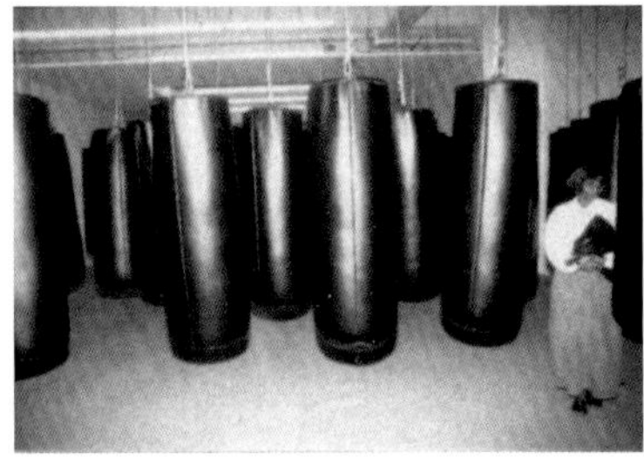

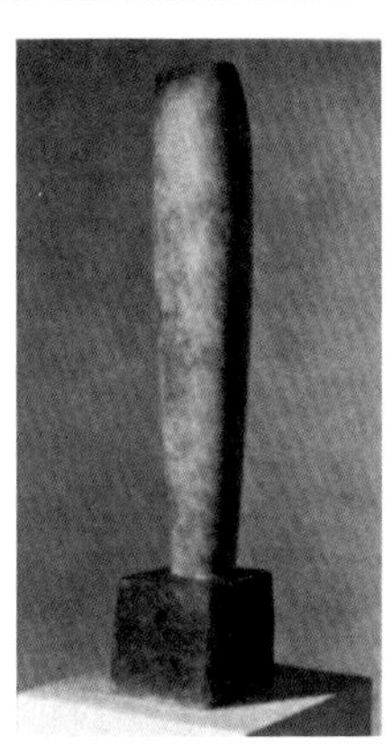

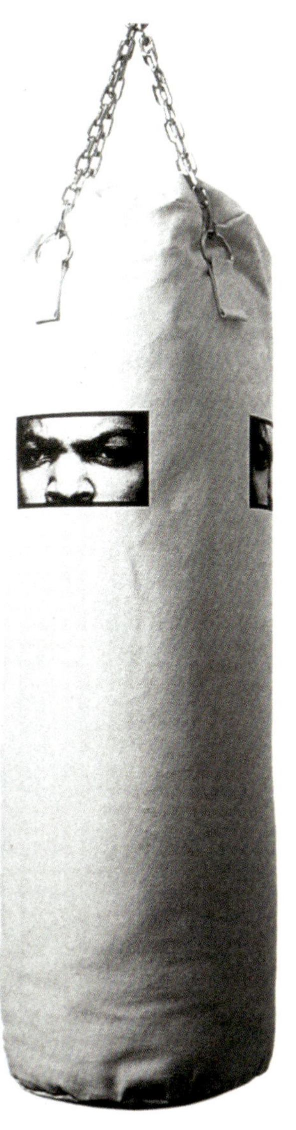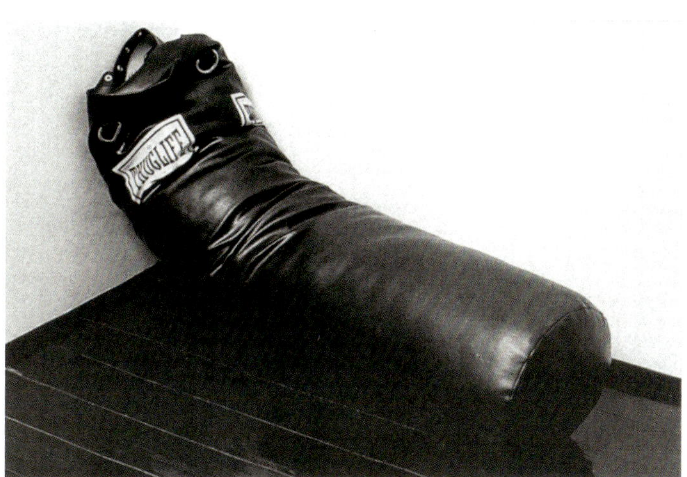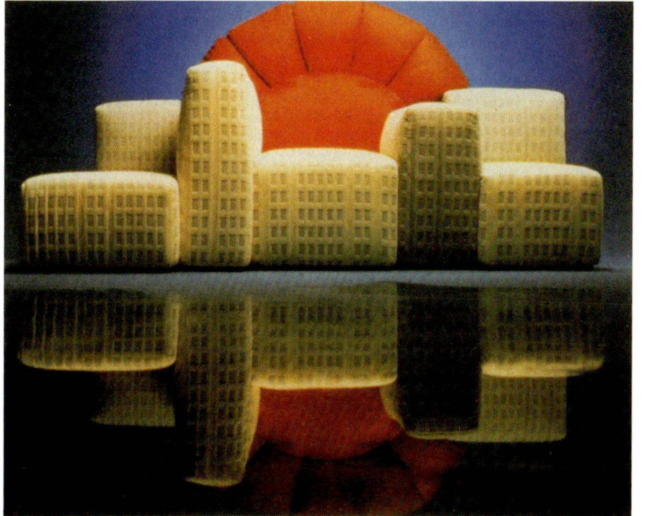

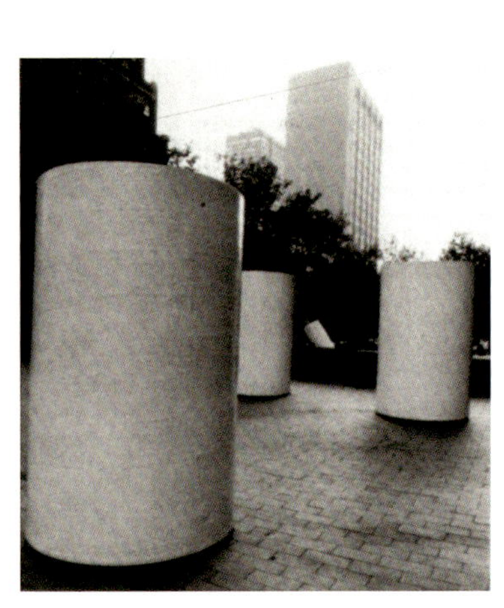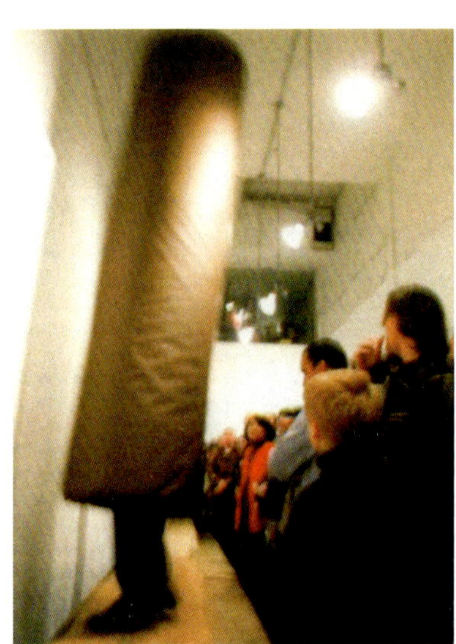

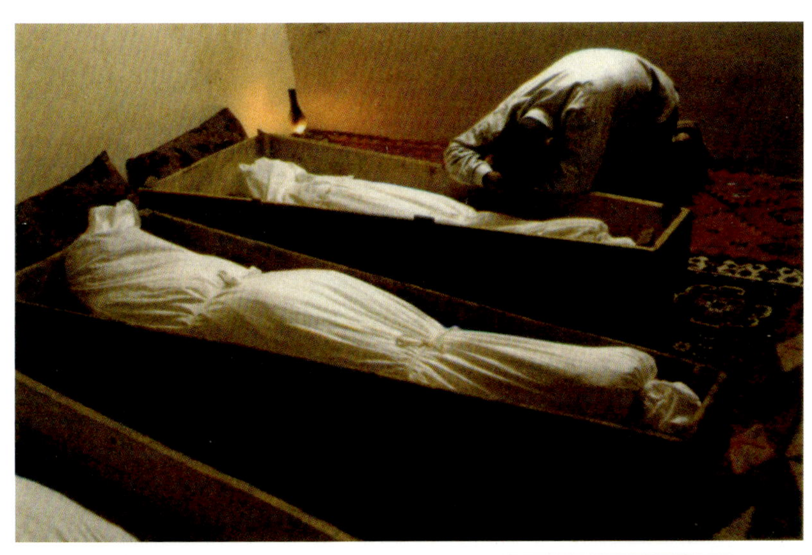

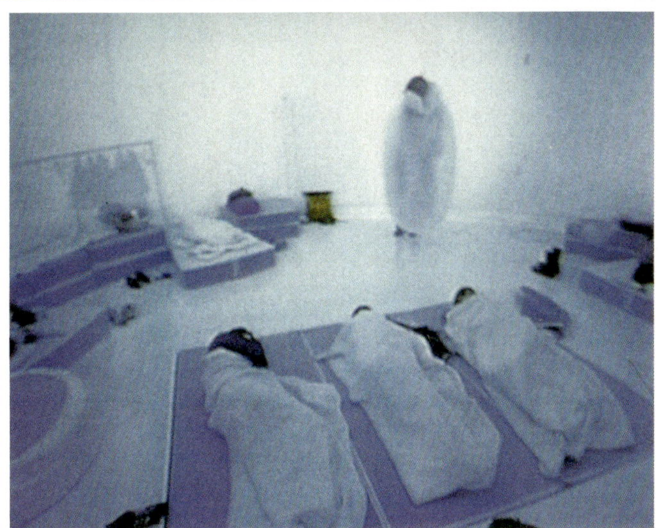

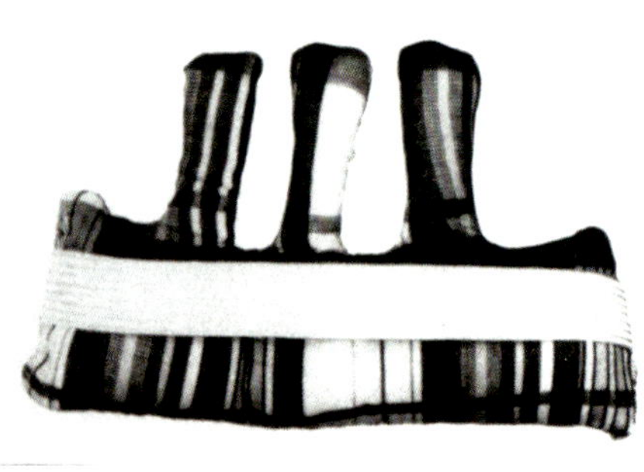
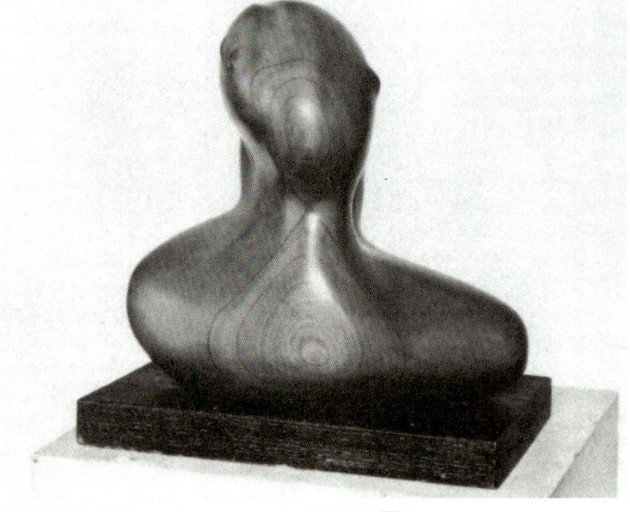
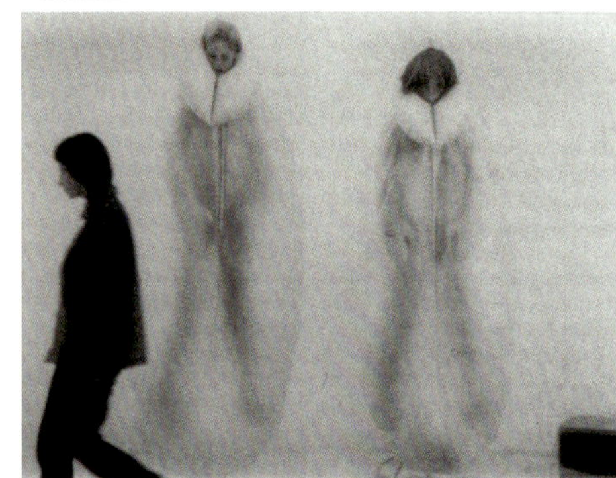
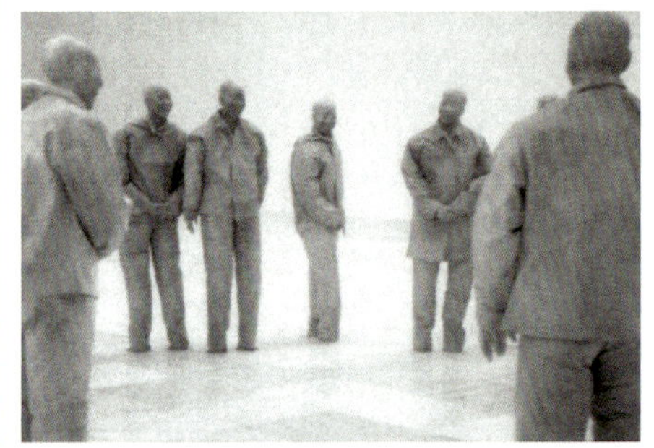
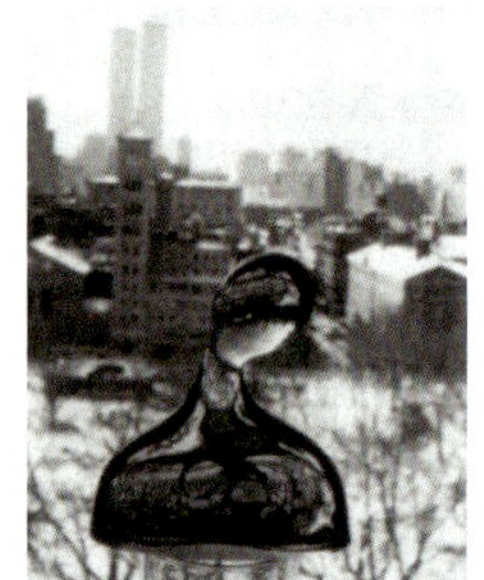
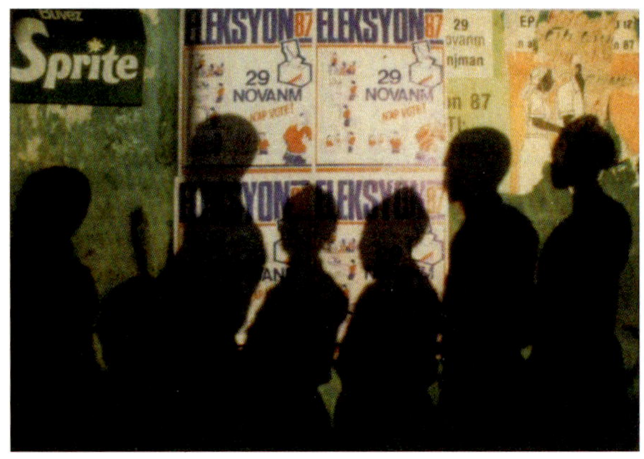
Sprite
ELEKSYON 87
ELEKSYON 87
29
NOVANM
29
NOVANM
87
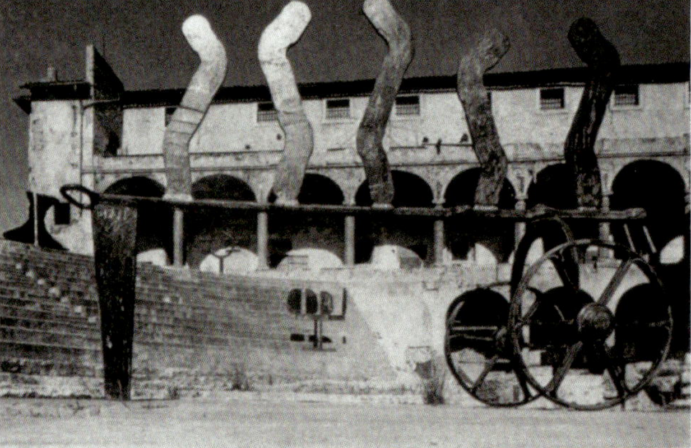

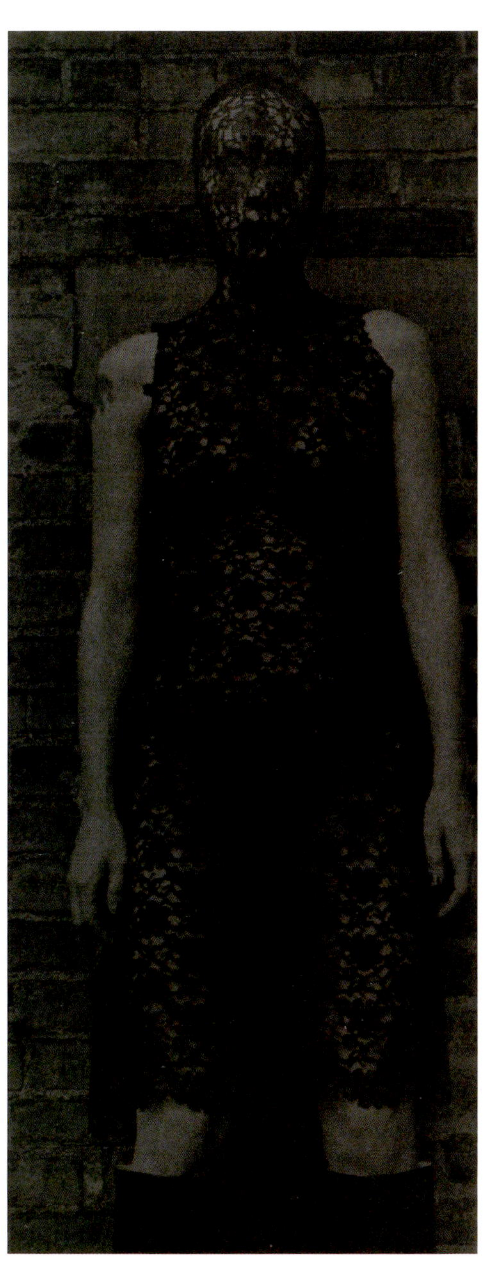

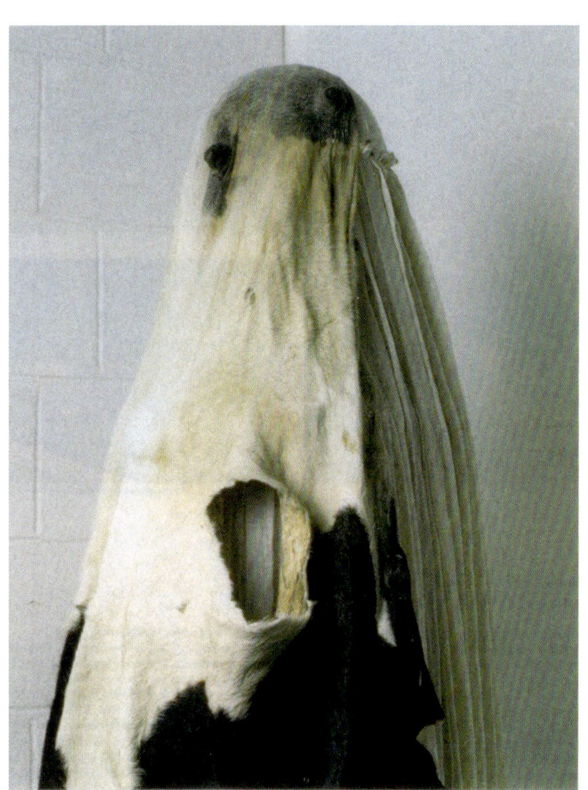

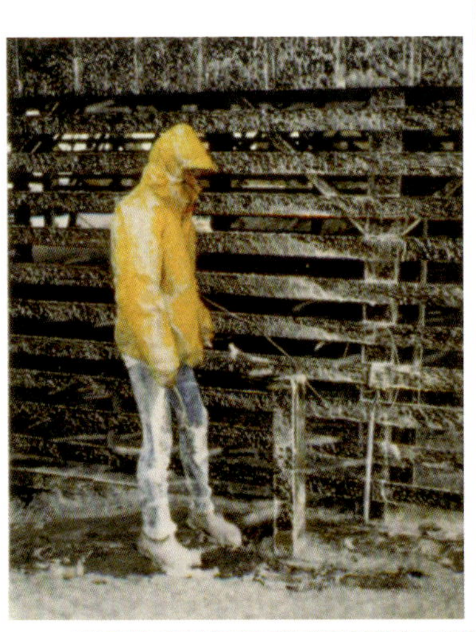
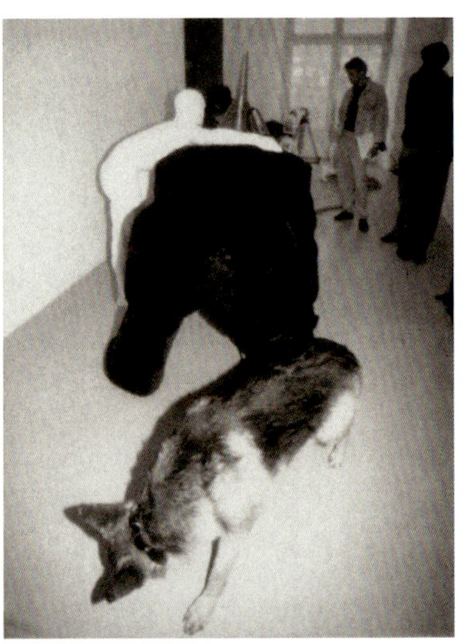
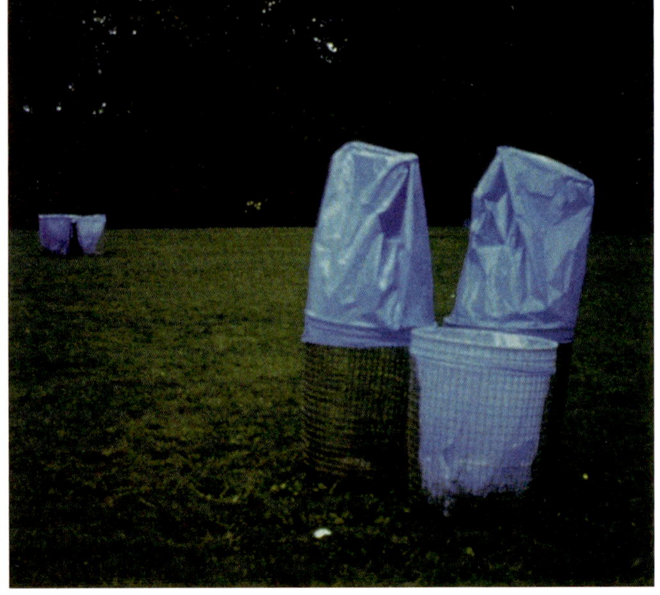

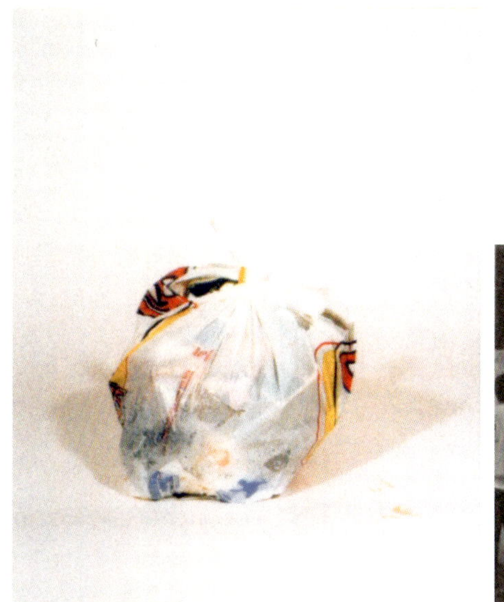
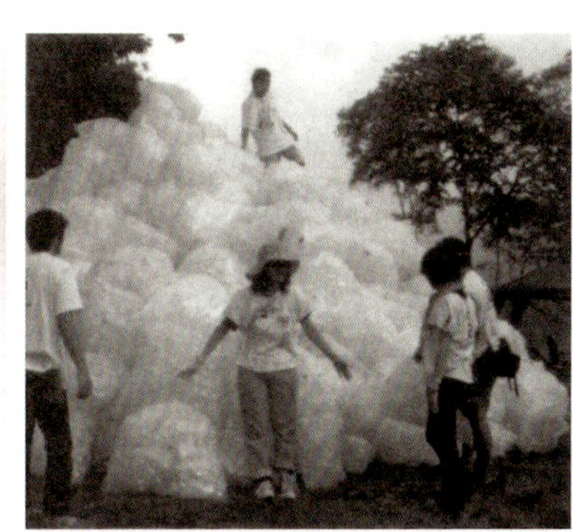
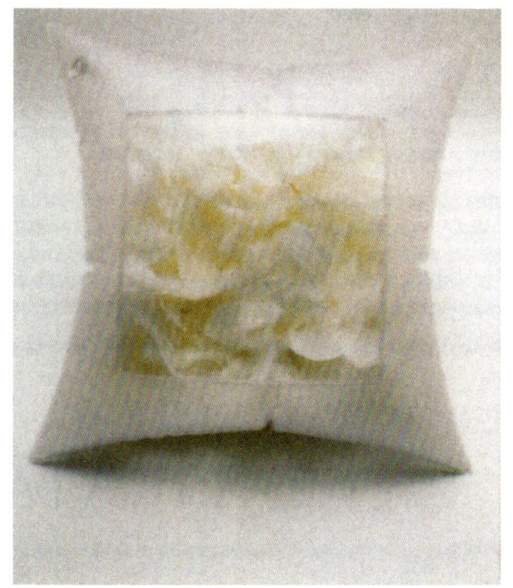
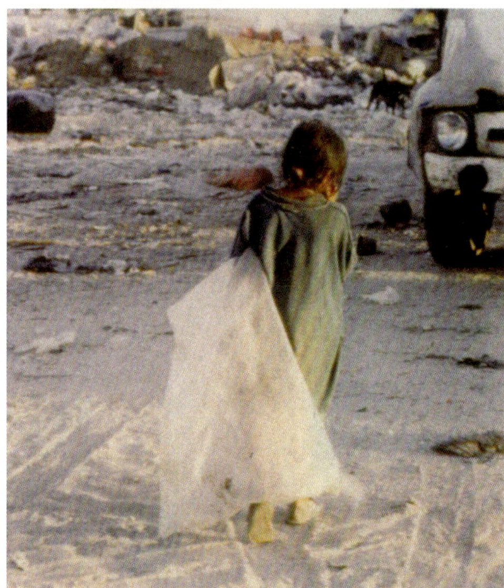

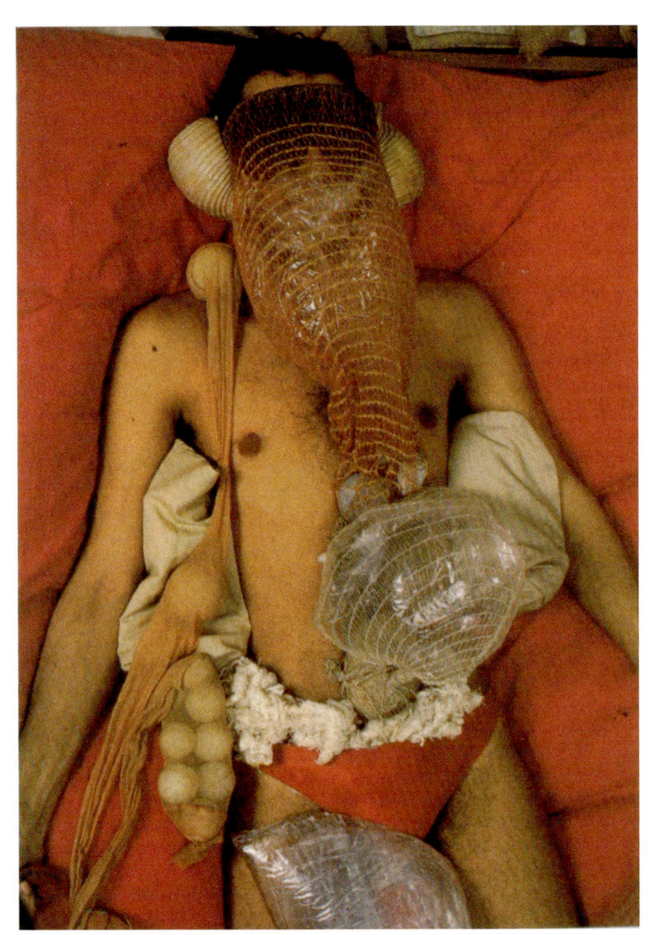

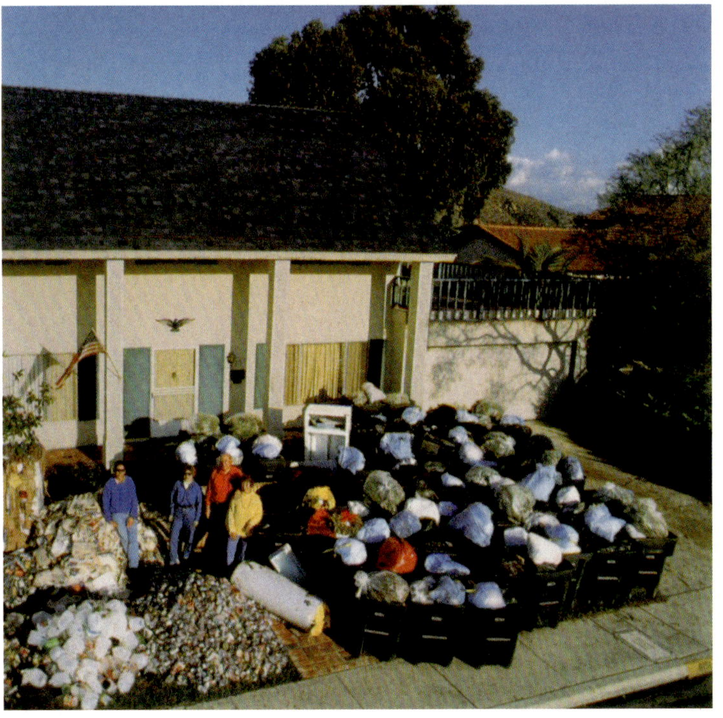

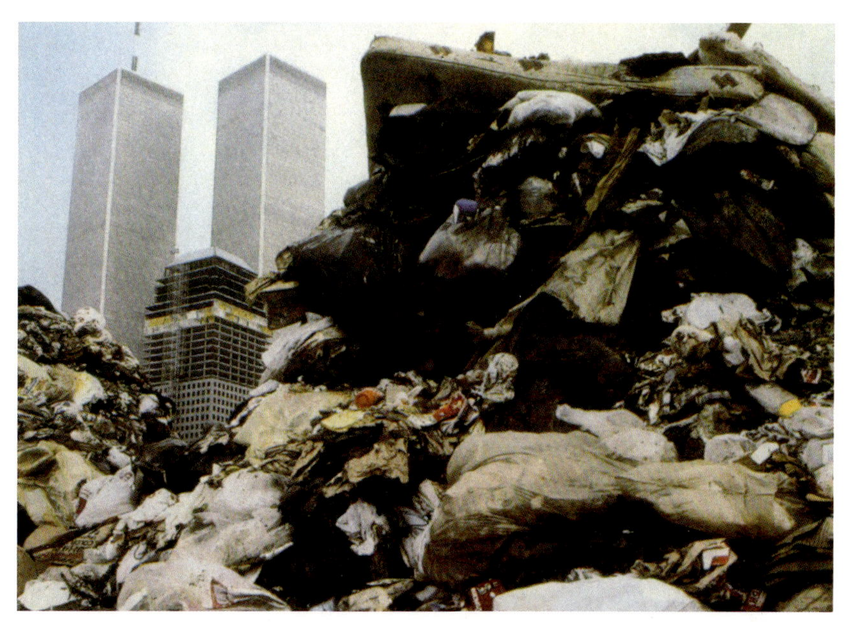

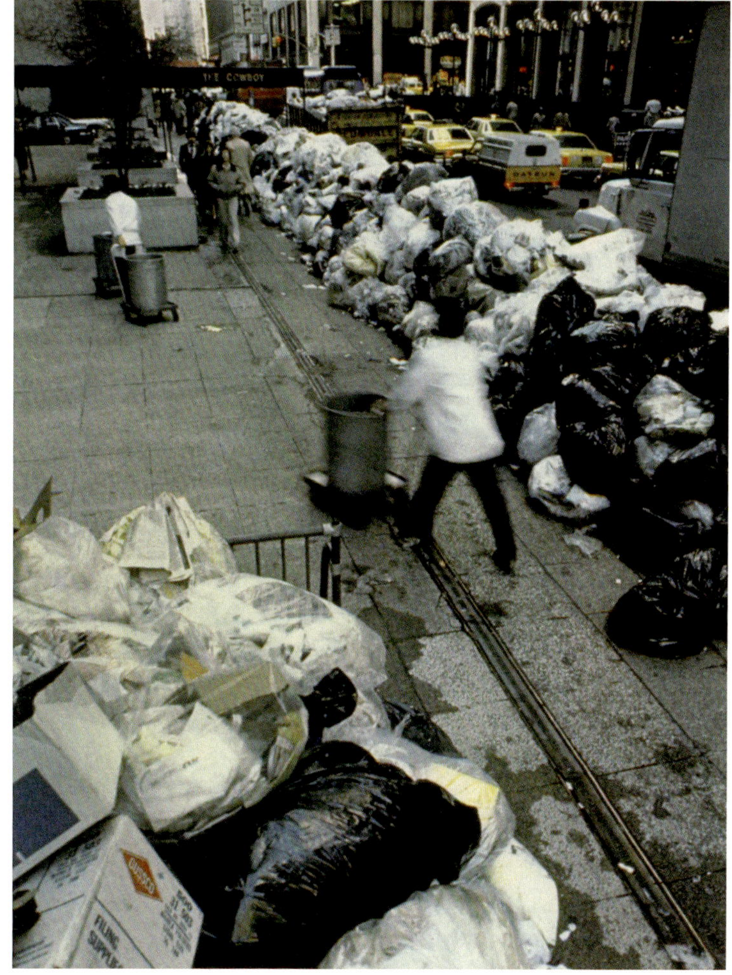

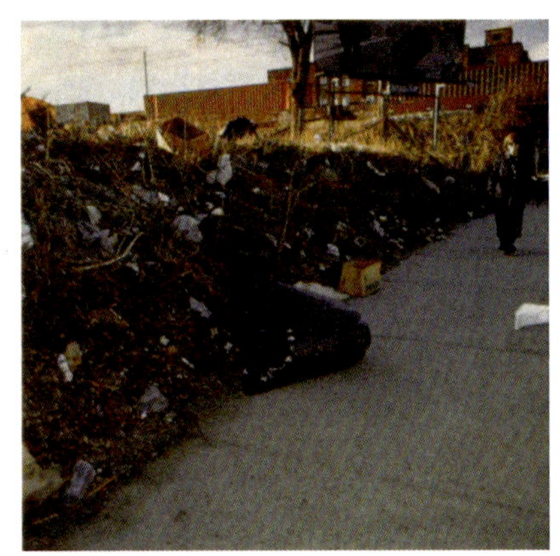
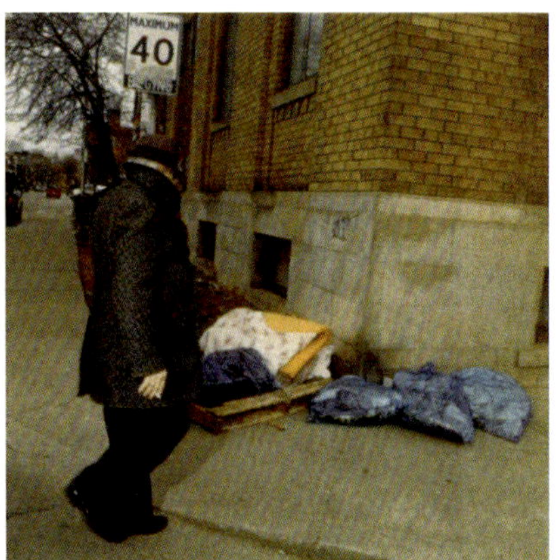
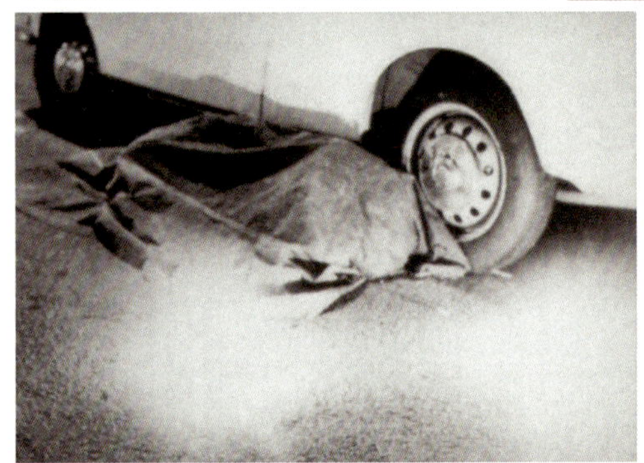
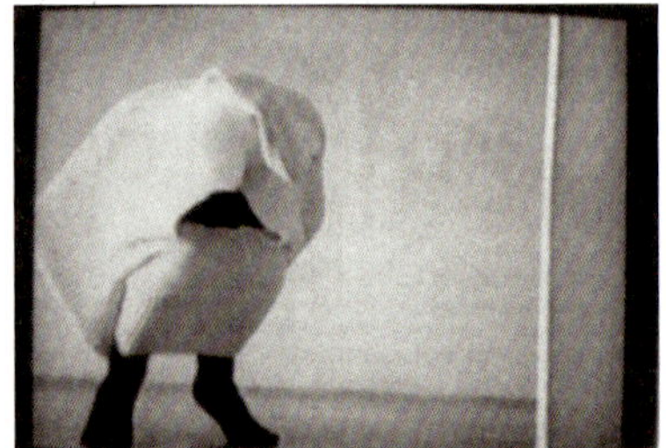
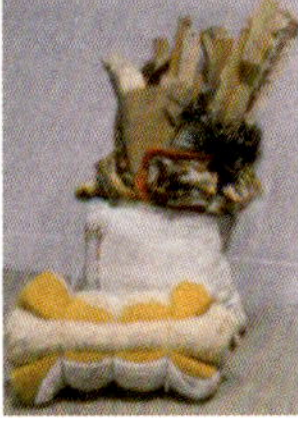
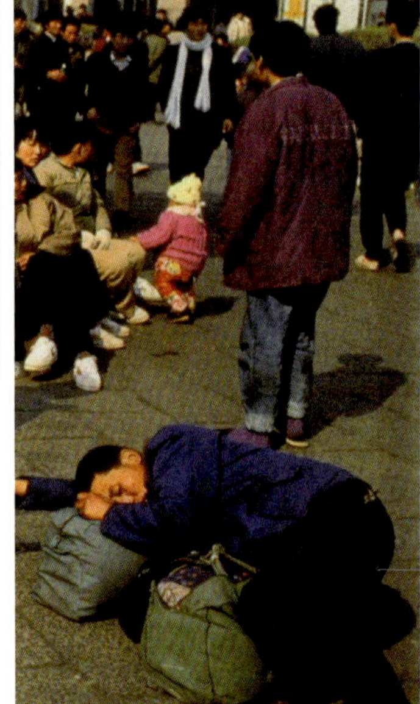

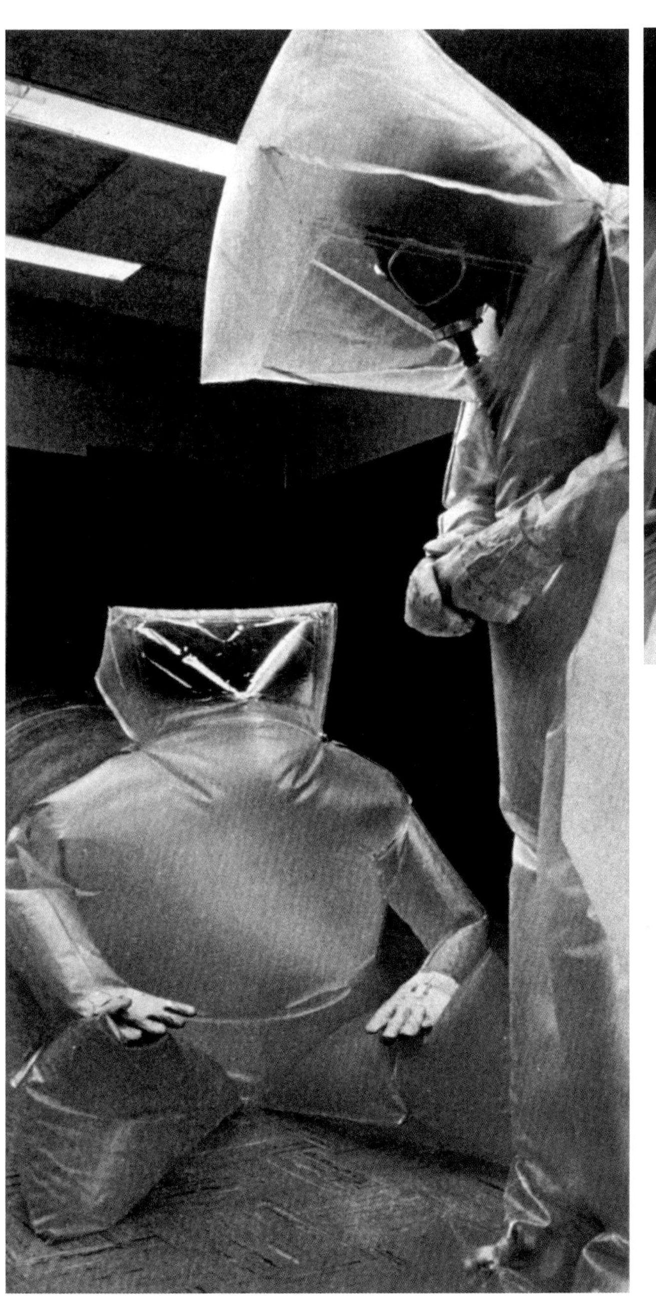
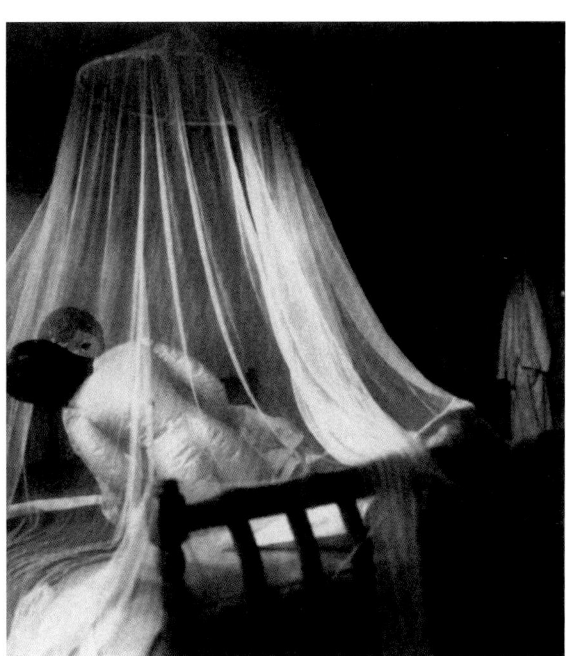

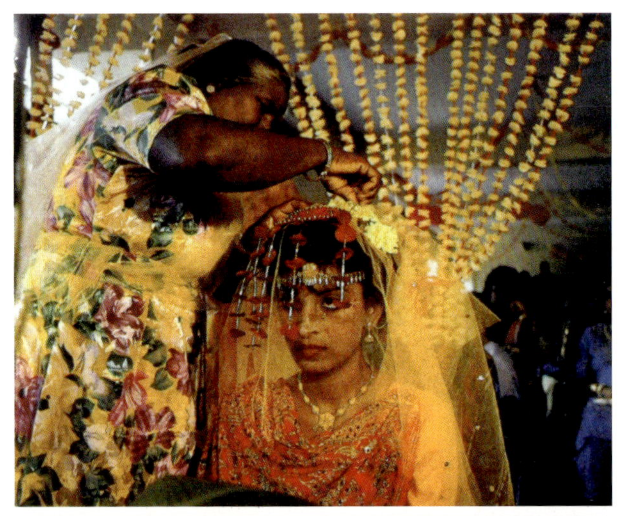

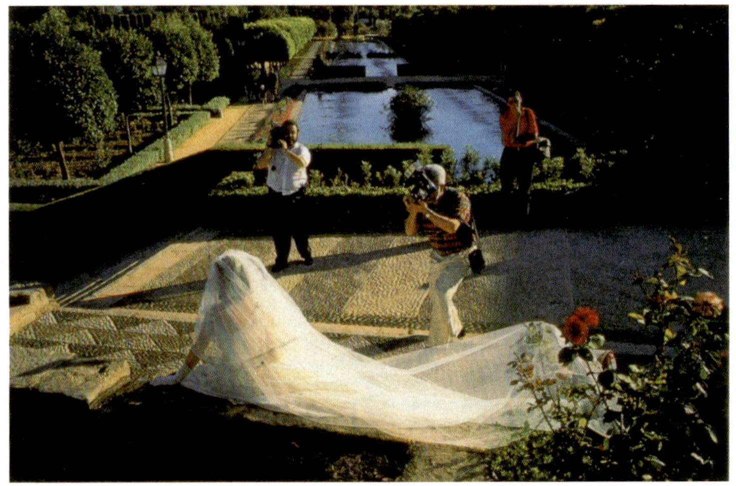

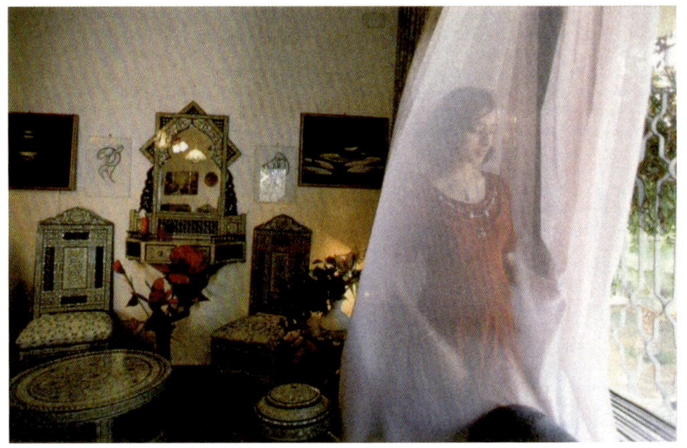

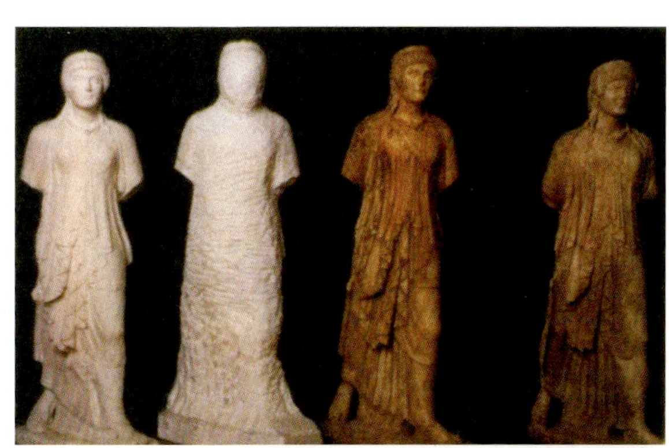
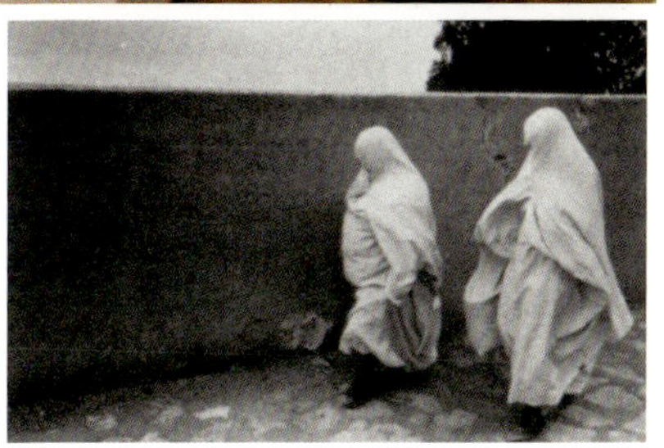

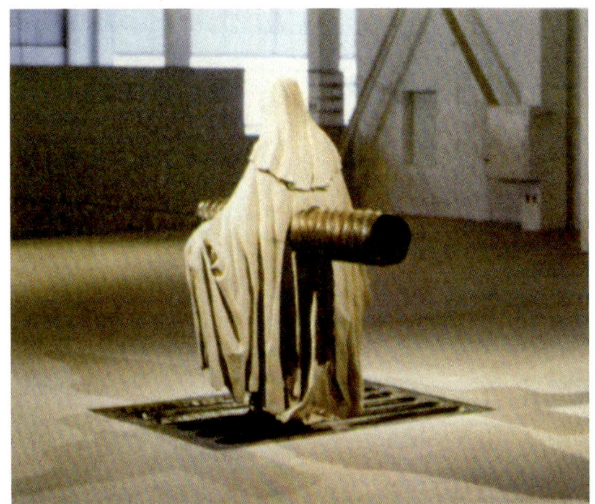

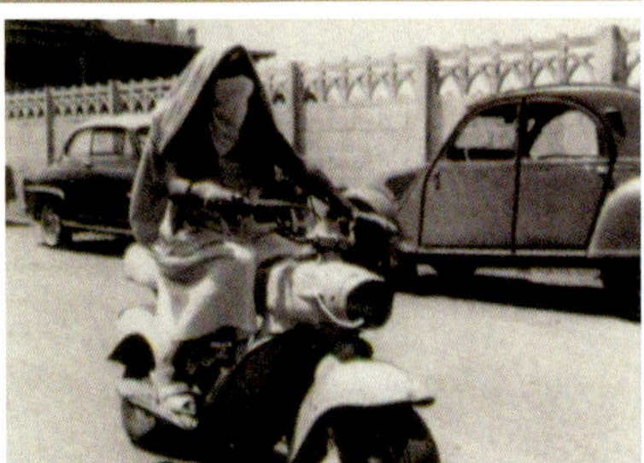

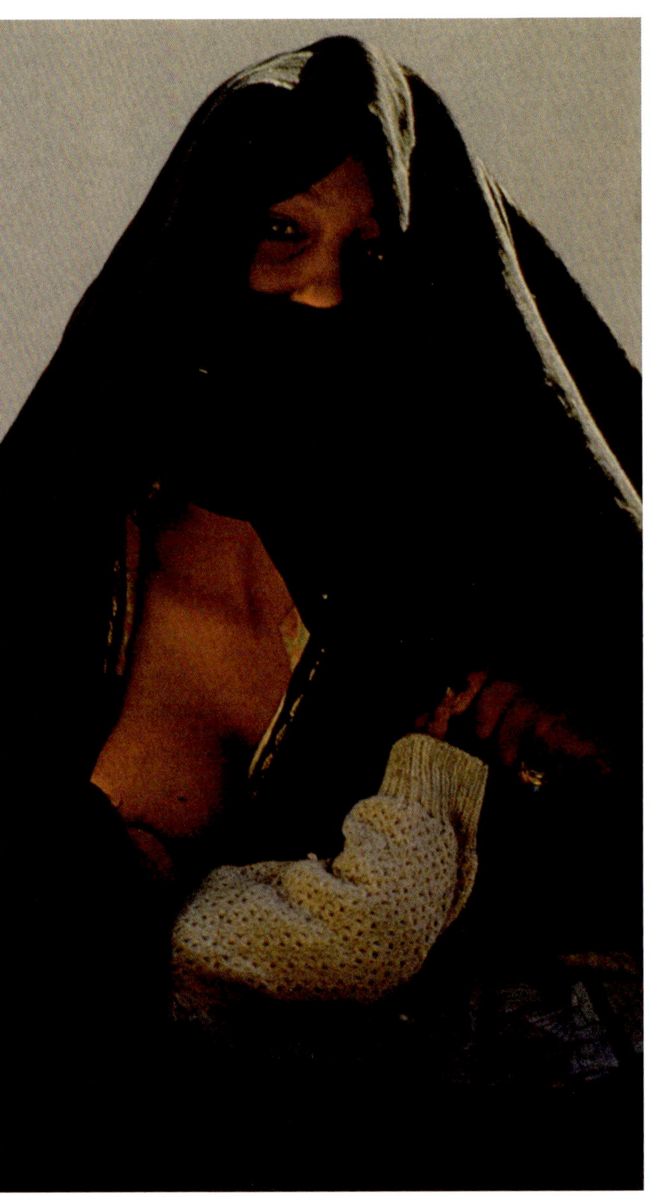

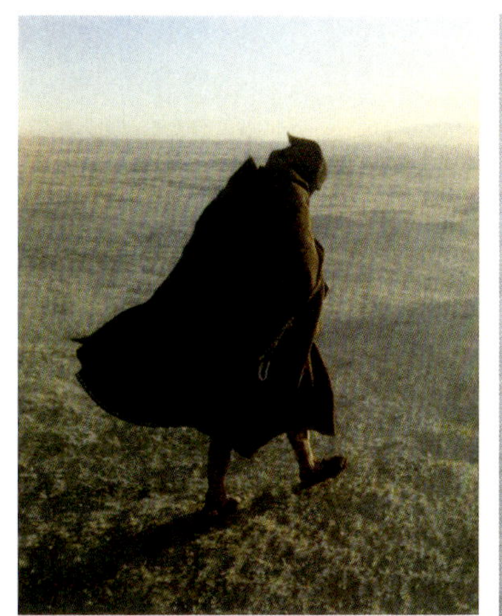
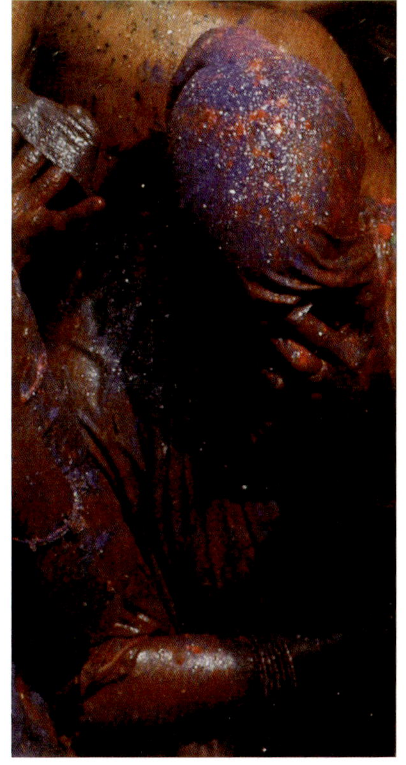
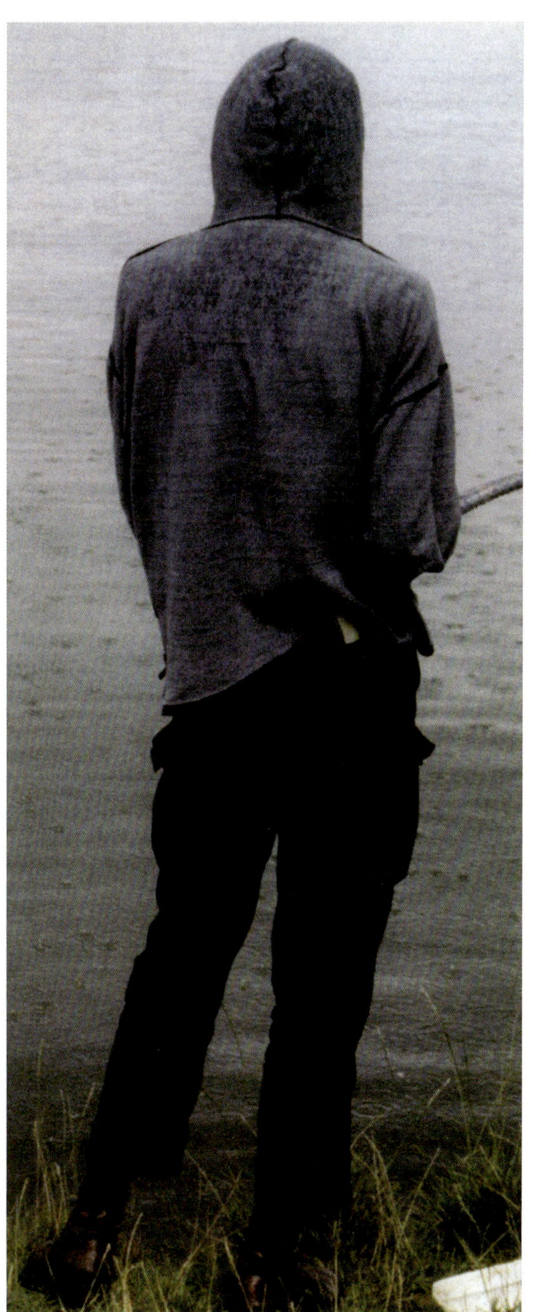

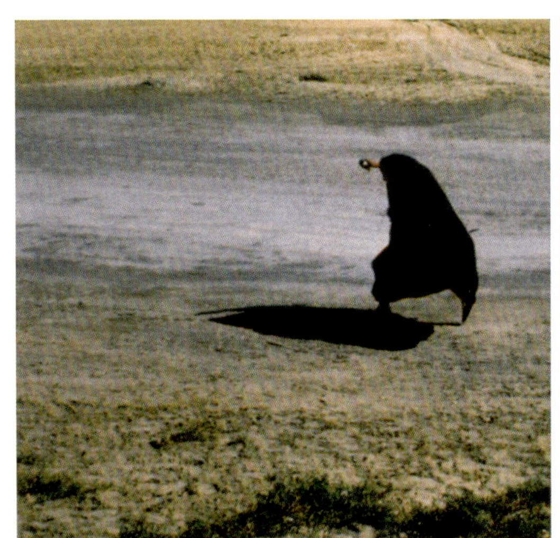
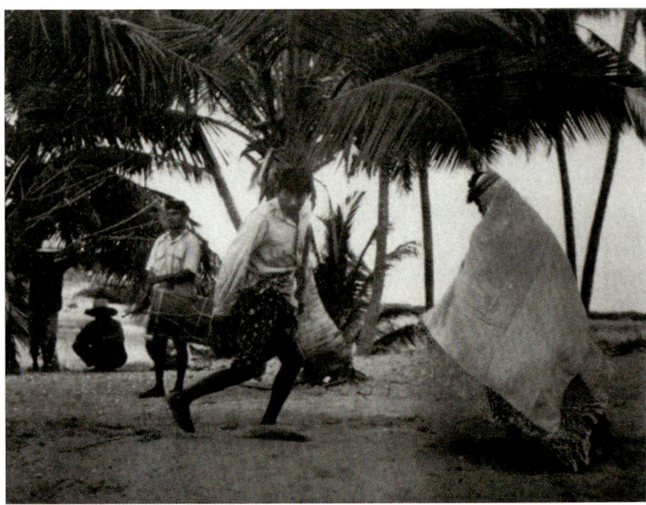
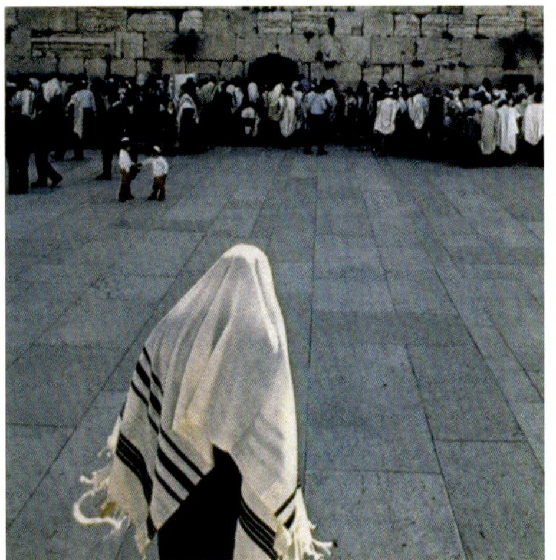
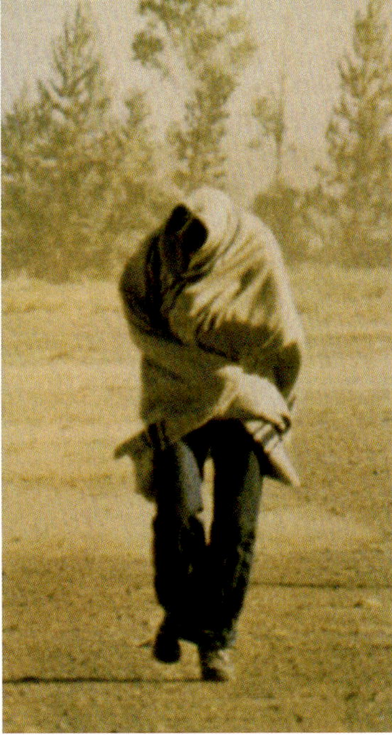
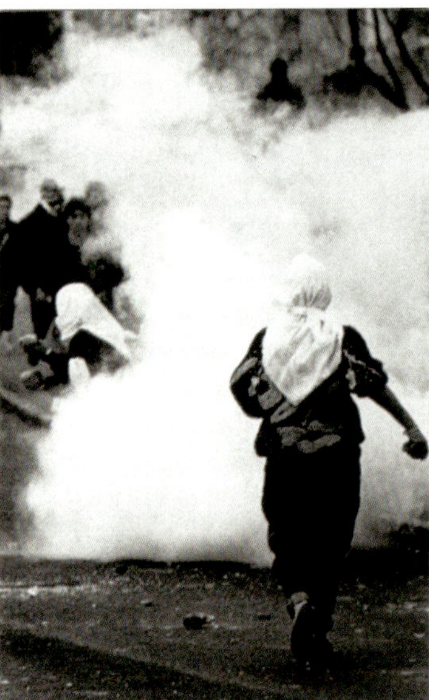

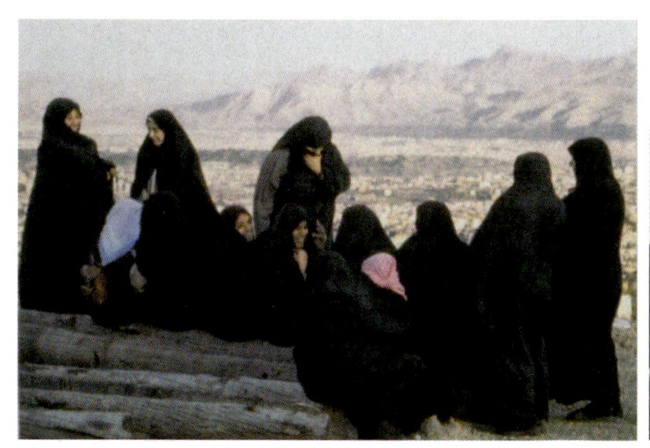

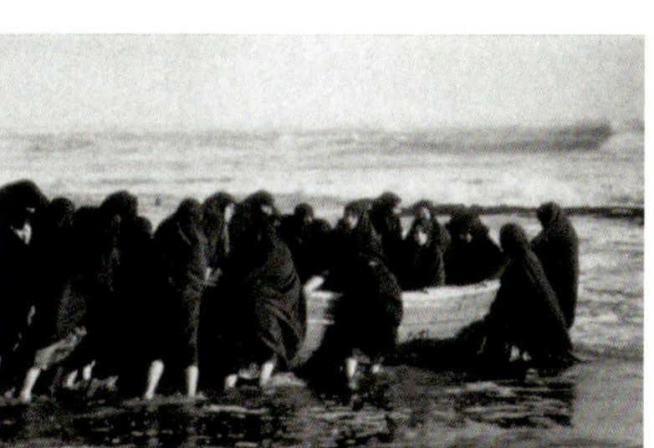

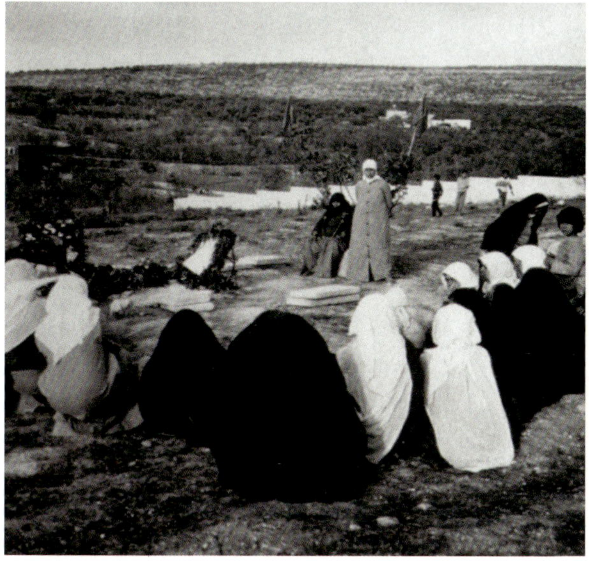

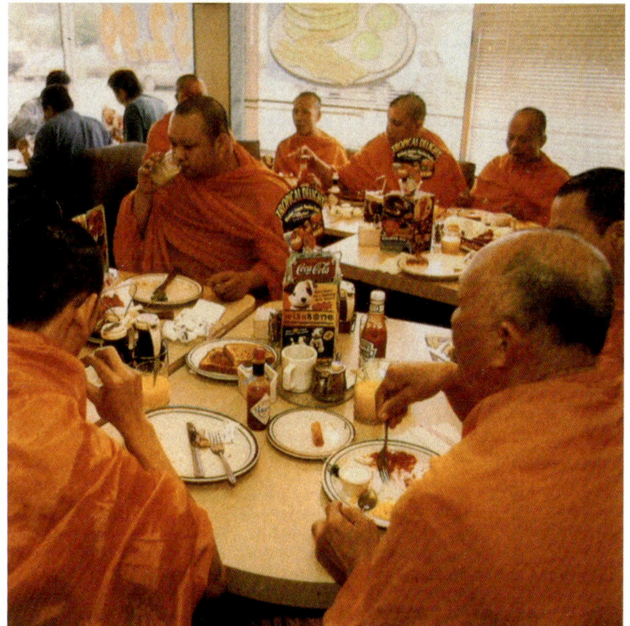

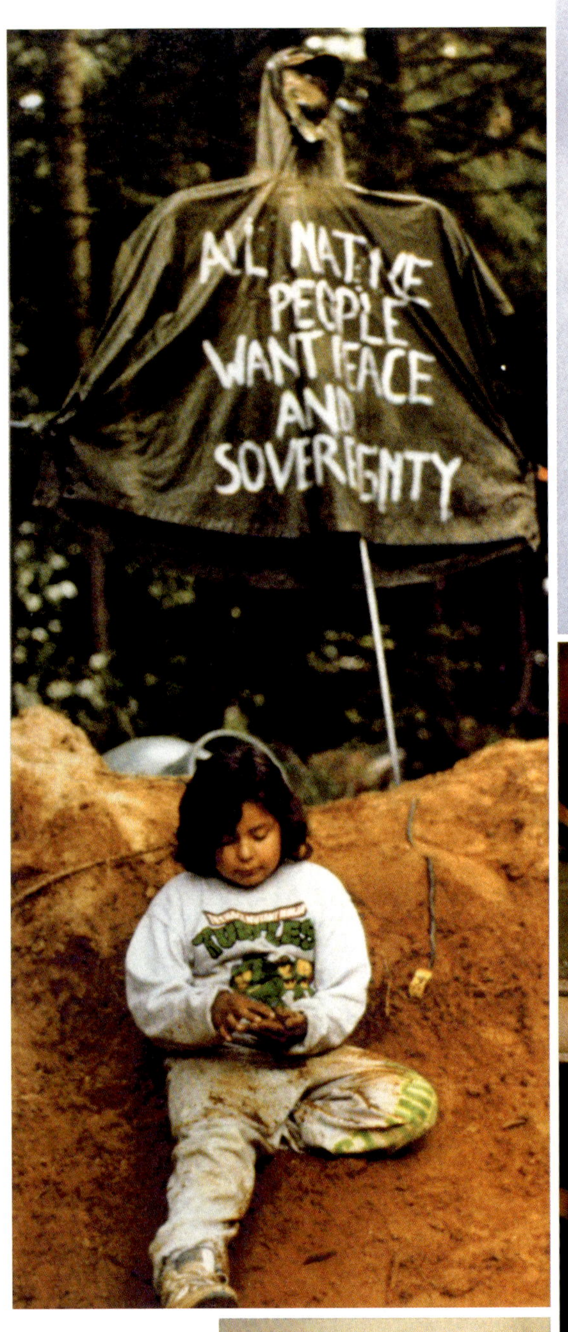

ALL NATIVE
PEOPLE
WANT PEACE
AND
SOVERIGNTY

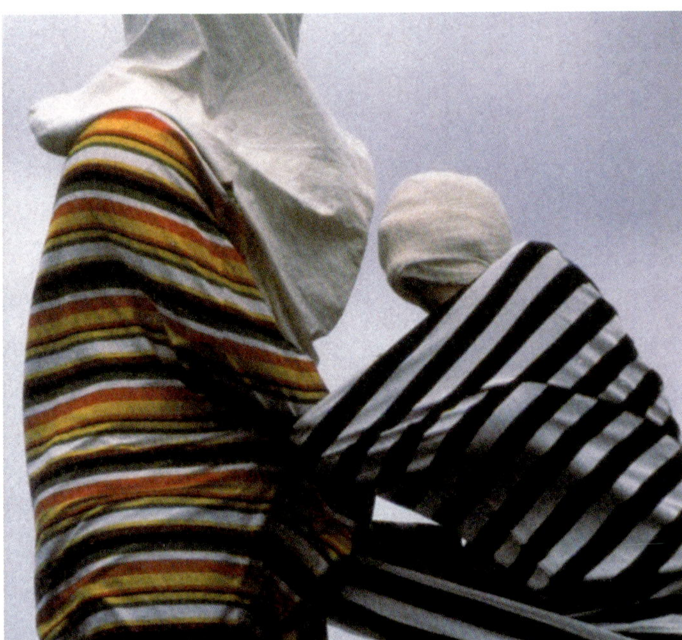

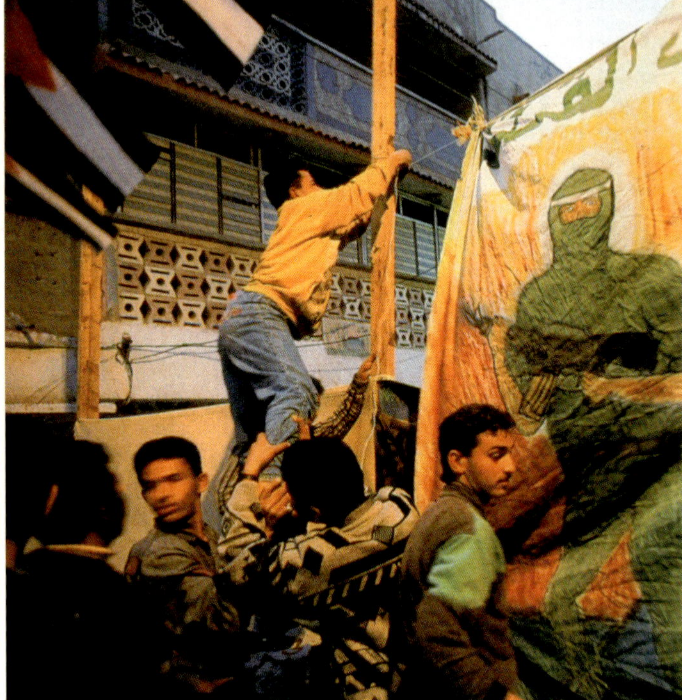

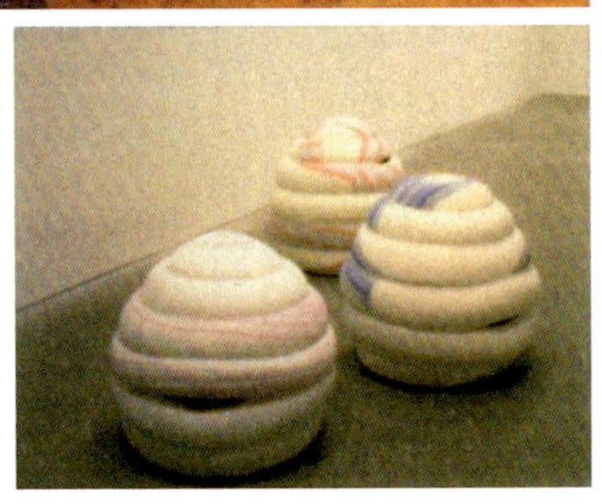

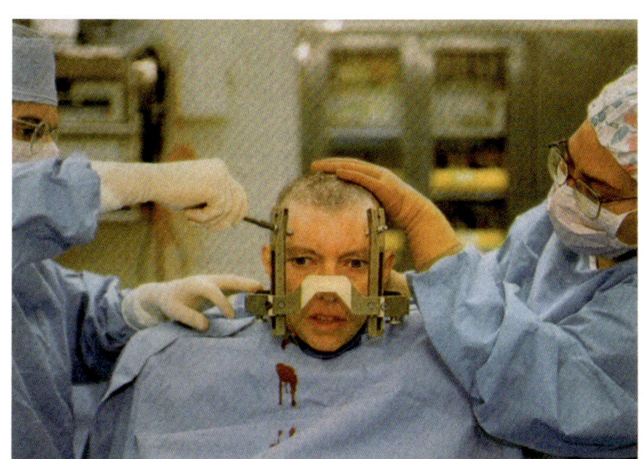

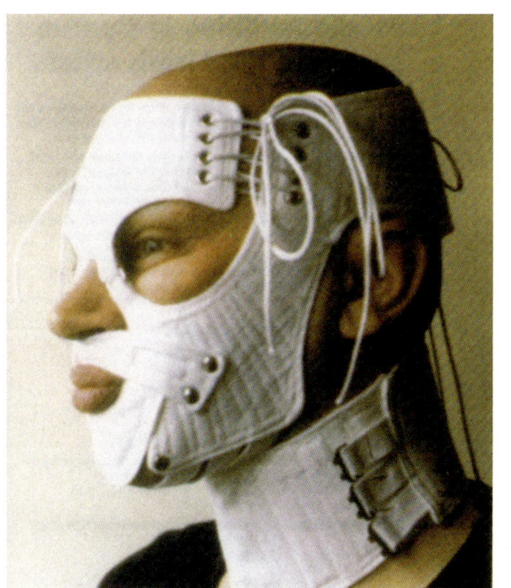

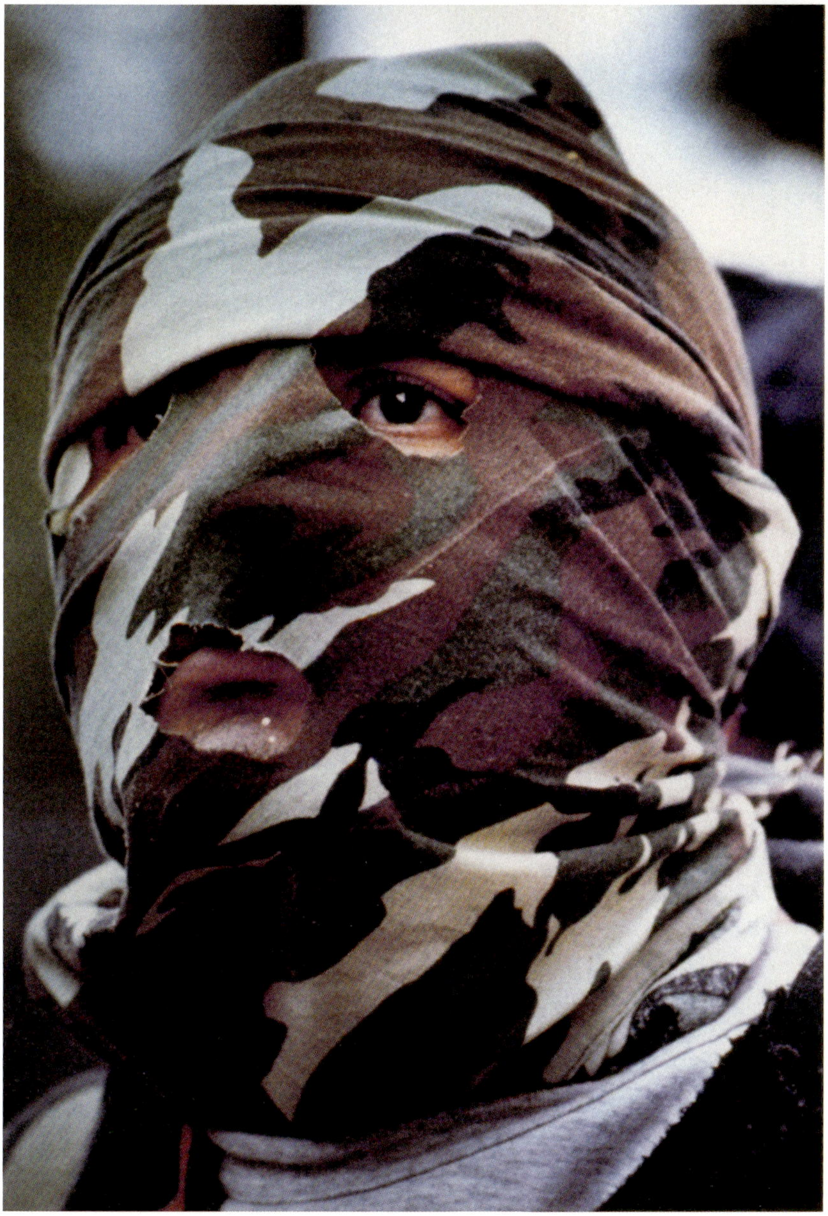

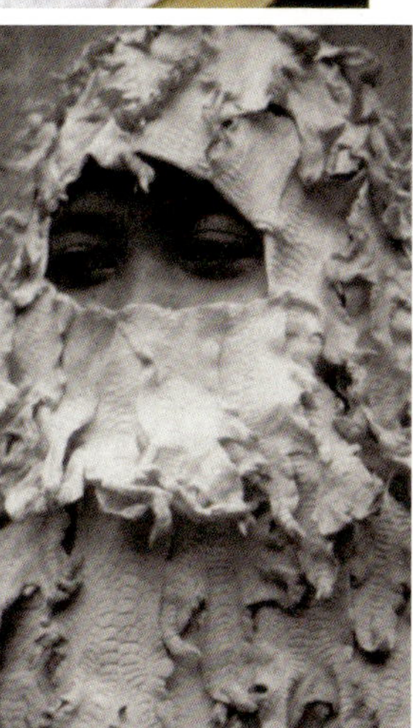

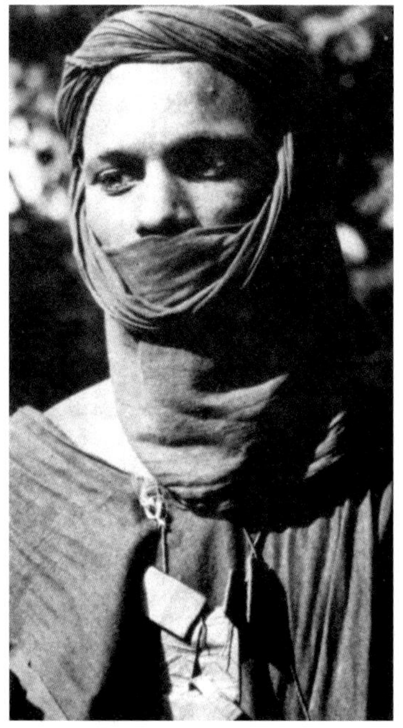
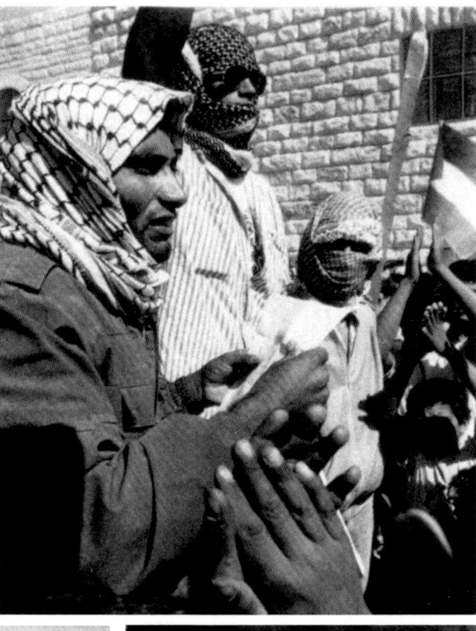
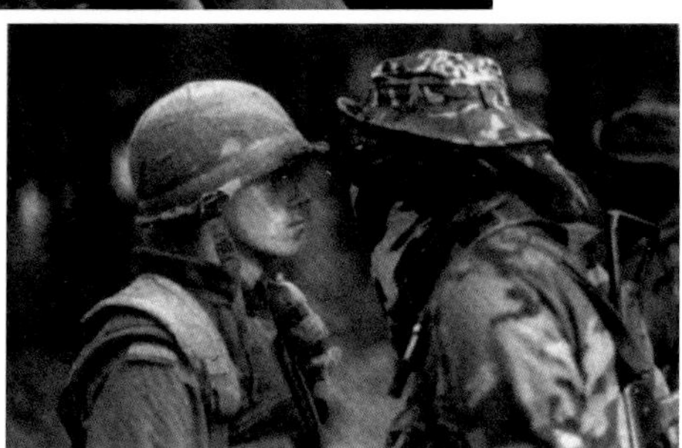
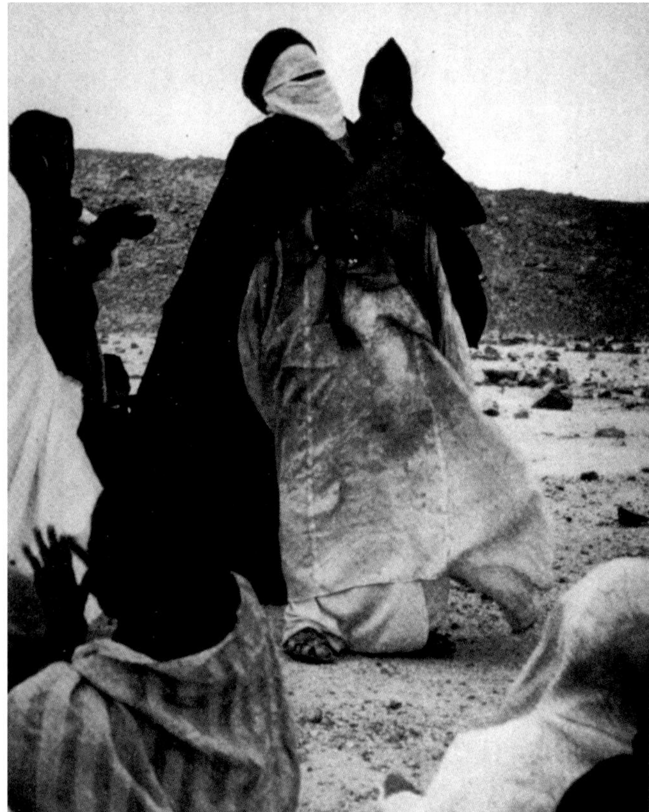
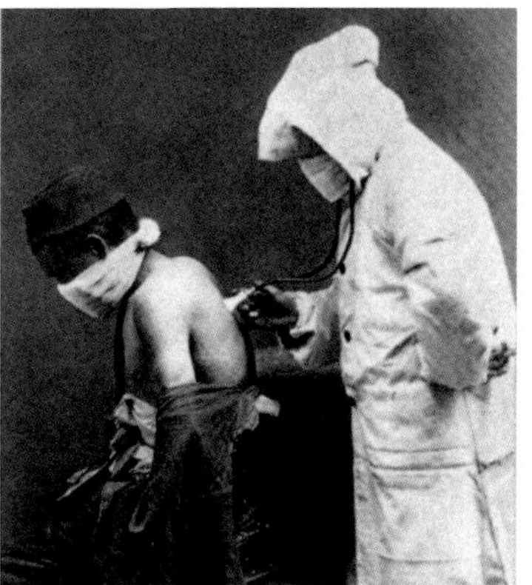

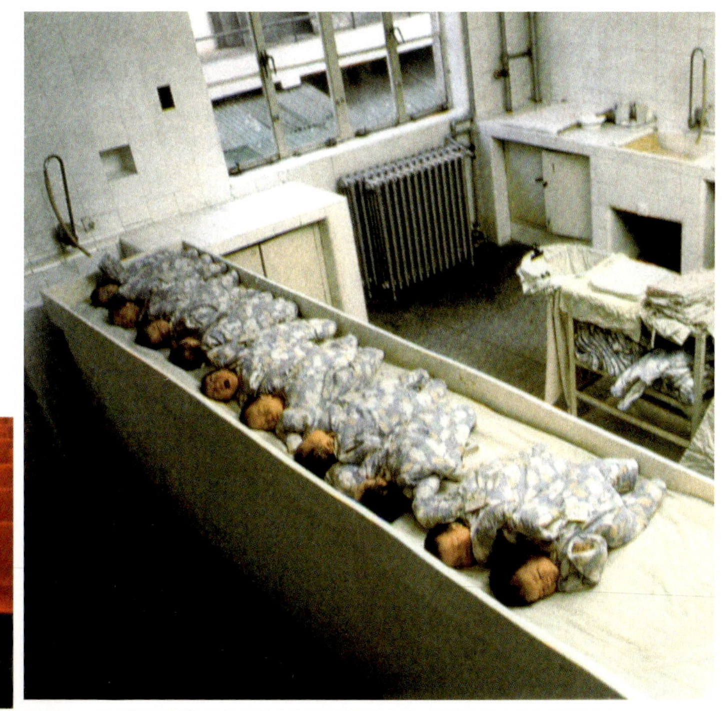

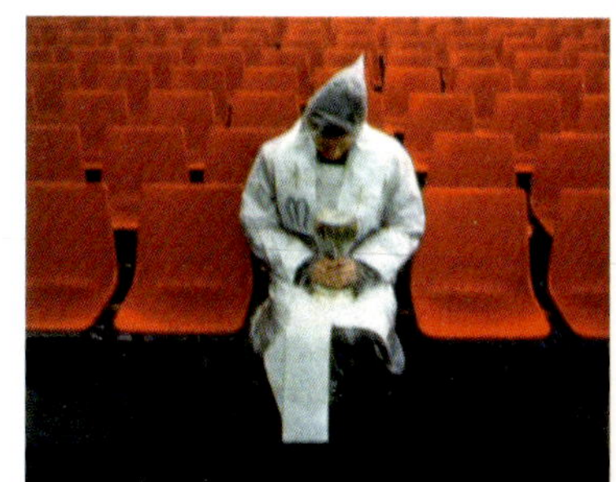

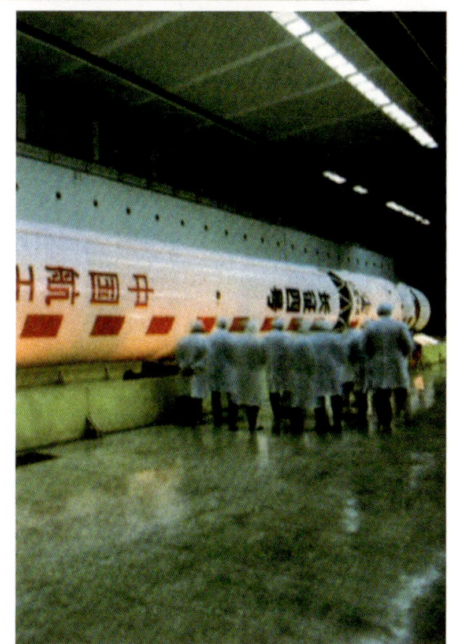

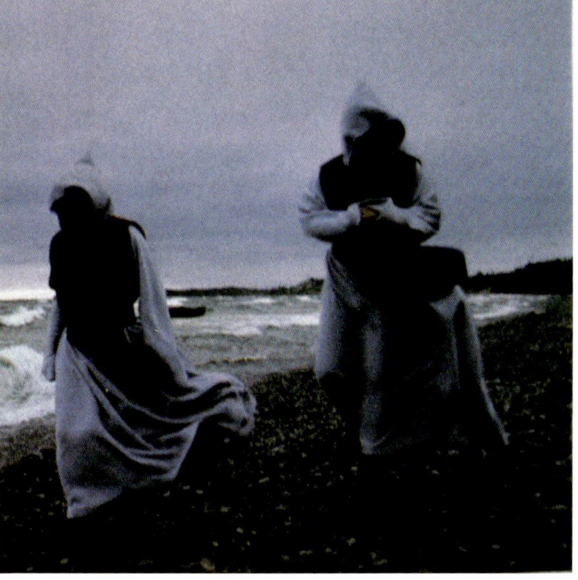

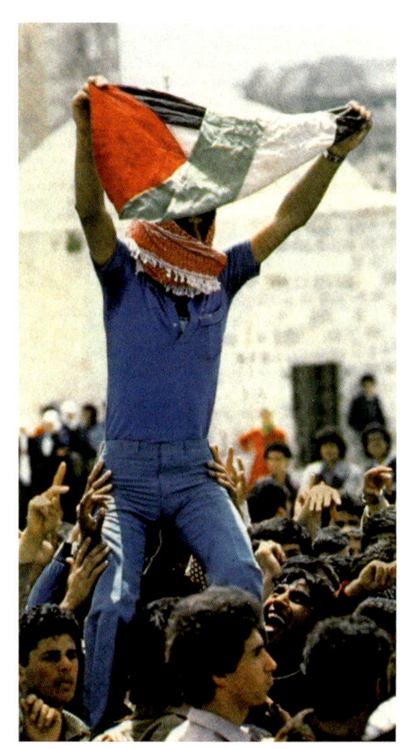
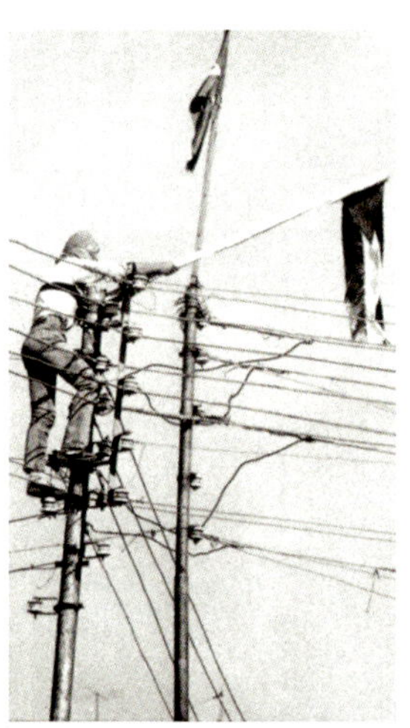
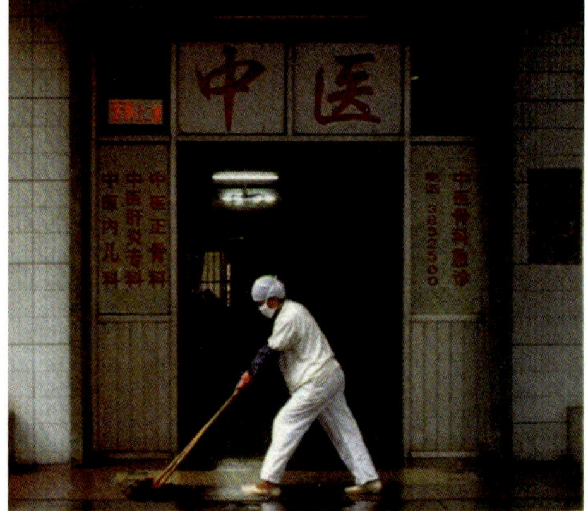
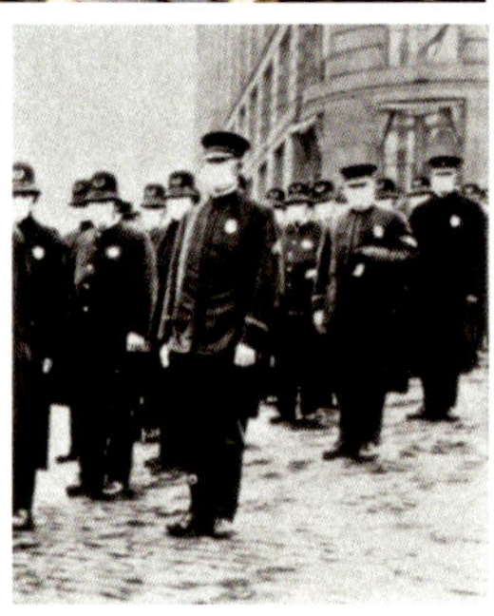

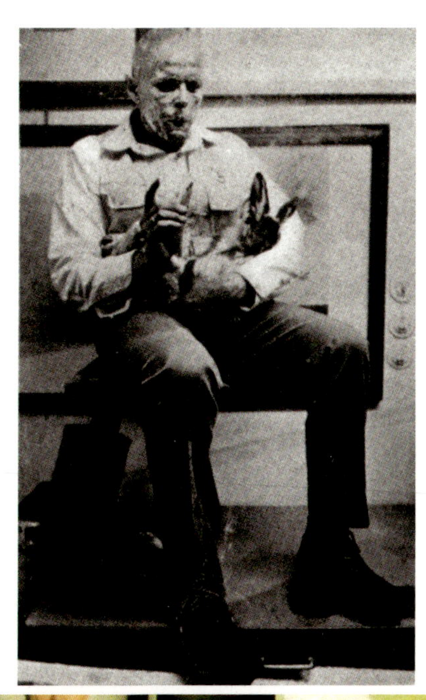

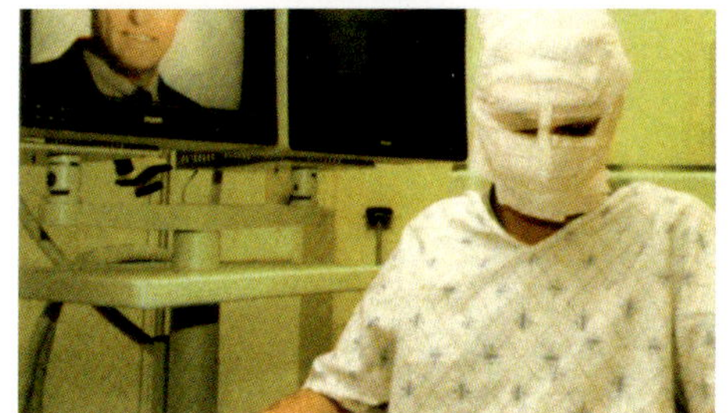

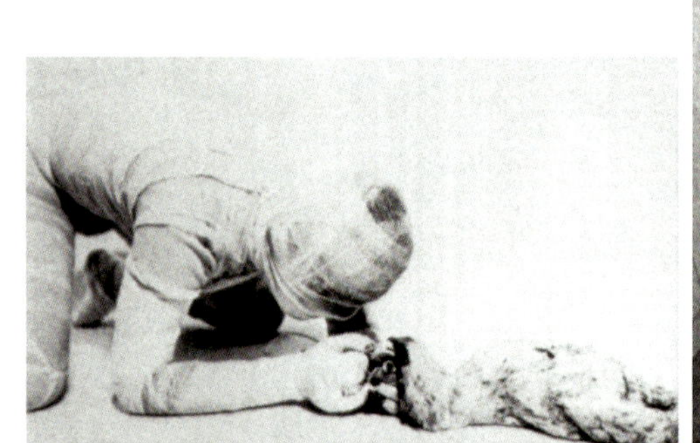
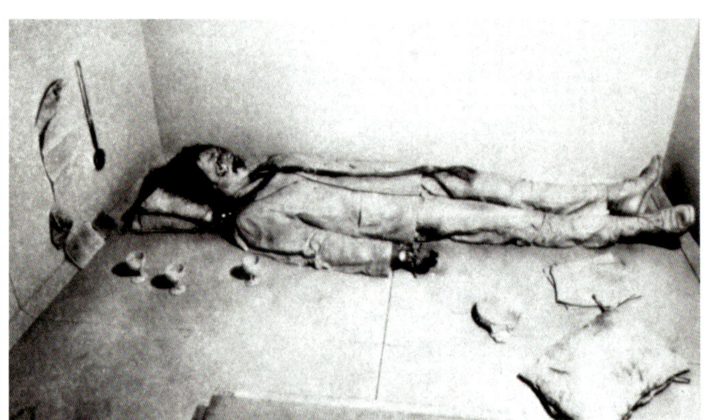
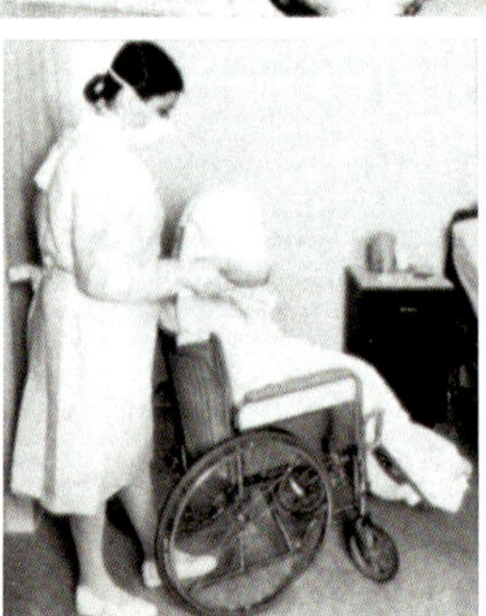
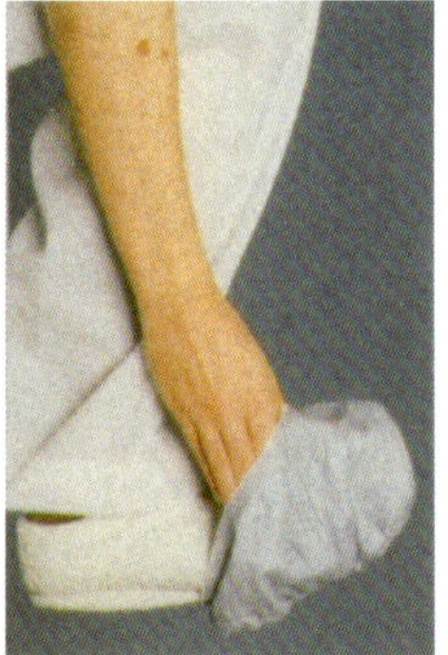
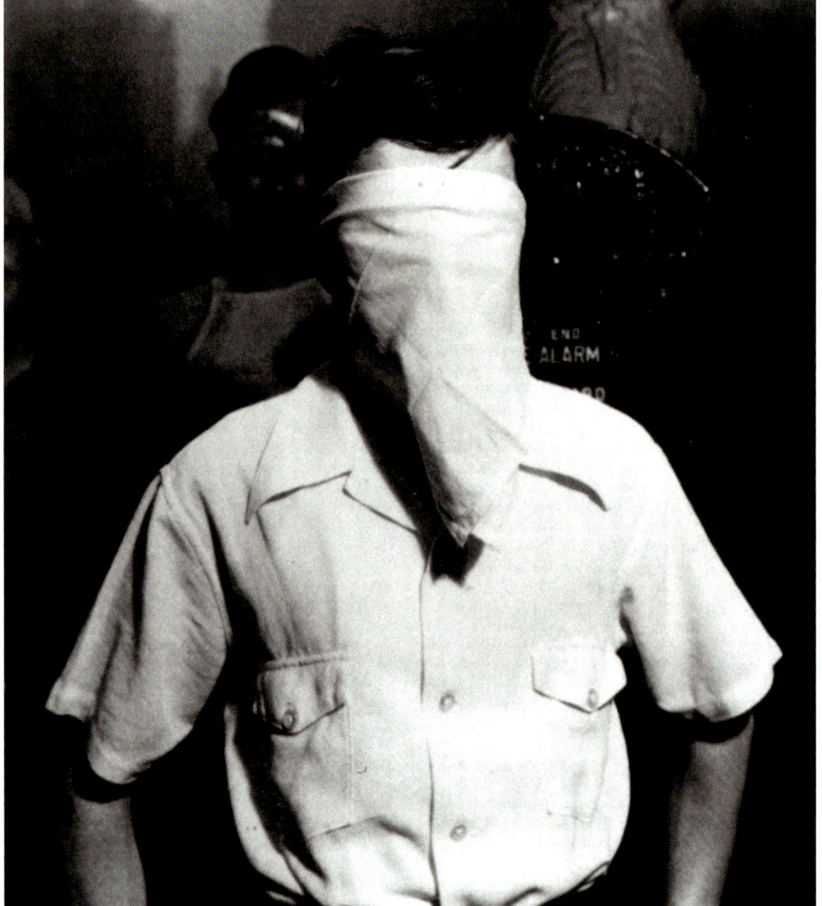

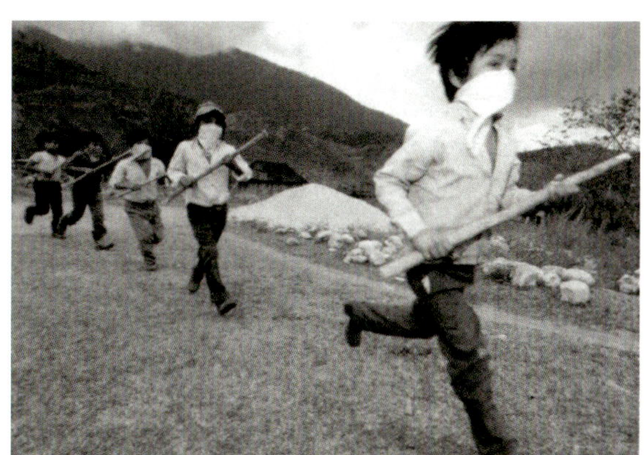

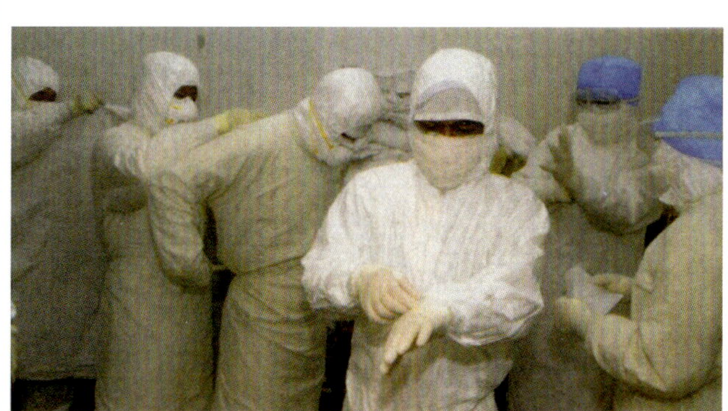

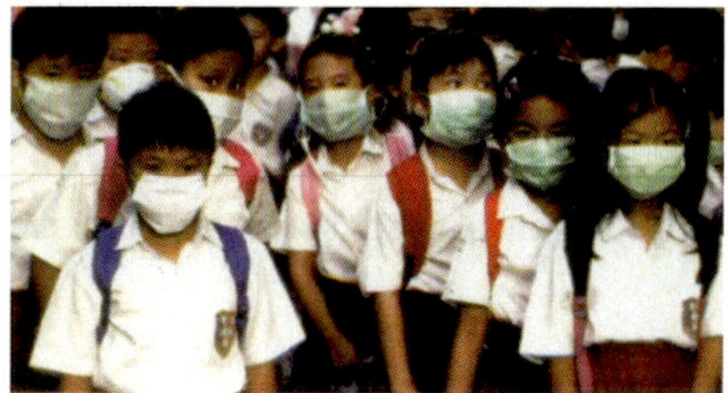

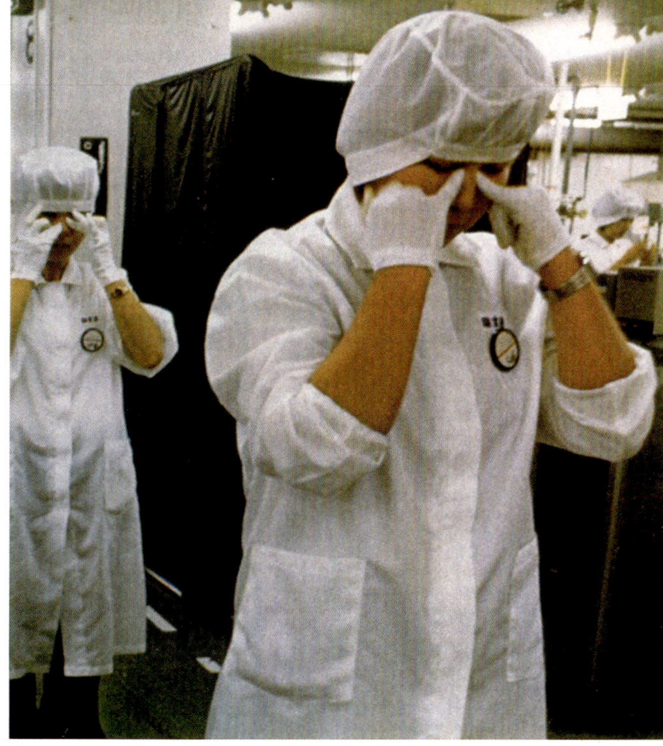

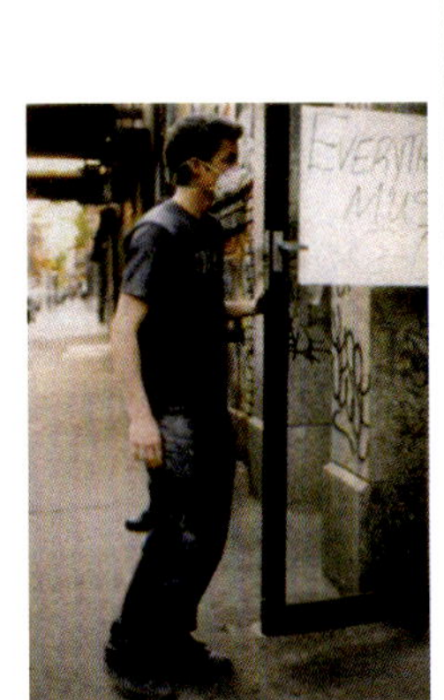
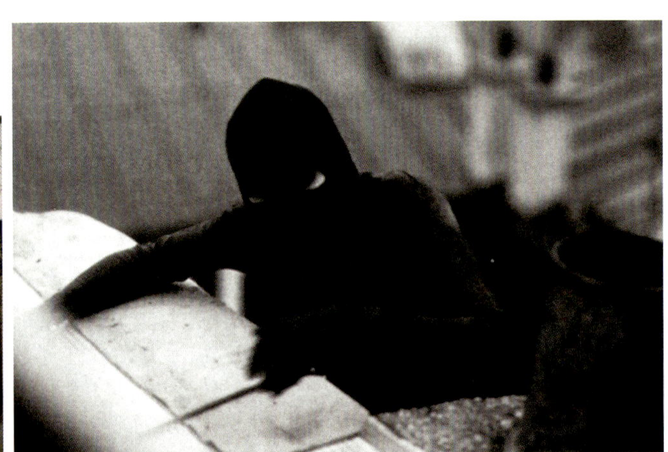
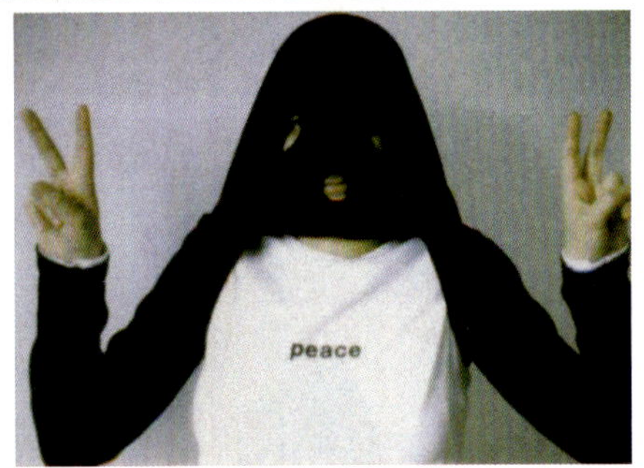

peace

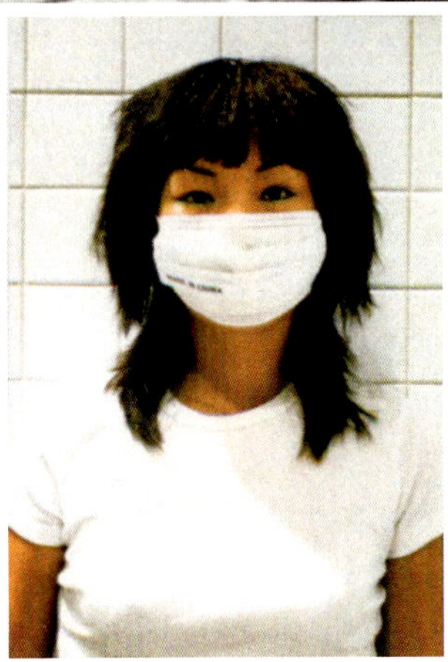

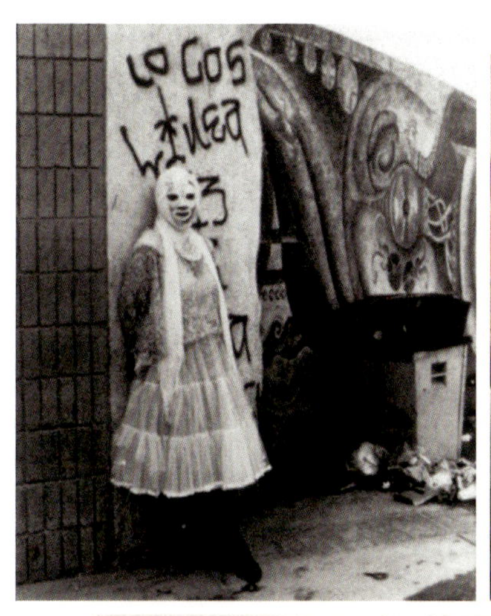
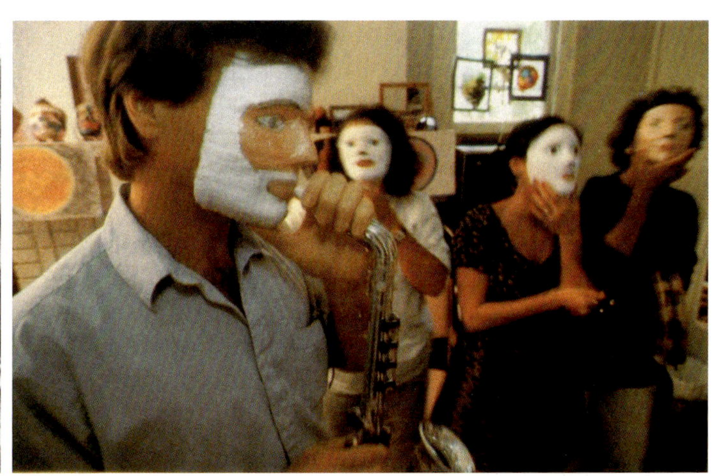
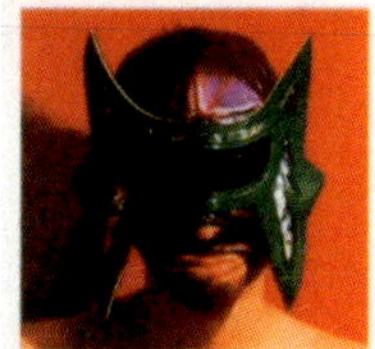
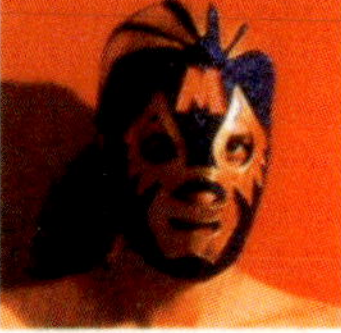
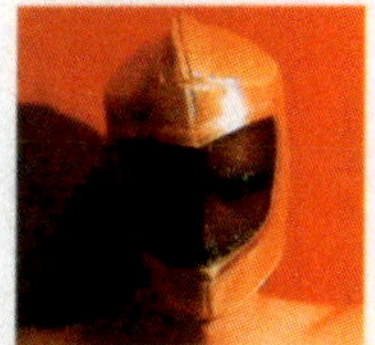
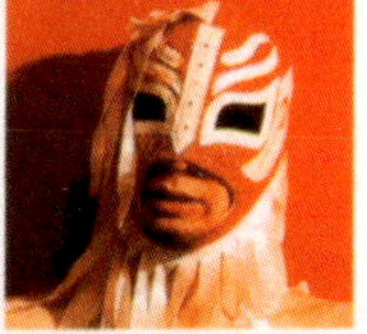
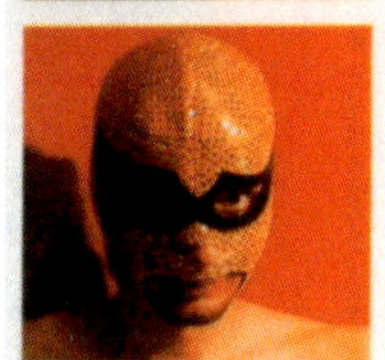
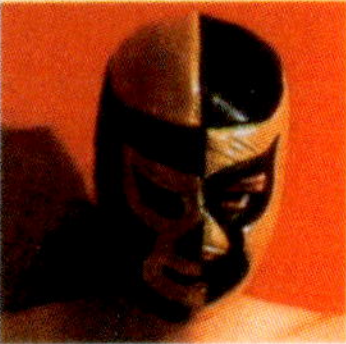
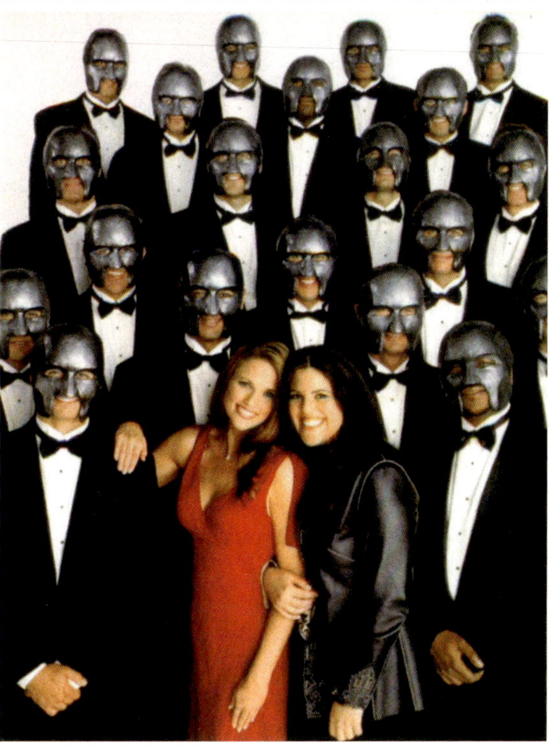

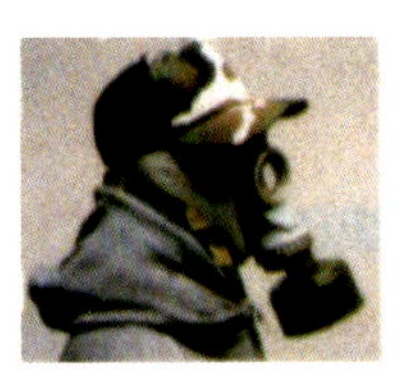
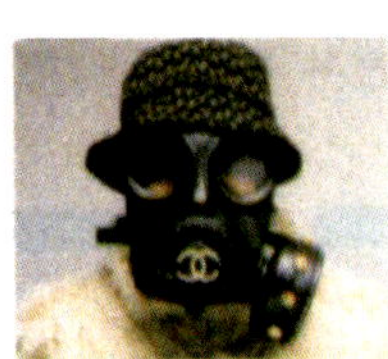
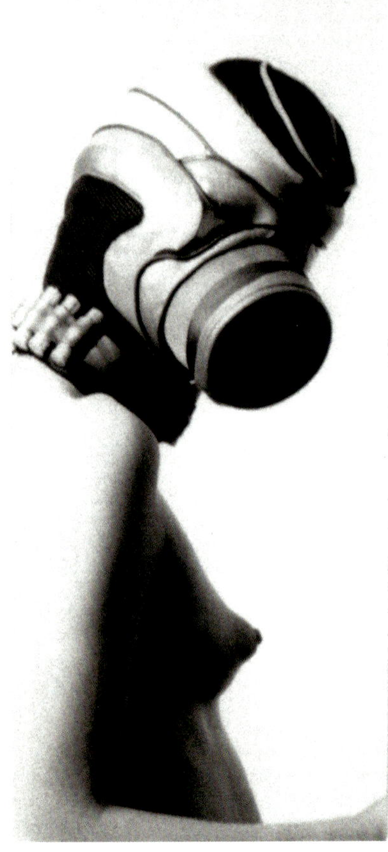

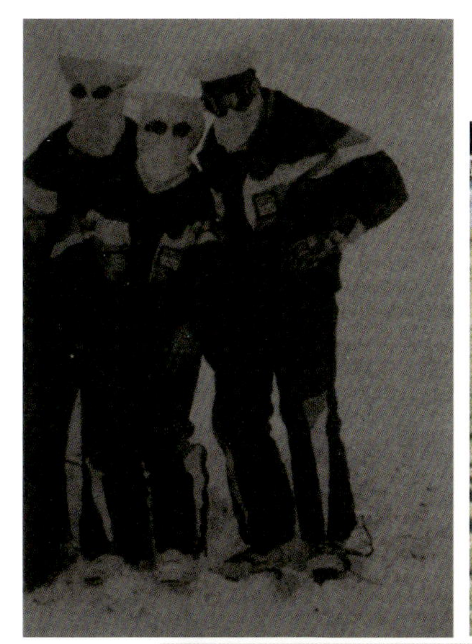
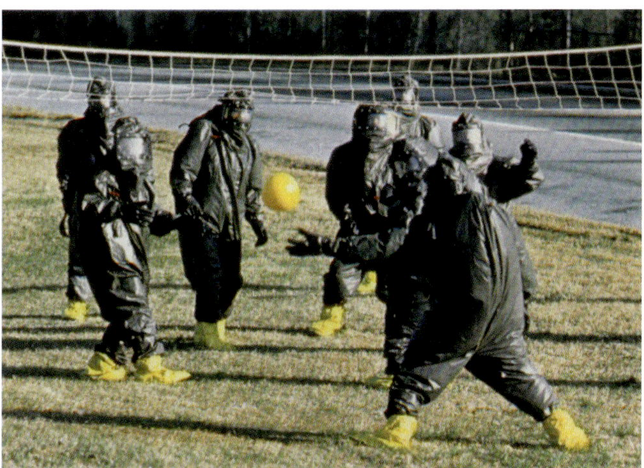
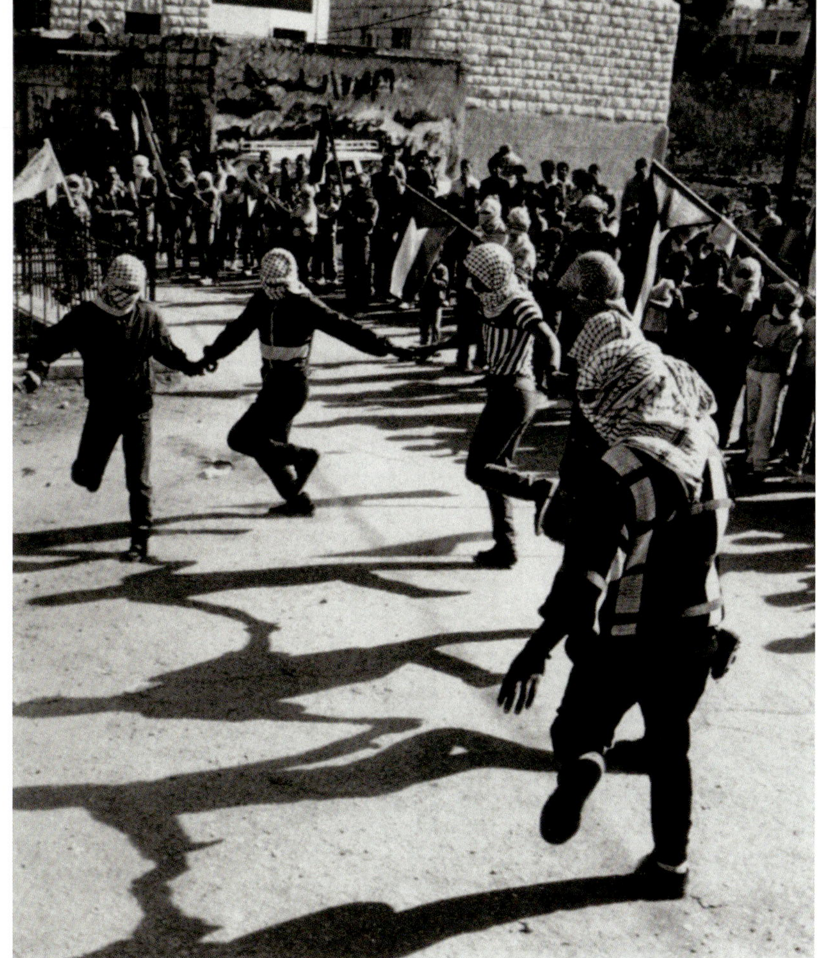

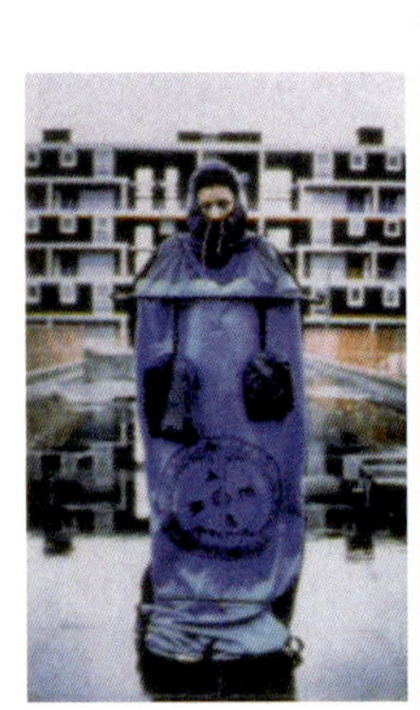
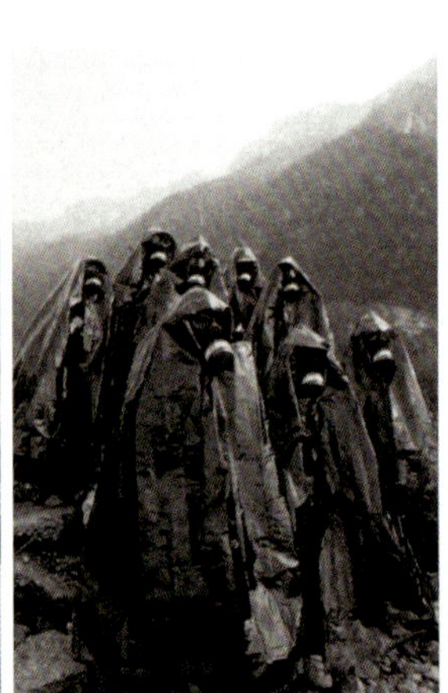
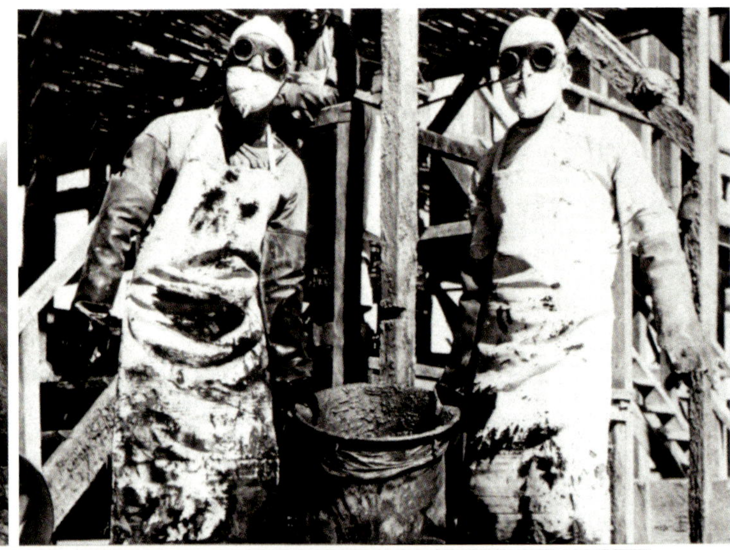
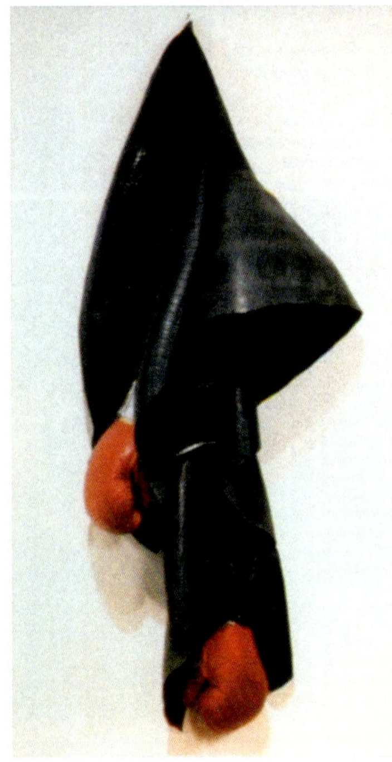
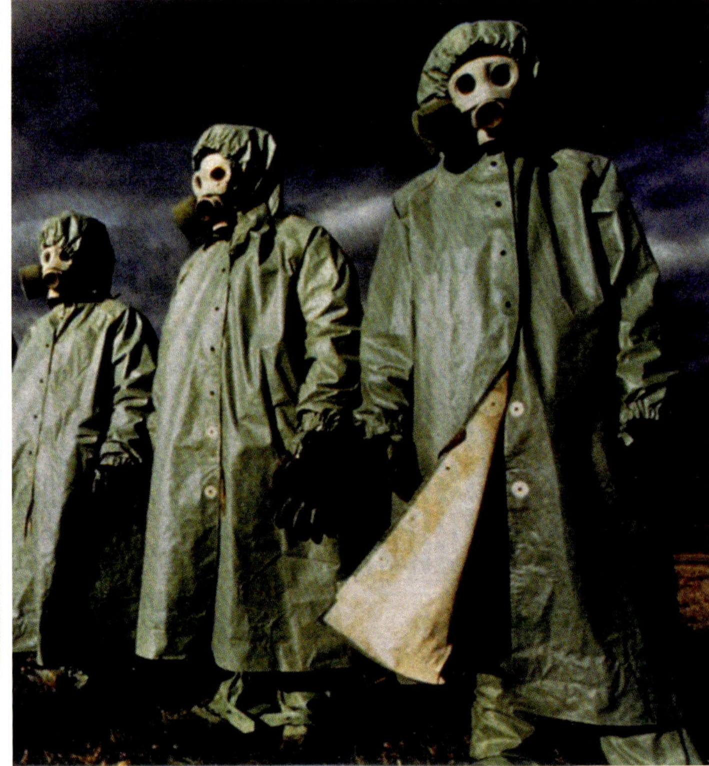

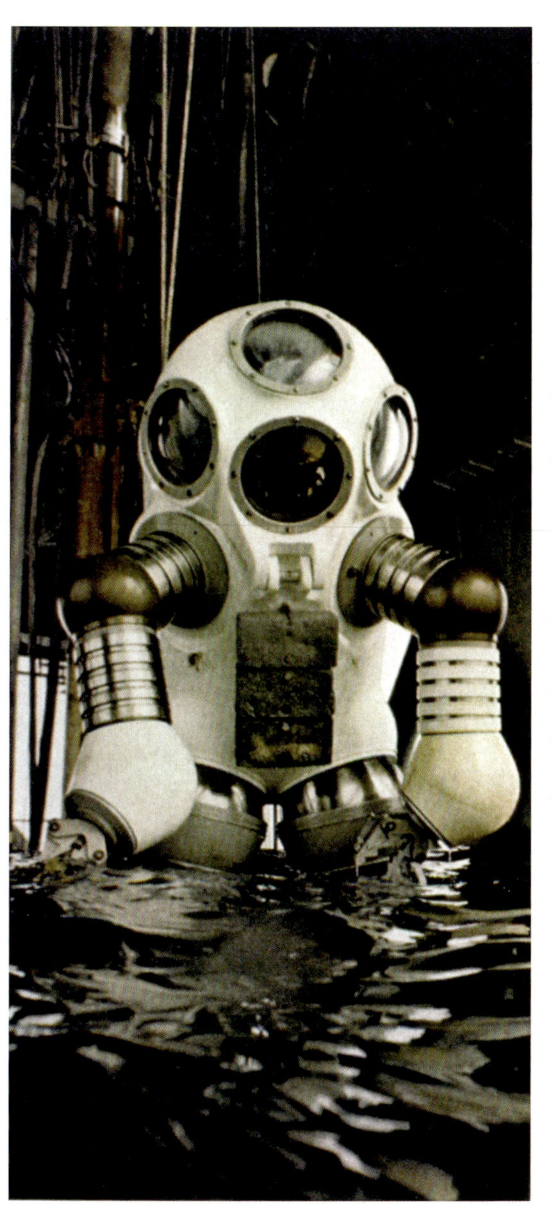
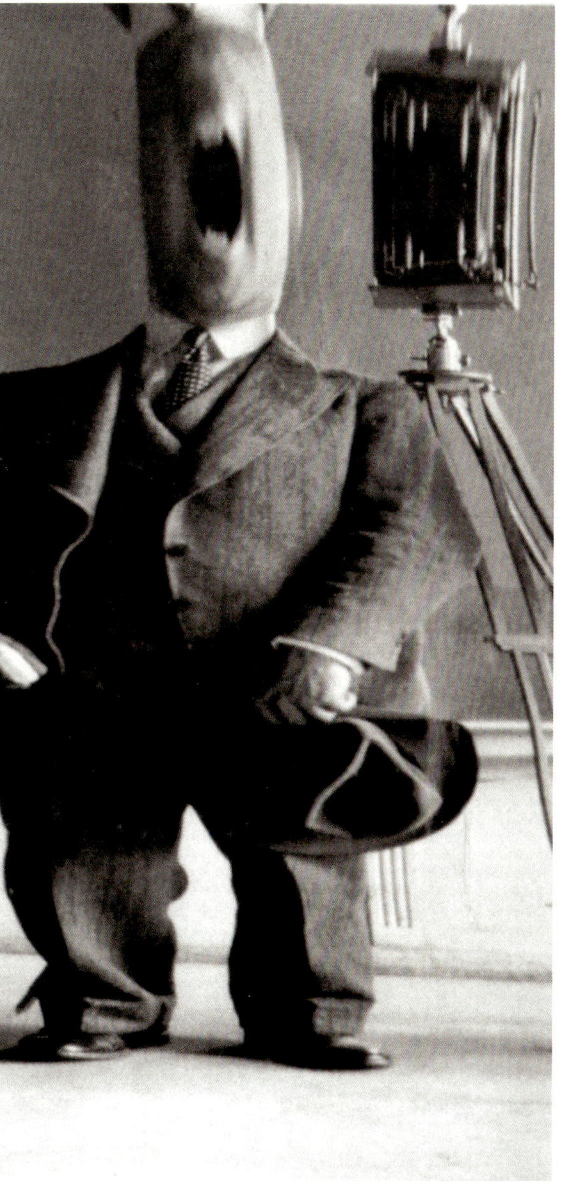

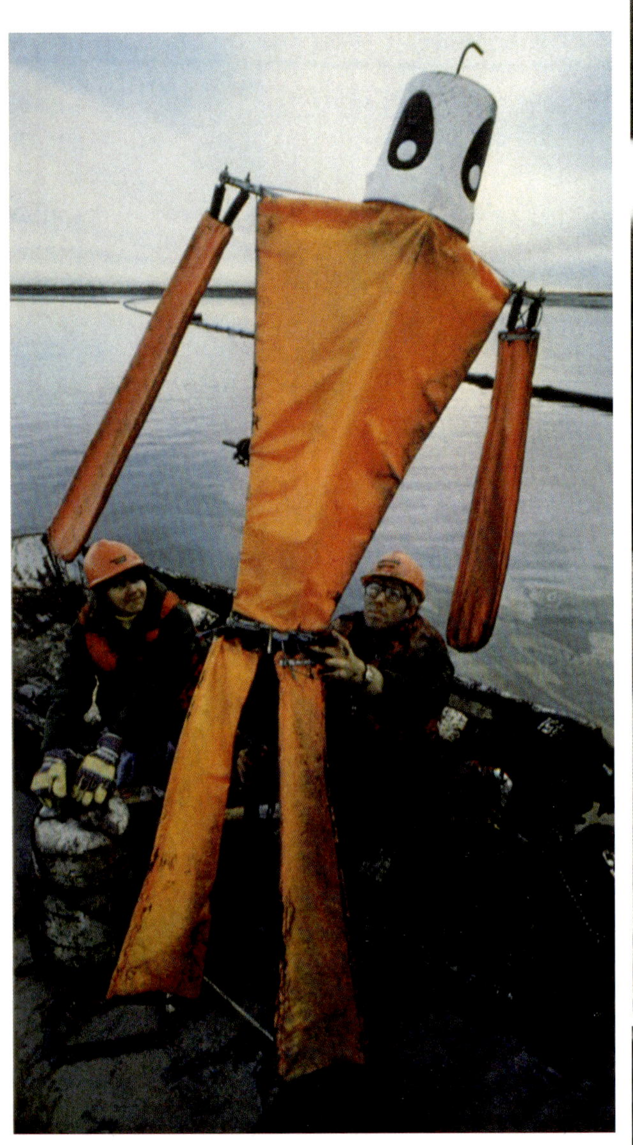

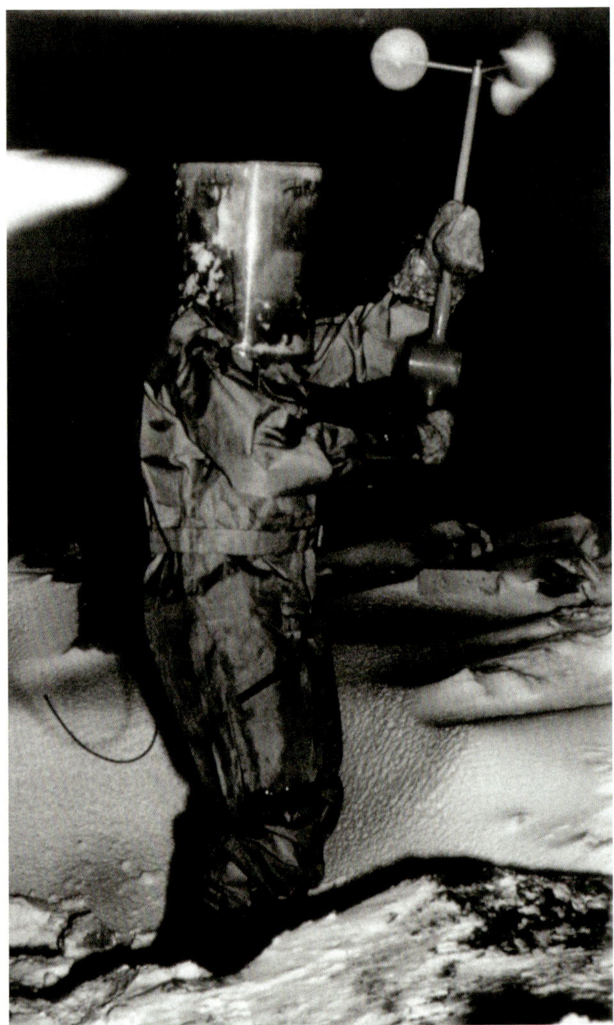

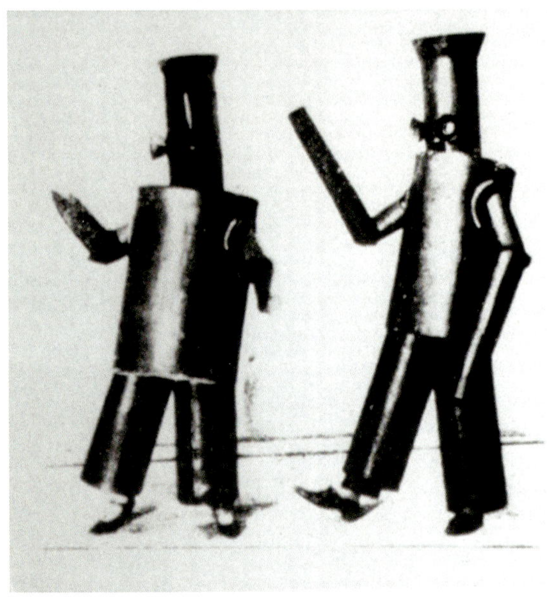

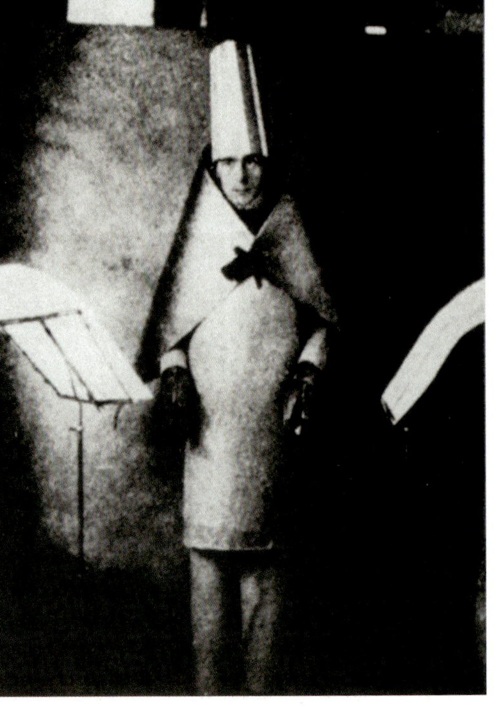

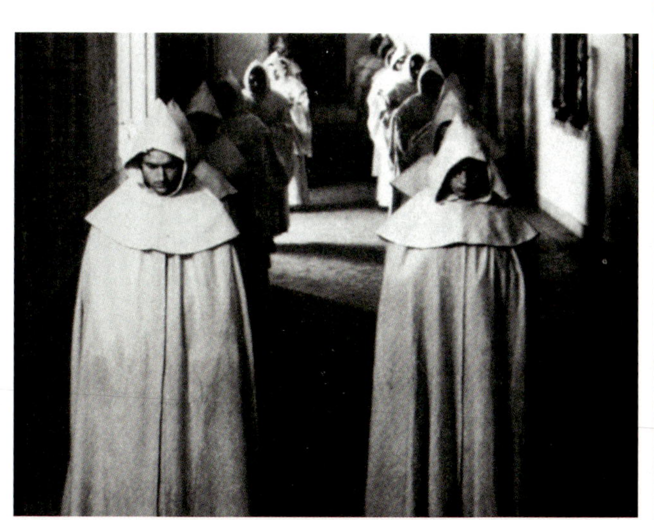
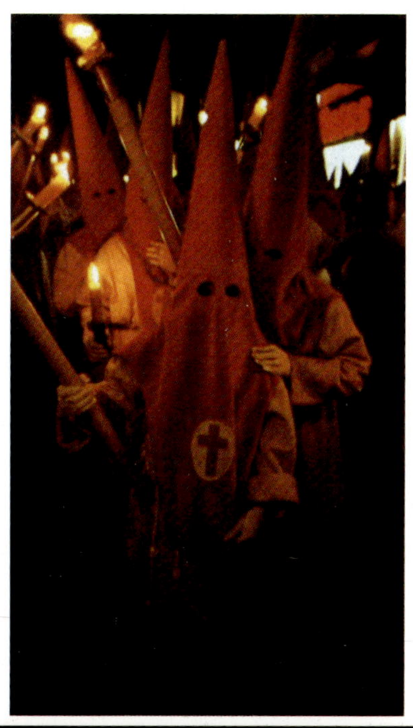
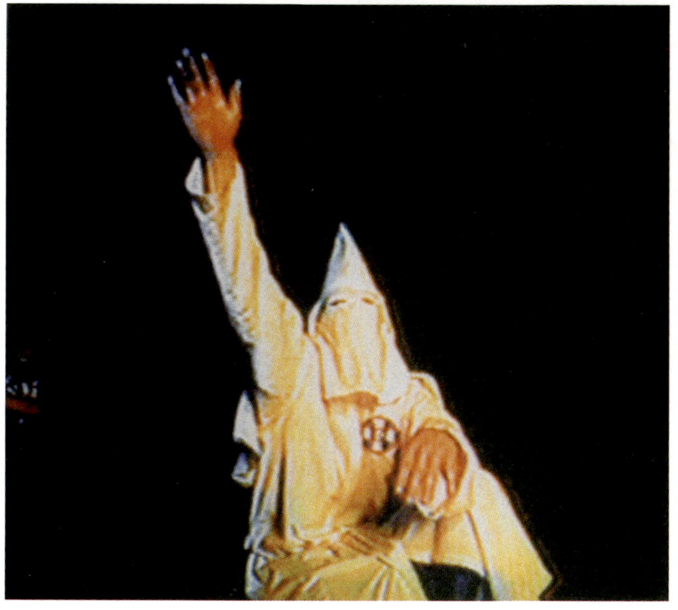
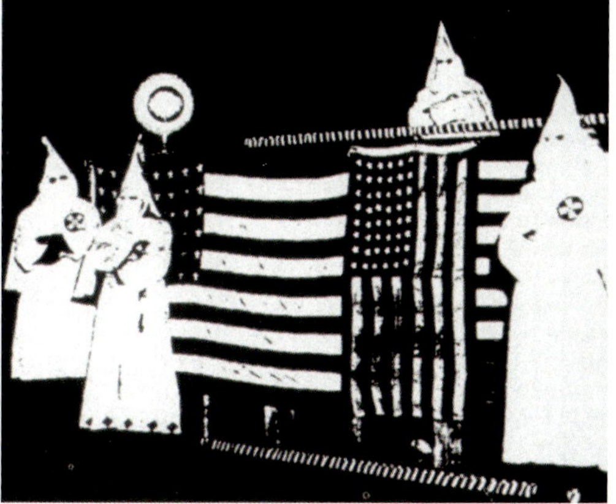

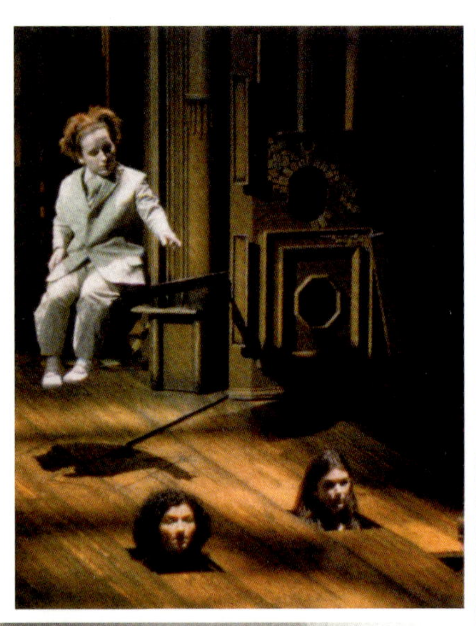
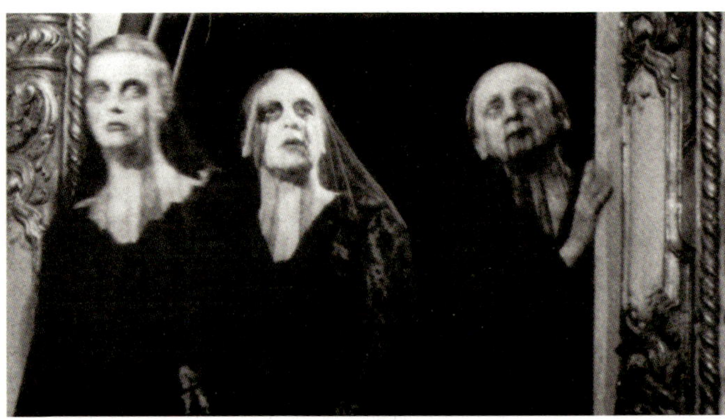
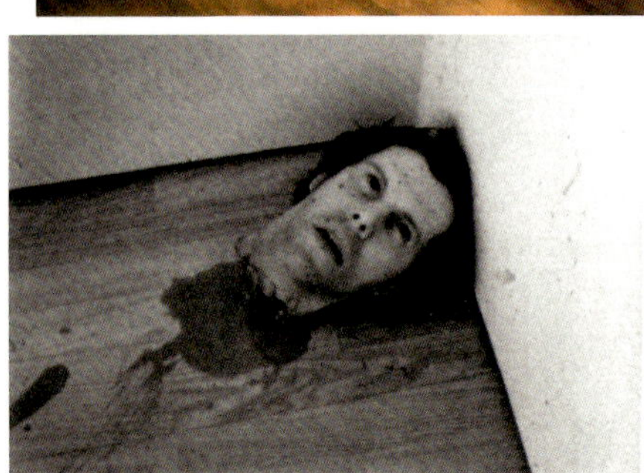
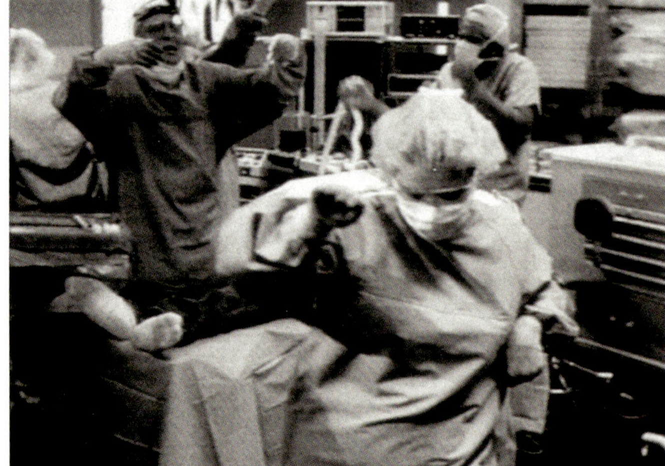

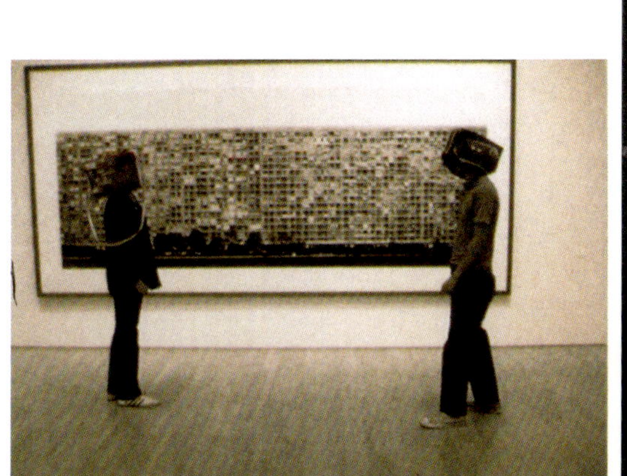
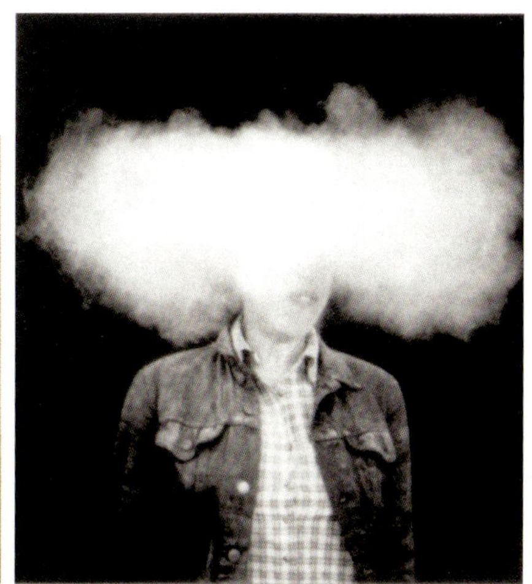
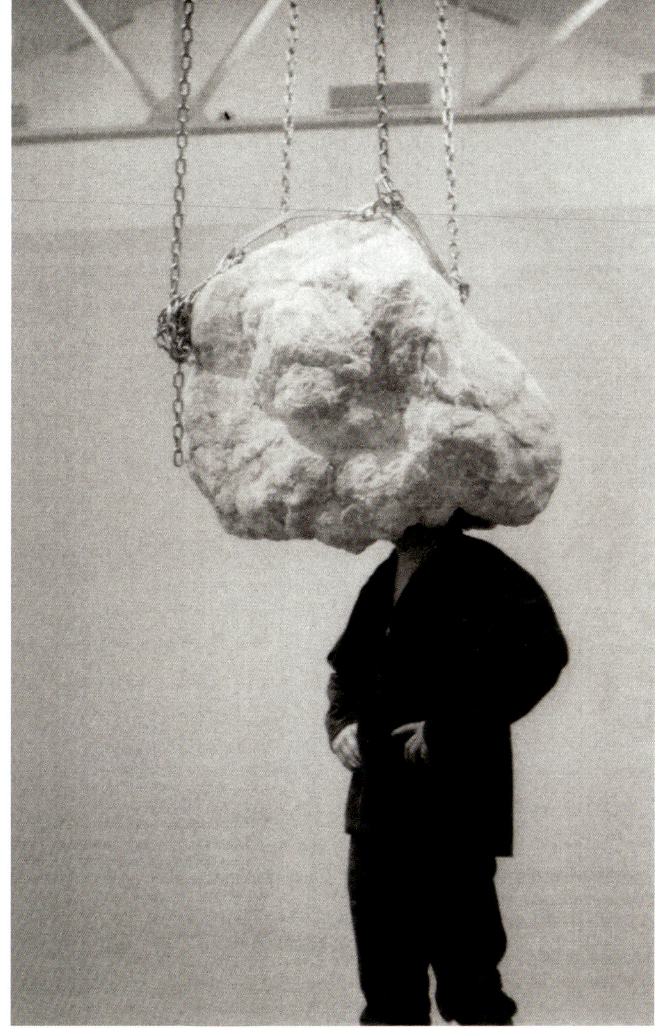

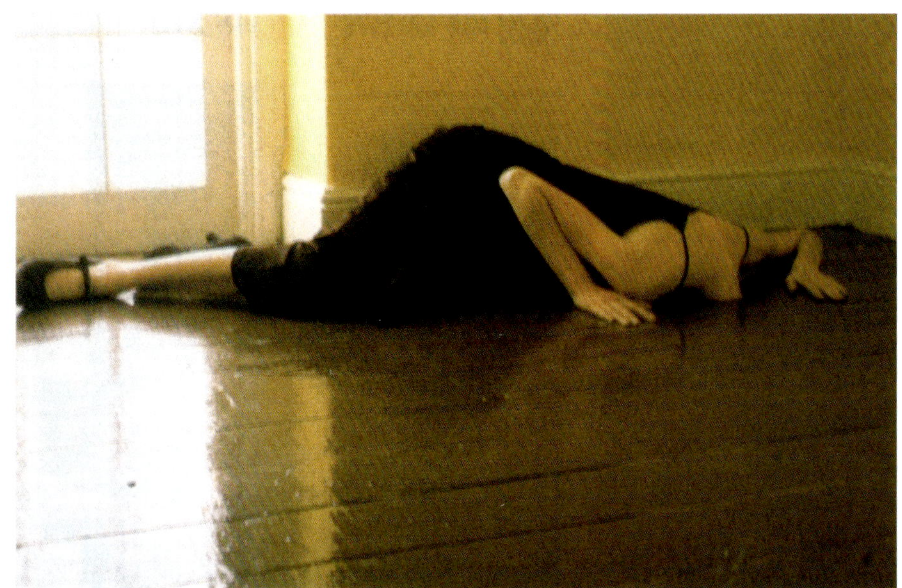

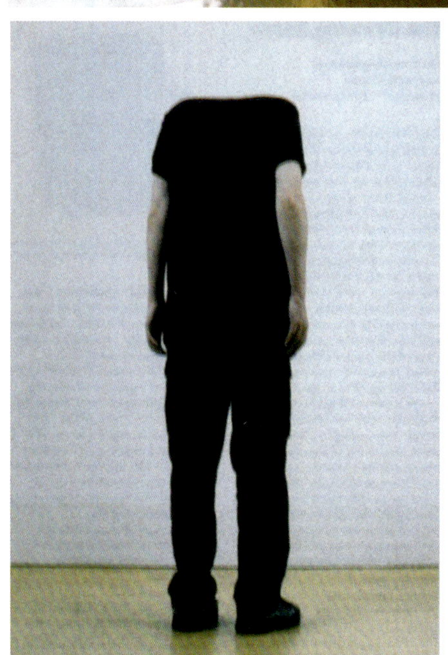

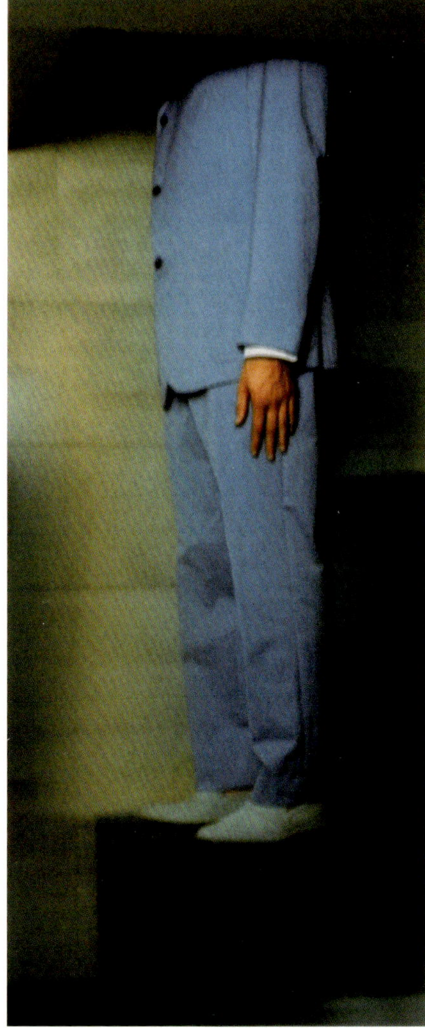

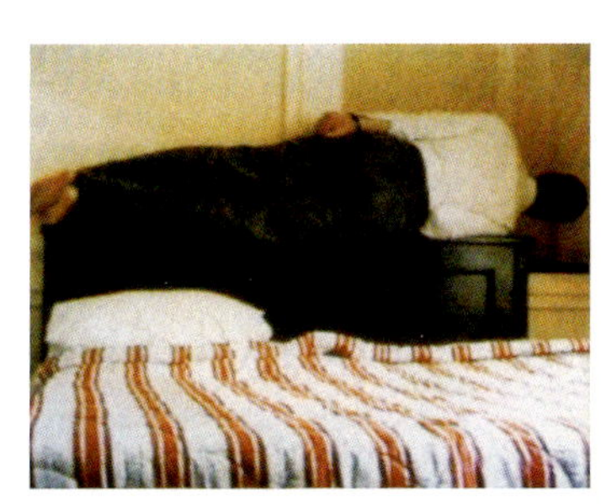
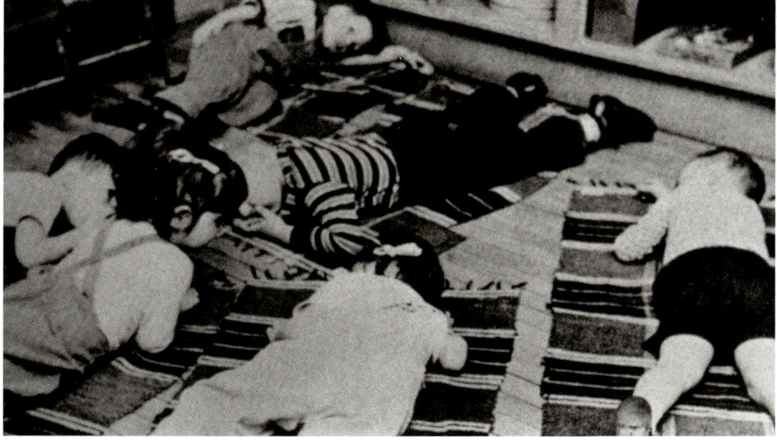
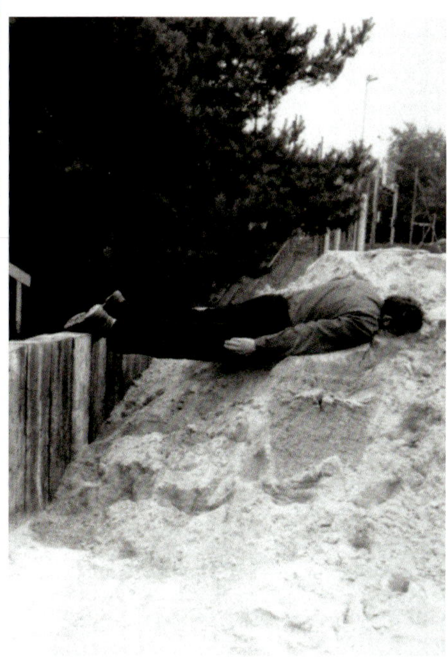

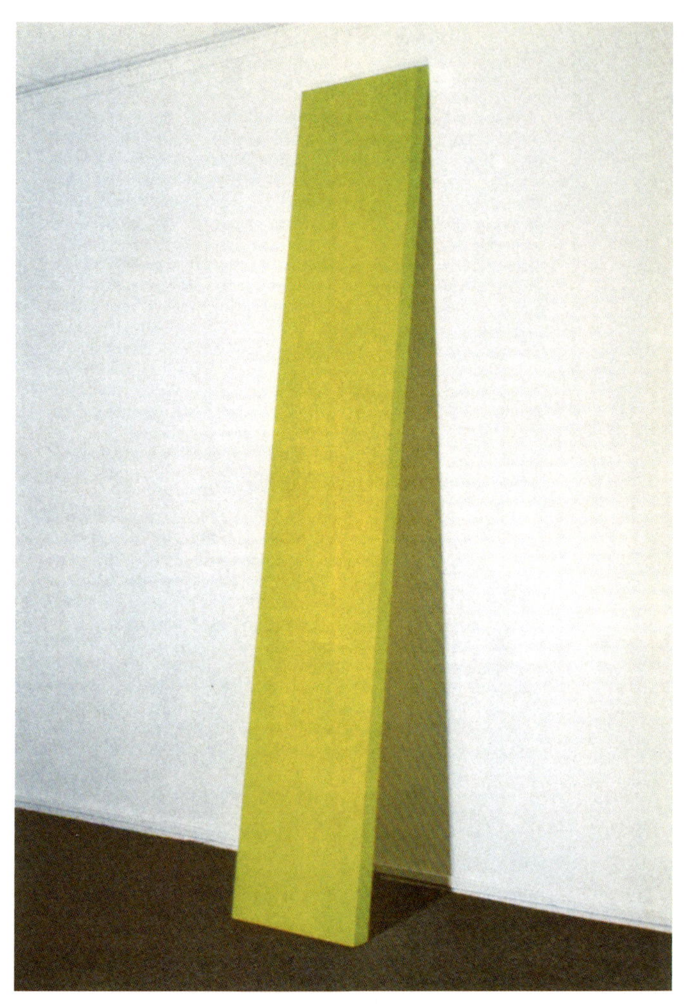

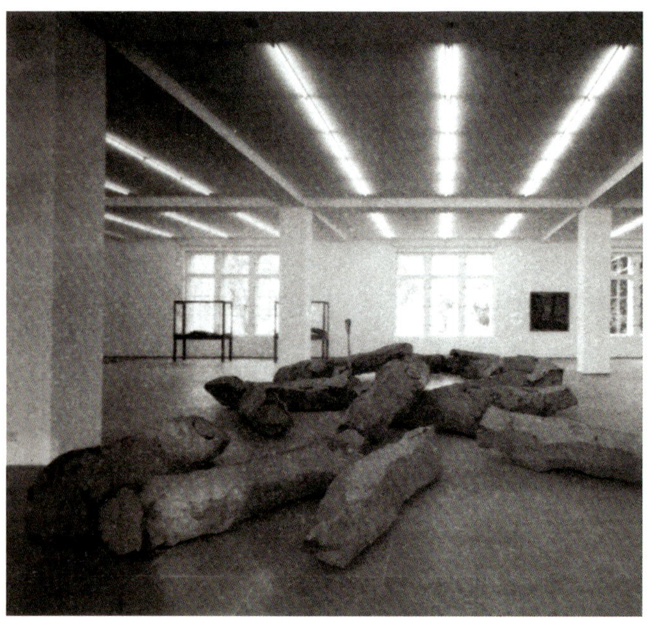

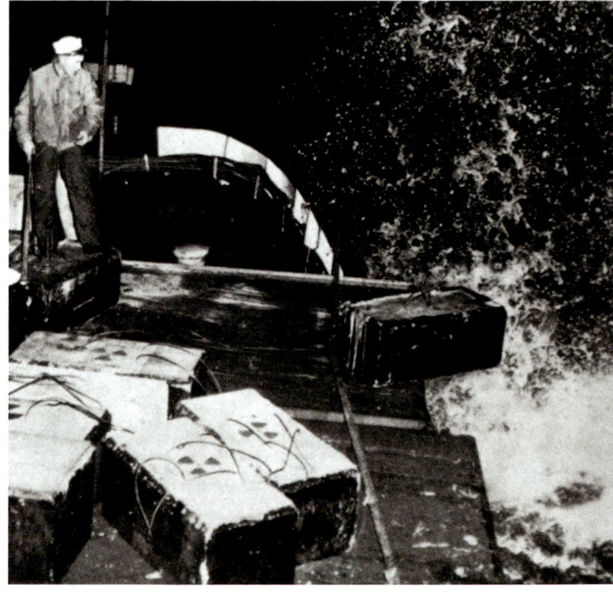

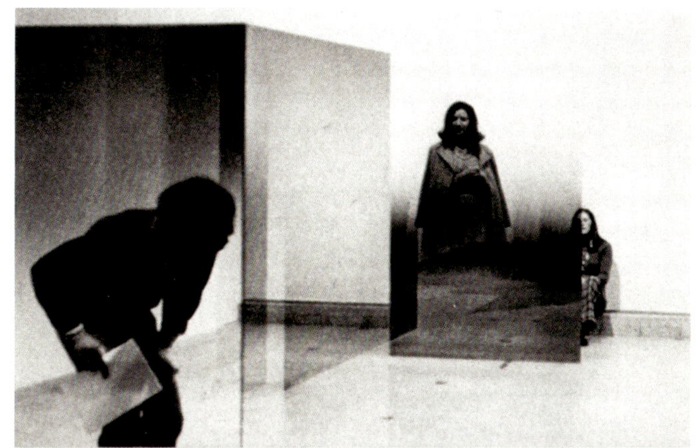

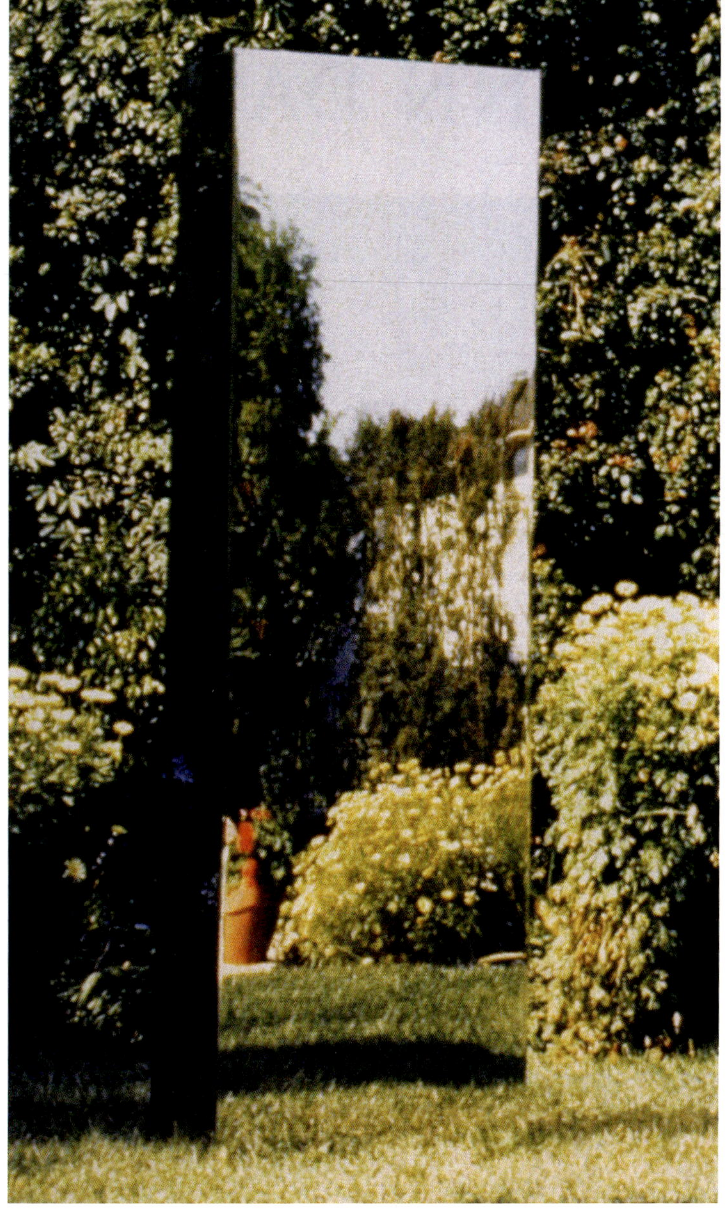

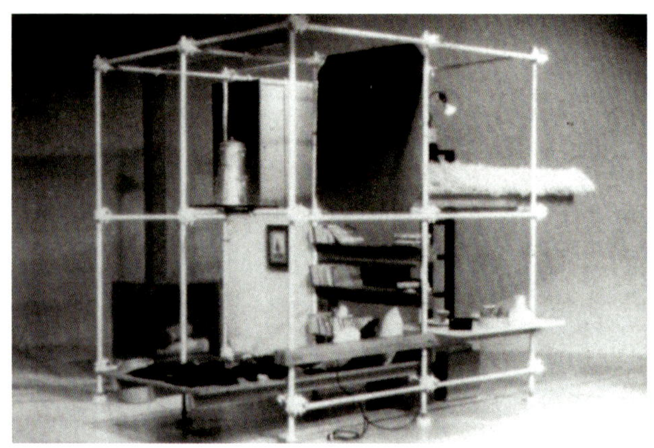
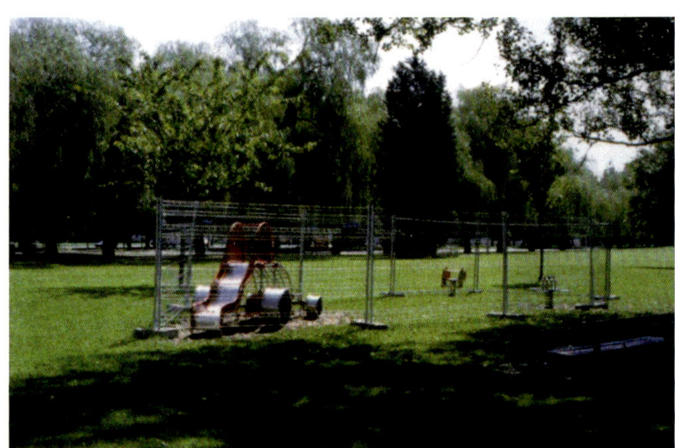
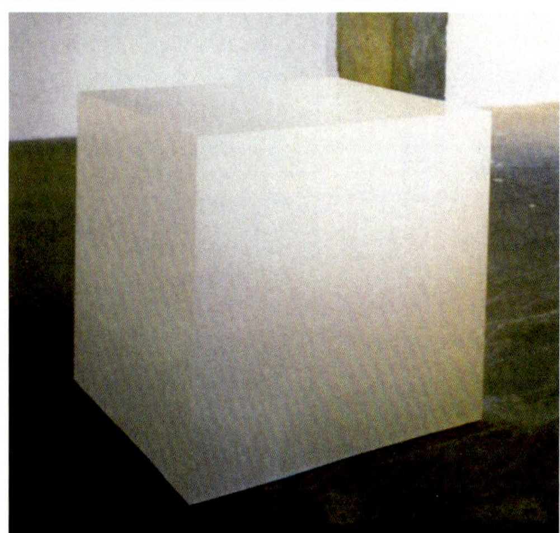
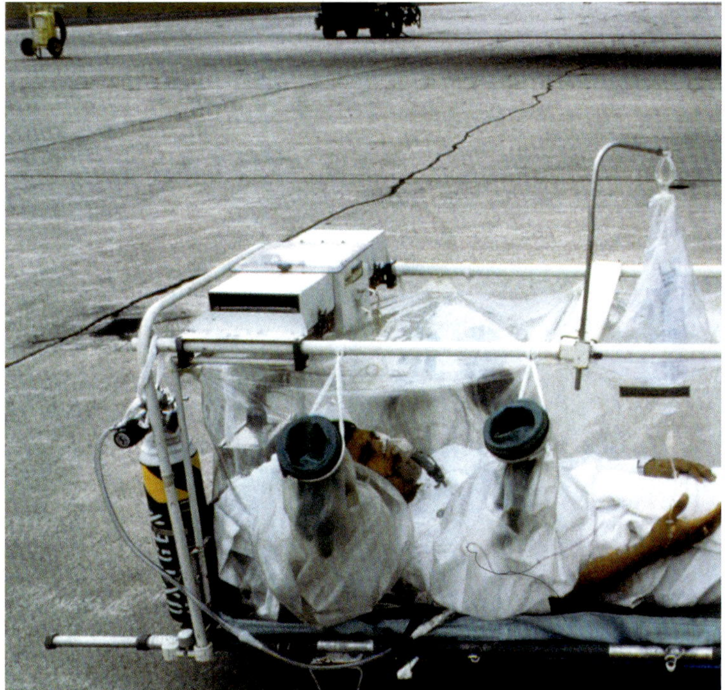
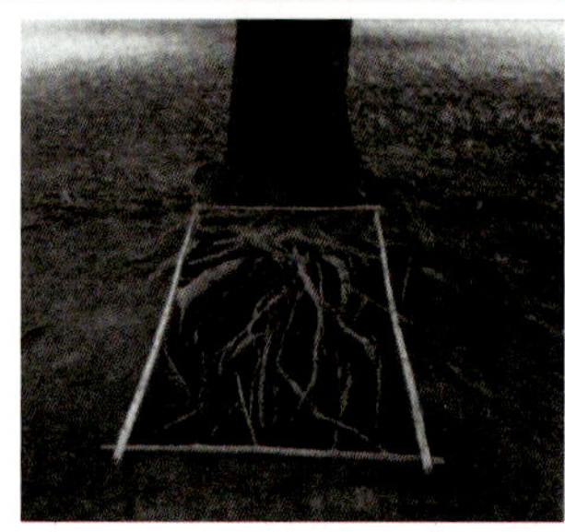

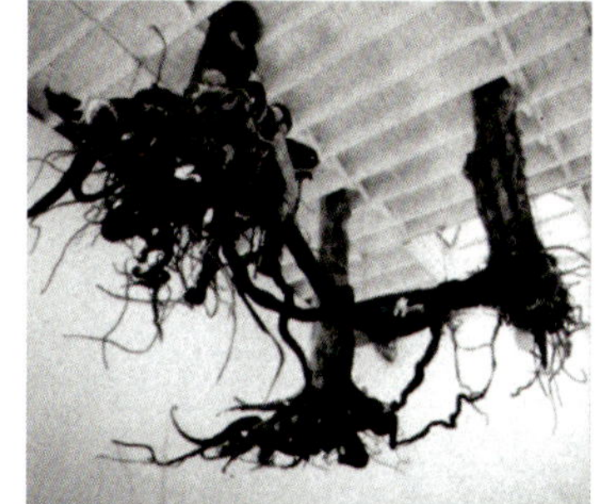

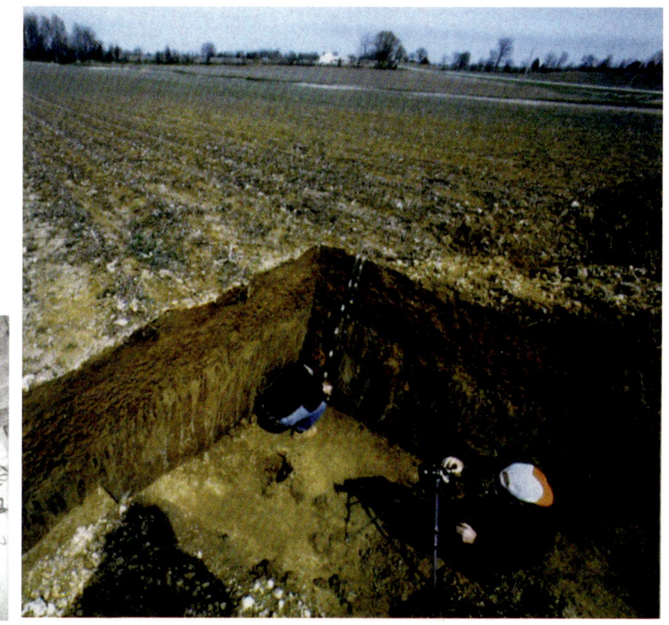

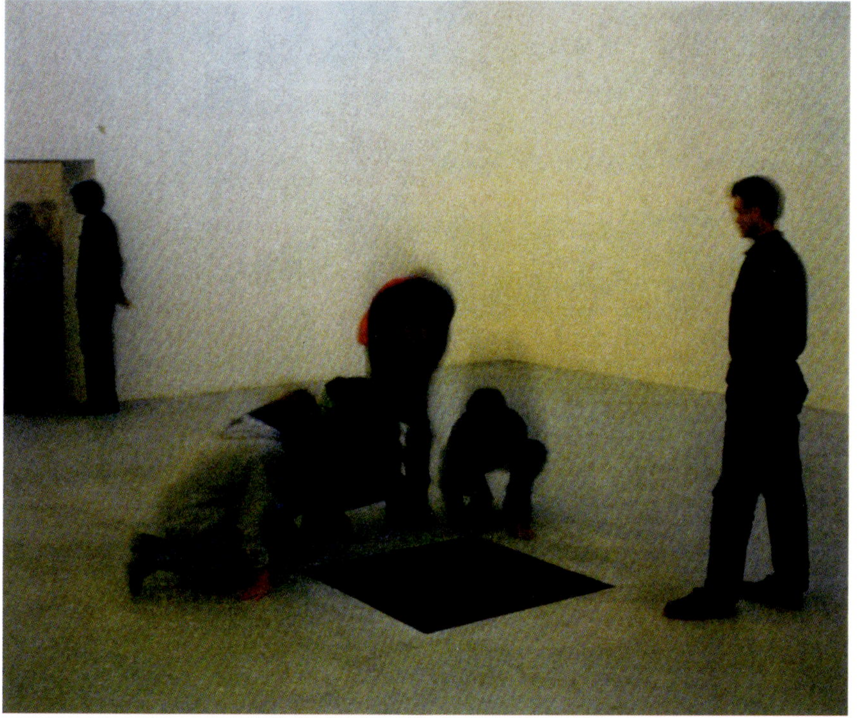

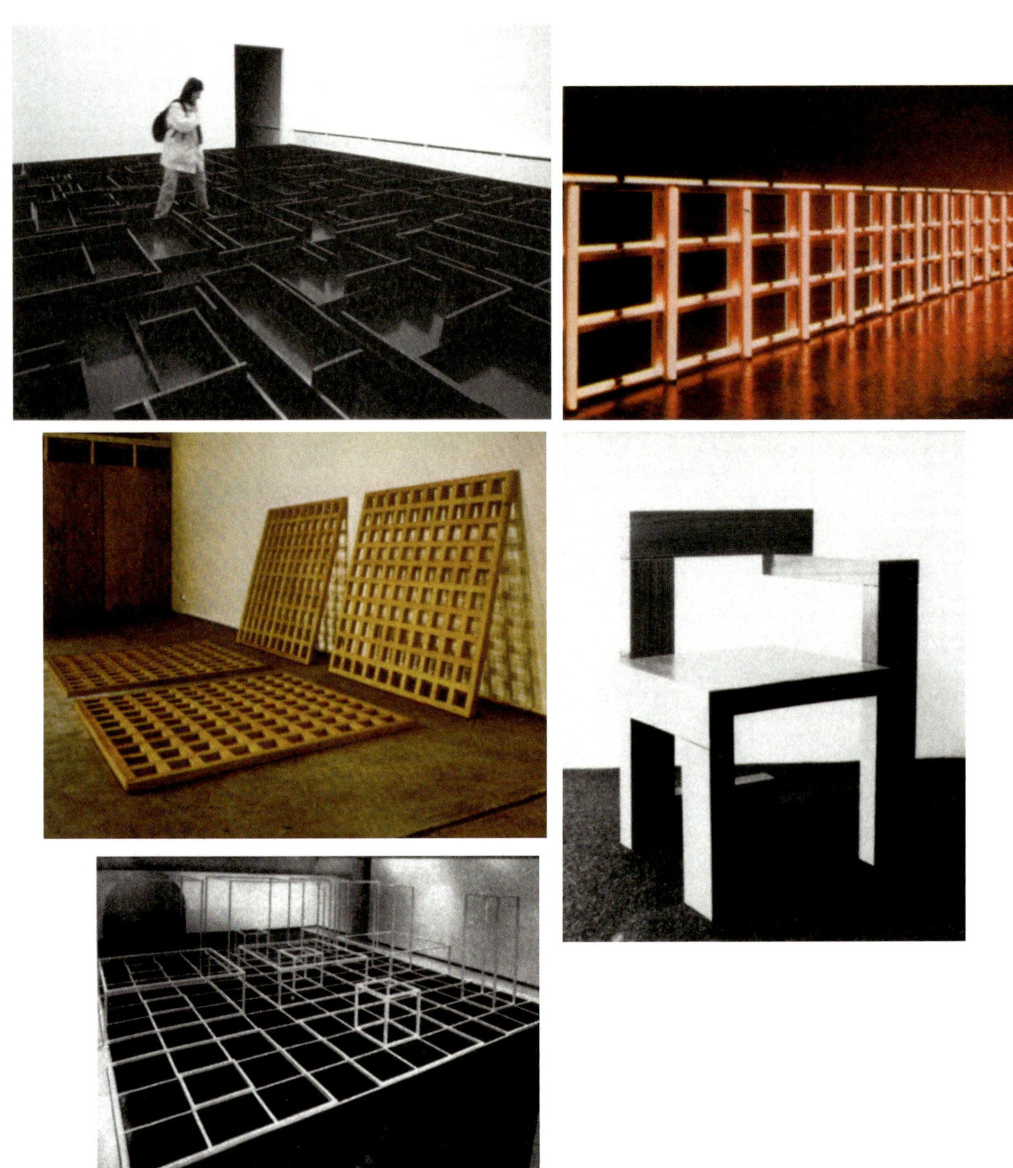

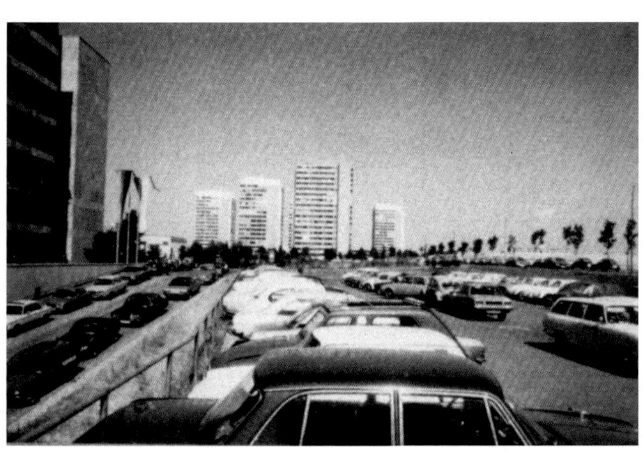
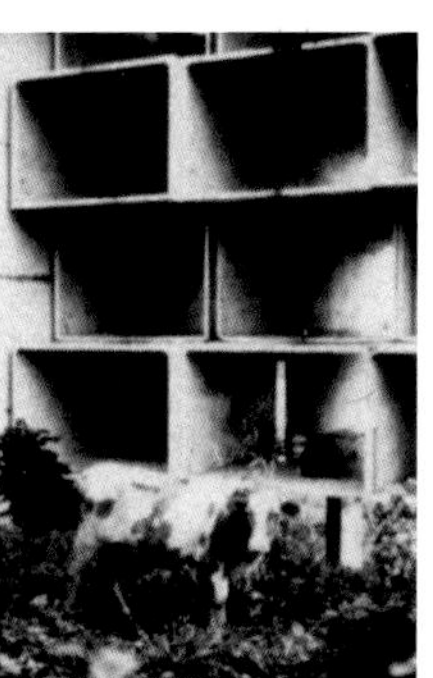
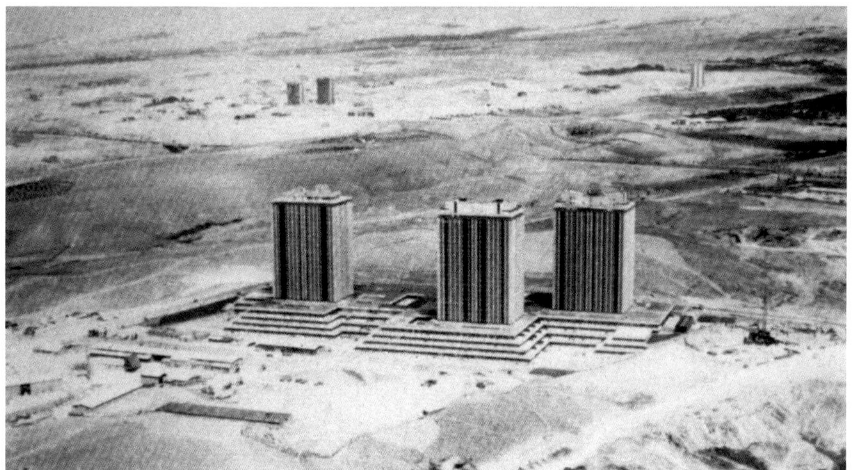

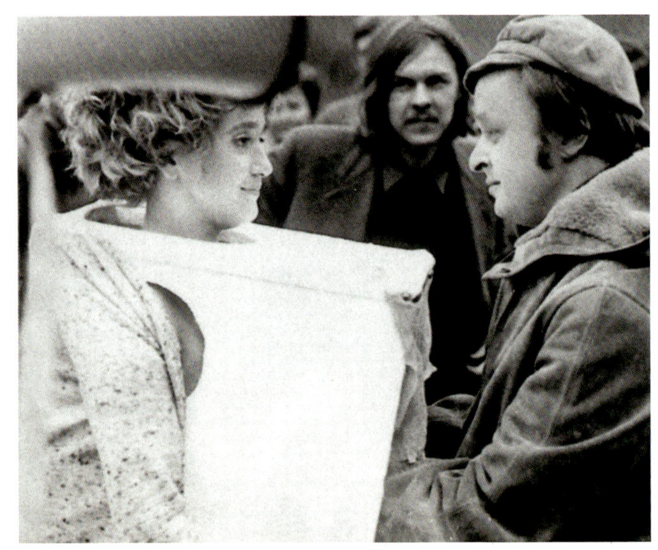

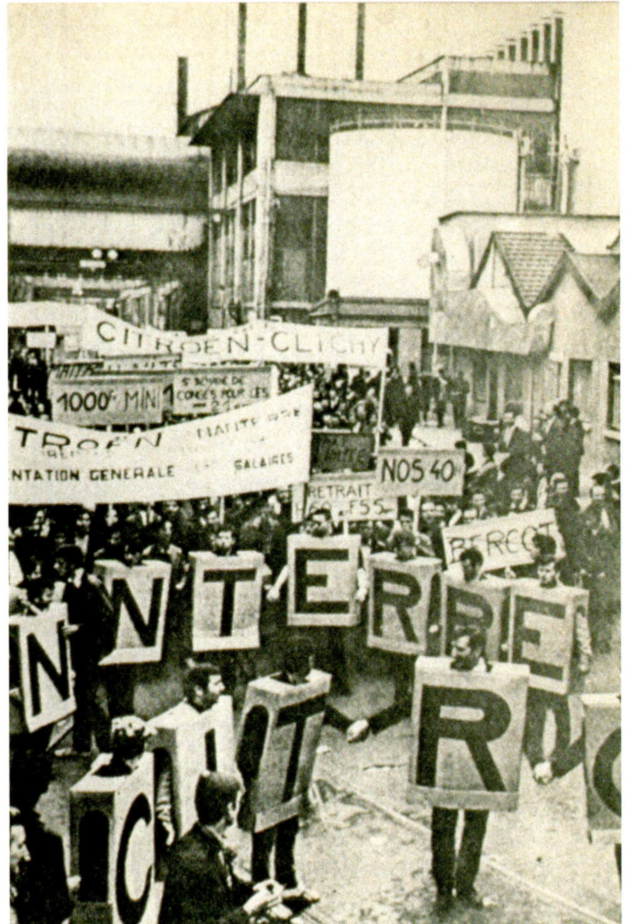
CITROEN-CLICHY
1000F MINI
5e SEMAINE DE CONGÉS POUR LES
TROEN
NTATION GENERALE DES SALAIRES
NOS 40
RETRAIT
60 FSS
BEROT
NTERIE
C
T
R

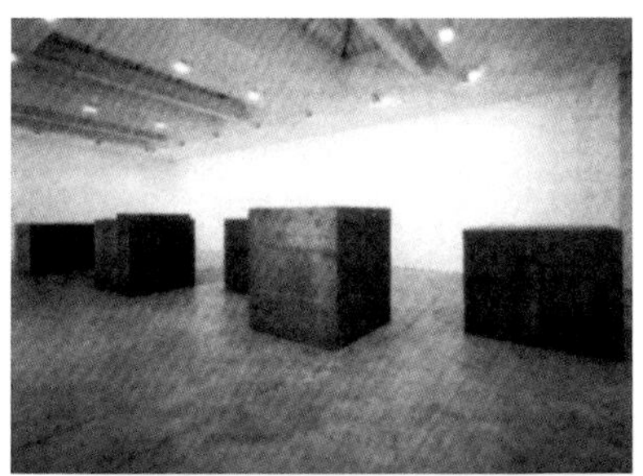

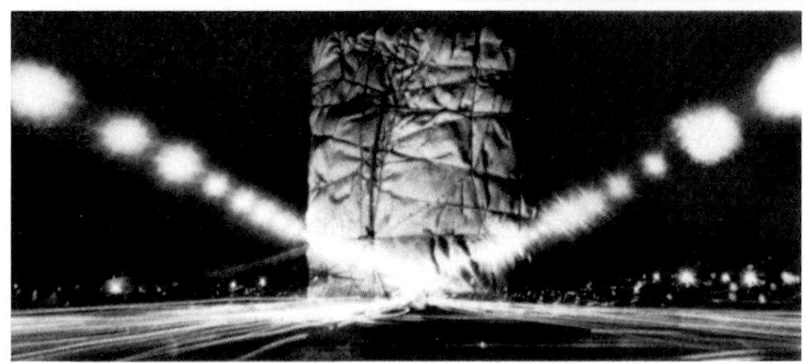
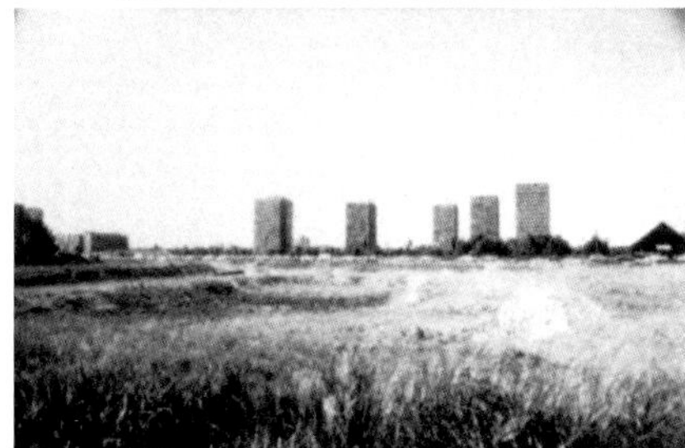
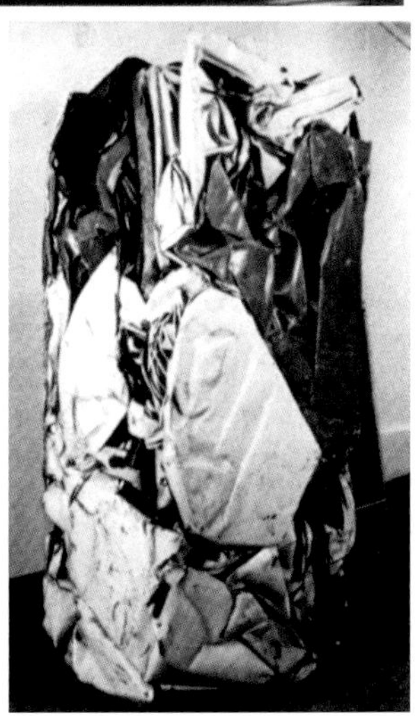
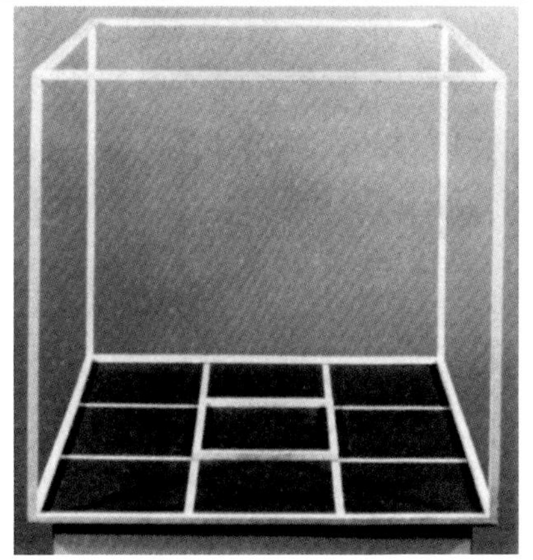

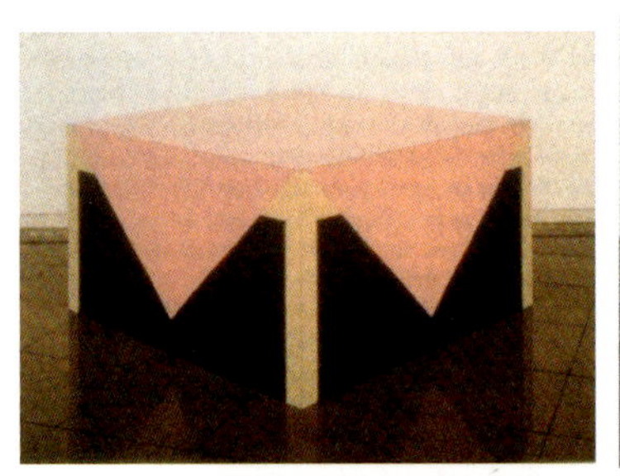
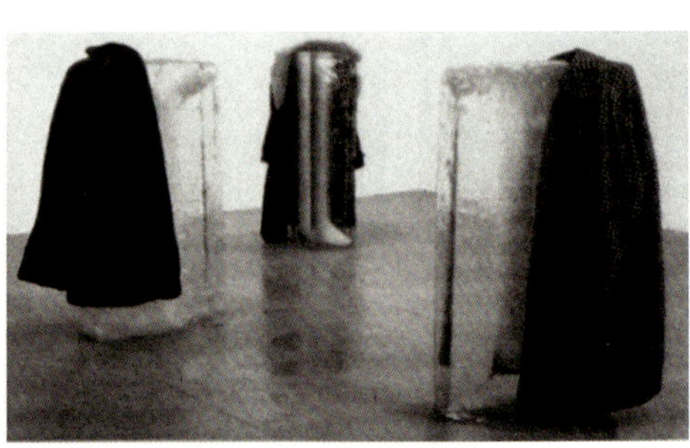
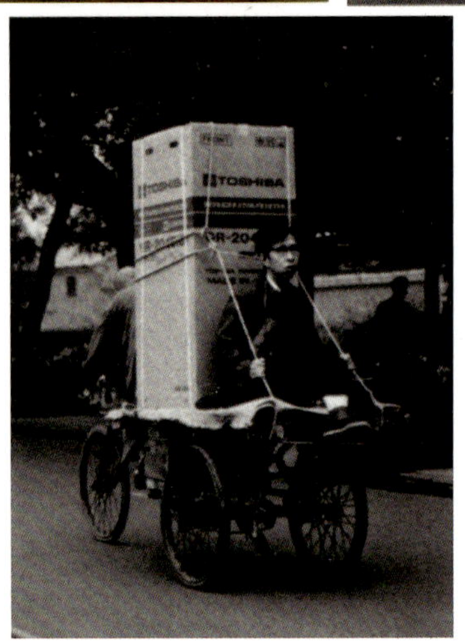
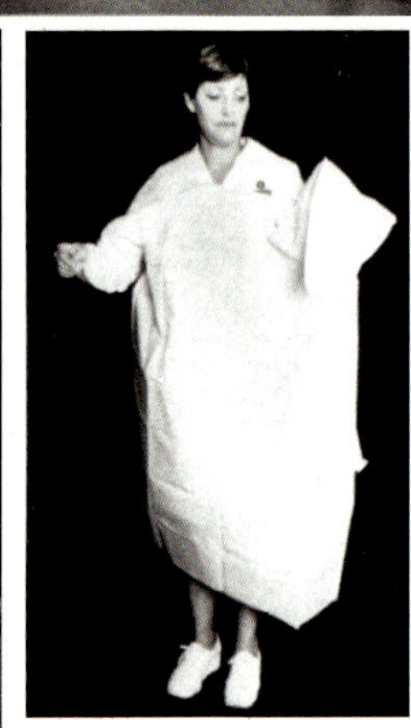

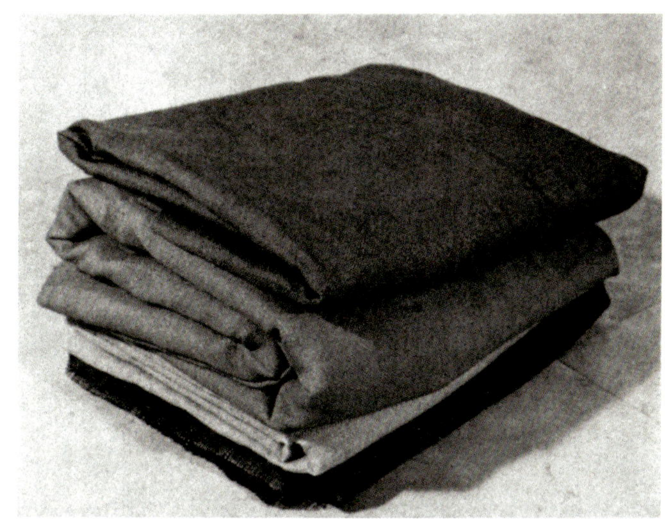

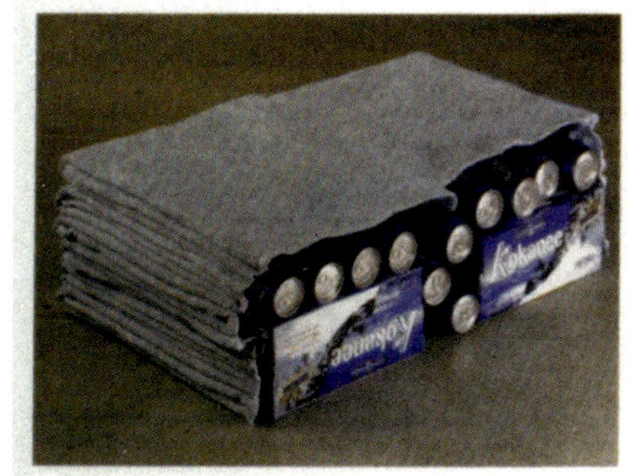

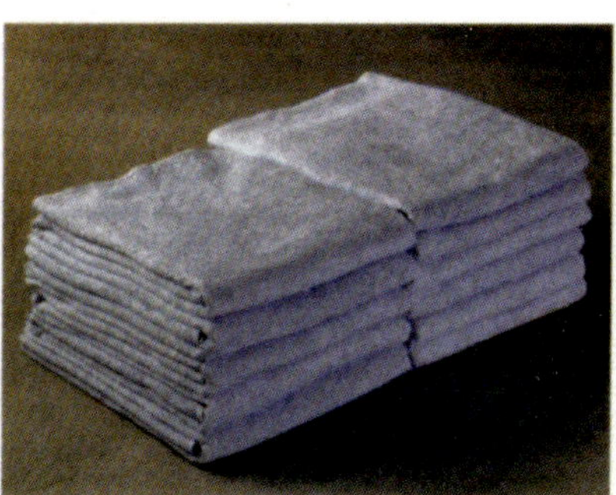

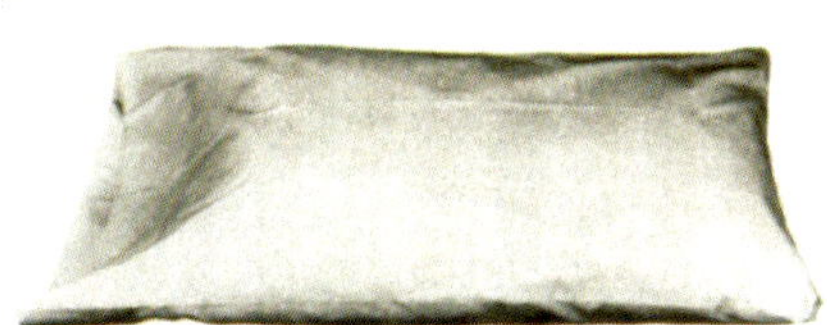

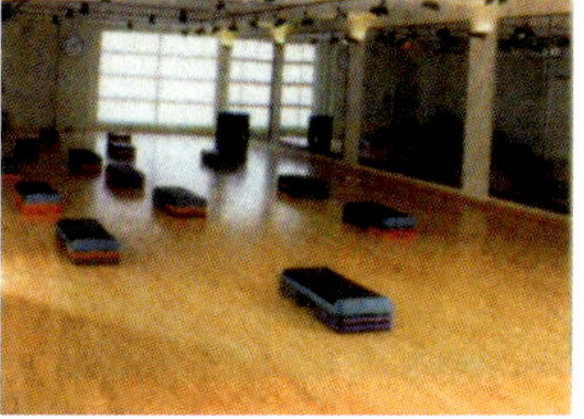

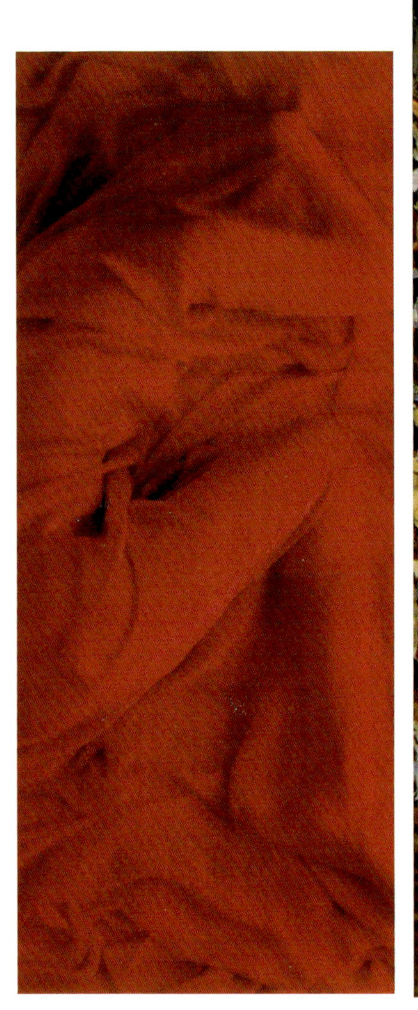
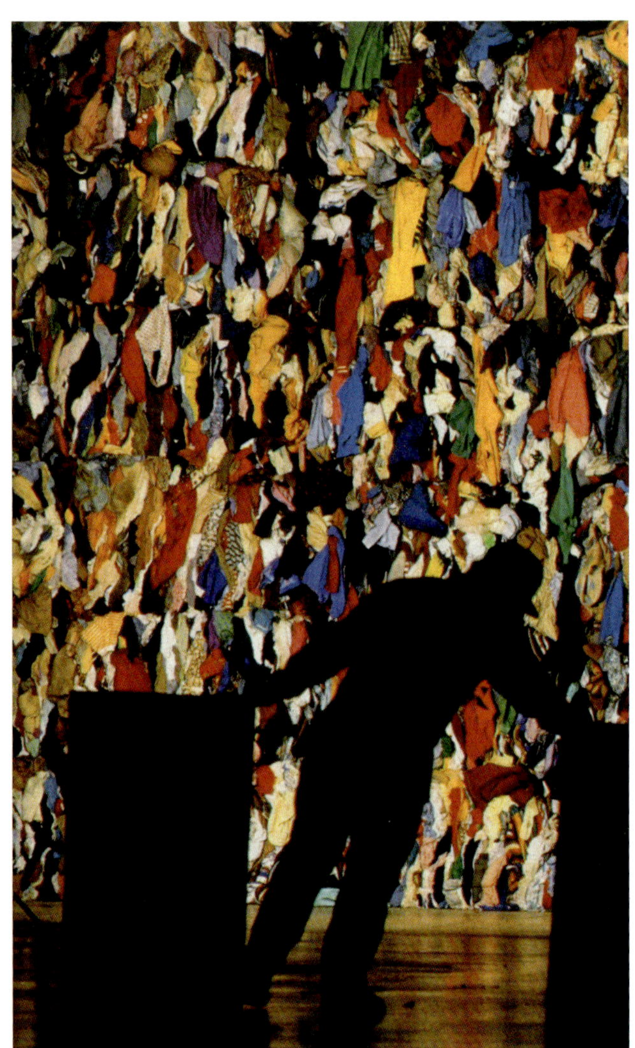

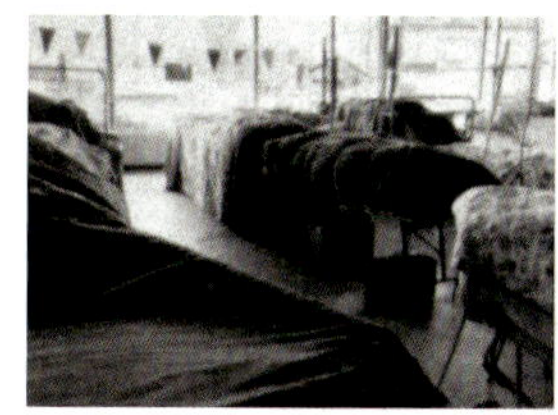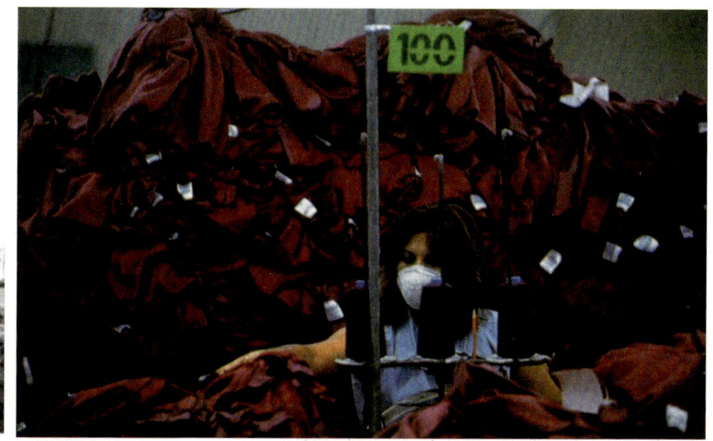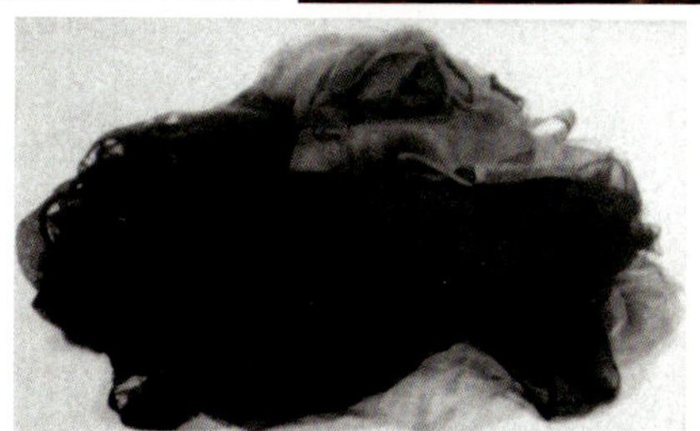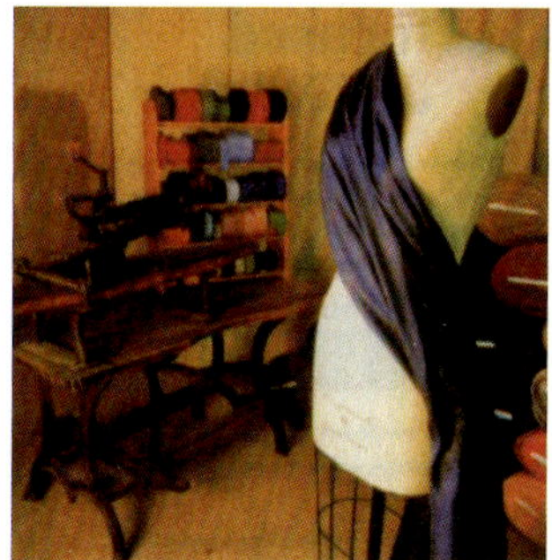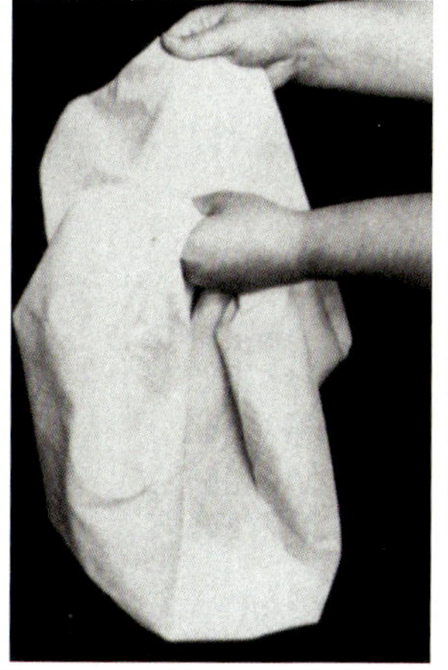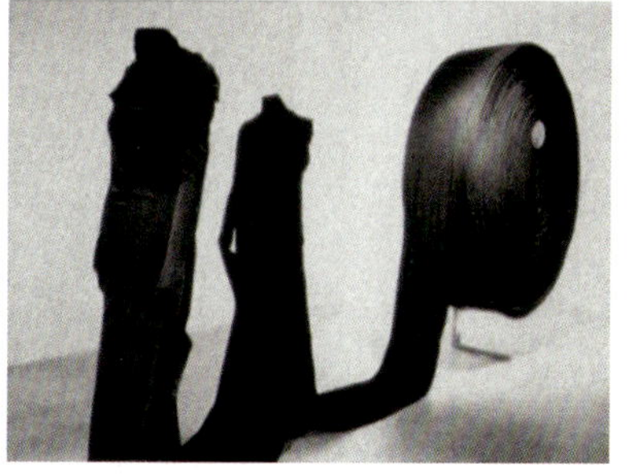

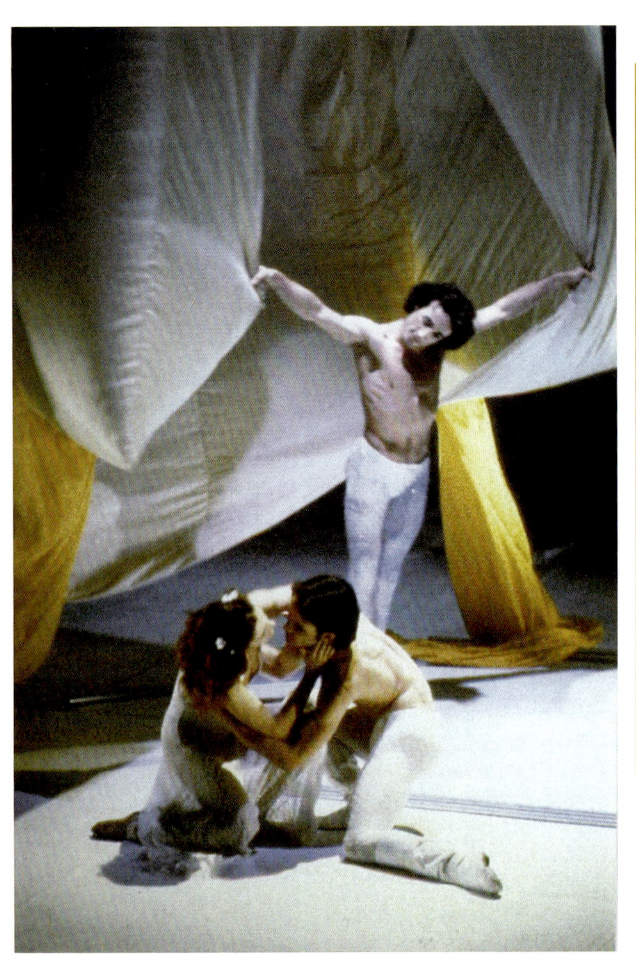
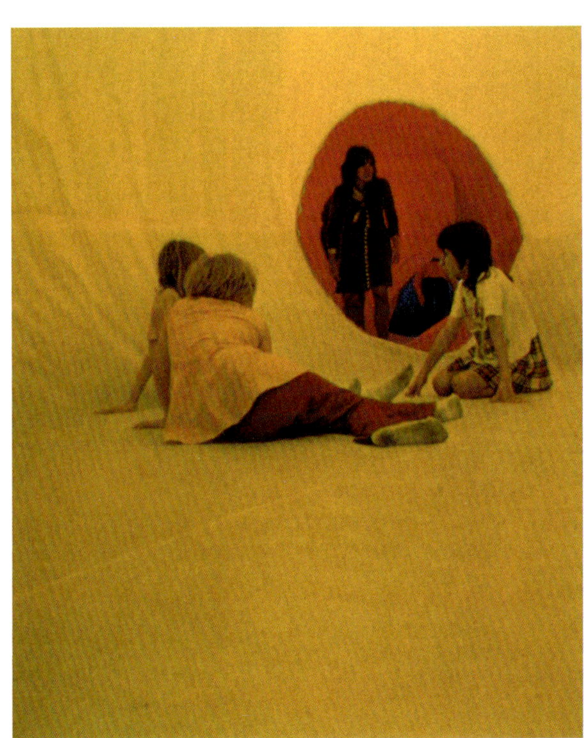

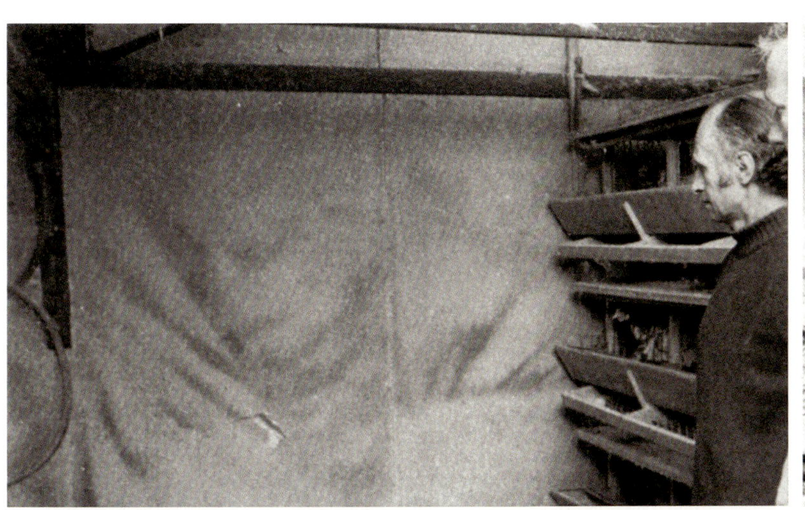
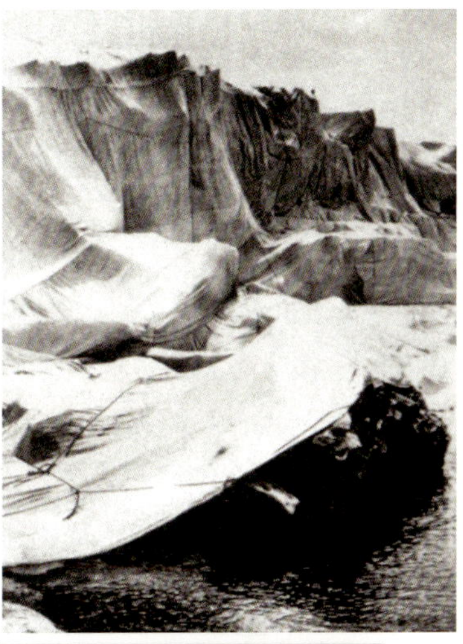
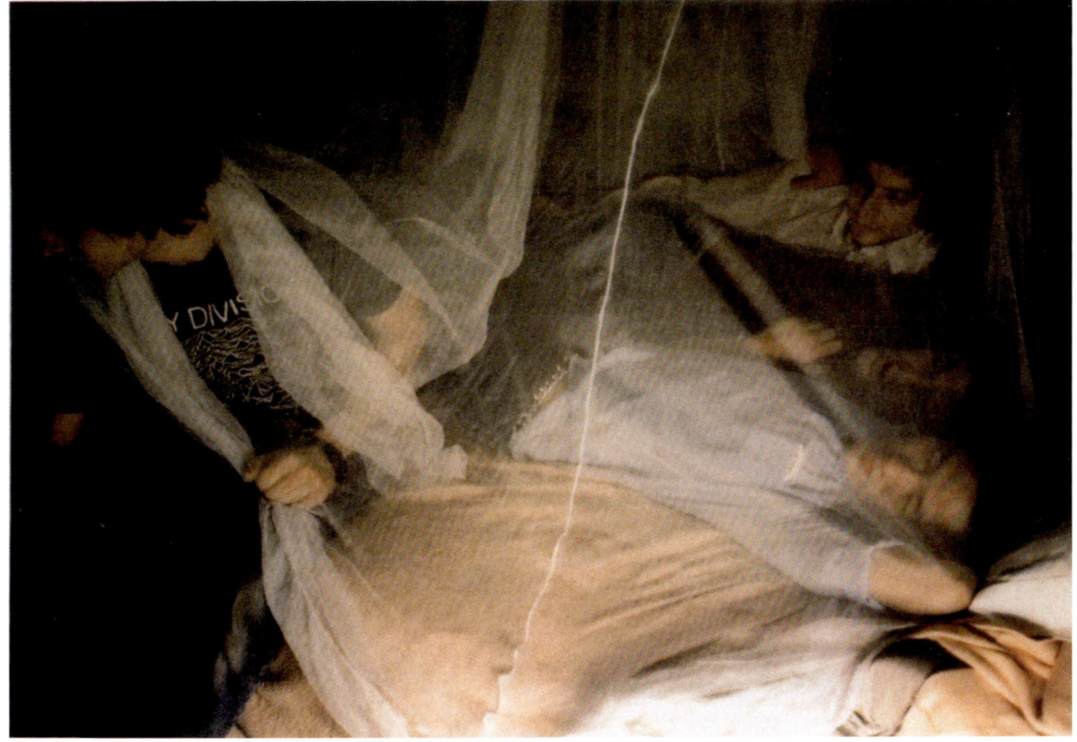

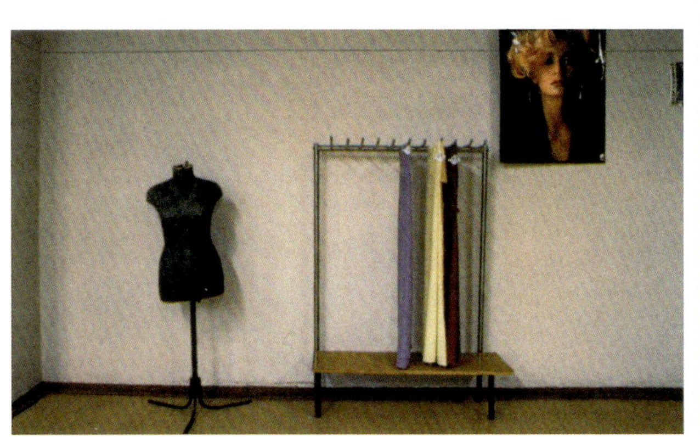
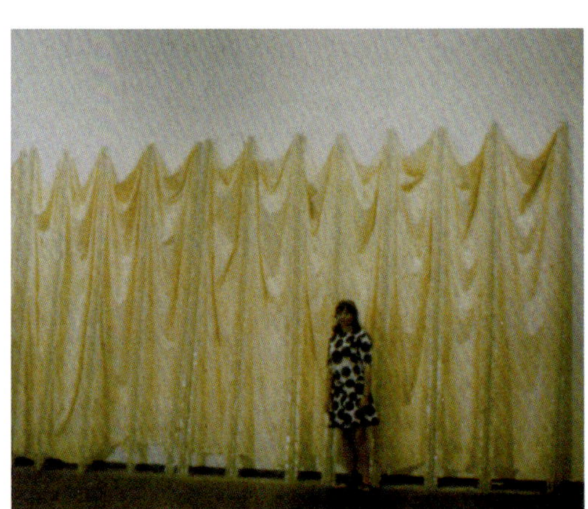
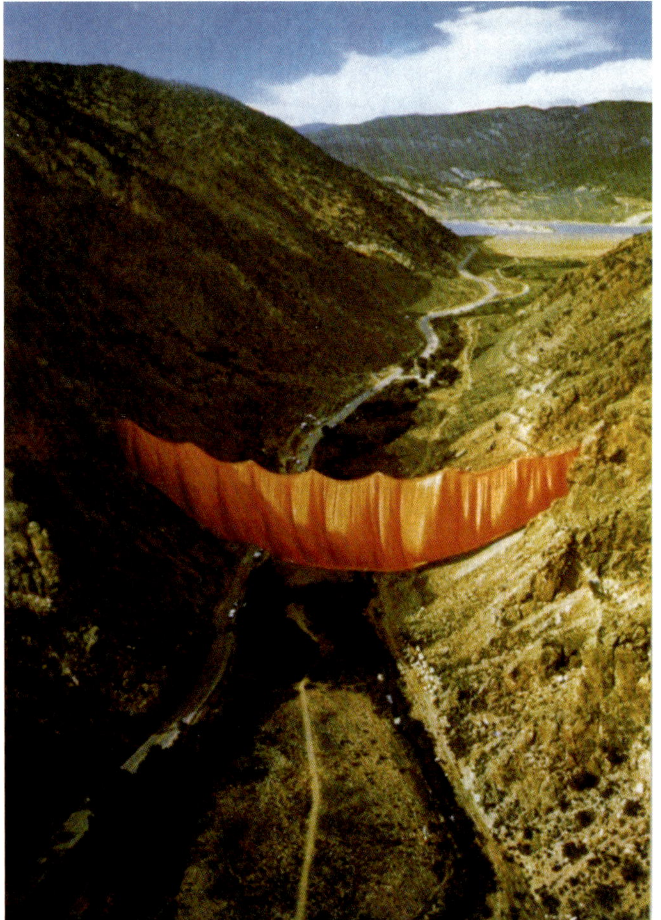
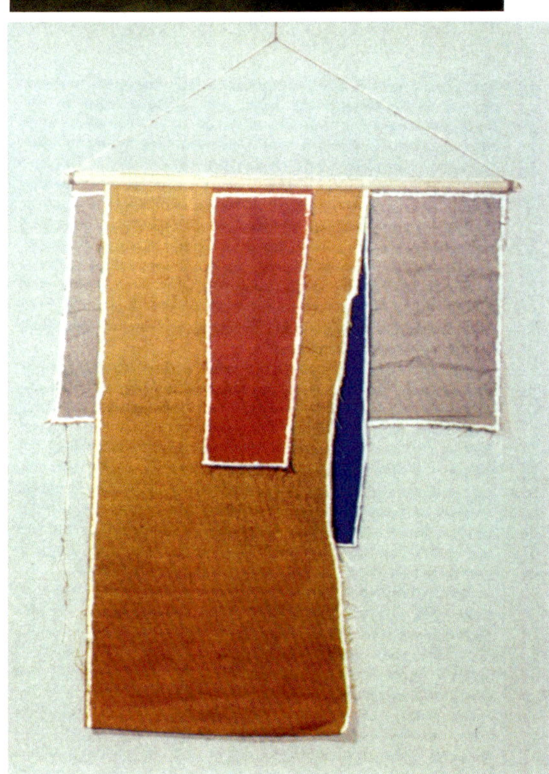

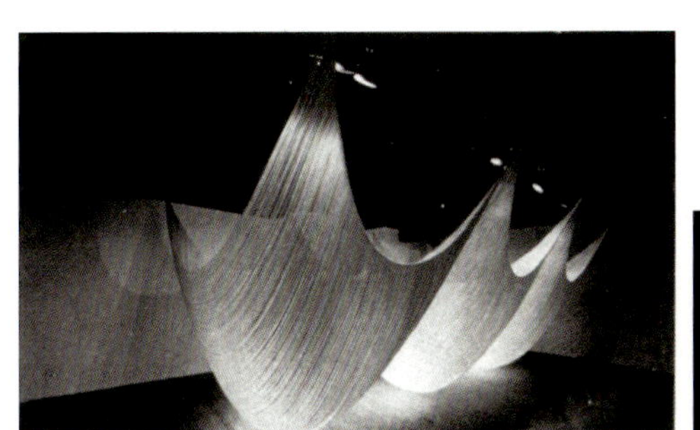
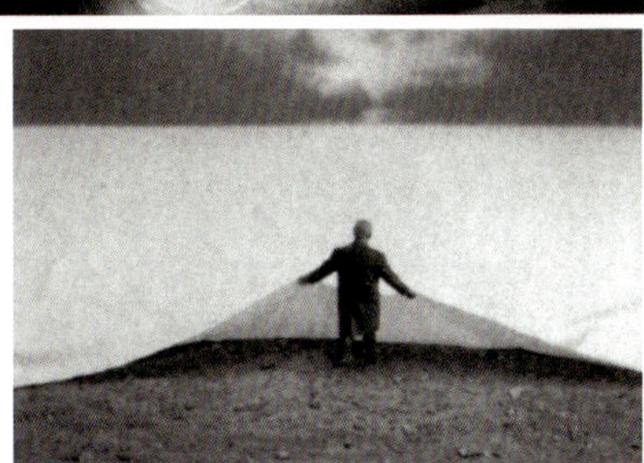
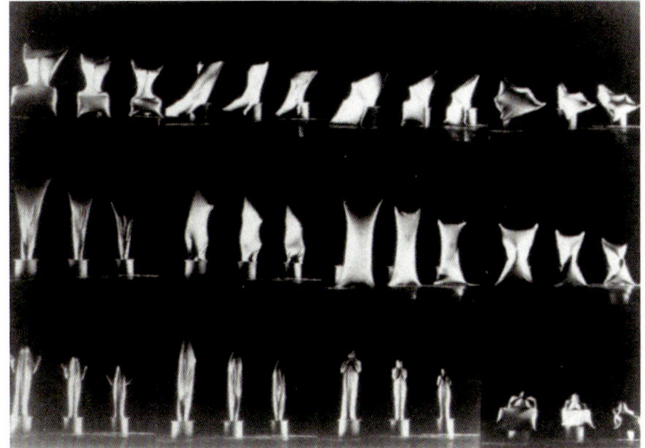
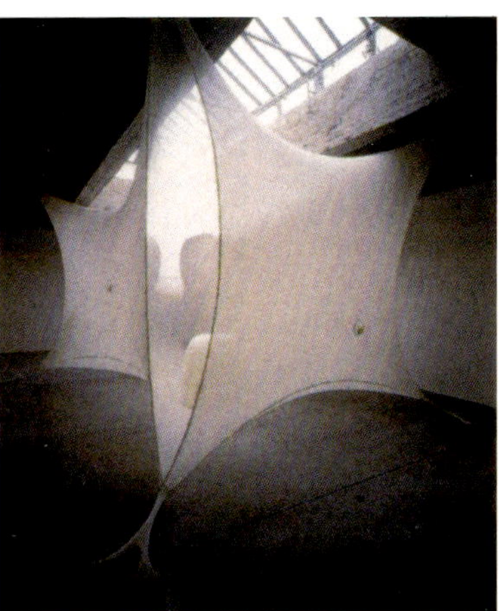
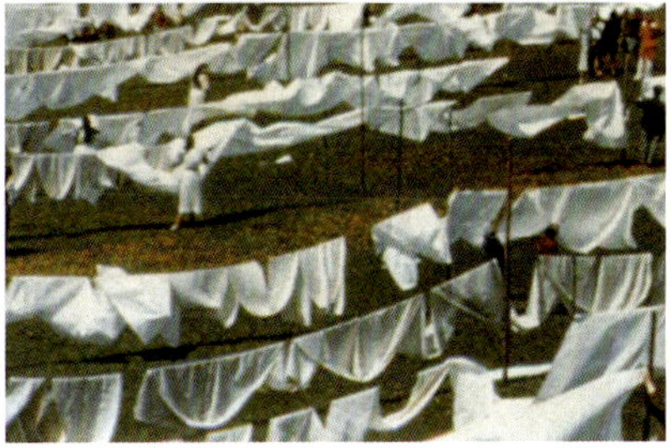

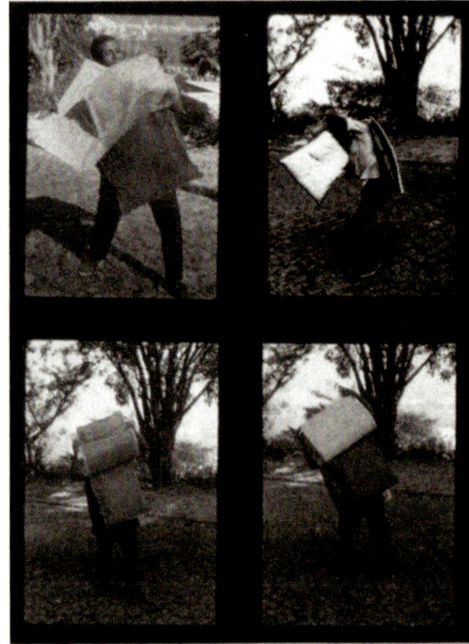

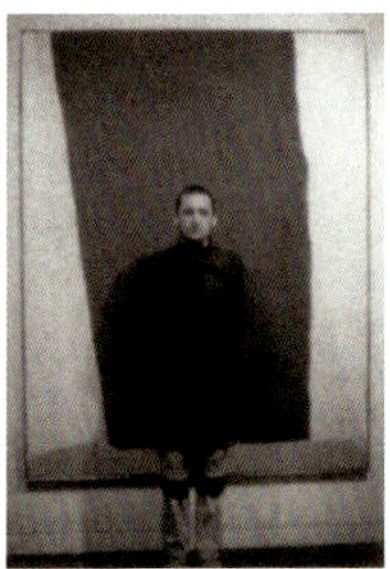

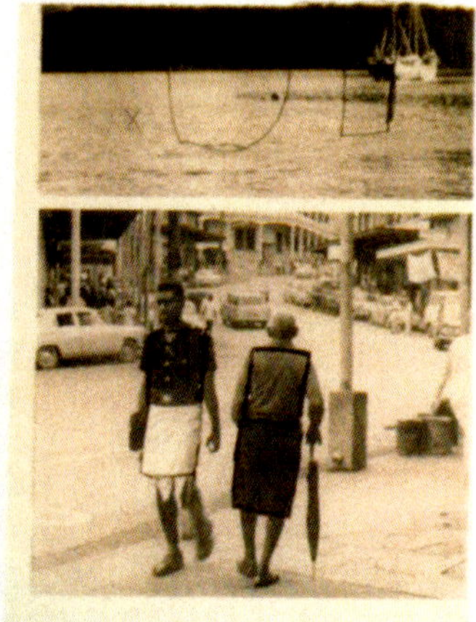

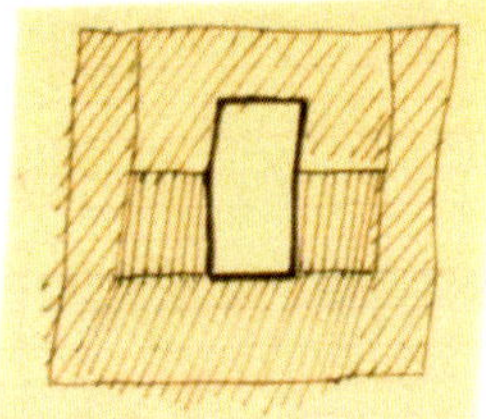

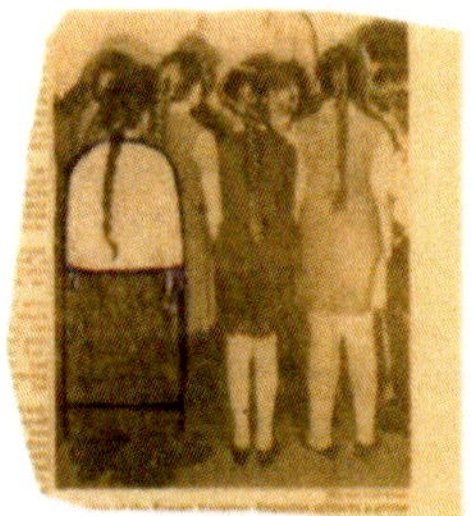

This page, top to bottom: **Ellsworth Kelly, *Four Sketches*, 1960,** ink and pencil, 15½ x 21". **Ellsworth Kelly, *Sketchbook #17*, 1951–52,** ink and pencil, 16½ x 5¼". Opposite page: **Ellsworth Kelly, *Lemon Branch*, 1964,** pencil on paper, 28½ x 22½". Collection of the Solomon R. Guggenheim Museum, New York.

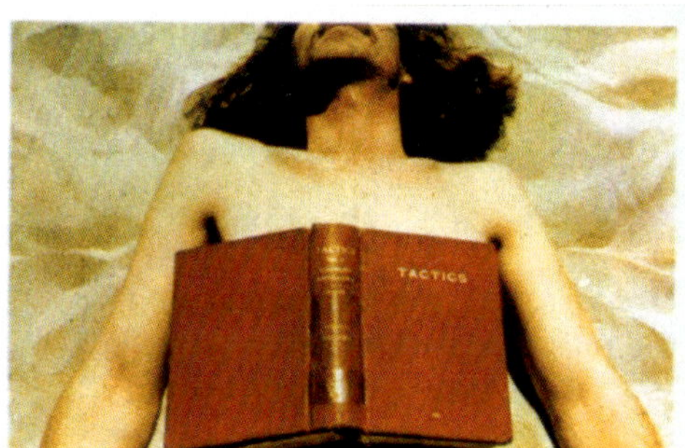
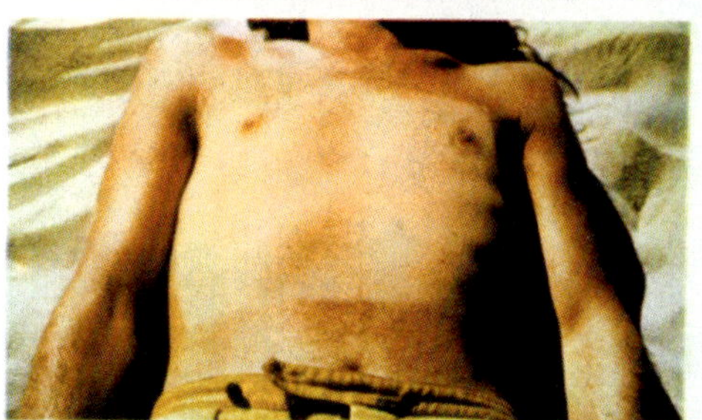
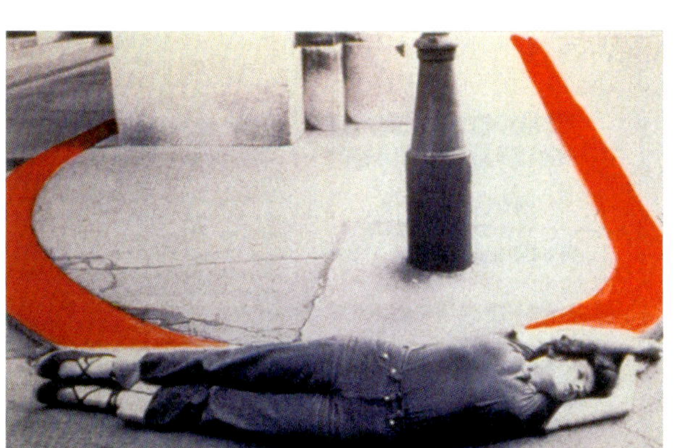
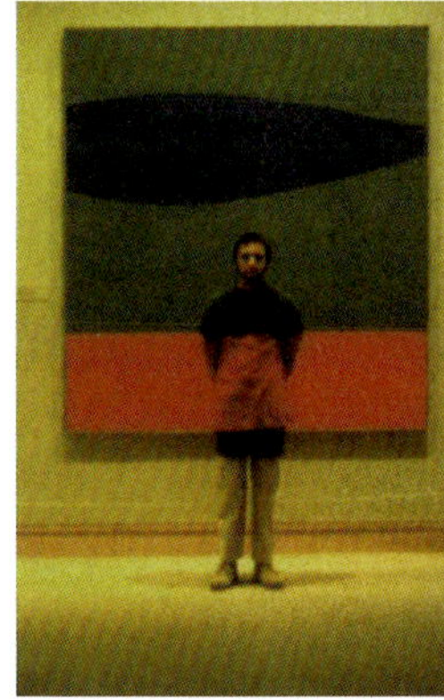
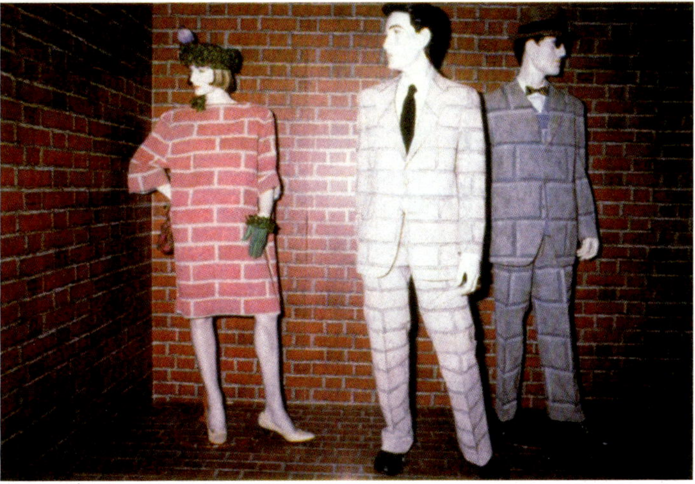

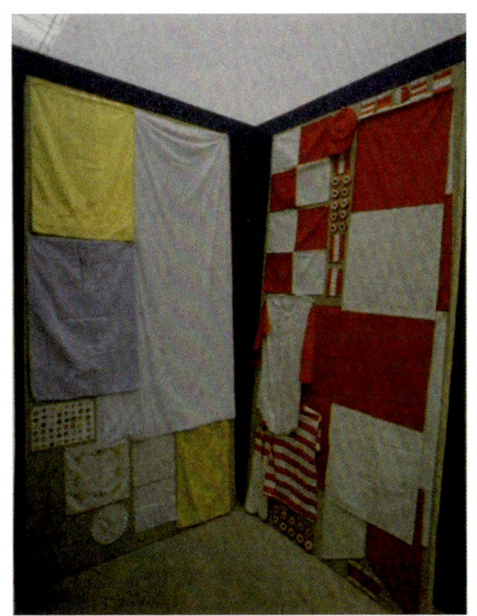
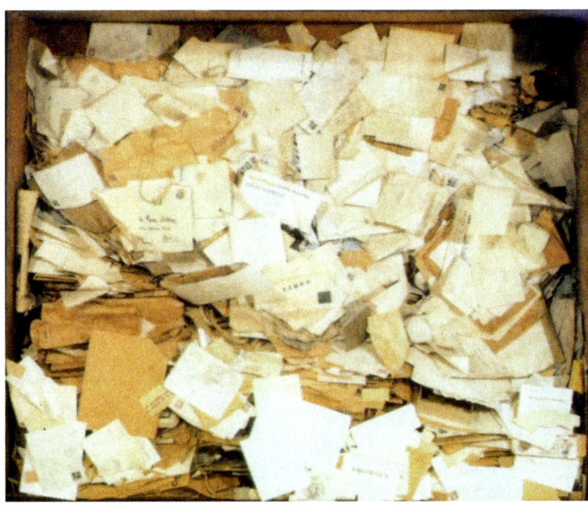
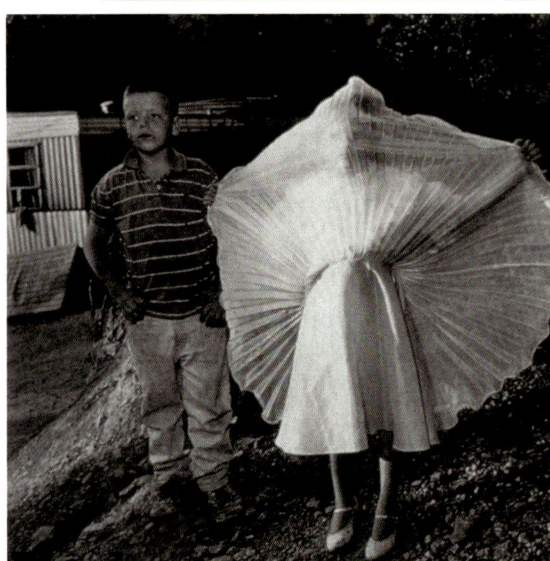
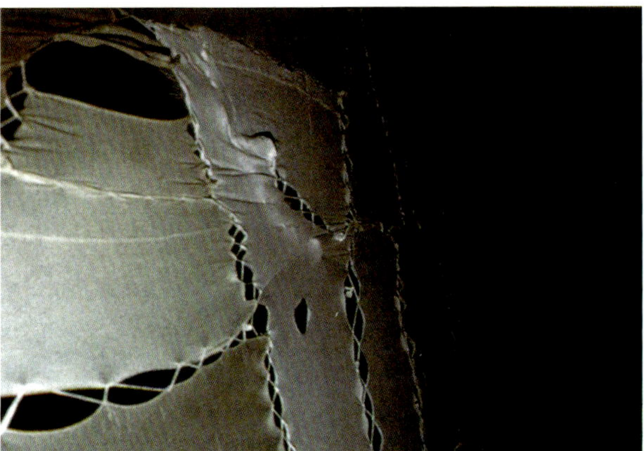
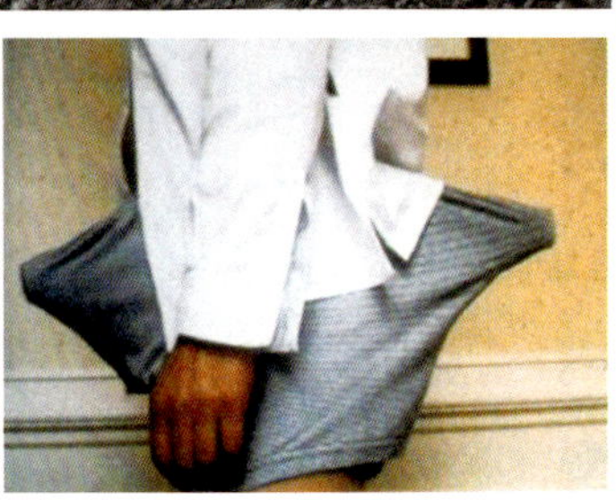
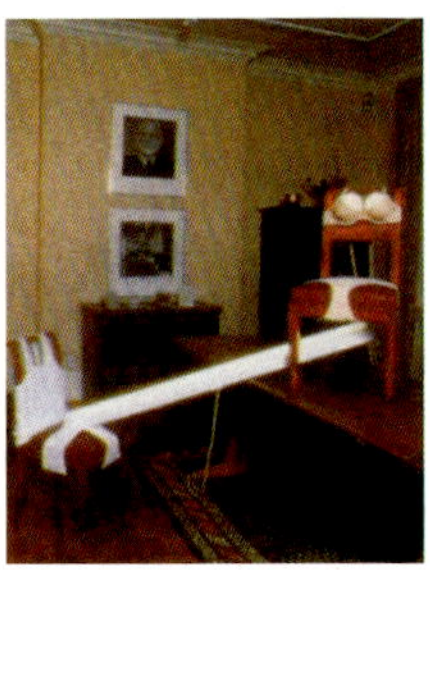
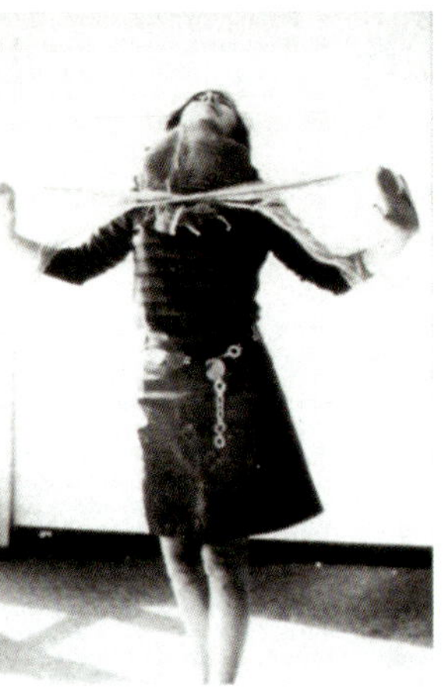

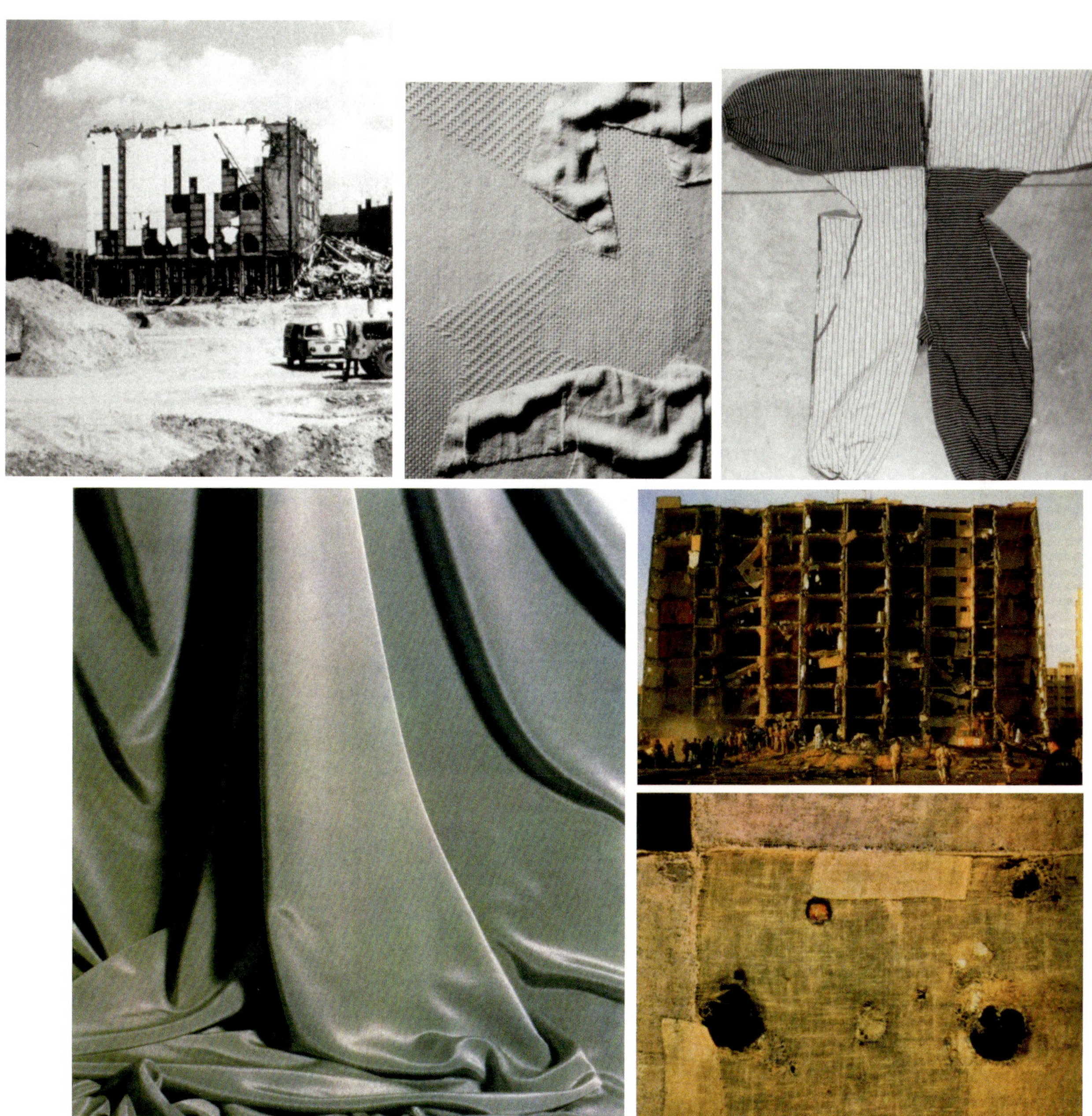

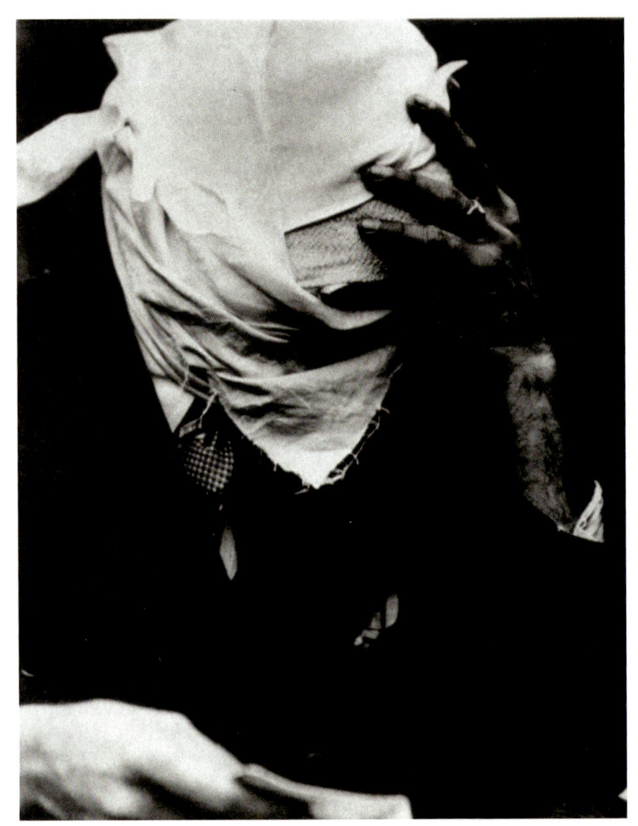

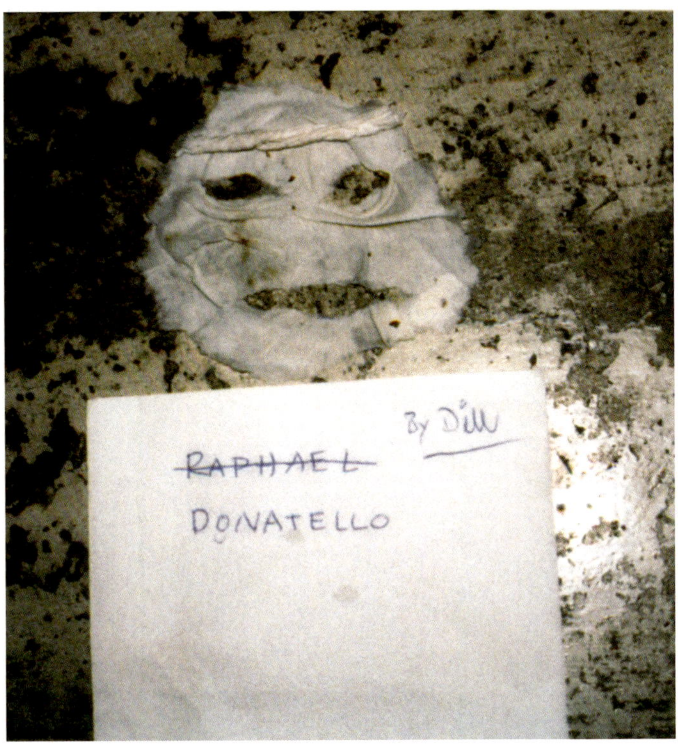
By Dill
RAPHAEL
DONATELLO

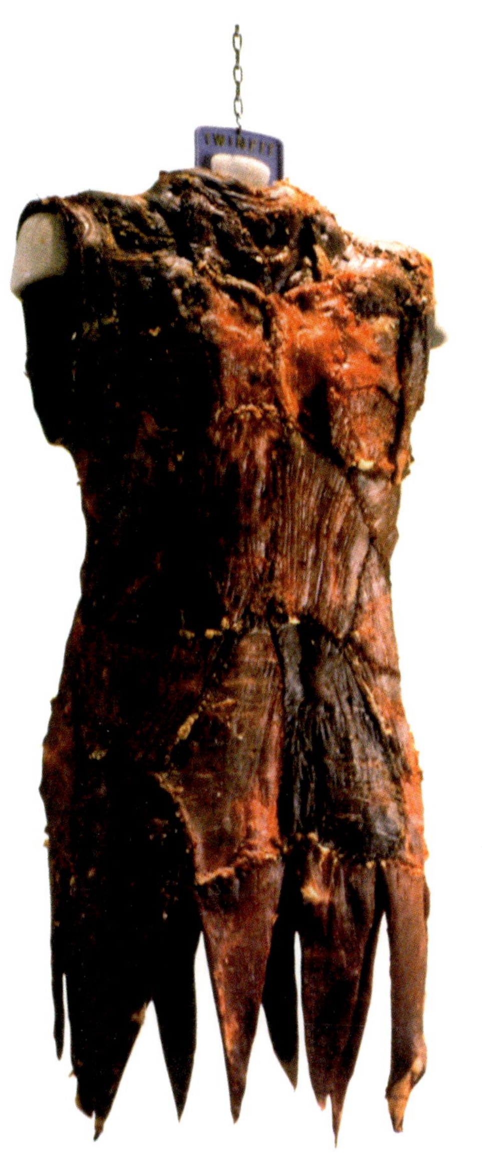
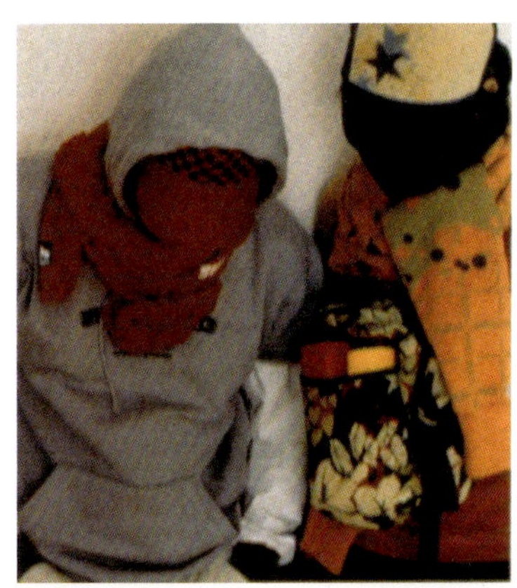
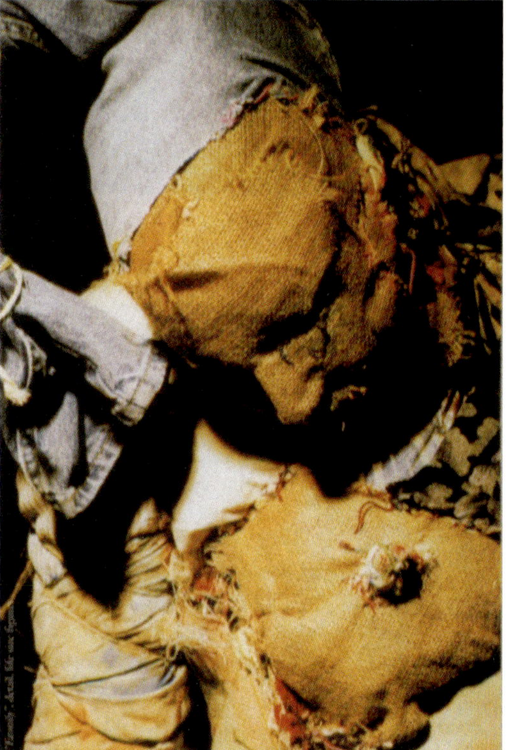
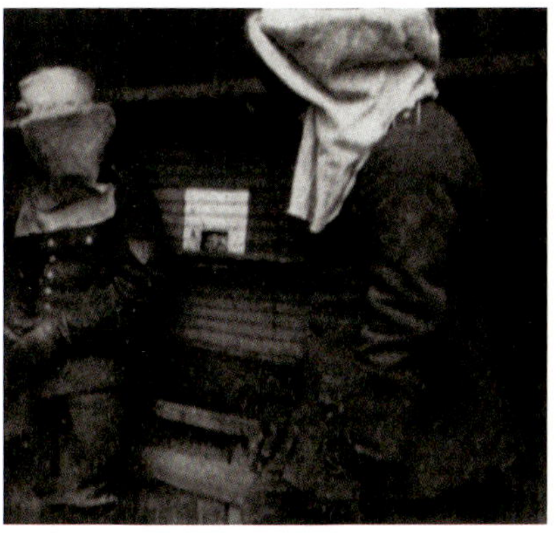
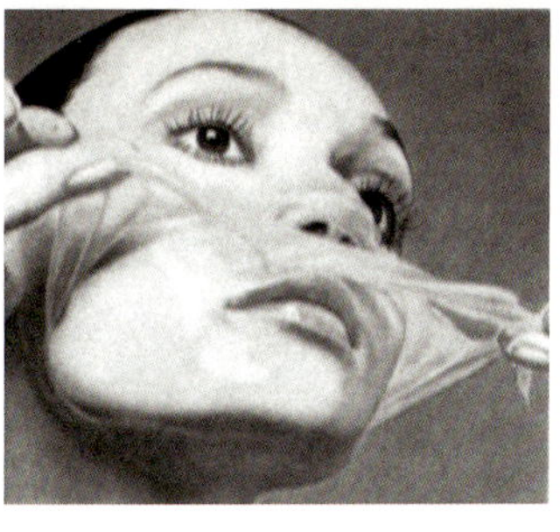

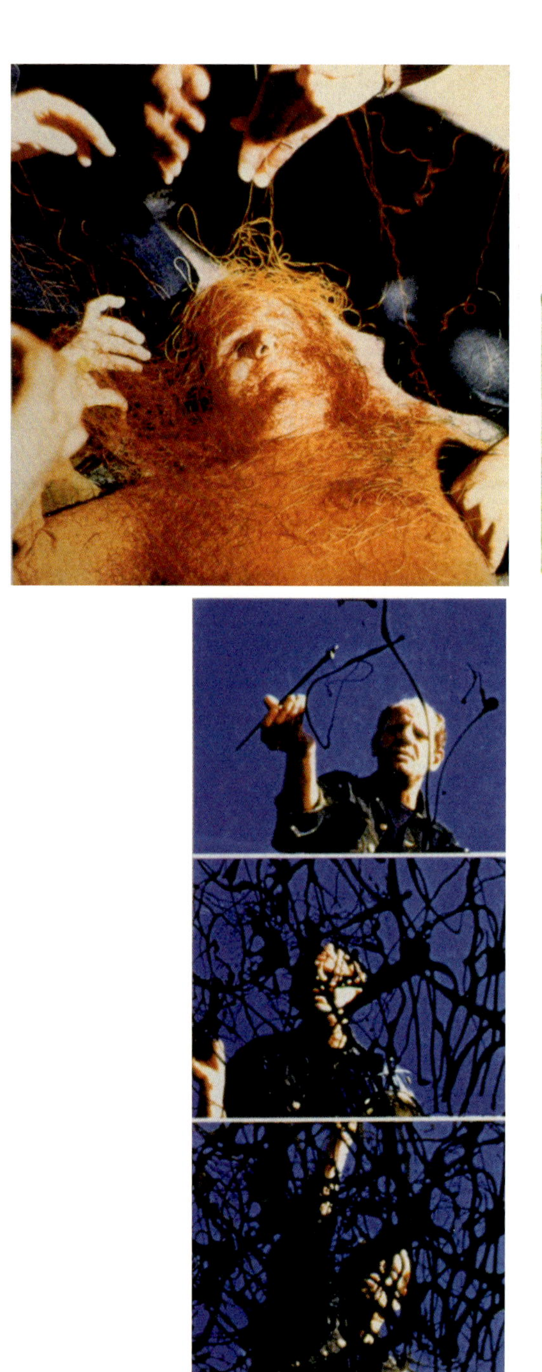
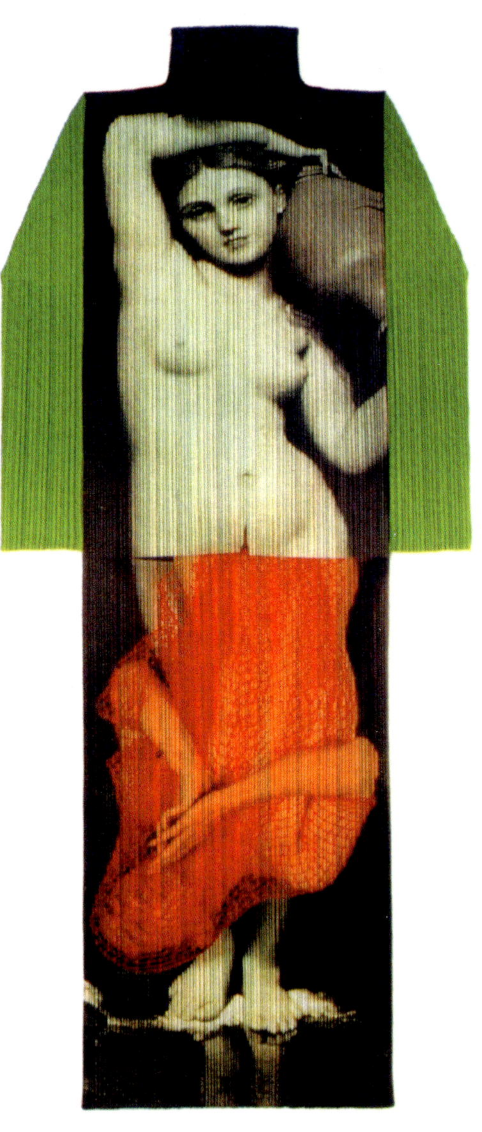

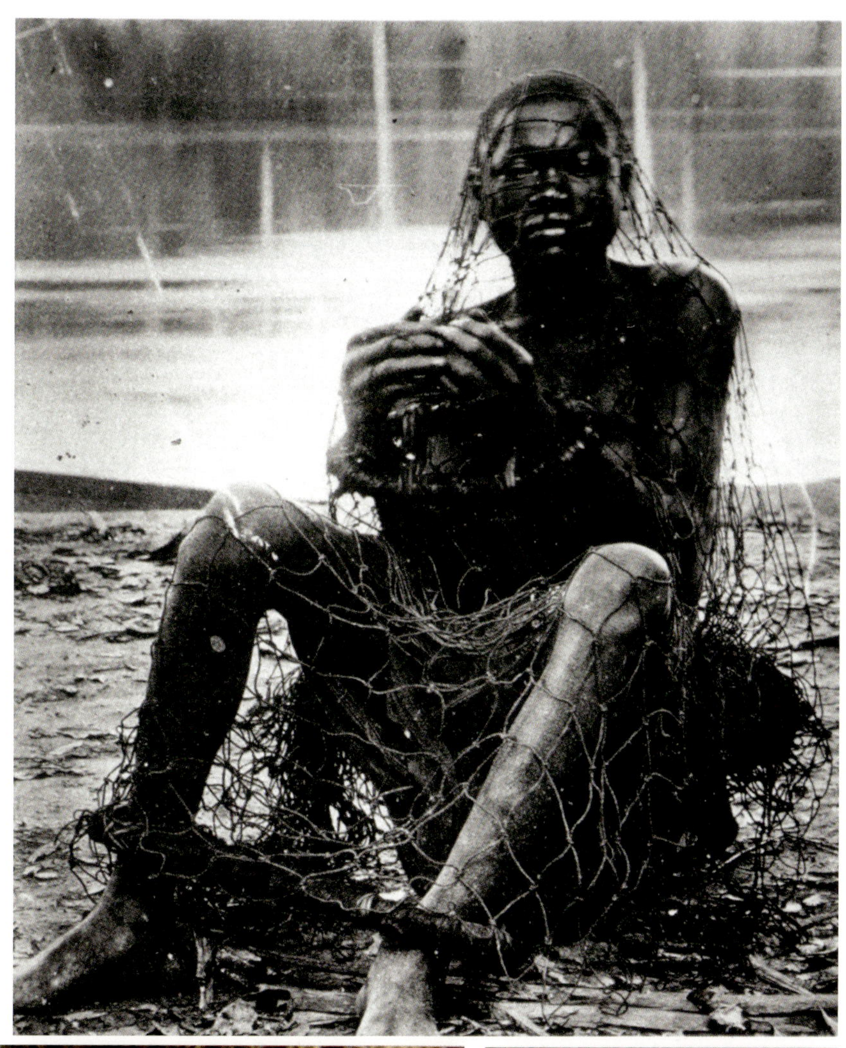

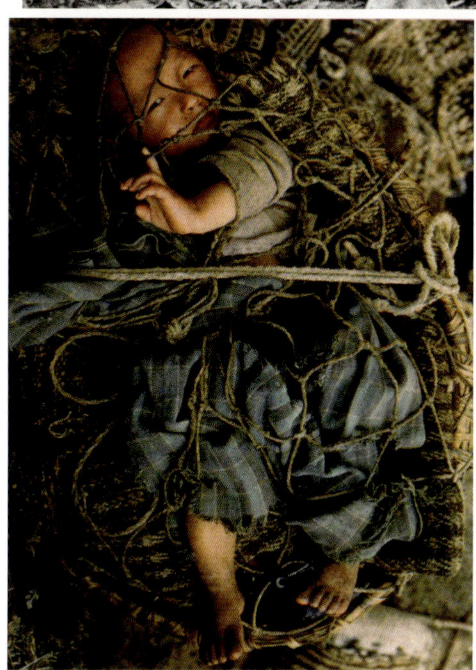

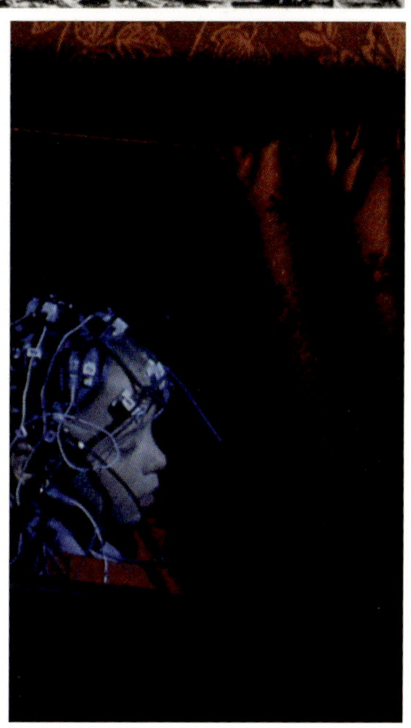

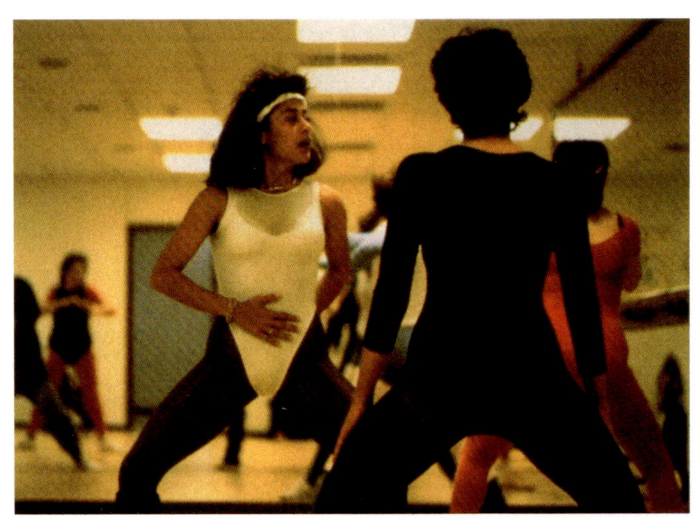

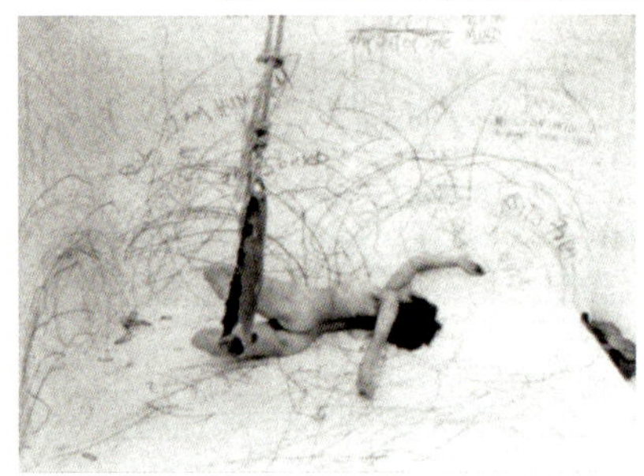

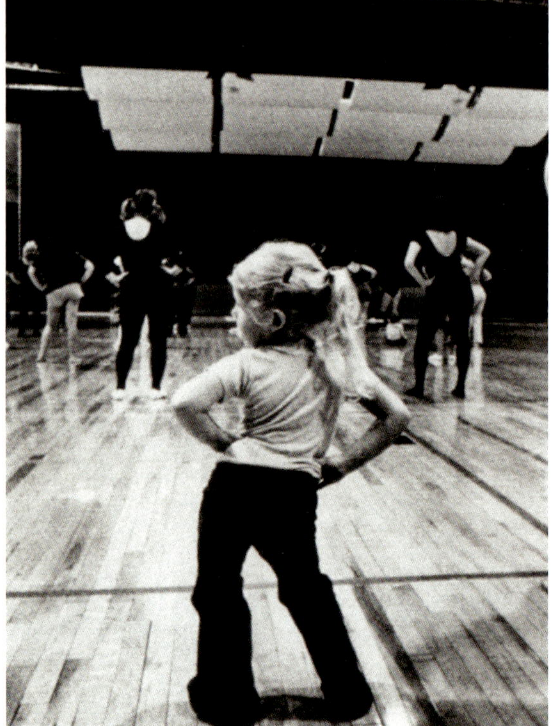

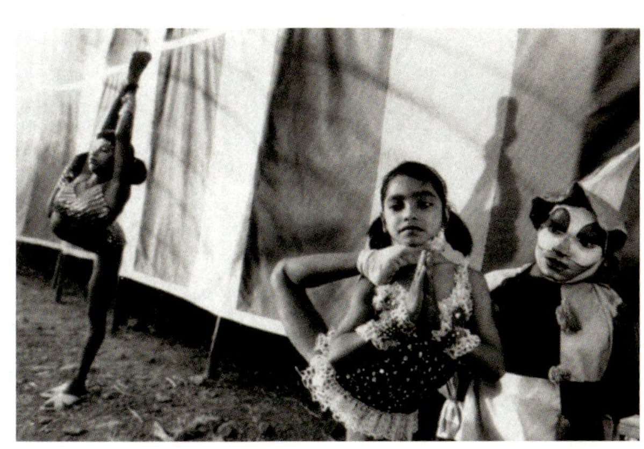

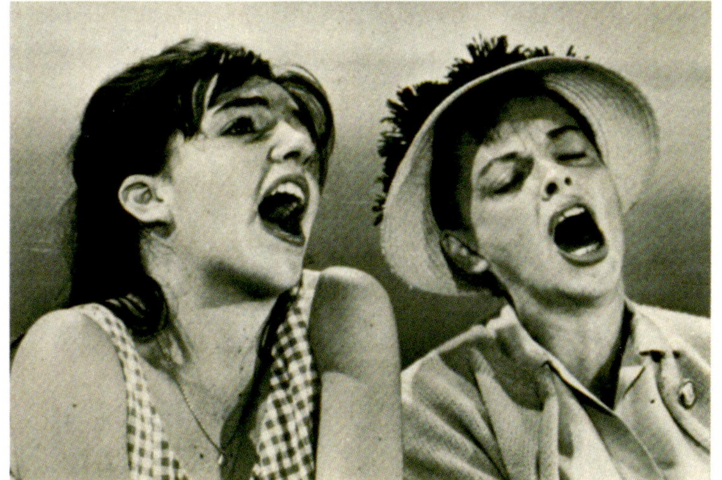

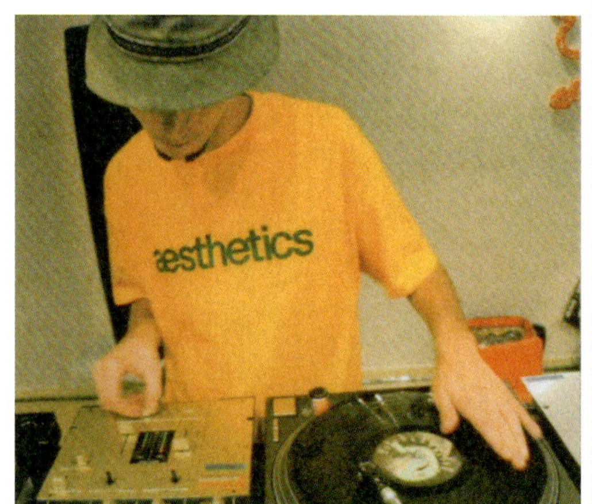

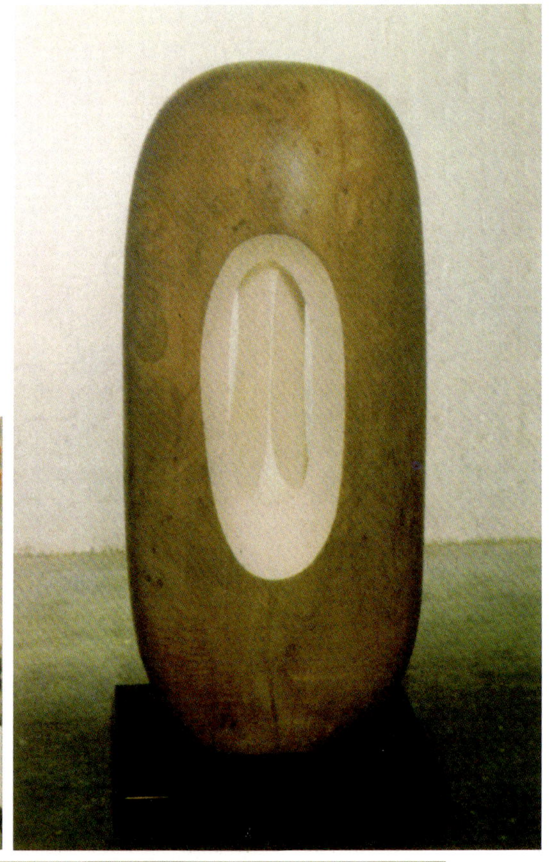

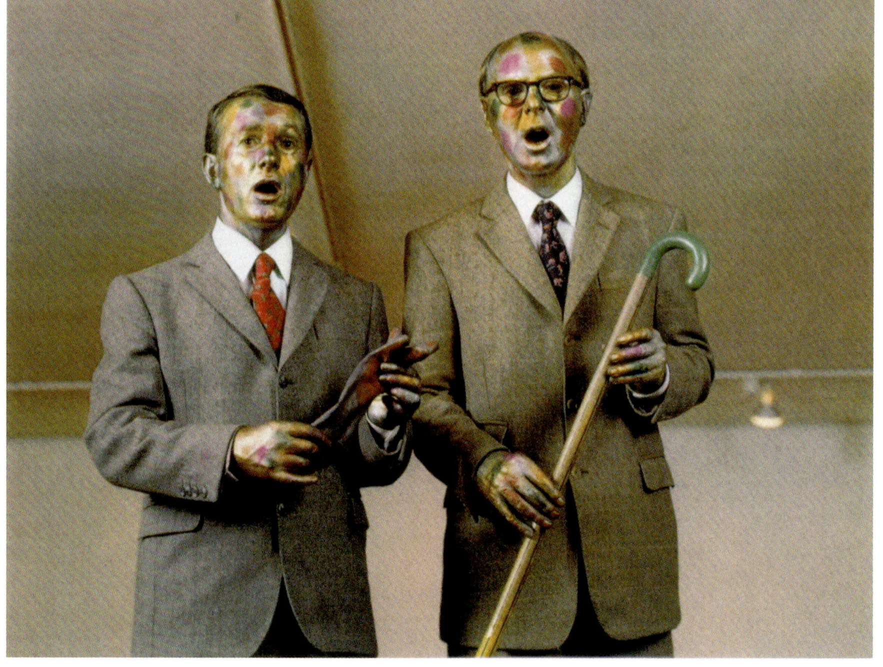

æsthetics

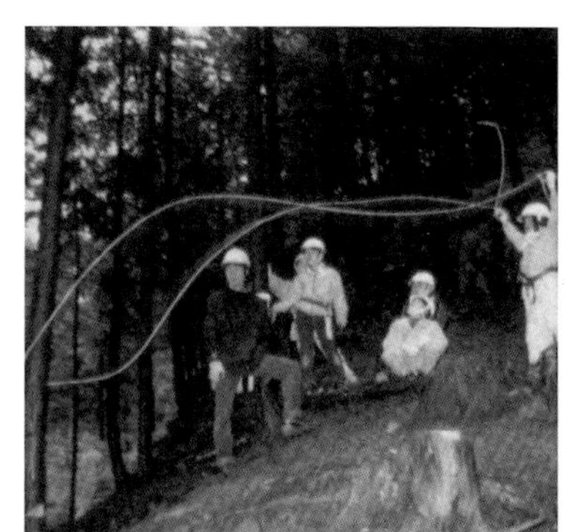
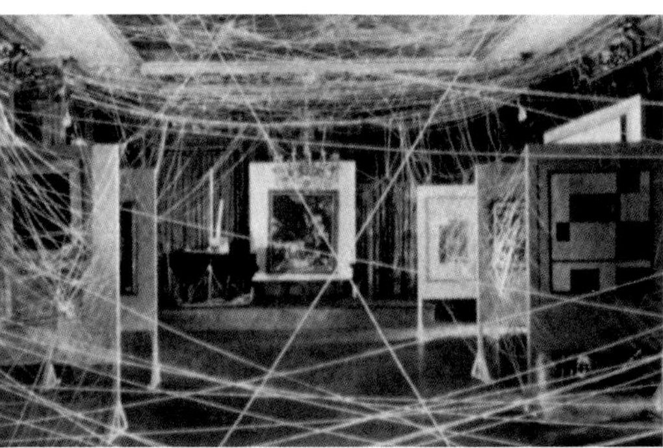
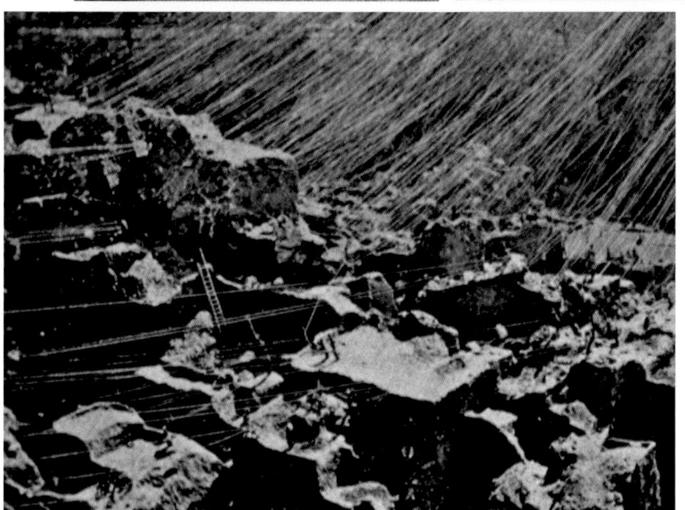
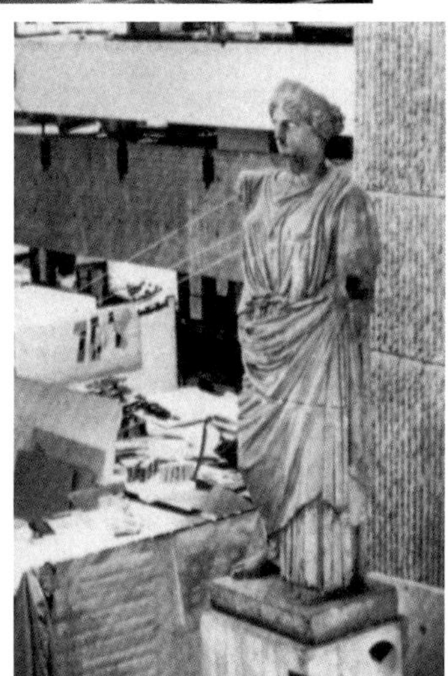

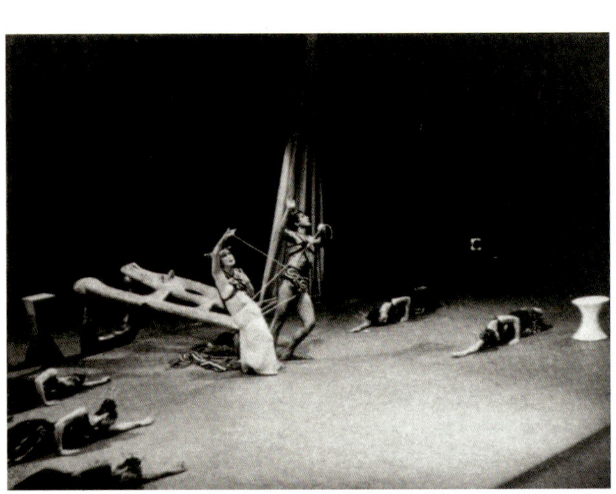
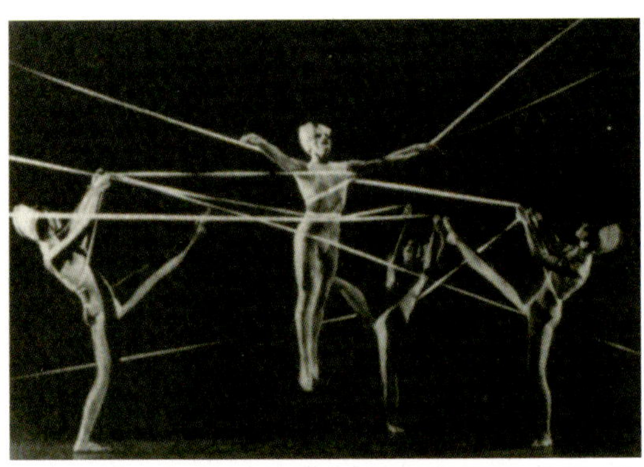
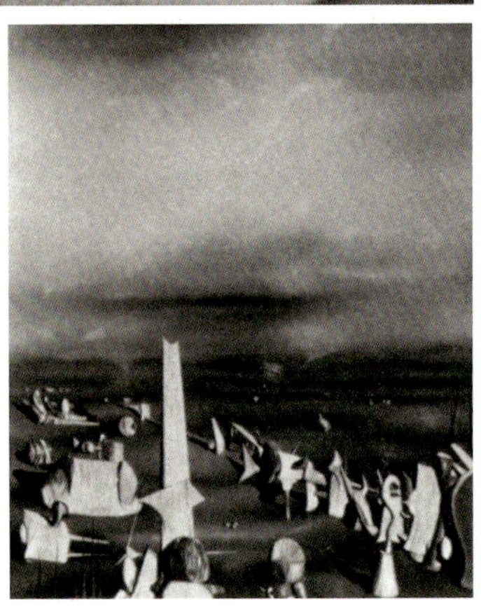
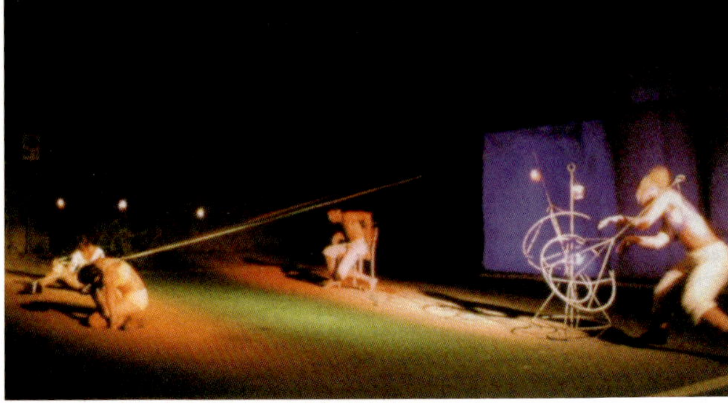
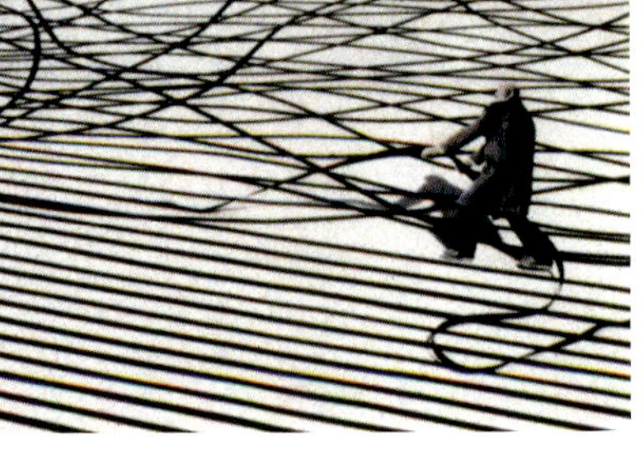

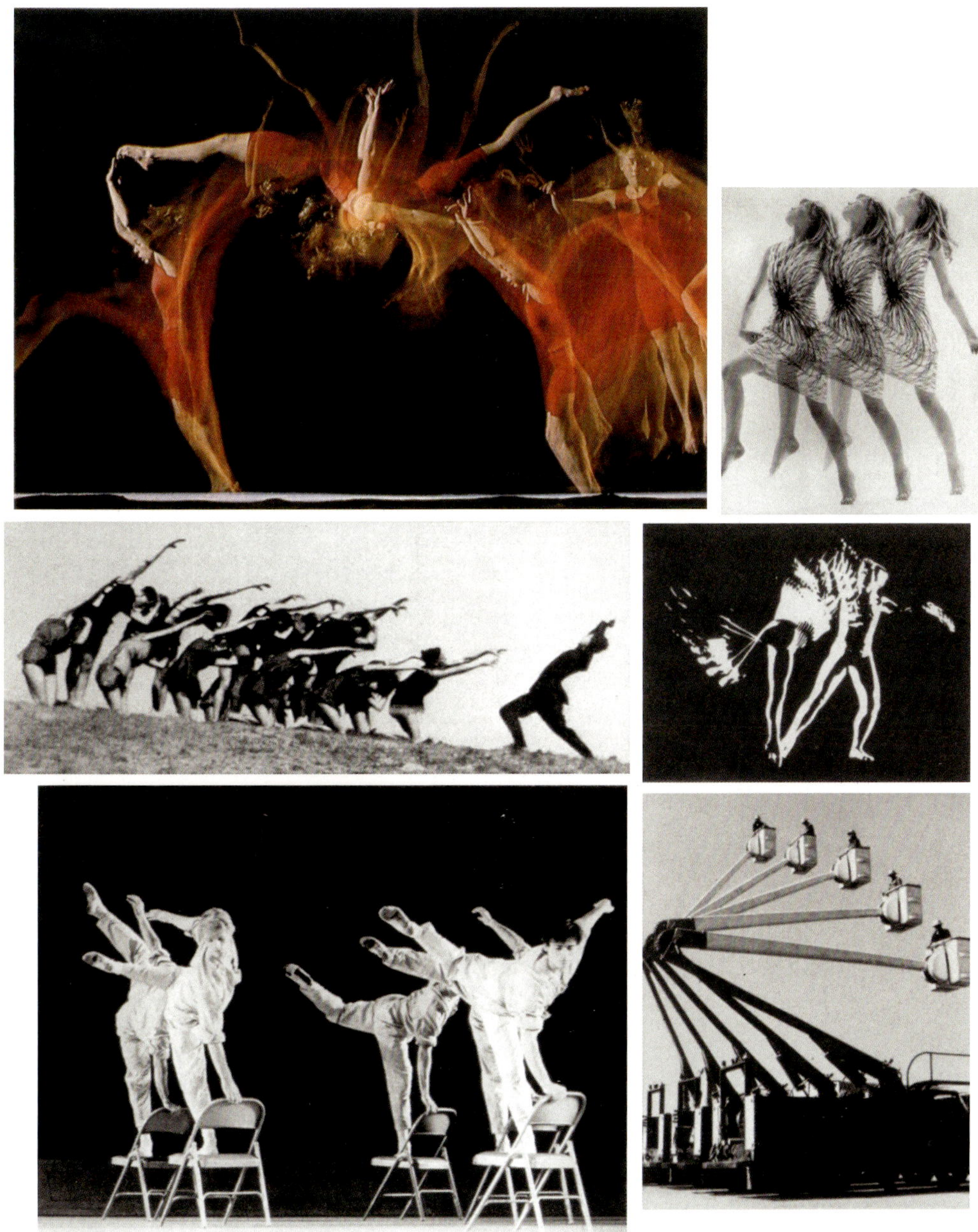

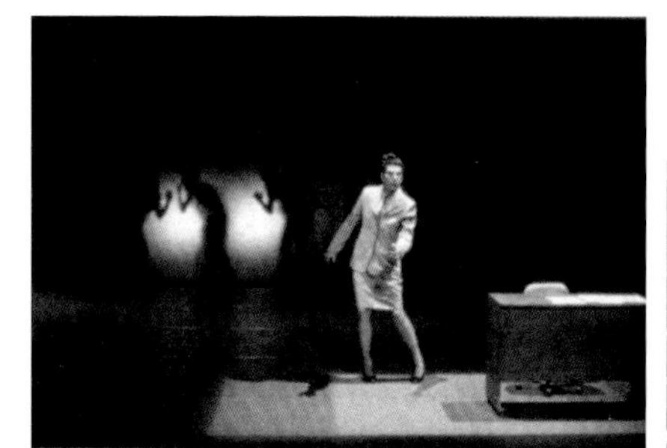
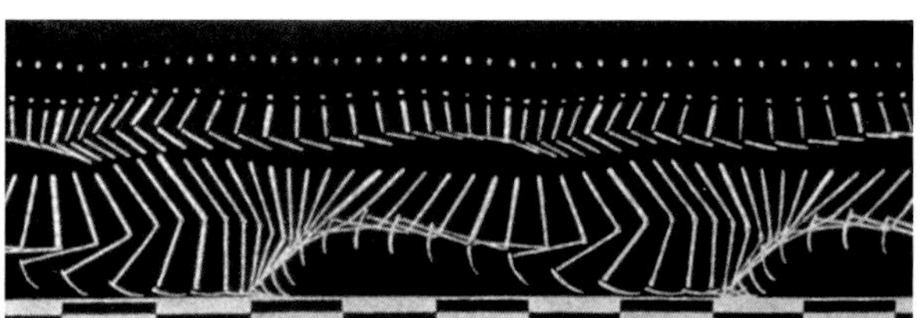
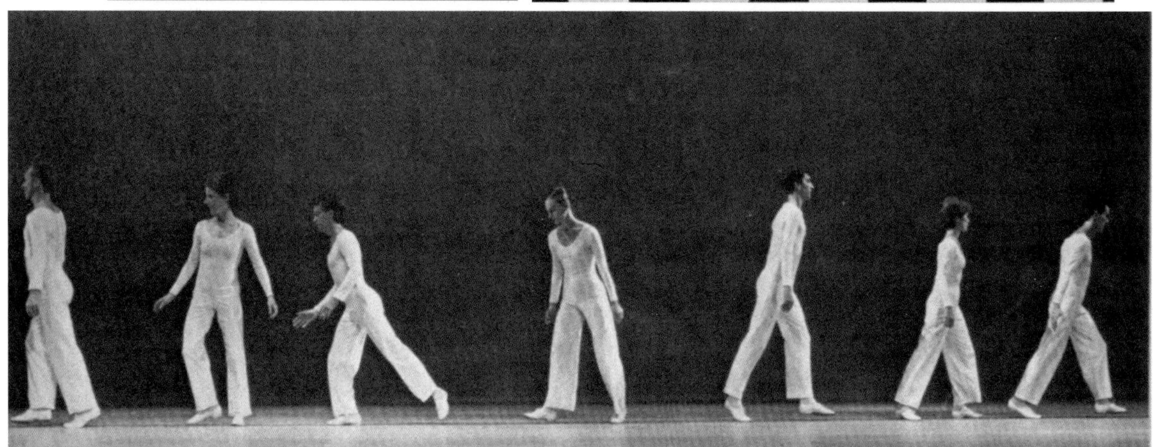
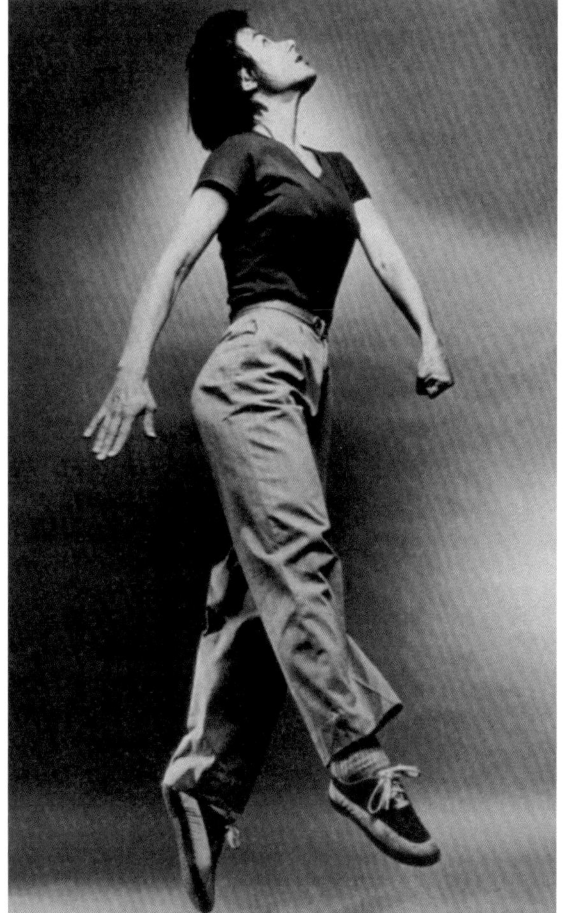
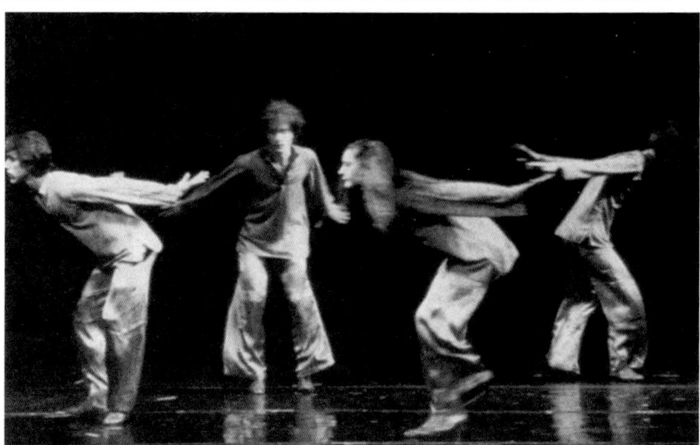
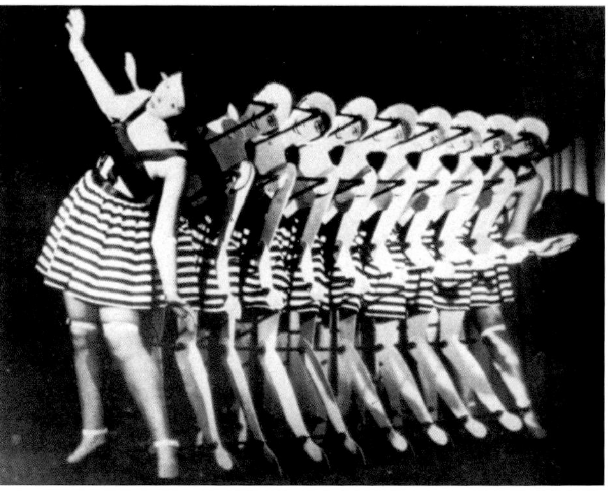

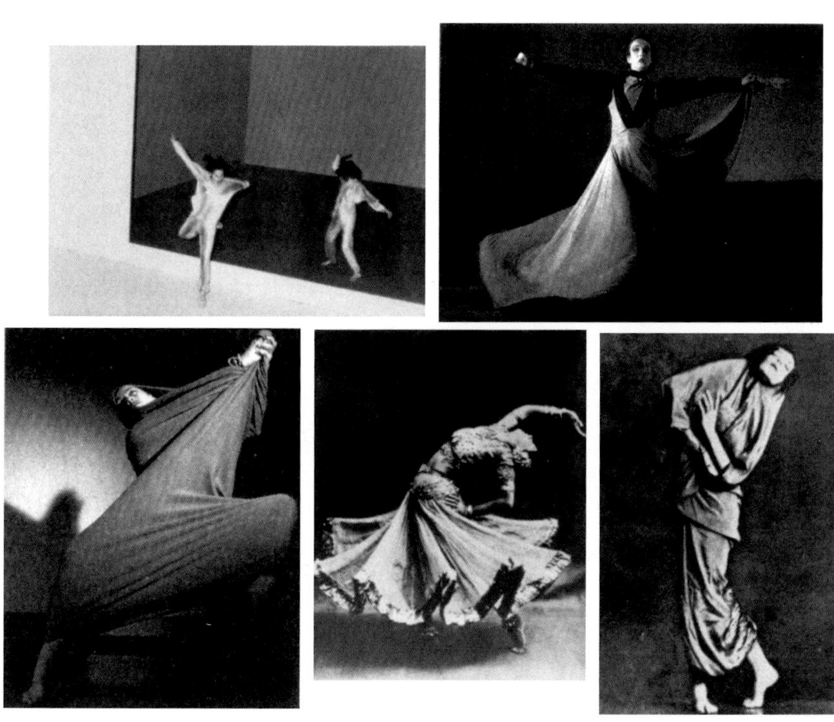

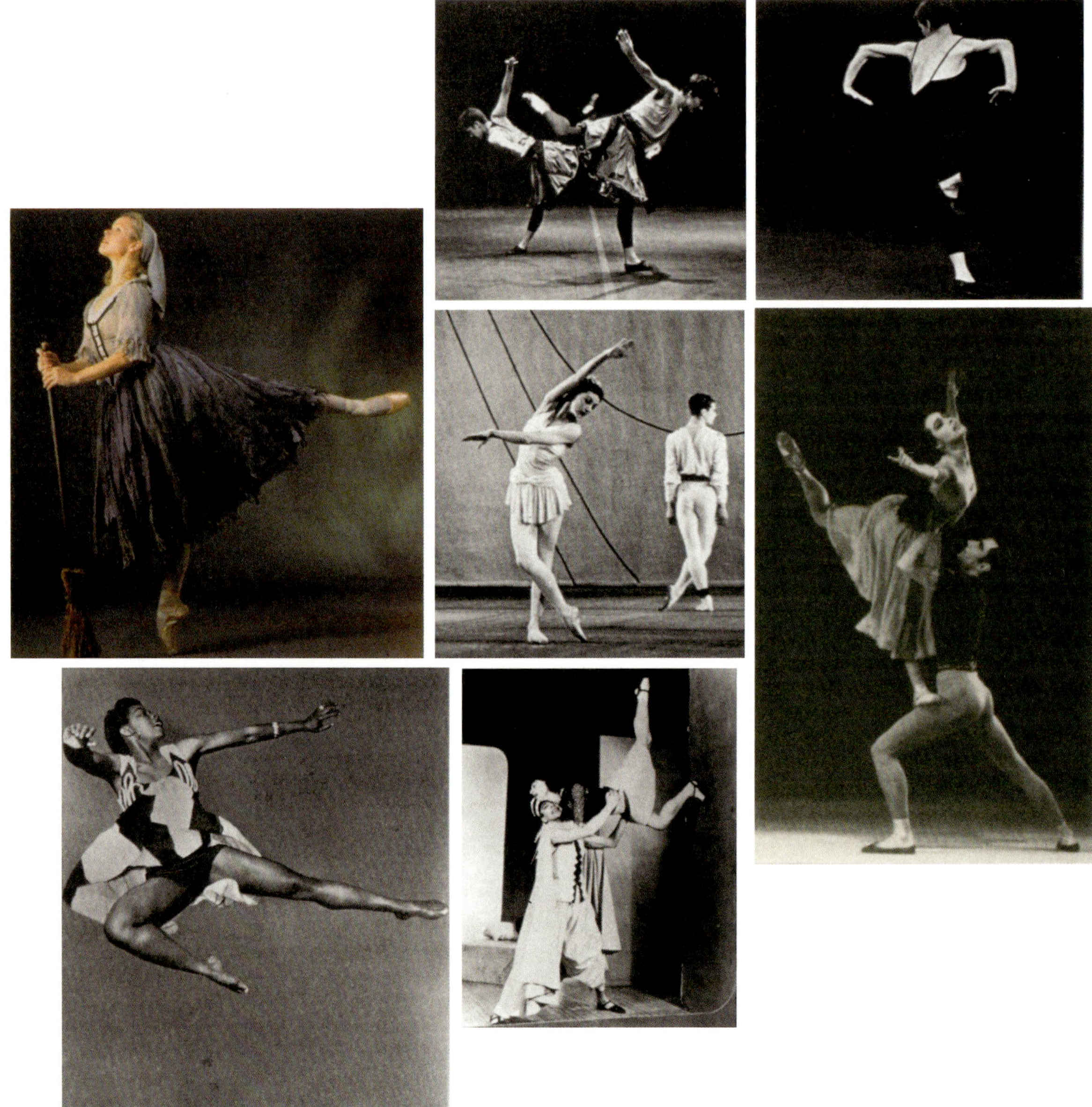

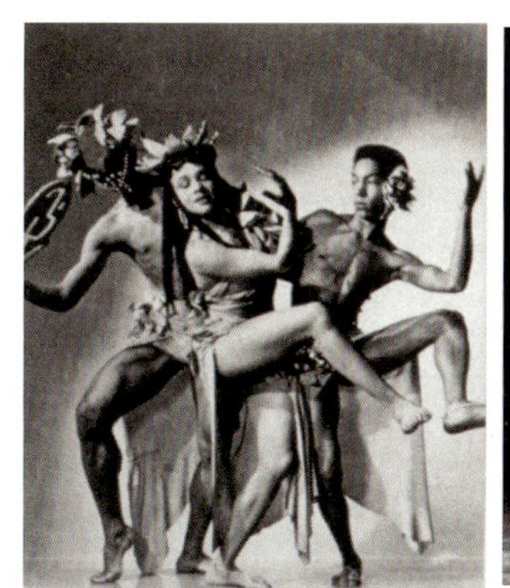
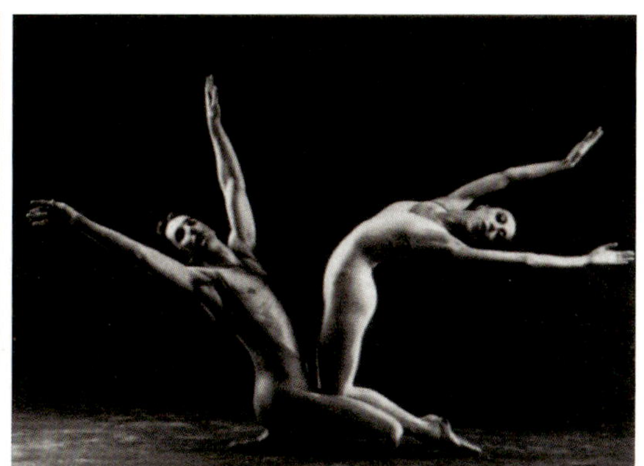
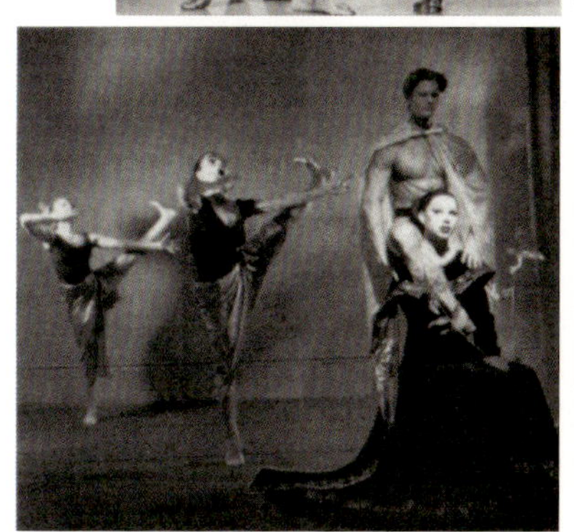
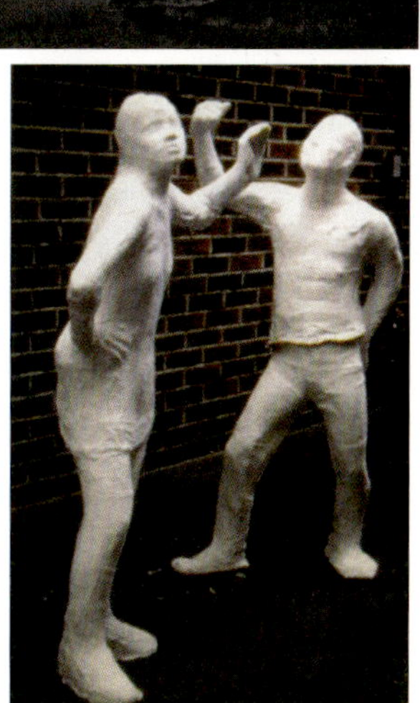
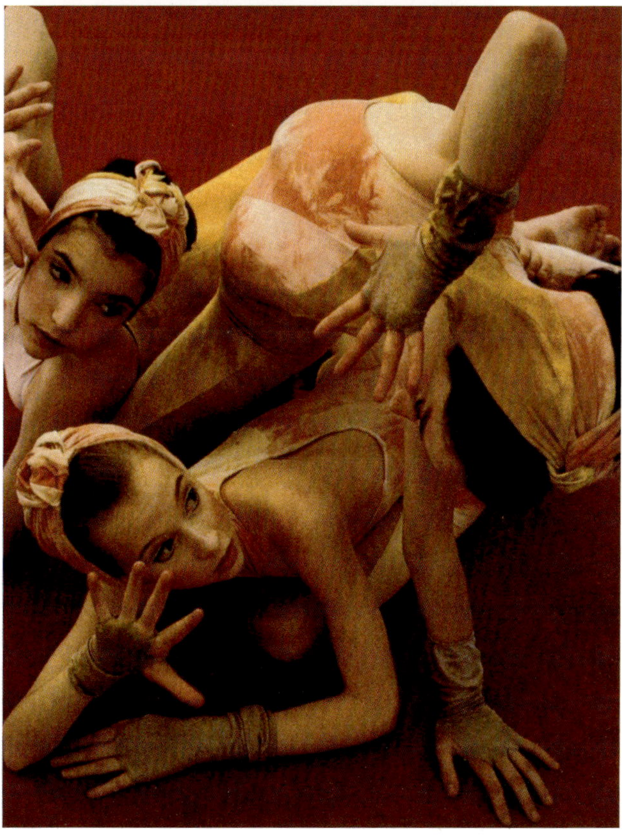

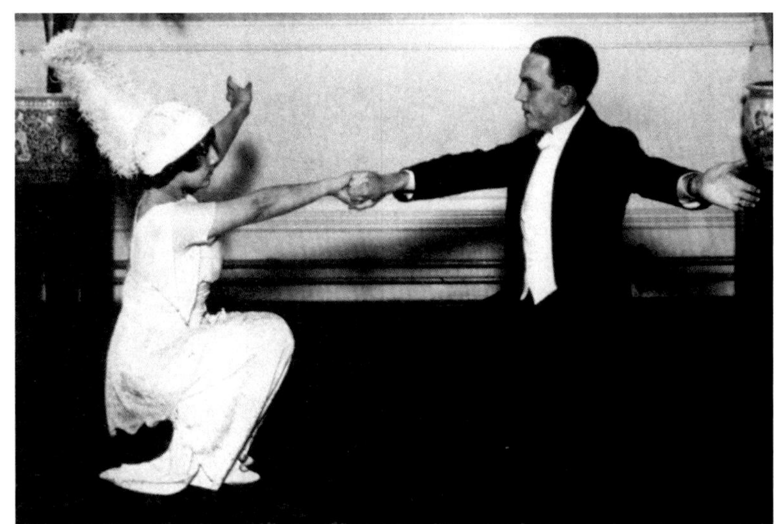

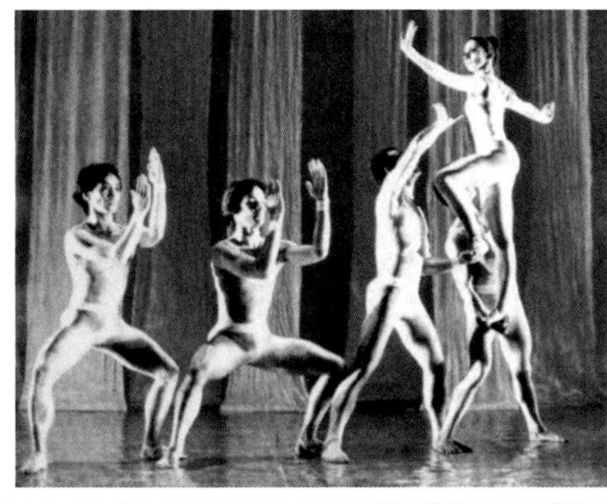

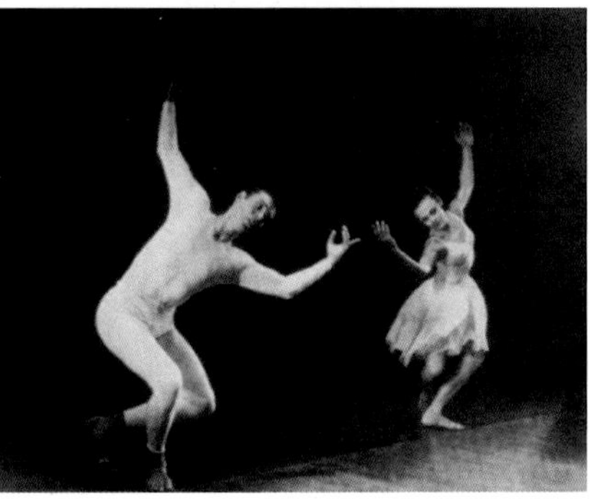

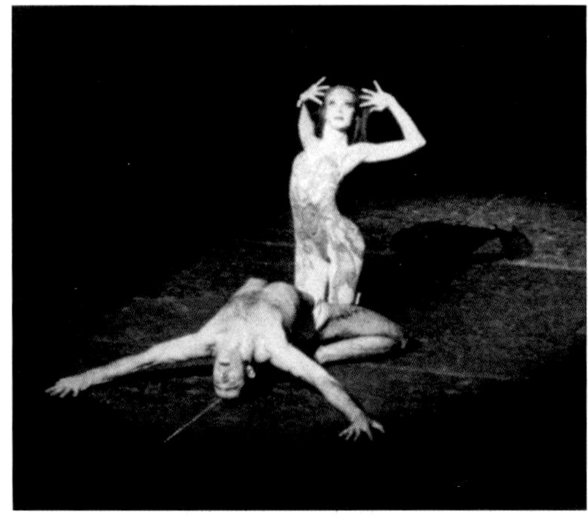

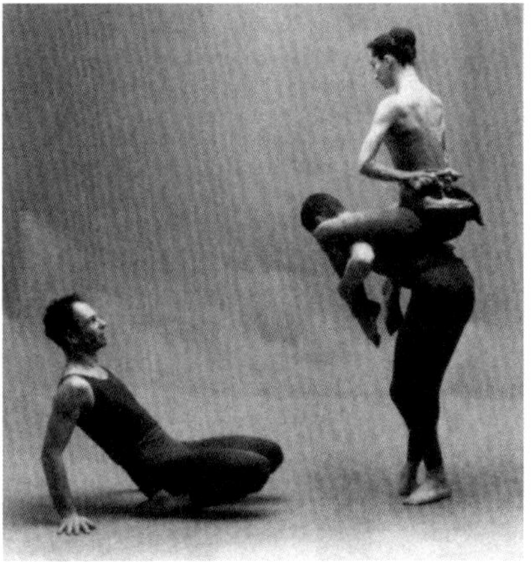

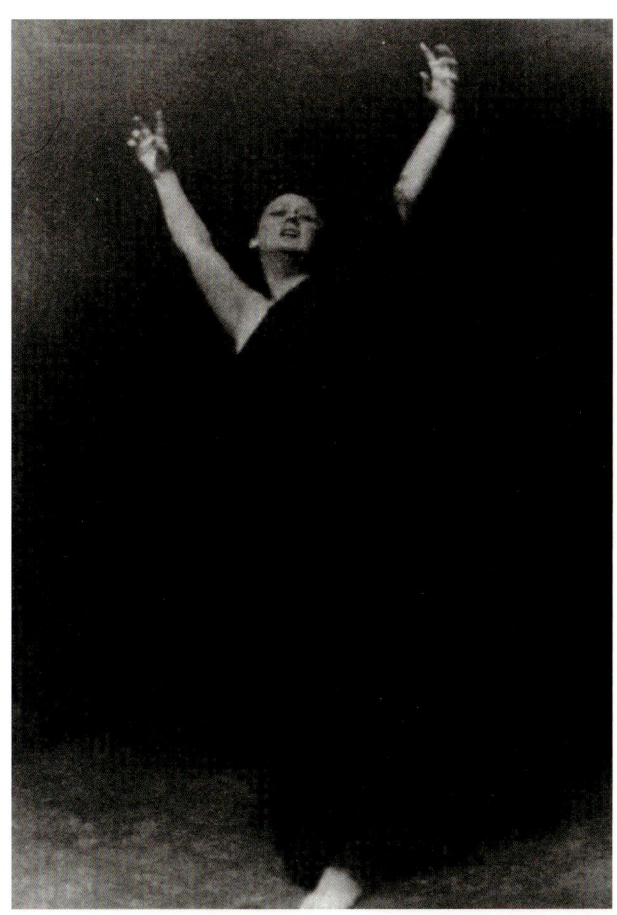
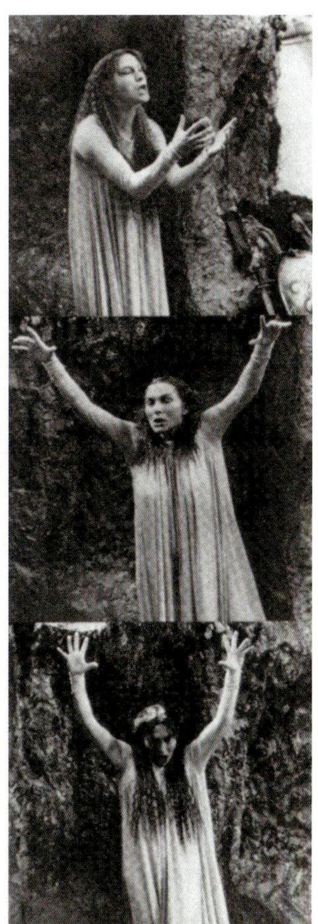
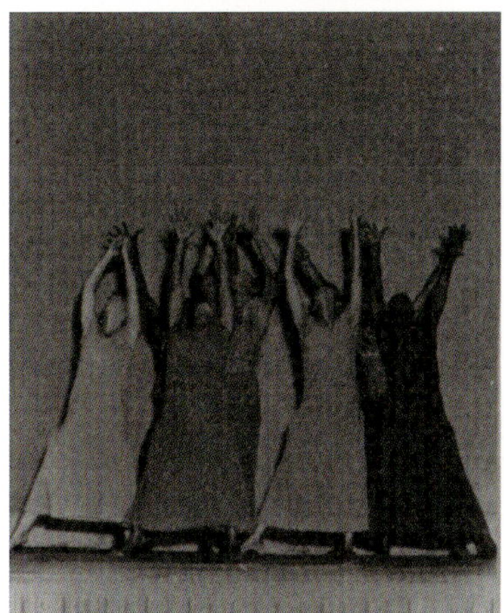
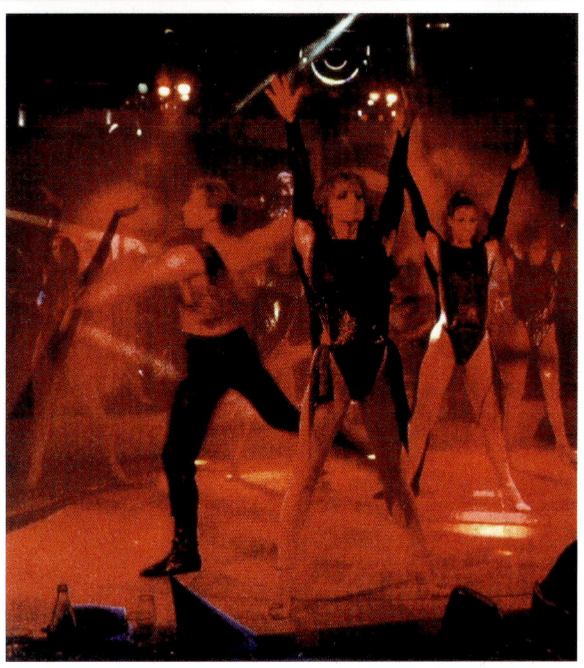

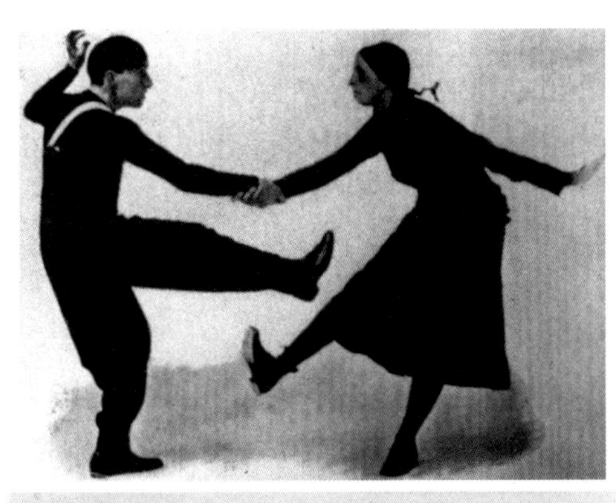

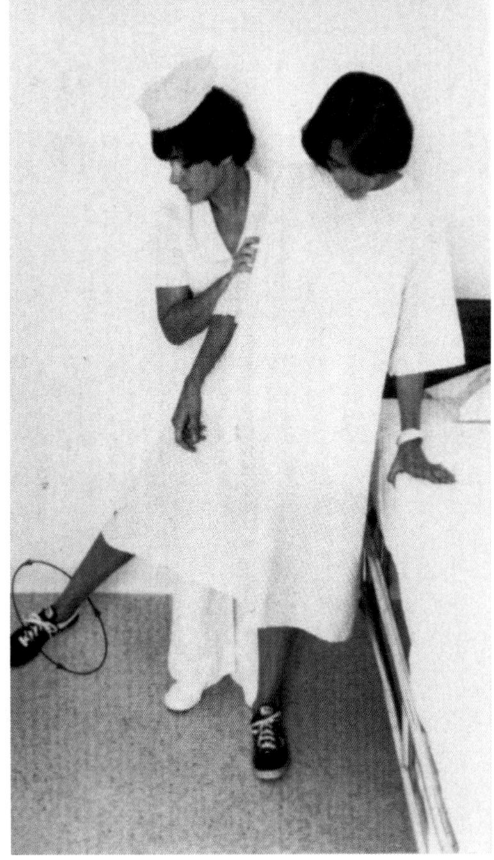

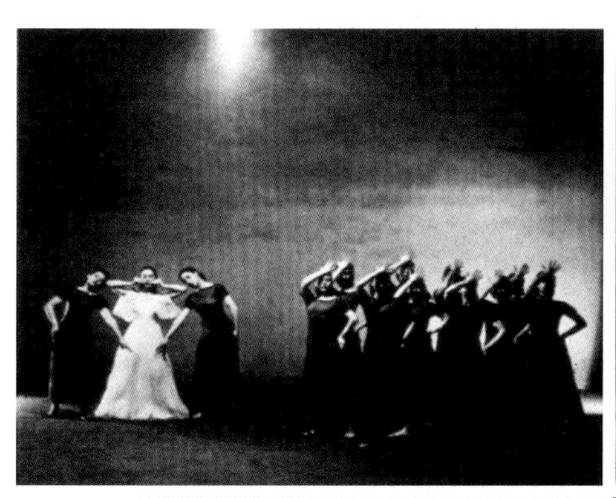
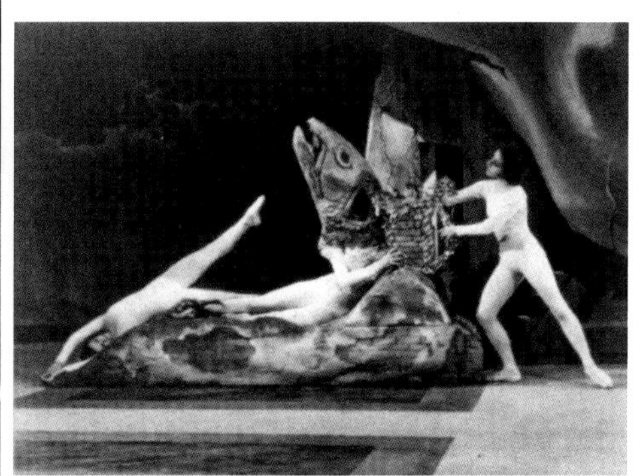
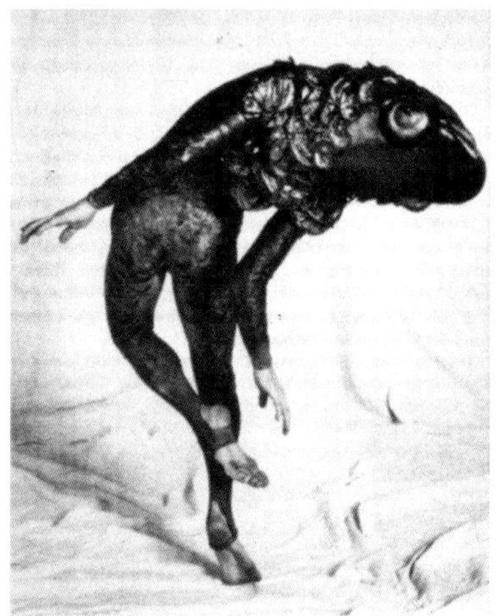
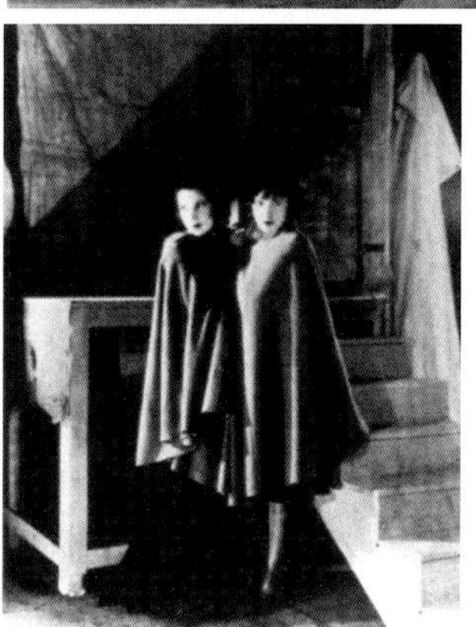

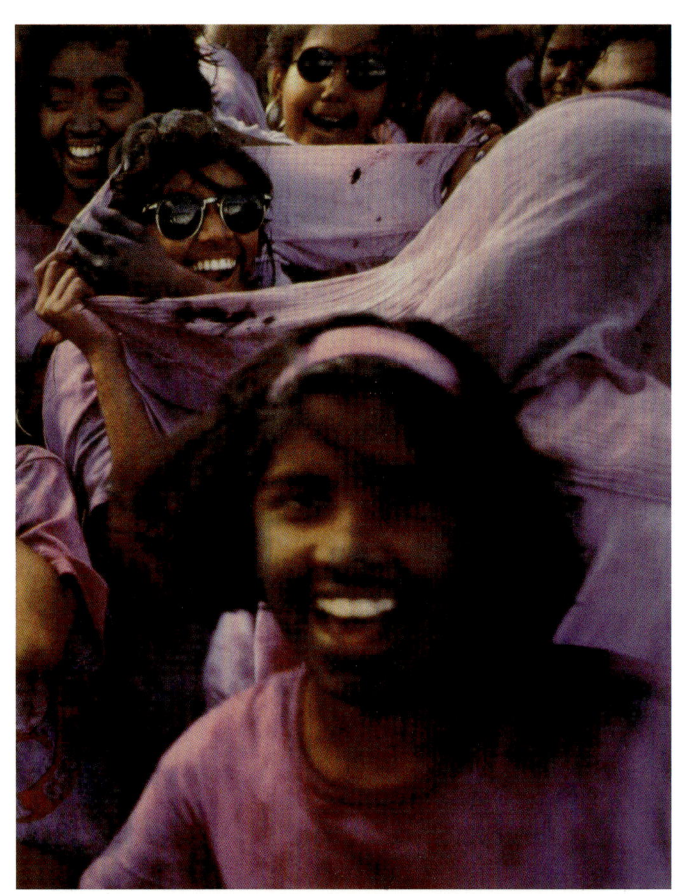

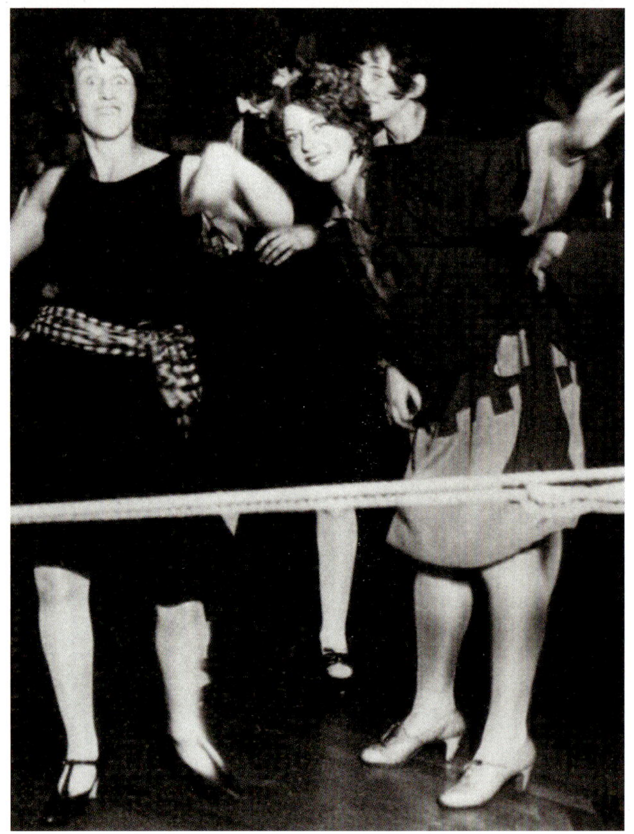

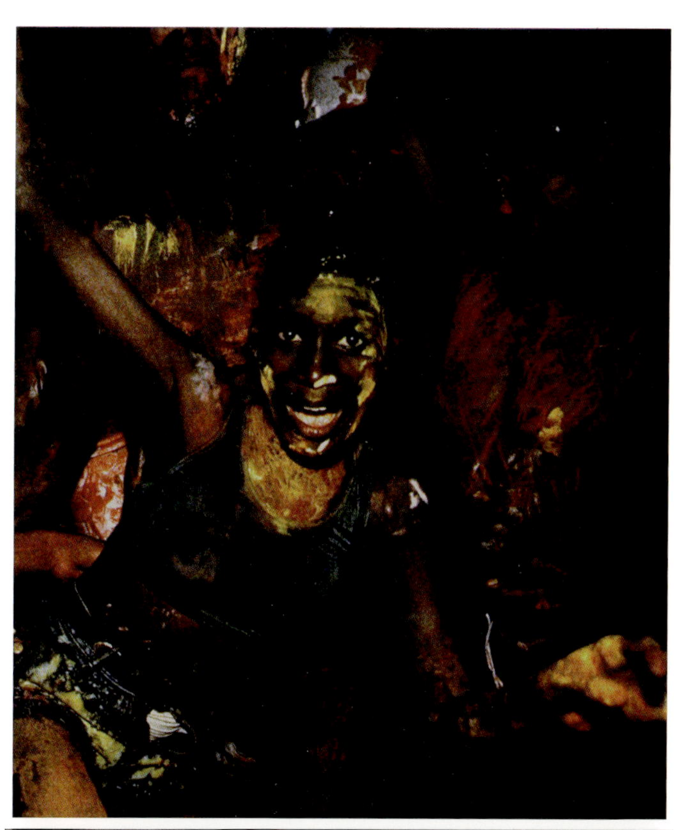

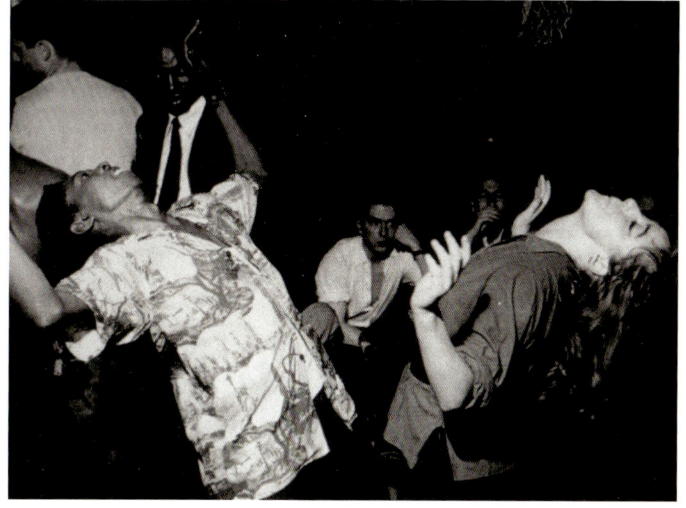

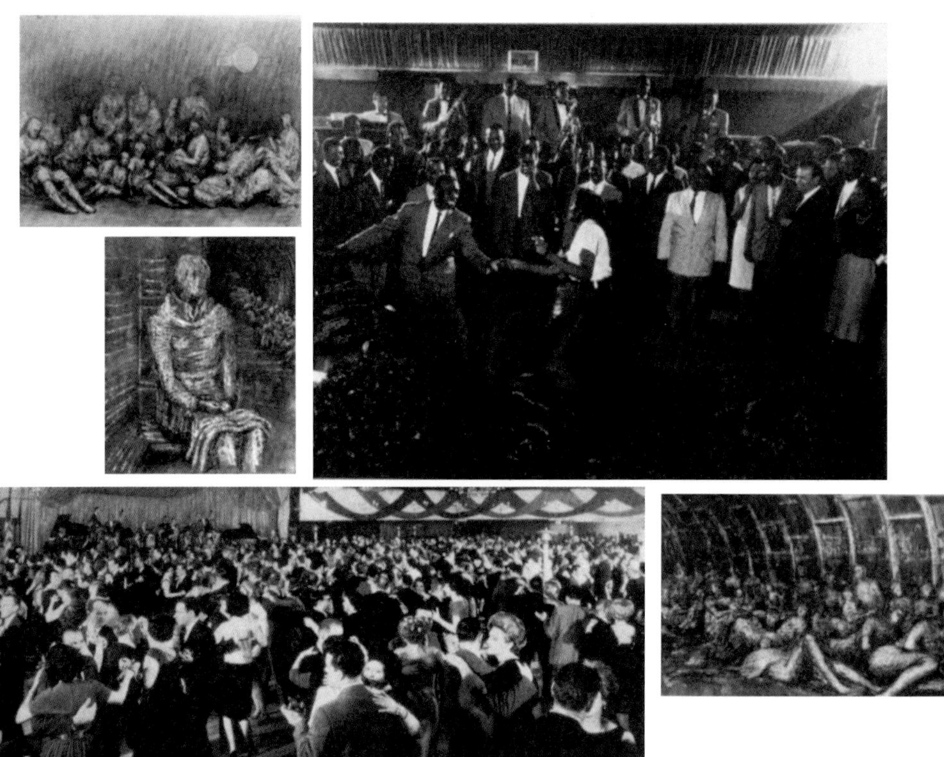

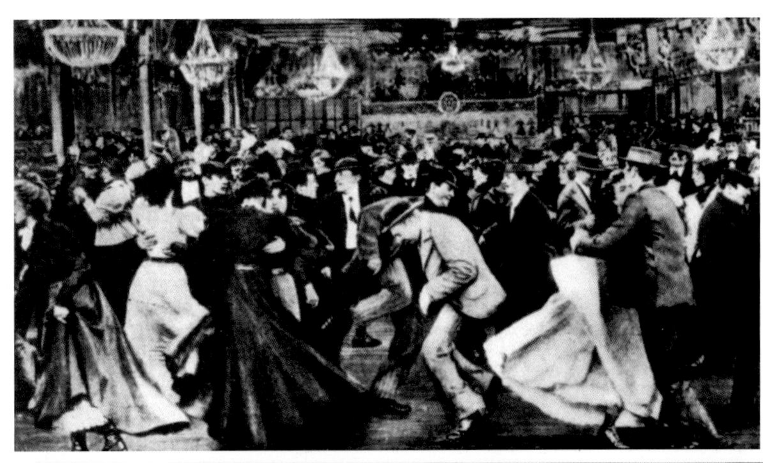

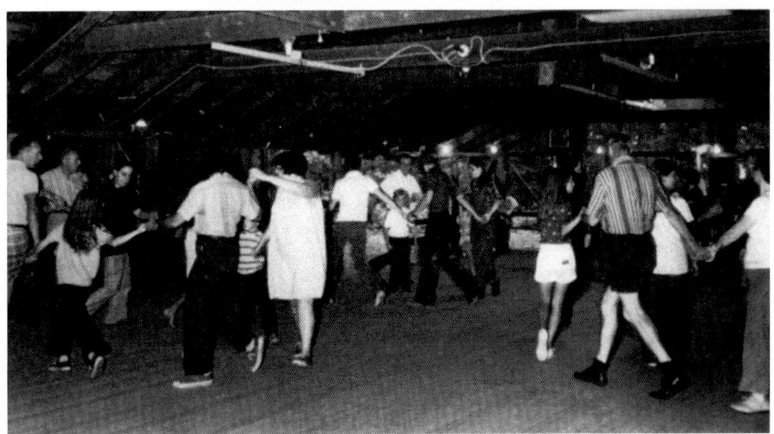

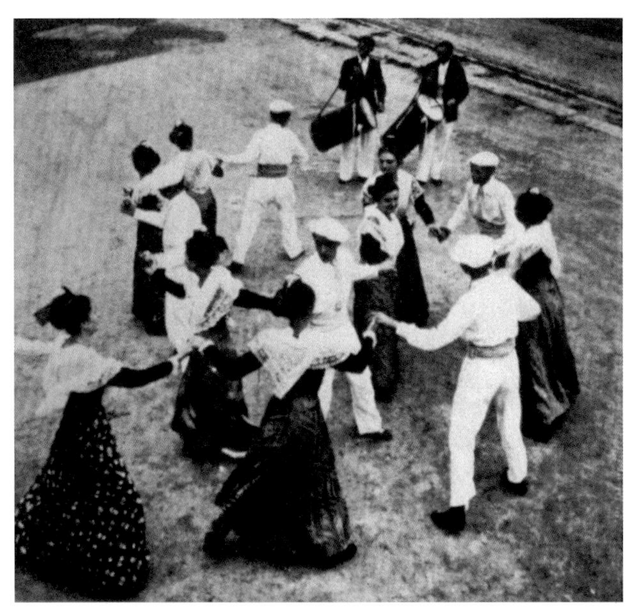

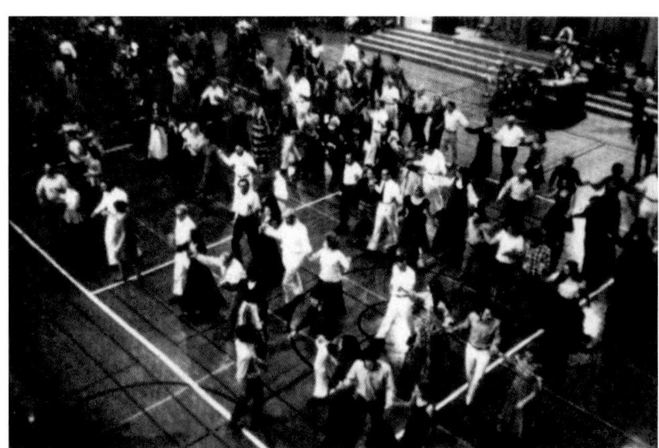

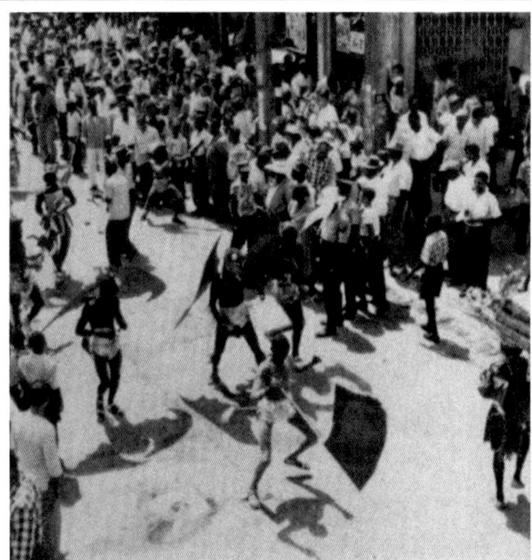

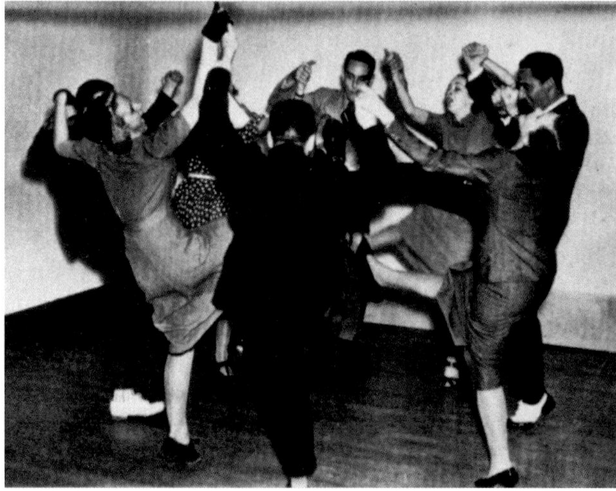

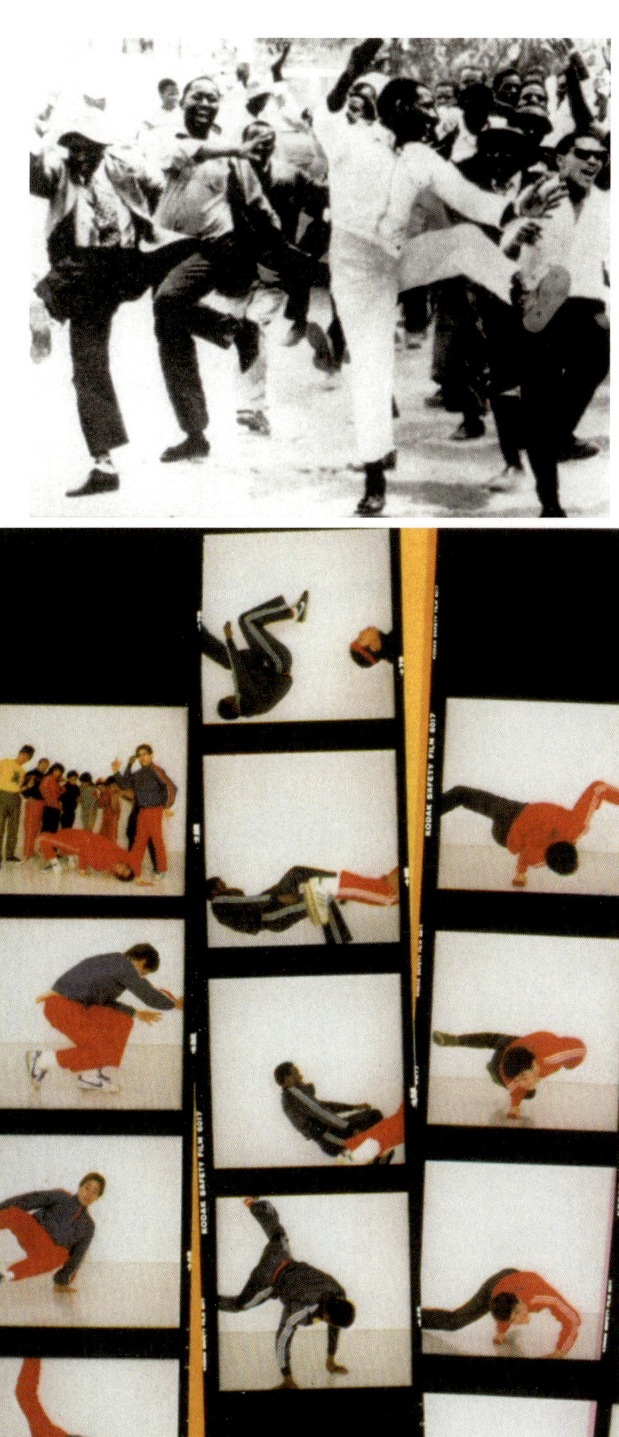

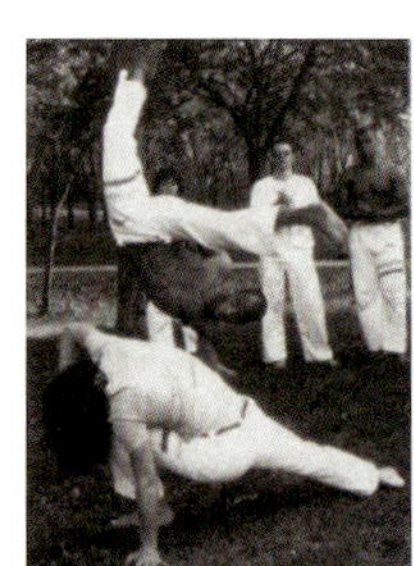
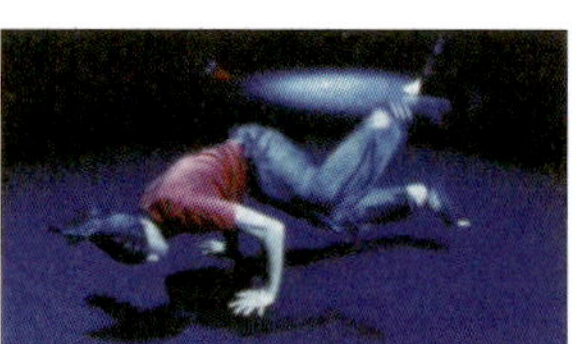
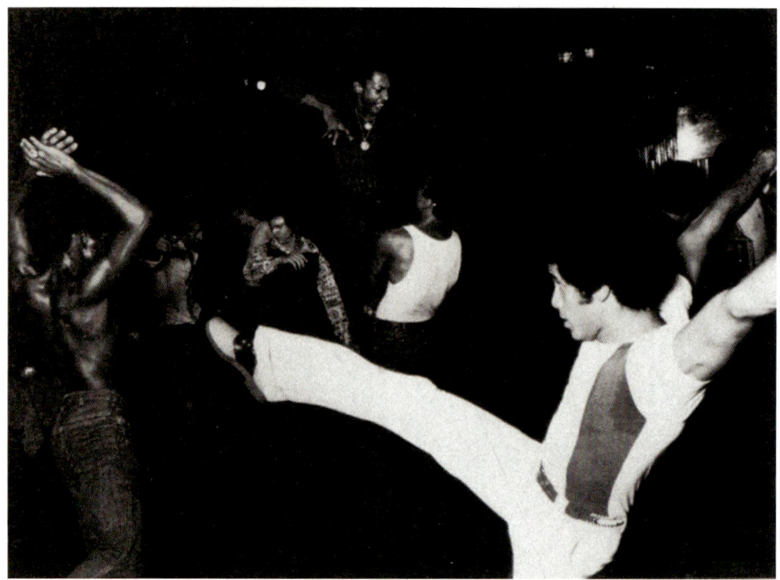

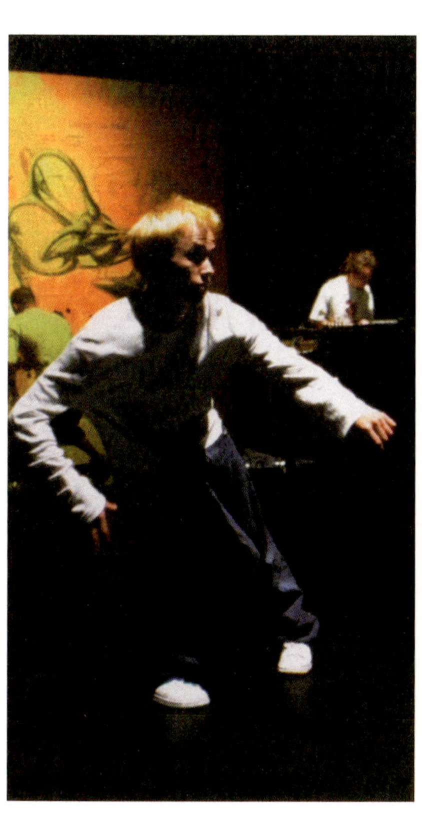
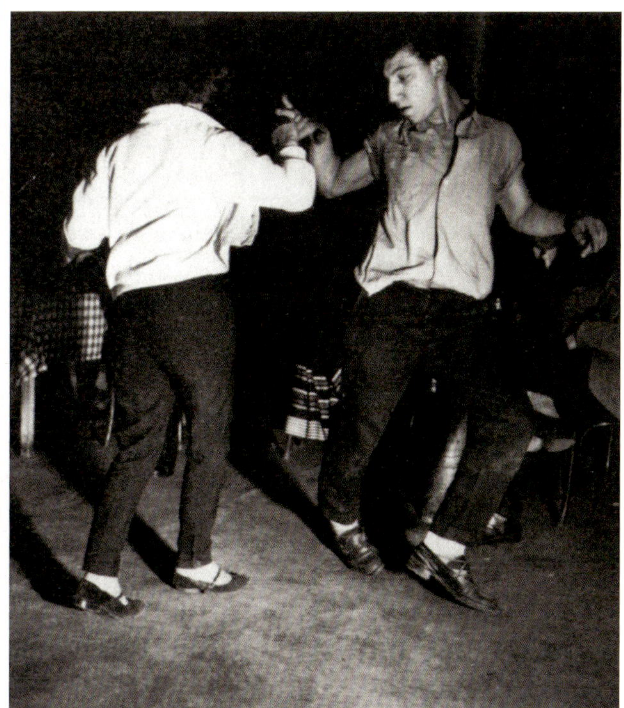

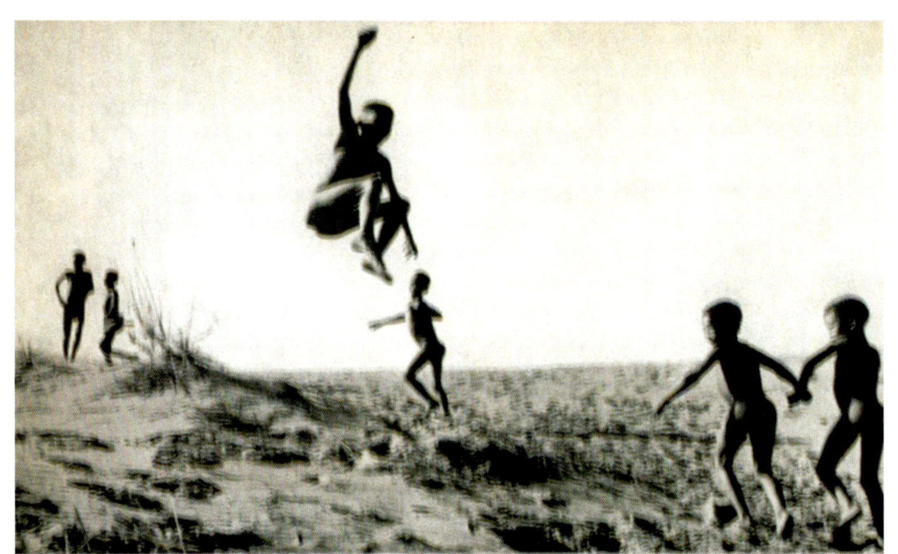

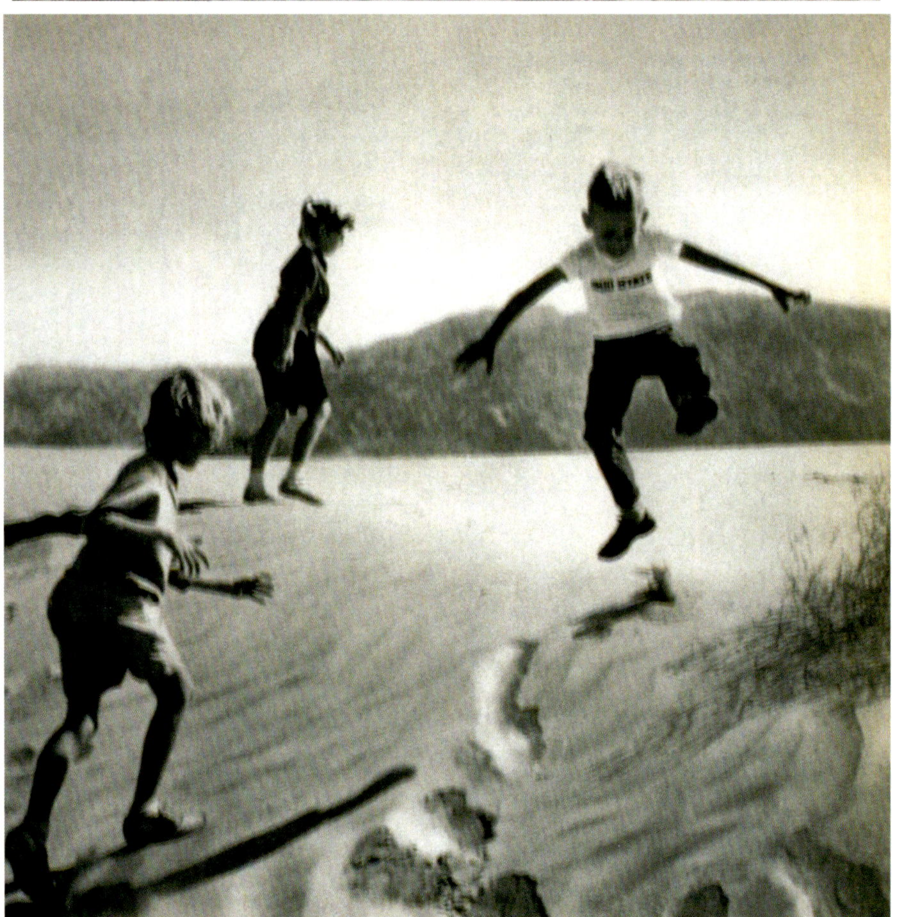

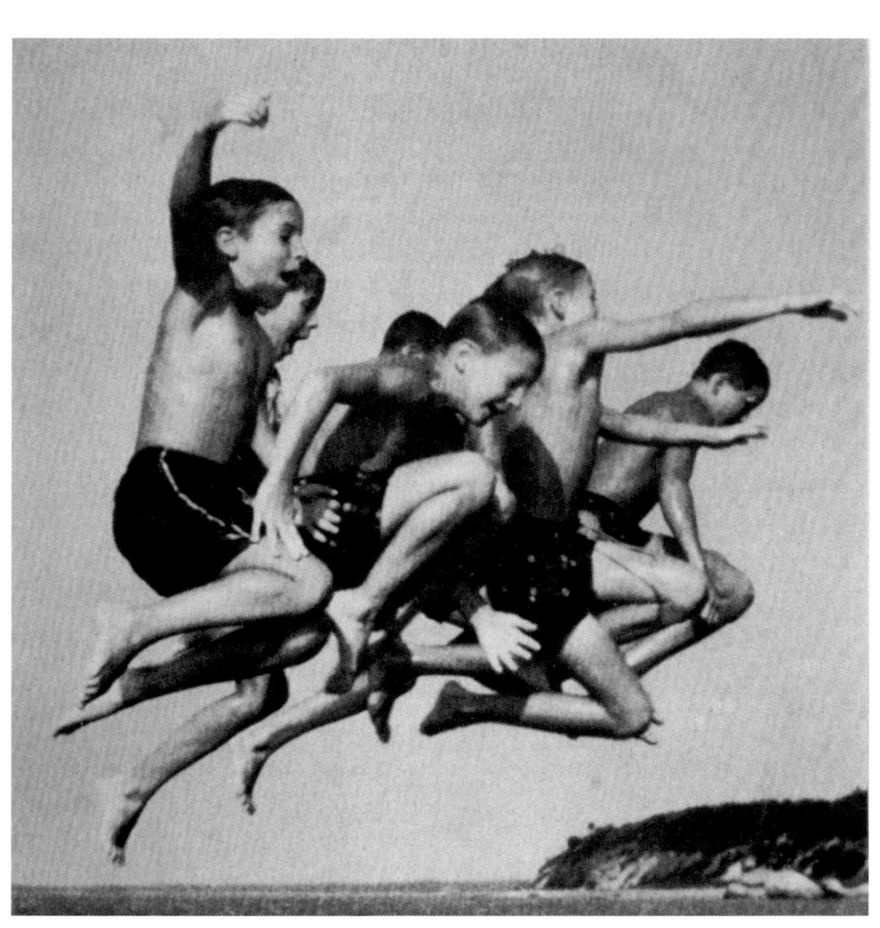

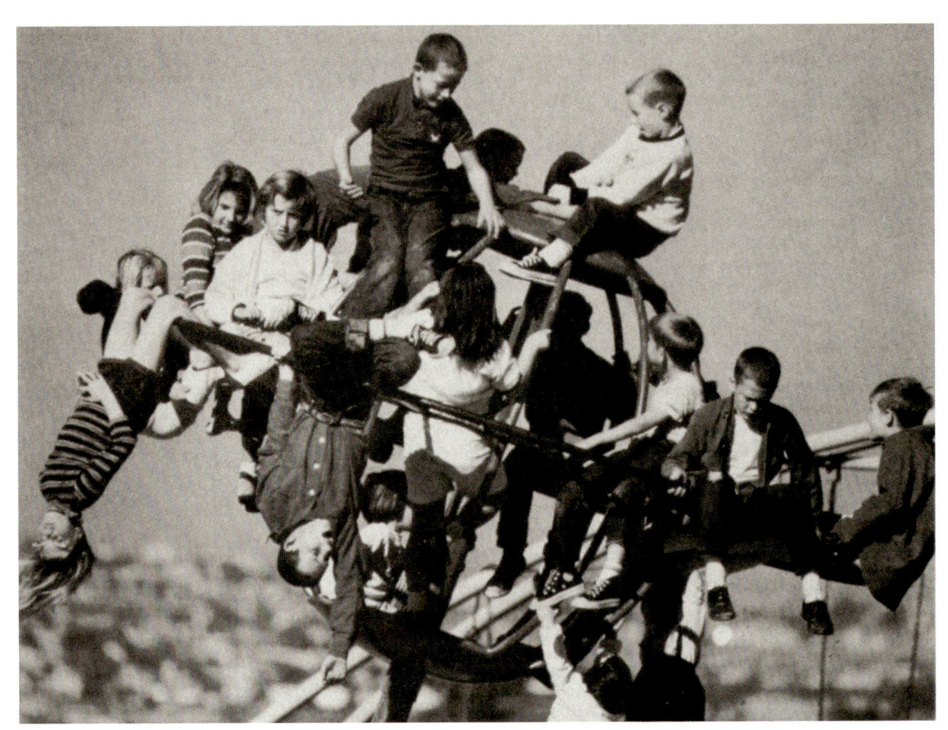

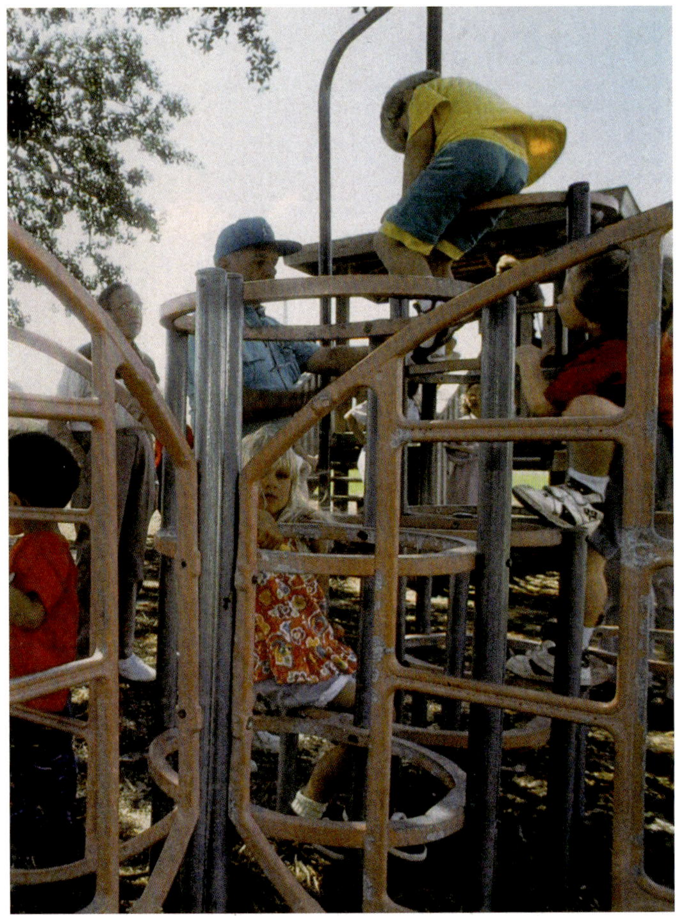

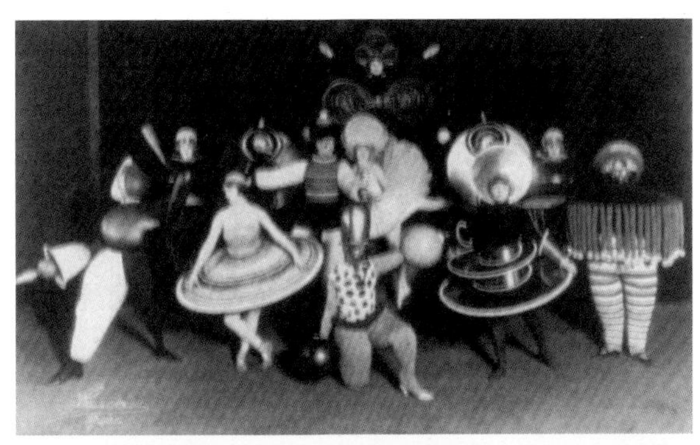

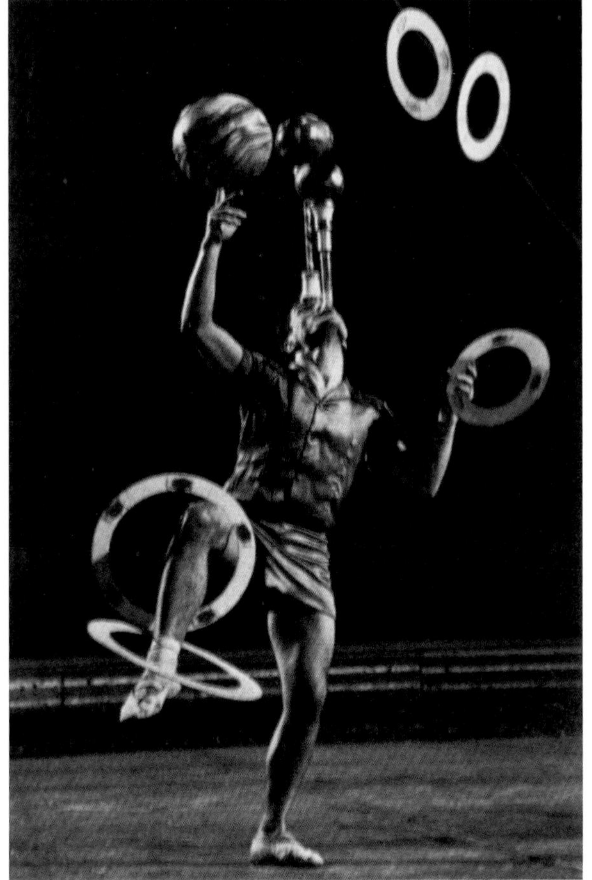

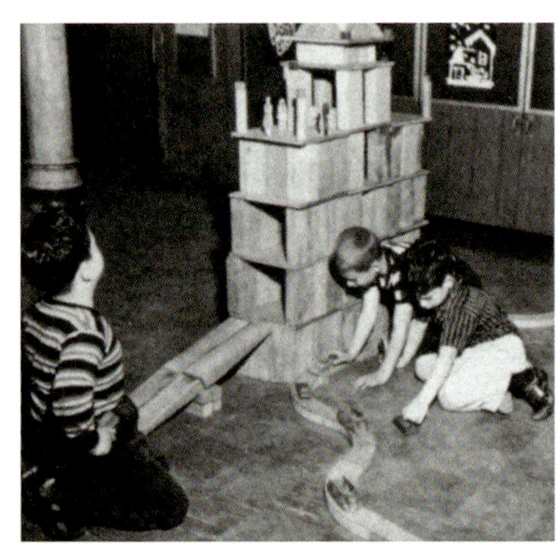
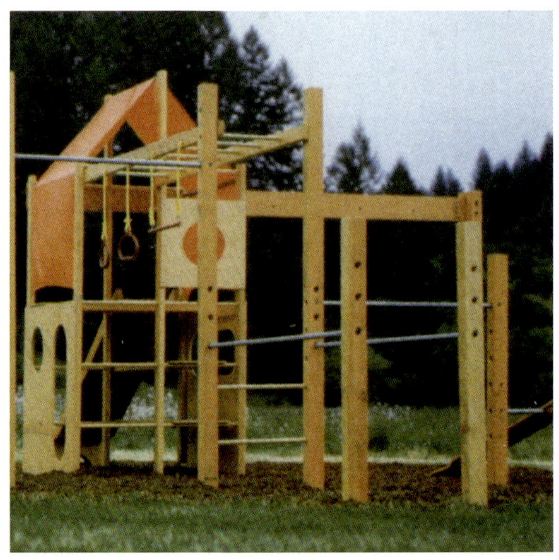
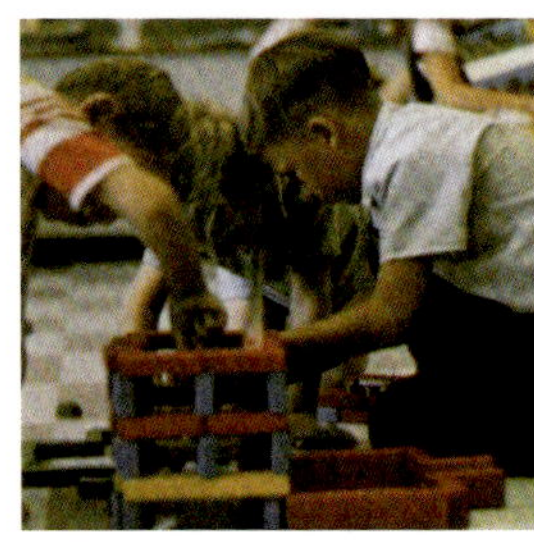
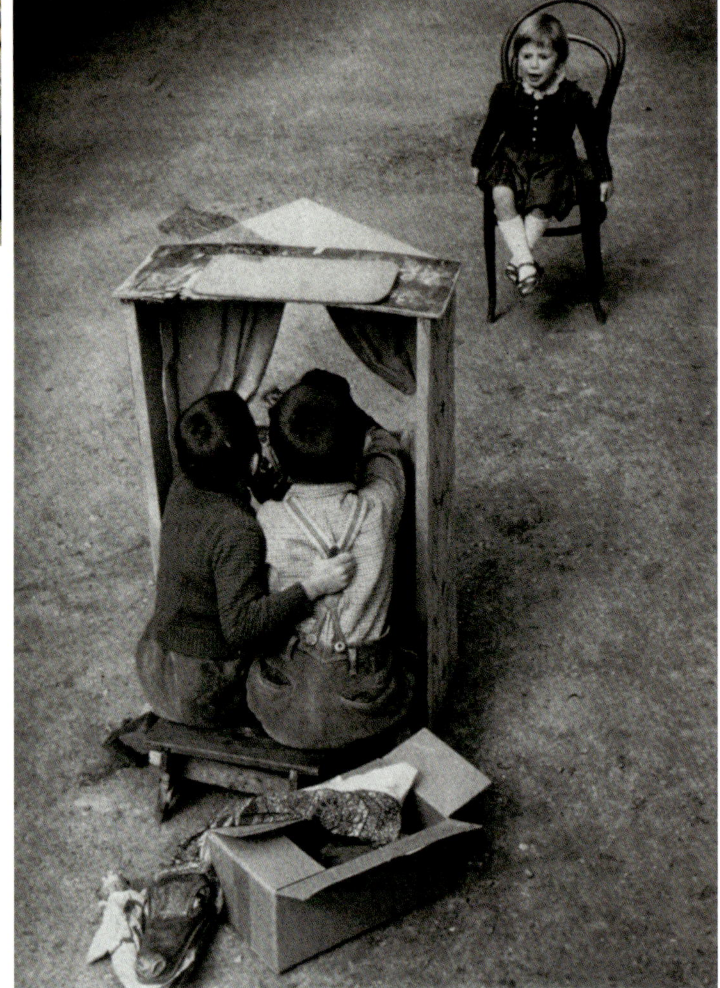

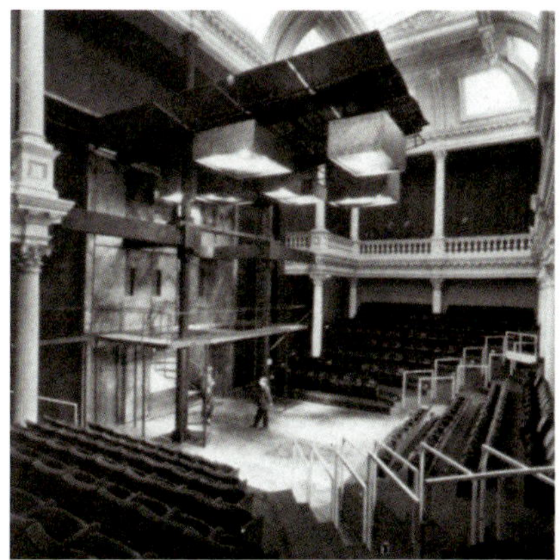
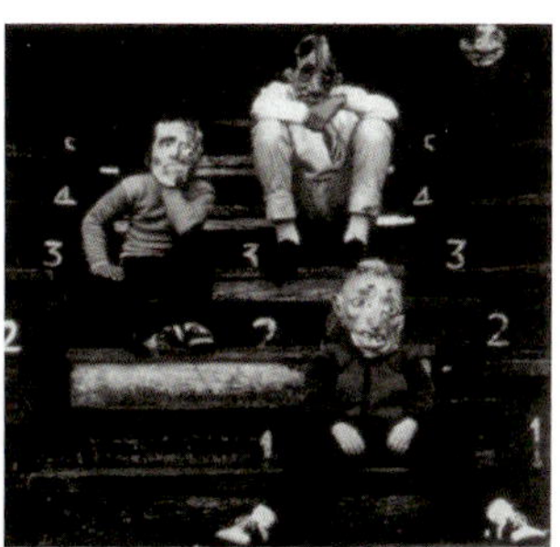

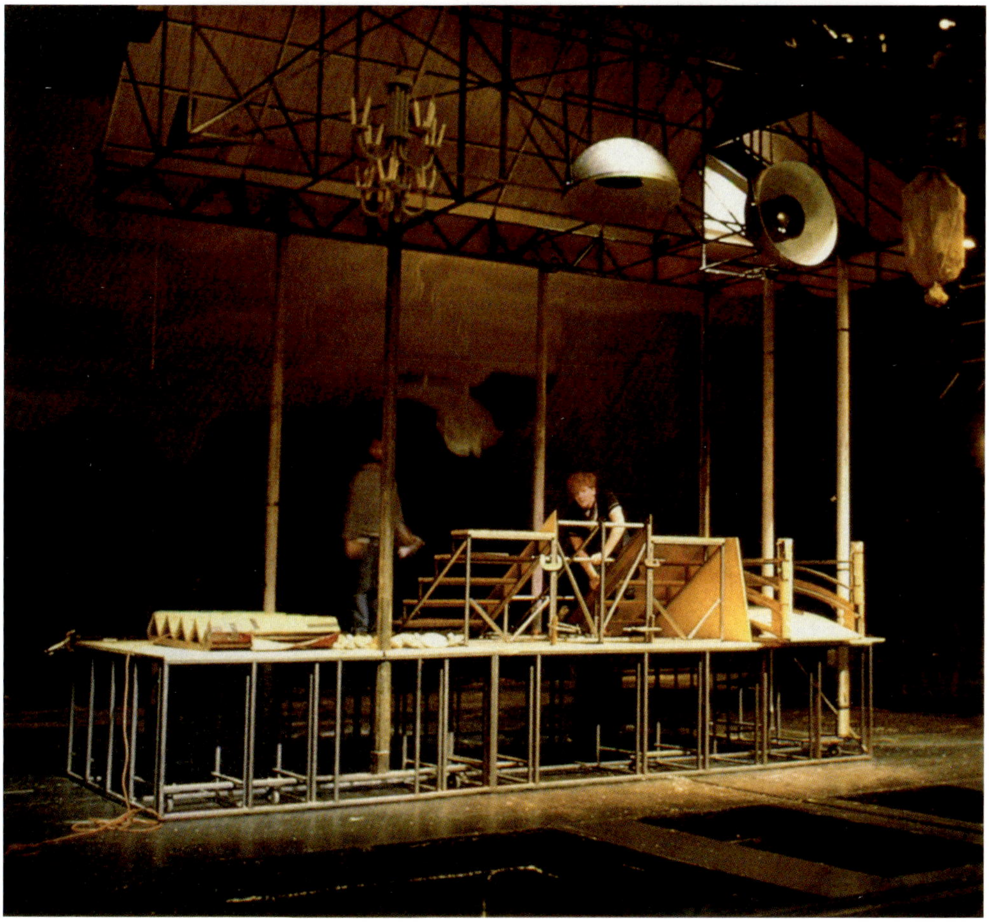

This artist book is published on the occasion of the exhibition of "Album III" at Documenta 12 (06/16 – 09/23/2007).

Thanks to Robert Gill, Allan Antliff, Lee Plested, Laura Rapp, Oliver Husain, Chris Curreri, and Birch Libralato (Toronto).

Concept and Layout by Luis Jacob
Production by Printmanagement Plitt, Oberhausen

Published by
Verlag der Buchhandlung Walther König, Köln
Ehrenstr. 4, 50672 Köln
Tel. +49 (0) 221 / 20 59 6-53
Email: verlag@buchhandlung-walther-koenig.de

Die Deutsche Bibliothek – CIP-Einheitsaufnahme
Ein Titelsatz für diese Publikation ist bei
Der Deutschen Bibliothek erhältlich

Printed in Germany

Outside Europe
D.A.P. / Distributed Art Publishers, Inc.
155 6th Avenue, 2nd Floor
New York, NY 10013
Tel: 212-627-1999
Fax: 212-627-9484
www.artbook.com

ISBN 978-3-86560-245-9